## Get the eBooks FREE!
(PDF, ePub, Kindle, and liveBook all included)

We believe that once you buy a book from us, you should be able to read it in any format we have available. To get electronic versions of this book at no additional cost to you, purchase and then register this book at the Manning website.

Go to https://www.manning.com/freebook and follow the instructions to complete your pBook registration.

That's it!
Thanks from Manning!

*Metaprogramming in .NET*

# Metaprogramming in .NET

KEVIN HAZZARD
JASON BOCK

MANNING

SHELTER ISLAND

For online information and ordering of this and other Manning books, please visit
www.manning.com. The publisher offers discounts on this book when ordered in quantity.
For more information, please contact

>    Special Sales Department
>    Manning Publications Co.
>    20 Baldwin Road
>    PO Box 261
>    Shelter Island, NY 11964
>    Email: orders@manning.com

♾ Recognizing the importance of preserving what has been written, it is Manning's policy to have
the books we publish printed on acid-free paper, and we exert our best efforts to that end.
Recognizing also our responsibility to conserve the resources of our planet, Manning books
are printed on paper that is at least 15 percent recycled and processed without the use of
elemental chlorine.

Manning Publications Co.        Development editor:  Cynthia Kane
20 Baldwin Road                        Copyeditor:  Corbin Collins
PO Box 261             Technical proofreader:  Justin Chase
Shelter Island, NY 11964              Proofreader:  Elizabeth Martin
                                      Typesetter:  Dennis Dalinnik
                                  Cover designer:  Marija Tudor

ISBN: 9781617290268
Printed in the United States of America
    3 4 5 6 7 8 9 10 – SP – 19

# brief contents

# contents

viii  **CONTENTS**

# foreword

When I think about metaprogramming I view it through three sets of experience: as a computer scientist, a business developer, and a .NET framework author.

From a computer science perspective, it is clear that our industry has been largely stagnant from a language perspective for an extremely long time. The slow evolution of 3GLs (third-generation languages) from C to C++ to Java to C# has resulted in incremental improvements, but no major leaps in terms of developer productivity, maintainability of code, reduction of complexity, or other meaningful metrics.

(I chose the C language progression in my example because it is perhaps the most widely known. Comparable progressions exist for BASIC, Pascal, and many other language families.)

Metaprogramming offers interesting possibilities around the creation of domain-specific languages and other abstraction concepts that could eventually break us out of the 3GL world we've lived in for the past 20-30 years. Although this book doesn't focus on such a long-term goal, I think you can use *Metaprogramming in .NET* as a starting point to gain valuable perspective on myriad core ideas that might inspire you to think more about the future of our industry.

As someone who's been a business developer for over 25 years, I've watched as metaprogramming has become one of the most mainstream and important tools for software development. Metaprogramming enables development time code generation as well as software that can dynamically adapt its behaviors at runtime.

In the mid-1990s people mocked attempts by Microsoft and others to create "wizards" that generated code for various business application scenarios. Today, such code generation tools are considered invaluable in environments as varied as Ruby on Rails, Eclipse, and Visual Studio. Most business developers rely daily on massive amounts of code generated by their tools during the development and build process.

Similarly, developers rely on runtime-generated code created by test mocking frameworks, dynamic UI generation tools, rules engines, and more. Even more subtle aspects of metaprogramming, such as the use of introspection (reflection) to create data binding frameworks, are pervasive.

This book explores a number of the underlying technologies and techniques used to implement code generation and dynamic applications during the development, build, and runtime phases of an application's lifecycle. Understanding these concepts is important for effective use of existing tools, and critical for creating your own or improving those that exist.

Finally, I am the author of the widely used CSLA .NET business objects framework. Within my framework I make extensive use of many of the techniques discussed in this book, including reflection, dynamic type loading, and expression trees.

A framework such as CSLA .NET couldn't exist without these technologies, and without the basic concepts of metaprogramming. Nor is CSLA .NET unique in this regard. Many frameworks in the data layer, business layer, and presentation layer make heavy use of metaprogramming techniques to provide broad and flexible support for object-relational mapping, business rules, validation rules, data binding, and dynamic UI generation.

In my view, metaprogramming is extremely important because its core concepts are used in popular development and testing frameworks and tools, as well as to enable code generation tooling and dynamic application behaviors. It is also one of the most promising areas of focus for the future of our industry as we look for ways to improve maintainability and reduce the cost of software over its lifetime.

This book is an excellent way to get started down the road of understanding and fully using the power of metaprogramming.

ROCKFORD LHOTKA
CTO AT MAGENIC
CREATOR OF THE CSLA .NET FRAMEWORK

# *preface*

In software development, metaprogramming is one of those words that sounds fancy and sophisticated—and somewhat intimidating at the same time. But what does it mean to be doing metaprogramming? The *meta* prefix can mean changed or higher. It can also mean after or beside, depending on the context. All of those terms describe the various forms of metaprogramming that we cover in this book.

You may choose to do metaprogramming in order to change code to support a higher level of abstraction within your system or to inject some new behavior that suits your particular needs. You may choose to do these things at compile time, between compile time and deployment, or even at runtime. Because of the flexible nature of the *meta* prefix, all of these scenarios qualify as metaprogramming.

No matter your reasons for doing metaprogramming, you must have a firm grip on the larger architectural picture of your project to do it effectively. That's why metaprogramming is sometimes considered a dark art, to be practiced only by senior developers and architects. Nothing could be further from the truth. Everyone can do some form of metaprogramming. By manipulating code with other code the metaprogramming way, you can suddenly tackle classes of coding problems that you were never able to overcome before.

Your foray into metaprogramming may be to improve code reuse through simple templating or reflection. But soon you might also find yourself doing it to reduce the complexity of your systems. For example, weaving the code that does logging, performance monitoring, or transaction handling into a class library after it's been compiled can greatly increase developer comprehension by reducing code complexity. Hiding all of that plumbing with metaprogramming can benefit everyone on the team.

We love metaprogramming. We want to create beautiful pieces of code that can enable conventions in applications that make adding a new aspect easy. We want to be able to optimize our code at runtime so it can perform faster. We want to analyze our code so we can find issues before compilation. We want to shape whole bodies of templated code to schemas at runtime, perhaps even compiling them on the fly to get excellent performance. Metaprogramming helps realize all these goals. We'd also like for you to fall in love with metaprogramming so you can reach higher goals. That's really what we hope to instill in you with this book: a passion to view your code in a different, often more abstract way.

To be fair, it's not as easy to do metaprogramming in .NET compared to other languages like Ruby. At least it seems that way when you first dive in. Dynamic languages let you easily manipulate your code, and such concepts are exposed as first-class citizens in languages like Python and Ruby. C# and Visual Basic .NET are usually not touted as being *dynamic* or *malleable*. Surprisingly, though, there are a lot of ways to do real metaprogramming in .NET. They may not be obvious or easy to carry out at first, but they are there at almost every turn. Some metaprogramming features of .NET are baked into the Common Language Runtime (CLR). Some exist as code in the Framework Class Library (FCL). Still more metaprogramming capabilities show up as language features in C# and Visual Basic .NET. Once you understand how some of these features work, you'll be well on your way to seeing problems in a whole new light.

Writing this book has been laborious, time-consuming, and frustrating, but above everything else, a joy. As far as we're concerned, this is the "fun stuff" in software development. It's also the "stuff" that can truly transform your code into something amazing, as long as you're willing to stretch your boundaries. So take a deep, cleansing breath and dive in with us. You'll find that the metaprogramming waters aren't as choppy as they may seem at first glance. We believe that in the end, you'll be glad you made the journey.

We also believe that once you've mastered a new concept or two, you'll be ready to convince your peers that the metaprogramming seas are smooth enough for anyone to sail on them.

# acknowledgments

We'd like to thank Manning for taking a chance on us and letting us create a book that didn't follow the typical .NET technical paths. Specifically, we thank Cynthia Kane, Michael Stephens, and Maureen Spencer for being patient with us during our long wanderings through the material. It took far longer for us to finish than we originally thought, and we appreciate them for sticking with us—thank you very much! We also thank our production team of Corbin Collins, Dennis Dalinnik, Elizabeth Martin, Mary Piergies, and Janet Vail.

Special thanks to the following reviewers who spent the time perusing the text and the code for mistakes, odd phrasings, and other quirks: Andrew Kirsch, Arun Noronha, Bill Wagner, Bryce Darling, Danish Gite, Eddy Vluggen, Harry Cummings, Jon Von Gillern, Matt Warren, Mick Wilson, Rama Krishna Vavilala, Rob Grainger, Rupert Wood, Sander Rossel, Scobie Smith, Timo Bredenoort, Timothy Cluff, and William Lee.

Finally, we're grateful to Rockford Lhotka for contributing the foreword to our book and to Justin Chase for his careful tech proofread of the manuscript during production.

KEVIN HAZZARD

I would like to thank

- My wife Donna and our five lovely children, for giving up husband and dad for the year that it took to produce this book. Donna, you will always be my lobster.
- Jason, for teaching me a lot about authorship and many things about metaprogramming that I didn't know when I began this work. Jason has patience

beyond all reckoning which I bent nearly to the breaking point more often than I should have. You're a real gem, Jason.

JASON BOCK

I would like to thank

- Magenic, especially Greg Frankenfield and Paul Fridman, for creating and growing a great place to work. I've been with Magenic for 11 years for many reasons, one being that I find tremendous satisfaction in solving problems for our clients. Some challenges are technical, others require "innovative thinking" to come up with ways to move forward. And all of them educate me. With that experience, I feel like I've grown far more than I ever have anywhere else. I'm thankful that I've found a place where I feel like I fit in.
- Kevin, for giving up his time to coauthor this book. Your knowledge and insight have added so much to the material in this book, and I feel that your writing style forced me to stop being so technical and focus on the story at hand. Thanks for everything you've done in this book. Well done!
- My wife Liz and my two sons Hayden and Ryan. I thought I'd never write another book, but when this opportunity presented itself, I had to do it, even though I knew it would cut into family time. I truly appreciate my amazing family and feel so fortunate that they've been supportive of me when "Dad's writing his book on his laptop...*again!*" To each of them: I love you very much.

# *about this book*

*Metaprogramming in .NET* requires you to move beyond the canonical material of interfaces, virtual methods, and events to more advanced and probably unknown concepts like reflection, assembly rewriting, expressions, and code analysis. If you've never encountered these APIs or techniques, it may feel a little daunting to even approach the first chapter!

We don't "pontificate on the profound"—that is, although you'll be exposed to new ideas, you won't read about every extreme, esoteric corner of metaprogramming. Rather, you'll be guided into these realms with an understanding of *why* you need to learn about these techniques. At the end of the day, we want you to not only gain an appreciation of how powerful metaprogramming is, but how to *use* this material in your day-to-day coding experiences.

Throughout this book, you'll learn about different techniques and frameworks. They all have their strengths and weaknesses. Some work well in some areas of an application, and others shine somewhere else. You'll understand when it's best to use one tool, and what the trade-offs are in using a particular approach.

## Roadmap

- Chapter 1 provides a broad introduction into the world of metaprogramming. We provide high-level examples to explain just what metaprogramming is all about.
- Chapter 2 moves into the world of reflection, describing how to query code, find out what it contains, and manipulate it.

- Chapter 3 discusses code generation with T4. You'll discover how the template engine works and where it makes sense to use code generation in an application.
- Chapter 4 covers the CodeDOM and why it's still an applicable API to use in certain development scenarios.
- Chapter 5 dives into the Reflection.Emit API. You'll learn about the inner workings of an assembly and how to dynamically create code at runtime with this API.
- Chapter 6 is all about expressions, specifically LINQ expressions. You'll see how to create small snippets of code and change their behavior at runtime.
- Chapter 7 takes the Emitter API one more step and shows how to rewrite assemblies, providing a path where you can inject reusable bits of code to enhance compiled code.
- Chapter 8 covers the Dynamic Language Runtime, or DLR. You'll learn all about binding, dynamic objects, and other things the DLR provides.
- Chapter 9 looks at other tools and frameworks, as well as other languages that make it easier to use metaprogramming within .NET.
- Chapter 10 rounds out the book with a look into the future with Project Roslyn, a compiler API from Microsoft that will provide a view into your code like you've never had from them before.
- There are two appendixes. Appendix A is an overview of Windows 8 and how metaprogramming in .NET works in Windows Store applications. Appendix B is a usage guide summary of the techniques presented in chapters 2–10.

## Who should read this book?

If you're a .NET developer who wants not only to learn more than just how to "do" dependency injection and "use" controllers, but also to create frameworks that provide useful services to other developers, then this book is for you. Many popular .NET frameworks that make hard problems simple usually end up using one or more of the techniques presented in this book, but they structure their work in such a way that you probably don't see it (which is usually a good thing). If you want to create these components, you'll need to know how these techniques work, and this book provides that guidance.

We assume that you're familiar with the base competencies that a .NET developer would have. For example, we expect that you know what a class is, the difference between a virtual and a non-virtual method, and what *sealed* means in C#.

## Code conventions and downloads

This book contains numerous code examples. All the code is in a `fixed-width font like this` to separate it from ordinary text. Code members such as method names, class names, and so on are also in a fixed-width font.

Source code examples in this book are fairly close to the samples that you'll find online. But for brevity's sake, we may have removed material such as comments from the code to fit it well within the text.

Annotations accompany many of the source code listings, highlighting important concepts. In some cases, numbered bullets link to explanations that follow the listing.

The source code for the examples in the book is available for download from the publisher's website at www.manning.com/Metaprogrammingin.Net. It is also available from http://metadotnetbook.codeplex.com.

To run the samples, you'll need to download some of the tools and languages we use in this book. We provide links in the text to places where you can get the relevant files.

## Author Online

The purchase of *Metaprogramming in .NET* includes free access to a private web forum run by Manning Publications, where you can make comments about the book, ask technical questions, and receive help from the authors and from other users. To access the forum and subscribe to it, point your web browser at www.manning.com/Metaprogrammingin.NET. This page provides information on how to get on the forum once you are registered, what kind of help is available, and the rules of conduct on the forum.

Manning's commitment to our readers is to provide a venue where a meaningful dialogue between individual readers and between readers and authors can take place. It's not a commitment to any specific amount of participation on the part of the authors, whose contributions to the forum remain voluntary (and unpaid). We suggest you try asking the authors some challenging questions, lest their interest stray!

The Author Online forum and archives of previous discussions will be accessible from the publisher's web site as long as the book is in print.

## About the authors

KEVIN HAZZARD is a director for CapTech Consulting, a management consulting and software development firm of 375 consultants based in Richmond, Va., with offices in Philadelphia, Charlotte, and Washington, D.C. Kevin was a Microsoft C# MVP for years until moving into the Windows Azure MVP group. Although his head is in the *clouds* these days, Kevin still considers himself to be a *languages* guy, focusing most of his attention on functional and dynamic languages like F# and Python.

Kevin has served as a leader for the Richmond Code Camp (http://richmondcode-camp.org), the Richmond .NET User Group, the Richmond SQL Server User Group, the Richmond Software Craftsmanship Group, and the Mid-Atlantic Developer Expo (http://madexpo.us). He also speaks regularly at conferences around the Midwest and Mid-Atlantic states, directing most of his attention these days to teaching programming and robotics to children.

Kevin taught computer programming language courses in the Virginia Community College system for more than a decade, but gave that up in 2011 to run for office and become elected to his county's K-12 School Board. You can follow Kevin at http://twitter.com/KevinHazzard or befriend him at http://facebook.com/wkhazzard to stay in touch.

JASON BOCK is a principal lead consultant for Magenic (www.magenic.com) and a
Microsoft C# MVP. He's worked on a number of business applications using a diverse
set of substrates and languages, such as C#, .NET, and Java. He's the also the author of
*Applied .NET Attributes* (Apress, 2003), *CIL Programming: Under the Hood of .NET* (Apress,
2002), and *Visual Basic 6 Win32 API Tutorial* (Wrox, 1998). He's written numerous articles on software development, has presented at a number of conferences and user
groups, and is a leader of the Twin Cities Code Camp (www.twincitiescodecamp.com).
Jason holds a master's degree in electrical engineering from Marquette University.
Visit his website at www.jasonbock.net.

# about the cover illustration

The figure on the cover of *Metaprogramming in .NET* is captioned a "Man from Japodes." The Japodes, also called Lapydes or Giapidi, were an ancient people who dwelt north of and inland from Liburnia, a region on the northeastern Adriatic coast in what is now Croatia. This illustration is taken from a recent reprint of Balthasar Hacquet's *Images and Descriptions of Southwestern and Eastern Wenda, Illyrians, and Slavs* published by the Ethnographic Museum in Split, Croatia, in 2008. Hacquet (1739–1815) was an Austrian physician and scientist who spent many years studying the botany, geology, and ethnography of many parts of the Austrian Empire, as well as the Veneto, the Julian Alps, and the western Balkans, inhabited in the past by peoples of many different tribes and nationalities. Hand-drawn illustrations accompany the many scientific papers and books that Hacquet published.

The rich diversity of the drawings in Hacquet's publications speaks vividly of the uniqueness and individuality of Alpine and Balkan regions just 200 years ago. This was a time when the dress codes of two villages separated by a few miles identified people uniquely as belonging to one or the other, and when members of an ethnic tribe, social class, or trade could be easily distinguished by what they were wearing. Dress codes have changed since then and the diversity by region, so rich at the time, has faded away. It is now often hard to tell the inhabitants of one continent from another and the residents of the picturesque towns and villages on the Adriatic coast are not readily distinguishable from people who live in other parts of the world.

We at Manning celebrate the inventiveness, the initiative, and the fun of the computer business with book covers based on costumes from two centuries ago brought back to life by illustrations such as this one.

# Part 1

## Demystifying metaprogramming

What is metaprogramming? What does it look like? What does it mean to use metaprogramming? Part 1 (chapters 1 and 2) gives you a tour of the foundations of metaprogramming.

In chapter 1 you'll see simple, clear examples that explain what metaprogramming is and why it's beneficial to understand what it's about.

Chapter 2 covers the need for reflection and its practical uses. Numerous uses of metaprogramming via the Reflection API will be presented throughout the chapter.

# Metaprogramming concepts

## In this chapter

- Defining metaprogramming
- Exploring examples of metaprogramming

The basic principles of object-oriented programming (OOP) are understood by most software developers these days. For example, you probably understand how encapsulation and implementation-hiding can increase the cohesion of classes. Languages like C# and Visual Basic are excellent for creating so-called coarsely grained types because they expose simple features for grouping and hiding both code and data. You can use cohesive types to raise the abstraction level across a system, which allows for loose coupling to occur. Systems that enjoy loose coupling at the top level are much easier to maintain because each subsystem isn't as dependent on the others as they could be in a poor design. Those benefits are realized at the lower levels, too, typically through lowered complexity and greater reusability of classes. In figure 1.1, which of the two systems depicted would likely be easier to modify?

Without knowing what the gray circles represent, most developers would pick the diagram on the right as the better one. This isn't even a developer skill. Show the diagrams to an accountant and she'll also choose the one on the right as the less

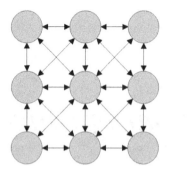 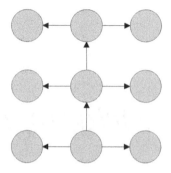

Figure 1.1   Which system is easier to change?

complex. We recognize simplicity when we see it. Our challenge as programmers is in seeing the opportunities for simplicity in the systems we develop. Language features like encapsulation, abstraction, inheritance, data-hiding, and polymorphism are great, but they only take you part of the way there.

---

**The I in SOLID**

Along the way, we'll refer to some of the five SOLID (single responsibility, open-closed, Liskov substitution, interface segregation, and dependency inversion) principles of object-oriented design (OOD). While we're thinking about coupling and cohesion, it's a good time to discuss the "I" in SOLID—the interface segregation principle (ISP). The ISP says that many client-specific interfaces are better than one general-purpose interface.

This seems to contradict the notion that high cohesion is always a good thing. If you study the ISP along with the other four SOLID principles, though, you'll discover that it speaks to the correctness of the middle ground in software development. The diagram on the left in figure 1.1 may represent absurdly tight coupling and low cohesion. The one on the right may embody the other extreme. The ISP tells us that there may be an unseen middle design that's best of all.

---

The metaprogramming style of software development shares many of the goals of traditional OOP. Metaprogramming is all about making software simpler and reusable. But rather than depending strictly on language features to reduce code complexity or increase reusability, metaprogramming achieves those goals through a variety of libraries and coding techniques. There are language-specific features that make metaprogramming easier in some circumstances. For the most part, however, metaprogramming is a set of language-independent skills. We use C# for most of the examples in this book, but don't be surprised when we toss in a bit of JavaScript or F# here and there when it helps to teach an idea at hand.

If you know a little bit about metaprogramming, you may scoff at the idea that metaprogramming reduces complexity. It's true that some types of metaprogramming require a deeper understanding of tools that may be out-of-sight from your perspective today. You may have been told in the past that to do metaprogramming, you must understand how compilers work. Many years ago that was largely true, but today you can learn and use highly effective metaprogramming techniques without having to know much at all about compilers. After all, complexity is in the eye of the beholder, as the saying goes. As perceived complexity from the end user's standpoint goes down, internal complexity of the design often goes up. Complexity reduction when metaprogramming follows the same rules. To achieve simplicity on the outside, the code on the inside of a metaprogramming-enabled component typically takes on added responsibilities.

For example, so-called Domain-Specific Languages (DSLs) are often built with metaprogramming tools and techniques. DSLs are important because they can fundamentally change the way that a company produces intellectual property (IP). When a DSL enables a company to shift some of its IP development from traditional programmers to analysts, time to market can be dramatically reduced. Well-designed DSLs can also increase the comprehension of business rules across the enterprise, allowing people into the game from other roles that have been traditionally unable to participate in the process. A flowcharting tool that produces executable code is a good example of such a DSL because it enables business stakeholders to describe their intent in their own vocabulary.

The trade-off is that DSLs are notoriously difficult to design, write, test, and support. Some argue that DSLs are much too complex and not worth the trouble. But from the consumer's vantage point, DSLs are precious to the businesses they serve precisely because they lower perceived complexity. In the end, isn't that what we do for a living? We make difficult business problems seem simple. As you study metaprogramming throughout this book, keep that thought in mind.

**NOTE** *DSLs in Action* by Debasish Ghosh (www.manning.com/ghosh) and *DSLs in Boo* by Oren Eini writing as Ayende Rahien (www.manning.com/rahien) are both excellent choices if your goal is to learn how to create full-featured DSLs.

At times, you may struggle as you try to learn so many new things at once. There will be enough promise in each new thing you learn to prove that the struggle is worthwhile. In the end, you'll have many new tools for fighting software complexity and for writing reusable code. As you begin to put metaprogramming to work in your projects, others will study what you've done. They'll marvel at the kung fu of your metaprogramming skills. Soon they'll begin to emulate you, and, as they say, imitation is the sincerest form of flattery.

Let's begin by defining what metaprogramming is. Then we'll dive into a few interesting examples to show how it's used.

## 1.1   Definitions of metaprogramming

The classic definition for a metaprogram is "a computer program that writes new computer programs." This sounds a lot like the definition of a compiler. A compiler for a programming language like C# could be thought of as the ultimate metaprogram, because its only job is to produce other programs from source code. But to call the C# compiler a metaprogram is a stretch. Unstated in the definition of a traditional compiler is the idea that the execution step is fixed in time, and the existence of the compiled outputs are somewhat unseen by end users. Also, metaprogramming techniques are clearly different because they're almost always used to deal with some sort of ever-changing stimulus.

There may be semistructured documents that need parsing on the fly. You may need a way to express trading restrictions from your partners that change daily. Database schemas change from time to time, and you may need a way to make your programs adapt gracefully. All of these problems are perfect for metaprogram-based solutions. They don't require compilers in the traditional sense. They do require the flexibility that a compiler affords to adapt to situations at hand.

The C# compiler in its current form is almost always invoked by programmers during a build process to produce a new program. In the near future, that will be changing with the release of Microsoft's Roslyn (code name) tools. Roslyn opens the black box of the C# and VB compilers to make them available before, during, and after the deployment of your applications. When that happens, we expect to see Microsoft's compilers used in many metaprogramming scenarios.

> **DEFINITION**   *Metaprogramming* may be among the most misunderstood terms in computer jargon. It's certainly one of the more difficult to define. To make learning about it easier, each time you see the word *metaprogramming* in this book, try to think of it as *after*-programming or *beside*-programming. The Greek prefix *meta* allows for both of those definitions to be correct. Most of the examples in this book demonstrate programming after traditional compilation has occurred, or by using dynamic code that runs alongside other processes. For each example, ask yourself which kind of metaprogramming you're observing. Some of the more in-depth examples demonstrate both kinds simultaneously.

Also inherent in the classic definition of metaprogramming is the notion that the code-generation process is embedded within an application to perform some type of dynamic processing logic. The word *dynamic* gets tossed around a lot in discussions about metaprogramming because it's often used to add adaptive interfaces to a program at runtime. For example, a dynamic XML application might read XML Schema Definitions (XSD) at runtime to construct and compile high-performance XML parsers that can be used right away or saved for future use. Such an application would perform well and be highly adaptable to new types of XML without the need for recompilation.

Another common definition for metaprogramming is "a computer program that manipulates other programs at runtime." Scripting languages often fit this mold, providing the simple but powerful tools for doing metaprogramming. A program that manipulates another program doesn't have to be a scripting language. The dynamic keyword in C# can be used to emit a kind of manipulating code into a compiled application, like this:

```
dynamic document = DocumentFactory.Create();
document.Open();
```

Using the dynamic keyword, the call to the Open() method shown here is embedded into a bit of C# code known as a CallSite. We dive into CallSites in great detail later in chapter 8. For now, all you need to understand is that what appears to be a type-safe call to the Open() method in the document object is implemented through C#'s runtime binder using the literal string "Open." When you dig around in the Intermediate Language (IL) emitted by the compiler for the preceding snippet, you may be surprised to see the literal string "Open" passed to the binder to invoke the method. The C# code certainly didn't look like a scripting language, but what was emitted certainly has that flavor. Through the various runtime binders for interfacing with plain old CLR objects (POCO), Python scripts, Ruby scripts, and COM objects, C# CallSites exhibit the second definition of metaprogramming rather well. In chapter 8, we show you how to interface with all those languages and object types using C# dynamic typing.

Writing new programs at runtime and manipulating programs at runtime aren't mutually exclusive concepts. Many of the metaprogramming examples you'll encounter in this book do both. First, they may use some sort of code-generation technique to create and compile code on the fly to adapt to some emerging set of circumstances. Next, they may control, monitor, or invoke those same programs to achieve the desired outcome.

### More metaprogramming jargon

There are a few more terms that you may encounter when you start reading articles and other books on metaprogramming. You may run across the term *metalanguage* to refer to the language used in the original program (the one that's writing the others). We prefer the term *metaprogram* because it's more generic. Remember that metaprogramming is largely a language-independent craft.

Other terms you're likely to hear are *target language* or *object language*, referring to the code produced by the metaprogram. Both those terms imply that there's an intermediate language that the metaprogrammer cares about in the process. As you'll soon discover, the output of a .NET metaprogram could be Common Intermediate Language (CIL) which, for all intents and purposes, you can regard as native code. In those cases, there's no target language in the classical sense.

## 1.2    Examples of metaprogramming

For most people, the best way to learn is by example. Let's examine a few examples of metaprogramming in action. We begin with the simplest of metaprogramming concepts: invoking bits of dynamically supplied JavaScript at runtime. This prototype will give you an appreciation for the flexibility that metaprogramming can add to a web application, even though the example is contrived for simplicity.

Next, we look at how to use introspective interfaces to drive application behavior at runtime. Through it you'll learn how to do simple reflection to peer into objects at runtime. But the real purpose of that example is to help you understand the performance considerations when deciding to metaprogramming-enable an interface to make it friendlier and more adaptive at runtime.

The third example in this section concerns code generation, arguably the classic definition of metaprogramming. We show you two runtime types of code generation: creating source code from a so-called object graph assembled by hand and creating executable IL from a lambda expression. For the second type, we let the C# compiler do the heavy lifting first. Then we build the lambda expressions by hand before turning them into runnable code.

The last example in this section demonstrates how you can use the dynamic features of the C# 4 compiler to do some fairly interesting metaprogramming with little effort. You'll learn a little bit about how the `CallSite` and `CSharpRuntimeBinder` types work. The real goal of that example, though, is to highlight some of the best practices around using dynamic types in C#.

The examples here are designed to provide basic prototypes that you'll need to learn faster when reading future chapters. Also, by examining several simple approaches to metaprogramming in rapid succession, we hope to give you a more holistic view of this important programming paradigm.

### 1.2.1    Metaprogramming via scripting

There are many dynamic programming languages. Some of them are also considered to be scripting languages. Languages like Python or Ruby would work well for our first example because they have clean, easy-to-understand syntaxes and they're loaded with great metaprogramming capabilities. But rather than starting with one of those languages, which could steepen the learning curve if you don't know them, let's begin, in the following listing, with the two most popular languages in the world.

**Listing 1.1   Dynamic Number Conversion (HTML and JavaScript)**

```
<!DOCTYPE html>
<html>
    <head>
      <script type="text/javascript">
      function convert() {
        var fromValue = eval(fromVal.value);
        toVal.innerHTML = eval(formula.value).toString();
      }
```

```
      </script>
    </head>
    <body>
      <span>fromValue:</span> 
      <input id="fromVal" type="text"/><br/>

      <span>formula:</span> 
      <input id="formula" type="text"/><br/>

      <input type="button" onclick="javascript:convert();"
        value="Convert" /><br/>

      <span>toValue:</span> <span id="toVal"></span>
    </body>
</html>
```

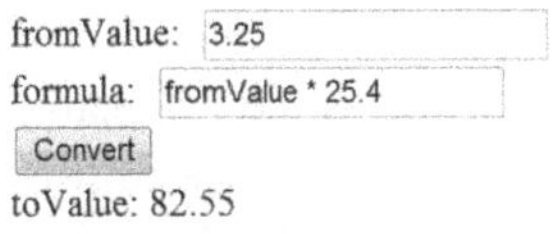

The admittedly unattractive web page created by this markup demonstrates a core metaprogramming concept. After locating the DynamicConversion.htm file in the book's sample source code, load it up and enter some values into the fromValue and formula fields, as shown in figure 1.2. Be sure to use the token fromValue somewhere in the formula to refer to the numeric value that you type into the fromValue field.

fromValue: 3.25
formula: fromValue * 25.4
Convert
toValue: 82.55

**Figure 1.2
DynamicConversion.htm—
converting inches to
millimeters**

Figure 1.2 shows a calculation that multiplies the user-supplied fromValue by 25.4, which is the simple formula for converting inches to millimeters. Typing in a fromValue such as 3.25 and clicking Convert shows that 3.25 inches is equivalent to 82.55 millimeters. There are two bits of JavaScript code in this web page that make it work: a function called convert() and the onclick event handler for the Convert button, which invokes the convert() function when the button is clicked. In the convert() function, the HTML Document Object Model (DOM) is used to fetch the value from the first text box on the page, the one named fromVal. The string is evaluated by the JavaScript DOM by passing it to the aptly-named eval() function:

```
var fromValue = eval(fromVal.value);
```

This is a neat trick, but how does it work? When we typed the string "3.25" into the fromVal element, we weren't thinking of writing JavaScript per se. We were trying to express a numeric value. But the eval() function did interpret our input as JavaScript because that's all it can do. The eval() function gives you direct access to JavaScript's compiler at runtime, so the string "3.25" compiled as JavaScript code is treated as the literal value for the floating point number we know as 3.25. That makes sense. The parsed literal number is then assigned to a local variable defined in the script named fromValue. The next line of code in the convert() function uses eval() once again:

```
toVal.innerHTML = eval(formula.value).toString();
```

The string "fromValue*25.4" looks a bit more like a script than the first input because it contains a mathematical expression. The result of executing that script is a number that's converted into a string and written back to the web page for the user to see. Once again, in that single line of code, you can see the HTML DOM and the JavaScript DOM working together to accomplish what's required.

The bit of metaprogramming lurking in this example is the way that the predefined JavaScript variable called `fromValue` is referenced within the formula provided by the user. The token `fromValue` in the user-supplied formula is somehow *bound* by the second `eval()` statement to the value of the predefined variable in the DOM's local execution scope. This kind of *late binding* is fairly common in metaprogramming. With JavaScript, writing a script that can refer to objects defined in the larger execution context, otherwise called the script scope, is simple to do. When you use libraries like jQuery or the Reactive Extensions for JavaScript (RxJS) for the first time, how they can do so much in so few lines of code seems utterly magical. The magic lies in the metaprogramming foundation upon which JavaScript was conceived, which we examine at the end of this chapter. If JavaScript didn't expose its compiler in this ingeniously simple way, neither jQuery nor RxJS would exist.

Defining the local variable `fromValue` is a convention in the design of this particular web page. Rather than using a variable with a specific name, you could inject your own variable into the local scope and use it instead, as shown in figure 1.3.

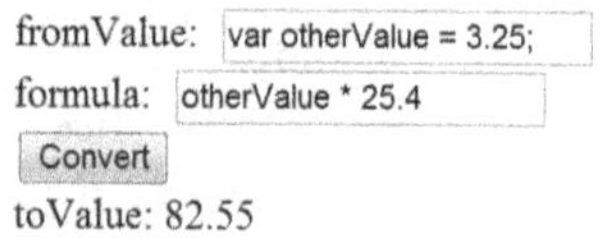

fromValue: var otherValue = 3.25;
formula: otherValue * 25.4
Convert
toValue: 82.55

**Figure 1.3**
**DynamicConversion.htm—**
**injecting variables into**
**JavaScript**

As you can see in figure 1.3, the value in the predefined `fromValue` variable is no longer being used in the user-supplied formula. This example takes advantage of the fact that when the first `eval()` statement runs in the `convert()` function, any JavaScript code can be provided to the compiler. A new variable named `otherValue` is injected into scope which the formula references instead. This *side effect* functions properly because the inches to millimeters calculation produces the correct output.

If you can create whole new objects using the JavaScript DOM, who knows what else you might be able to reference from a user-supplied script at runtime? You might have access to some of JavaScript's built-in libraries, for example. Let's give that a try. The example shown in figure 1.4 uses JavaScript's built-in `Math` class to calculate the tangent value at 45 degrees. In case you don't remember your college trigonometry, the tangent line on a circle at 45 degrees should have a slope of 1.

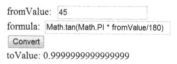

fromValue: 45
formula: Math.tan(Math.PI * fromValue/180)
Convert
toValue: 0.9999999999999999

**Figure 1.4**
**DynamicConversion.htm—using**
**JavaScript's `Math` class**
**dynamically**

The `tan()` function needs radians, not degrees. The formula first converts the degrees supplied by the user to radians using the constant for pi from JavaScript's `Math` class. In JavaScript, getting the constant for pi is as *easy as pie*, as the saying goes. Then the `Math` class is used again to compute the tangent value using the trigonometric `tan()` function. The result shows a slight rounding error, but it's pretty close and neatly illustrates the idea of using JavaScript's libraries from a dynamic script.

As you can see, the name chosen for the convert() function is wearing a bit thin as you begin to realize that this number converter can become pretty much whatever the user wants. For example, pass a single-quoted string for the from-Value and invoke one or more JavaScript strings in the formula to manipulate it. As you'll observe, the user-supplied input doesn't have to be a number at all. So it goes with metaprogramming in general. You'll often find that the metaprogramming-enabled interfaces you encounter seem simple from the outside. Beneath the surface, however, a lot of interesting and useful functionality is often waiting to be discovered.

Having studied the important metaprogramming concepts of late binding and runtime compilation, let's turn our attention to another popular technique that's used throughout the .NET Framework Class Library (FCL) to make code easier to write and comprehend.

### 1.2.2 *Metaprogramming via reflection*

The surface simplicity that many metaprogramming-enabled interfaces expose is often quite deliberate. As you'll see throughout this book, metaprogramming is commonly used to hide complexity by providing natural interfaces to complicated processes. Let's take a look at one of the simplest uses of this idea. Imagine that a ListBox control exists named listProducts. Your goal is to load the control with a list of (you guessed it) Product objects from a data context. Each Product contains a string property named ProductName and an integer property named ProductID. You want ProductName to be visible to the user, and when they click an item in the ListBox, you want the associated ProductID to be the selected value. Since .NET 1.0, the code to do that has been this simple:

```
listProducts.DisplayMember = "ProductName";
listProducts.ValueMember = "ProductID";
listProducts.DataSource = DataContext.Products;
```

In English, this code might be read as, "Bind these Product objects to this ListBox, displaying each ProductName to the user and setting the ProductID for each item as the selectable backing value." Notice how the declarative quality of the code makes it easy to understand what's going on. In fact, the C# code and the English rendering of it are quite similar.

You may have written code that does data binding as we've described dozens of times, but have you ever stopped to think about what's going on behind the scenes? How can strings be used in a statically typed language like C# to locate and bind property values by name at runtime? After all, the strings assigned to the Display-Member and ValueMember properties could have been variables instead of string literals. The treatment of them by Microsoft's data-binding code must be performed completely at runtime.

The answer is based on something known as the reflection application programming interface (API), which can *illustrate* the inner workings of a class at runtime,

## Declarative programming

In 1957, the FORTRAN programming language appeared—the great-grandparent of all the so-called imperative programming languages. In English, the word *imperative* is used to mean *command* or *duty*. FORTRAN and its descendants are called imperative languages because they give the computer commands to fulfill in a specific order. Imperative languages are good for instructing computers *how* to do work using specific sequences of instructions. The data binding example at hand hints at the power of a programming style called *declarative* that aims to move you from demanding *how* the computer should work to declaring *what* you want done instead. You can express what you want, and Microsoft's data-binding code figures out how to do it for you.

hence the name. Microsoft's `ListBox` data-binding code uses reflection to use bits of metadata left behind by the compiler, as shown in the following listing.

**Listing 1.2   DataSource reflection logic (C#)**

```csharp
public System.Collections.IEnumerable DataSource
{
  set
  {
    foreach (object current in value)
    {
      System.Reflection.PropertyInfo displayMetadata =
        current.GetType().GetProperty(DisplayMember);
      string displayString =
        displayMetadata.GetValue(current, null).ToString();
      // ...

      System.Reflection.PropertyInfo valueMetadata =
        current.GetType().GetProperty(ValueMember);
      object valueObject =
        valueMetadata.GetValue(current, null);
      // ...
    }
  }
}
```

Keep in mind that Microsoft's real data binding code is quite a bit more optimized than this. As each element in the `DataSource` collection is iterated over, its type is obtained using the `GetType()` method, which is inherited from `System.Object`.

**NOTE**   If you have any doubts about how fundamental reflection is in the .NET ecosystem, think for a moment about the significance that the `Get-Type()` method is included in `System.Object`. The base class for all .NET types is quite sparsely populated yet the `GetType()` method, which is critically important for metadata discovery and metaprogramming, was deemed important enough to be exposed from every single .NET object.

The System.Type object returned from GetType() has a method called GetProperty() that returns a PropertyInfo object. In turn, PropertyInfo has a method defined within it called GetValue() that's used to obtain the runtime value of a property on an object that implements the metadata described by the PropertyInfo.

In the System.Reflection namespace, you may be interested in several of these Info classes for expressing the various types of metadata, such as FieldInfo, MethodInfo, ConstructorInfo, PropertyInfo, and so on. As seen in listing 1.2, these classes are categorical in nature. Once you have an Info class in hand, you must supply an instance of the type you're interested in to do anything useful. In listing 1.2, the current Product reference in the loop is passed to the GetValue() method to fetch the instance values for each targeted property. Now that you know the Info classes in reflection are categorical, you may be thinking about reusing them to optimize the data binding code. Now that's thinking like a metaprogrammer! The following listing shows an optimized version of the code.

**Listing 1.3  Optimized DataSource binding logic (C#)**

```csharp
public IEnumerable DataSource {
  set {
    IEnumerator iterator = value.GetEnumerator();
    object currentItem;
    do {
      if (!iterator.MoveNext())
        return;
      currentItem = iterator.Current;
    } while (currentItem == null);

    PropertyInfo displayMetadata =
      currentItem.GetType().GetProperty(DisplayMember);
    PropertyInfo valueMetadata =
      currentItem.GetType().GetProperty(ValueMember);

    do {
      currentItem = iterator.Current;
      string displayString =
        displayMetadata.GetValue(currentItem, null).ToString();
      // ...

      object valueObject =
        valueMetadata.GetValue(currentItem, null);
      // ...
    } while (iterator.MoveNext());
  }
}
```

The first portion of the optimized DataSource data binding code shown in listing 1.3 iterates until it finds a non-null current item. This is necessary because you can't assume that the collection supplied as the DataSource has all non-null elements. The first elements could be empty. Once an element is located, some of its type metadata is cached for later use. Then the iteration over the elements uses the cached Property-Info objects to fetch the values from each element. As you can imagine, this is a more efficient approach because you don't have to perform the costly metadata resolution for every single object in the collection. Using caching and other optimizations to improve runtime performance is a common metaprogramming practice.

---

**The magic string problem**

One of the drawbacks of any metaprogramming approach that uses literal strings to drive application behavior at runtime is the fact that compile-time verification by compilers can't be performed. What would happen if you misspelled the `DisplayMember` value as `"ProductNane"`? You would discover that error during testing quickly. But what if you allowed the user to specify that string through an application setting, or worse, via a query parameter? Malicious users could begin probing for so-called *magic strings* that could be used to exploit your code by injecting new behaviors. An entire class of related exploits known as SQL injection attacks still plagues poorly designed websites, despite the fact that fixing the problem takes only a few minutes.

---

For brevity, Microsoft's `DataSource` binding implementation isn't shown here. It includes many interesting optimizations you can learn from. When you're ready, use the skills you pick up in chapter 2 to *introspect* into Microsoft's real data-binding code. You'll learn a lot from that exercise.

Next, we turn our attention to the idea of code generation, which is how most developers define metaprogramming.

### 1.2.3   *Metaprogramming via code generation*

So far we've looked at scripting and reflection as tools for metaprogramming. Now let's focus on generating new code at runtime. To ease into the subject, we focus on two of the simpler approaches to code generation using the Microsoft .NET Framework:

- Generating source code with the CodeDOM
- Generating IL with expression trees

To be as illustrative as possible, the approaches are quite different, but the outcomes only vary by the fact that one approach produces source code text, and the other emits new functions that are immediately executable.

#### CREATING SOURCE CODE AT RUNTIME WITH THE CODEDOM

Document-oriented programming models are common in software design because the document is such a powerfully simple metaphor for organizing information. You may have used the HTML DOM and the JavaScript DOM to do web development, for example. Microsoft has included something known as the CodeDOM in the .NET Framework. As its name implies, the CodeDOM allows you to take a document-oriented approach to code generation.

The CodeDOM comes from the early days of .NET and reflects some of the most primitive thinking about creating a standardized code-generation system for Microsoft's platform. The term *primitive* isn't pejorative in this case because the CodeDOM, despite the fact that Microsoft hasn't focused its attention there in recent years, is still an elegant code-generation system that many metaprogrammers still enjoy using. The CodeDOM uses a so-called *code graph*-based approach to creating code on the fly.

For all of the CodeDOM snippets shown in this section, the following namespace imports are required:

```
using System;
using System.IO;
using System.Text;
using System.CodeDom;
using System.Diagnostics;
using System.CodeDom.Compiler;
```

To understand how the CodeDOM functions as a source code generator, let's begin by exploring which .NET programming languages the CodeDOM supports. The `CodeDom-Provider` class is one of the central classes in the `System.CodeDom.Compiler` namespace and it includes a handy, static method called `GetAllCompilerInfo()`, which returns an array of `CompilerInfo` objects. Each `CompilerInfo` object has a method called `GetLanguages()` you can use to obtain the list of tokens that can be used to instantiate the language provider, like this:

```
foreach (System.CodeDom.Compiler.CompilerInfo ci in
  System.CodeDom.Compiler.CodeDomProvider.GetAllCompilerInfo())
{
  foreach (string language in ci.GetLanguages())
    System.Console.Write("{0}     ", language);
  System.Console.WriteLine();
}
```

Running this snippet in a console application or in LINQPad generates the list of synonyms for each of the installed language providers in the system. Figure 1.5 shows LINQPad acting as a sort of C# scratchpad to execute this bit of code.

As you can see in the LINQPad output, five language providers are installed on our system: C#, Visual Basic, JavaScript, Visual J#, and Managed C++. Each provider allows for the use of three or four synonyms for instantiating them. We come back to provider instantiation near the end of this example.

Notice that F# isn't among the supported languages. Microsoft hasn't been putting much effort into the CodeDOM in the last several years. There have been small enhancements and corrections in recent releases of the .NET Framework, but don't expect to see whole new language providers appear, for example. Microsoft still uses the CodeDOM heavily in its own major subsystems. The Text Templating Transformation Toolkit (T4) engine and the ASP.NET page generator still depend on the Code-DOM for code generation. Going forward, however, Microsoft will almost certainly continue to focus its research and development dollars for code generation in tools like the Roslyn API.

Next, let's take a look at dynamically generating a class. The CodeDOM uses the concept of a *code graph* to assemble .NET objects programmatically. As a C# source

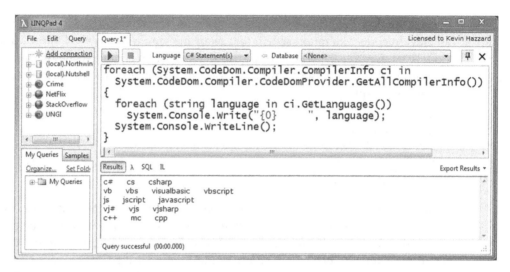

**Figure 1.5   Enumerating the synonyms for the CodeDOM language providers using LINQPad**

---

**LINQPad: A tool that every .NET developer needs**

It's not often that we speak categorically about development tools. As *polyglot* programmers, we admire most development tools in a somewhat egalitarian fashion. Once in a while though, a tool comes along that's so valuable we feel we must recommend it to every developer we meet. LINQPad, written by Joe Albahari, is such a tool. It can be used as a scratchpad for your .NET code. As its name implies, it's also good at helping to write and debug LINQ queries. As of this writing, you can freely download LINQPad from http://LINQPad.net. If you don't already have it, we encourage you to download it and begin exploring right away.

---

file might start with the declaration of a namespace, a CodeDOM graph typically begins with the creation of a `System.CodeDom.CodeNamespace` object. The `Code-Namespace` serves as the root of the graph. Going back to the source code analogy, the curly braces following a `namespace` declaration in C# are used to contain the types that will be defined within it. The `CodeNamespace` type in the CodeDOM behaves the same way. It's a container in which various types and code can be defined. Before jumping into the code sample, let us take a moment to describe how the code works. Here are the steps:

1  Create a `CodeNamespace` that is the CodeDOM class that represents a CLR (Common Language Runtime) namespace. We'll call our example namespace `Meta-World` to make it memorable.

2  Create a `CodeNamespaceImport` to import the `System` namespace in the generated source code. These are like `using` declarations in C# or `Import` declarations in Visual Basic.

3 Create a `CodeTypeDeclaration` named "Program" for the class that will be generated. This is like using the `class` keyword in your code to declare a new type.

4 Create a `CodeMemberMethod` named "Main" that will serve as the entry point function in the `Program` class. The method object will be inserted into the `Program` class. This follows how source code is written. The `Program` class is defined in the namespace, and the `Main` function is defined in the `Program` class.

5 Create a `CodeMethodInvokeExpression` to call "Console.WriteLine" with a `CodePrimitiveExpression` parameter of "Hello, world!". This is the hardest part to understand because of the nested way in which the code is structured.

You can probably see where this is going. We'll be dynamically generating the time-honored "Hello, world!" program with the code shown in the following listing.

**Listing 1.4   Assembling the "Hello, world!" program with the CodeDOM (C#)**

```csharp
partial class HelloWorldCodeDOM
{
  static CodeNamespace BuildProgram()
  {
    var ns = new CodeNamespace("MetaWorld");
    var systemImport = new CodeNamespaceImport("System");
    ns.Imports.Add(systemImport);
    var programClass = new CodeTypeDeclaration("Program");
    ns.Types.Add(programClass);
    var methodMain = new CodeMemberMethod
    {
      Attributes = MemberAttributes.Static
      , Name = "Main"
    };
    methodMain.Statements.Add(
      new CodeMethodInvokeExpression(
        new CodeSnippetExpression("Console")
        , "WriteLine"
        , new CodePrimitiveExpression("Hello, world!")
      )
    );
    programClass.Members.Add(methodMain);
    return ns;
  }
}
```

**NOTE**   In chapter 4, we show in depth how to generate code dynamically using the CodeDOM. In the small example shown here, we used the `Code-SnippetExpression` for simplicity. Using that CodeDOM object can lock you into producing code for one specific language, which often defeats one purpose for using the CodeDOM to begin with.

The `BuildProgram()` method shown in listing 1.4 encapsulates the script outlined earlier, returning a `CodeNamespace` object to the caller. You haven't yet rendered the source code. That comes next. The `CodeNamespace` object can be used by a `CodeDom-Provider` to generate source code. Now you have to use one of the five language providers installed on our computer to do the work. The example in listing 1.5 performs the following steps to do that:

1  Create a `CodeGeneratorOptions` object to instruct the chosen compiler how to behave. You can control indentation, line spacing, bracing, and more with this class.

2  Create a `StringWriter` that the language provider will stream the generated source code into. An attached `StringBuilder` holds the generated source code.

3  Create a C# language provider and invoke the `GenerateCodeFromNamespace` method, passing the `CodeNamespace` constructed by the `BuildProgram()` method shown in listing 1.4.

Once completed, the `StringBuilder` will contain the source code you're after. The example program dumps the emitted source code to the console. But it could as easily be written to disk.

**Listing 1.5   Generating source code from a `CodeNamespace` (C#)**

```
partial class HelloWorldCodeDOM
{
  static void Main()
  {
    CodeNamespace prgNamespace = BuildProgram();
    var compilerOptions = new CodeGeneratorOptions()
    {
      IndentString = "  ",
      BracingStyle = "C",
      BlankLinesBetweenMembers = false
    };
    var codeText = new StringBuilder();
    using (var codeWriter = new StringWriter(codeText))
    {
      CodeDomProvider.CreateProvider("c#")
        .GenerateCodeFromNamespace(
          prgNamespace, codeWriter, compilerOptions);
    }
    var script = codeText.ToString();
    Console.WriteLine(script);
  }
}
```

Compile and run this little code-generator program to see the nicely formatted C# program it produces in the following listing.

**Listing 1.6   CodeDOM-generated C# source code for "Hello, world!"**

```
namespace MetaWorld
{
  using System;

  public class Program
  {
    static void Main()
    {
      Console.WriteLine("Hello, world!");
    }
  }
}
```

Generating C# source code is easy, isn't it? But what if you wanted to generate managed C++ source code for the same program? You might be surprised at how simple that change is. Modify the string that reads `"c#"` in the call to `CodeDomProver` `.CreateProvider()` in listing 1.5 to read `"c++"`, and the metaprogram will generate C++ code instead. The following listing shows the C++ version of the dynamically generated source code after making that small change.

**Listing 1.7   CodeDOM-generated C++ source code for "Hello, world!"**

```
namespace MetaWorld {
  using namespace System;
  using namespace System;
  ref class Program;

  public ref class Program
  {
    static System::Void Main();
  };
}
namespace MetaWorld {
  inline System::Void Program::Main()
  {
    Console->WriteLine(L"Hello, world!");
  }
}
```

The output of the slightly modified program is nicely formatted source code written in Managed C++, which you could save to disk for compilation in a future build step, for example. According to the output from the LINQPad run shown in figure 1.5, you could also have used the synonyms `"mc"` and `"cpp"` to instantiate the C++ language provider. The remaining providers for Visual Basic, JavaScript, and Visual J# are available to create well-formatted code in those languages, too. Give them a try to see that switching the output language when generating source code from a CodeDOM code graph is almost effortless.

We hope this example reveals how straightforward it is to generate source code at runtime. Yet we haven't answered the central question about why you would want to do such a thing. Why would you ever want to generate source code? Here are some ideas taken from real-world projects that have used code-generation techniques successfully:

- Creating entity classes from database metadata for an object-relational mapping (ORM) tool during a build process.
- Automating the generation of a SOAP client to embed features in the proxy classes that aren't exposed through Microsoft's command-line tools.
- Automating the generation of boundary test cases for code based on simple method parameter and return type analysis.

The list goes on and on. Whatever your reasons for wanting to generate source code, the CodeDOM makes it fairly easy. The CodeDOM isn't the only way to generate source code in the .NET Framework, but once you become comfortable with the classes in the

System.CodeDom namespace, it's not a bad choice. The preceding example is deliberately simple. When you're ready to dive deeper into the CodeDOM, see chapter 4, which is dedicated to the CodeDOM and which shows many advanced metaprogramming techniques with rich, reusable examples.

Now that we've delved into expressing code as data, let's turn our attention to a more recently introduced way to do that in the .NET Framework.

### CREATING IL AT RUNTIME USING EXPRESSION TREES

One of the most common metaprogramming techniques is expressing code as data. That may sound a bit odd at first. The CodeDOM example in the last section described code as a set of data structures to emit source code. An arguably more interesting metaprogramming practice involves compiling the data that represents a body of code into an assembly that can be saved to disk or executed immediately by the running application. This cuts out the step of having to compile intermediate source code files. Better still, if the code graph were somehow independent of the machine architecture, it could be serialized to a remote computer to be compiled and executed there. The remote computer need not be using the same operating system or even the same processor architecture, as long as it has the means for compiling the serialized data structure. Those types of in-memory compilation scenarios are quite a bit more common in metaprogramming than the ones for generating source in an intermediate step.

To demonstrate this idea of in-memory compilation, the code graph must somehow be assembled at runtime into IL. As it turns out, the CodeDOM classes you examined can compile code graphs and blocks of raw source code written in one of the supported languages into .NET assemblies. Those dynamically generated assemblies can be written to disk for future use or exposed as in-memory types for immediate use by the currently executing application. There are also classes in the Reflection.Emit namespace that are well-suited for IL generation. But both the CodeDOM and Reflection.Emit approaches are a bit too complex for an introductory chapter designed to bring developers up to speed who may be learning about metaprogramming for the first time. Both the CodeDOM and Reflection.Emit approaches are important, which is why we dedicate chapters 4 and 5, respectively, to them. To get comfortable with dynamic IL generation in .NET right now, expression trees are the best vehicle for learning the fundamentals.

To understand expression trees, you need to understand a bit of history concerning delegates in the .NET Framework and languages. Delegates were introduced in the first version of the Framework. They were pretty slow in the early days, so a lot of performance-conscious developers avoided using them for computationally intensive work. Early delegates, as expressed in C# and Visual Basic, also had to be named at compile time, which made them a bit awkward feeling. When the 2.0 Framework shipped, anonymous methods were added to the C# language. Under the covers, the runtime implementation of delegates also got a big performance boost at that time. These were steps in the right direction. Higher-order functions could now be declared inline without having to assign names to them. They performed well at

## From C++ function pointers to .NET expression trees

The C++ language uses so-called *function pointers* to pass functions around as parameters to other functions. Using this technique, a function caller can provide a variety of implementations at runtime, passing the one that best suits the current needs of the application. Does that sound familiar? Indeed, these so-called higher-order functions in C++ enable a rudimentary kind of application composition that can be used for metaprogramming.

The problem with this approach is that the compiler can't check that the parameters or the return type of the referenced functions correctly match the expectations of the caller. The .NET Framework 1.0 introduced delegates to deal with this problem. Delegates can be passed around like function references, but they fully enforce the call contract in a type-safe way. Through several revisions of the .NET Framework, the delegate concept has greatly evolved. Today we have .NET expression trees, which masterfully blend the concepts of higher-order functions with code as data and a runtime compiler into a rich instrument for everyday metaprogramming.

runtime, too. Anonymous methods made the C# delegate syntax much more coherent, but the language still lacked the overall expressive power of truly functional programming languages.

## What makes a programming language functional?

According to computer scientist Dr. John Hughes, in his research paper "Why Functional Programming Matters," programming languages can be considered functional if they have first-class support for both higher-order functions and lazy evaluation. Higher-order functions are those that accept other functions as parameters or return new functions to their callers. The C# language has had that capability since the beginning, courtesy of delegates in the Common Language Runtime (CLR). *Lazy evaluation* means waiting until a calculation is needed to perform it. The .NET class library includes the `Lazy<T>` type for deferring execution, but it's not a language construct. The C# and Visual Basic languages both support the `yield return` syntax in their iterator blocks which, when chained together as the LINQ standard query operators do, exhibits a useful kind of lazy evaluation for list comprehension. But this isn't the language-supported kind of lazy evaluation that Dr. Hughes was talking about. If you want true lazy evaluation capability in a .NET language today, you should take a look at F#, which is the only .NET language from Microsoft that supports it.

In 2006, Microsoft added expression trees to the Base Class Library (BCL) and lambda expression support to the C# and Visual Basic languages. These features were added to support LINQ. With LINQ, the .NET languages could seriously compete with more functional languages for constructing what are known as *list comprehensions*. That term goes way back into computer science history. For now, the best way to think about list comprehension is that it enables lists of objects to be created from other lists. That sounds as absurdly simple as it is. When you think about it, doesn't most of our work in software development involve list creation and manipulation? Indeed, list handling is one of those core concepts that can make or break a programming language.

With the new LINQ-oriented features added to C#, a function that generically accepts two parameters and returns a result could be expressed as follows:

```
public delegate TResult Func<in T1, in T2, out TResult>(T1 arg1, T2 arg2);
```

Functions that compare one integer to another and return a Boolean result would certainly fit this pattern. An instance of a function that tests whether a `Left` parameter is greater than a `Right` parameter might be expressed this way:

```
public bool GreaterThan(int Left, int Right)
{
  return Left > Right;
}
```

It may seem odd to think about "instances of functions," but that metaprogramming concept will become clearer in the next few minutes. The `GreaterThan` function as it's defined above is okay, but using it as a predicate for filtering query results, for example, is a bit cumbersome. The fact that it's an independently defined and named function is part of the problem. To use it, you'd have to wrap it in a specific delegate type or the closed generic type `Func<int,int,bool>`. C# now offers a much more succinct way to do this using a lambda expression:

```
(Left, Right) => Left > Right
```

The `=>` operator is read as "goes to," so for this expression in English, you might read it as "`Left` and `Right` parameters go to the result of testing if `Left` is greater than `Right`." Notice first of all that as a pure expression, there's no requirement that the `Left` and `Right` parameters be of any specific types. You could be comparing floating point numbers, integers, strings—who knows? But for compilers like C#, which isn't as good at doing deep type inference as F# is, you need to get more specific, like this:

```
Func<int, int, bool> GreaterThan = (Left, Right) => Left > Right;
```

Now the `Left` and `Right` parameters are both known by the compiler to be integer types.

We added the name `GreaterThan` back to the definition to show how this newfangled functional delegate described as a lambda expression links back to the old-fashioned function by the same name shown earlier. On the inside, both functions are identical. You could invoke either of them with code like this:

```
int Left = 7;
int Right = 11;
System.Console.WriteLine("{0} > {1} = {2}",
  Left, Right, GreaterThan(Left, Right));
```

This would print to the console 7>11=False as you'd expect. Being able to define functional delegates using lambda expressions sure makes the code more succinct. The compiler support for lambda expressions is nice, but using lambda expressions in

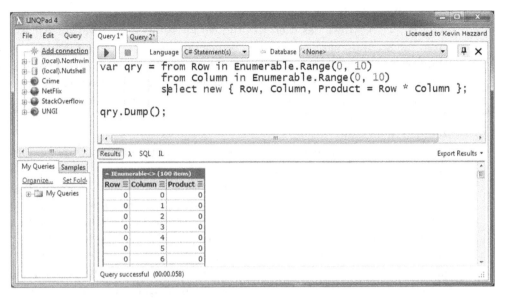

**Figure 1.6  Cross-joining two ranges in LINQ**

this way isn't how they add real value. Using them inline in LINQ expressions is more typical. Figure 1.6 shows LINQPad being used again. This time, we're performing a cross-join in LINQ to multiply one range of numbers against another. The `Dump()` function is a LINQPad feature that makes it easy to dump the results of an expression. If you were running the example code in a console application, you'd need to write out the results with custom code.

With two ranges of 10 values each, the result contains 100 items as shown in LINQPad's Results tab. Forty-five of those 100 results are redundant because the cross-joined ranges overlap and multiplication is commutative. You can eliminate the duplicates by comparing the row and column values in a predicate, by adding a filter like this:

```
qry.Where(a => a.Row >= a.Column).Dump();
```

Notice how the lambda expression passed to the `Where()` standard query operator looks a lot like the `GreaterThan Func<int,int,bool>` shown earlier. The difference is that rather than taking two parameters, the two compared values are accessed from properties of a single parameter. By using that expression in the `Where()` standard query operator, the results are filtered by it. We call this type of filtering function a *predicate*.

You could read the predicate expression `a=>a.Row>=a.Column` in English as "Return true for items where the `Row` number is greater than or equal to the `Column` number." If you're unaccustomed to LINQ, the way this expression is used in context may be a bit confusing. What's the a parameter? Where did it come from? What type is it? One of the clues can be found in the Results tab in LINQPad. Notice in figure 1.6 that the result of the `Dump()` is of type `IEnumerable<>`. The query must produce a list of something. Still, you don't know what type those items in the list have because the selectnew{…} syntax was used to produce an anonymous type which has no name from the programmer's perspective. You can tell from the output that each unnamed thing has a Row property, a Column property, and a Product property. Behind the scenes, the items in the list do have a named type, but you wouldn't want to read it. For anonymous types, the compiler generates a long, strange-looking name that only has value internally. If LINQPad were to show you the name in the Results, it would only get in the way.

Now that you understand that the query produces a list of anonymously typed objects, the parameter named a in the lambda expression might make a bit more sense. In this case, the name a was chosen because each of the objects passed to the function will be one of those anonymous types. You could have used any name for the parameter. But when lambda functions are embedded like this, we often use parameter names that are a bit more compact. This increases comprehension because the use of the function is so close to its definition, long descriptive names aren't often needed. When functions are declared the old-fashioned way, totally separated from their points of use, more descriptive parameter names tend to increase comprehension.

In figure 1.7, reading the numbers from top to bottom and left to right, you can visualize what the improved results of the filtered query look like.

The 45 duplicate values in the cross-join operation that would have appeared on the bottom and left sides have been filtered out by the predicate. Try the filtered query in LINQPad to see that it produces the result shown in figure 1.7. Then try using some other predicates to manipulate the results in interesting ways. After all, the best way to learn is to play.

Now that you understand how to filter queries using a lambda expression in LINQ, you're ready to understand an interesting metaprogramming connection. Asking the C# compiler to turn the lambda expression into a function is purely a compile-time process. It may be newfangled looking, but it's still sort of *old school*, as they say. What if you need to be able to pass in a variety of filter predicates based on the circumstances

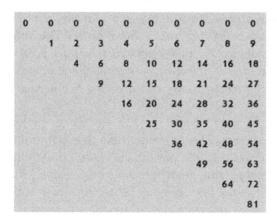

Figure 1.7   The results of filtering a cross-join of two ranges with a lambda predicate

## The importance of playfulness

For adults, some types of play are pure distraction. Blasting away at aliens in a first-person shooting game for hours at a time can certainly wash away the worries of the day, but it probably doesn't help to establish and refine the prototypes that your mind needs to absorb new ideas. Playfulness can be useful as a learning tool. Small children lack analytical skills, so they use play to build experience and knowledge about how the world works. As you get older, your play becomes more and more structured until eventually you may even forget how to do it. Throughout this book, we encourage you to be playful with the topics we're teaching you. When we show you one way to do something, try a few variations to cement what you've learned deep into your mind.

at the moment? Moreover, what if some of those *filtering algorithms* can't be known at compile time? Or perhaps they come from a remote process that can create new filters on the fly, sending them across the wire to your application to compile and use. Metaprogramming to the rescue!

Moving from the idea of concrete, compile-time functions to a more generic abstraction of those functions is fairly straightforward in .NET, thanks to so-called expression trees and the latest compilers from Microsoft. You've already seen how the C# compiler can turn a lambda expression into a real function that you can call like any other. Internally, compilers operate by parsing the text of source code into abstract syntax trees (AST). These trees follow certain basic rules for expressing code as data. When lambda expressions are compiled, for example, they fit into the resulting AST as any other .NET constructs would.

## What happened to Compiler-as-a-Service?

At the Microsoft Professional Developer Conference in 2008, Anders Hejlsberg hinted at things to come in future versions of the C# programming language. One of them was called Compiler-as-a-Service. The basic idea was to expose some of the C# compiler's black box functionality for developers outside of Microsoft to use. Microsoft has since dropped that name, but the ideas behind what was known as Compiler-as-a-Service are alive and well. Jump ahead to chapter 10 to find out more right away.

What if you could preserve the AST created by the compiler so that it could be modified at runtime to suit your needs? If that were possible, all sorts of interesting things would be possible. Unfortunately, as of this writing the parser and AST generator for C# is still exposed in such a way that the average developer can't use it to implement the dynamic execution scenarios just described. But the aptly named expression trees in the .NET Framework are an interesting step in that direction.

Expression trees were introduced into .NET 3.0 to support LINQ. Then they got great enhancements to support the Dynamic Language Runtime (DLR) in version 4.0 of the Framework. In addition to the expression tree enhancements in version 4.0, the

.NET compilers got the ability to parse C# and Visual Basic code directly into expressions. Think back to the `GreaterThan()` function defined as a lambda expression earlier. Remember the `Func<int,int,bool>` that created a real, callable function at compile time? Now evaluate the following line of code and look for the differences:

```
Expression<Func<int, int, bool>> GreaterThanExpr =
  (Left, Right) => Left > Right;
```

Syntactically, the `GreaterThan Func<>` has been *enclosed* in an `Expression<>` type and renamed to `GreaterThanExpr`. The new name will make it clearly different in the discussion that follows. But the lambda expression looks exactly the same. What's the effect of the change? First, if you try to compile an invocation of this new `GreaterThanExpr` expression, it will fail:

```
bool result = GreaterThanExpr(7, 11); // won't compile!
```

The `GreaterThanExpr` expression can't be invoked directly as the `GreaterThan` function could. That's because after compilation, `GreaterThanExpr` is data, not code. Rather than compiling the lambda expression into an immediately runnable function, the C# compiler built an `Expression` object instead. To invoke the expression, you need to take one more step at runtime to convert this bit of data into a runnable function.

```
Func<int, int, bool> GreaterThan =
  GreaterThanExpr.Compile();

bool result = GreaterThan(7, 11); // compiles!
```

The `Expression` class exposes a `Compile()` method that can be called to emit runnable code. This dynamically generated function is identical to the one produced by both the old-fashioned, separately defined method named `GreaterThan` and the precompiled `Func<>` delegate by the same name. Calling a method to compile expressions at runtime may feel a bit odd at first. But once you experience the power of dynamically assembled expressions, you'll begin to feel right at home.

### How LINQ uses Expressions

LINQ queries benefit directly from the way that `Expressions` can be compiled. But the various LINQ providers don't typically call the `Compile()` method as shown here. Each provider has its own method for converting expression trees into code. When a predicate like `a => a.Row > a.Count` is compiled, it might produce IL that can be invoked in a .NET application. But the same expression could be used to produce a WHERE clause in a SQL statement or an XPath query or an OData $filter expression. In LINQ, expression trees act as a sort of neutral form for conveying the intent of code. The LINQ providers interpret that intent at runtime to turn it into something that can be executed.

As you've seen in the previous example, the C# compiler can build an `Expression` for you at compile time. That's certainly convenient, but you can also assemble lambda expressions by hand which may be useful in some applications. The code in the following listing shows how to construct and compile an `Expression` class programmatically that implements the `GreaterThan` function seen previously.

**Listing 1.8  Assembling a lambda `Expression` manually**

```
using System;
using System.Linq.Expressions;

class ManuallyAssembledLambda
{
  static Func<int, int, bool> CompileLambda()
  {
    ParameterExpression Left =
      Expression.Parameter(typeof(int), "Left");
    ParameterExpression Right =
      Expression.Parameter(typeof(int), "Right");

    Expression<Func<int, int, bool>> GreaterThanExpr =
      Expression.Lambda<Func<int, int, bool>>
      (
        Expression.GreaterThan(Left, Right),
        Left, Right
      );

    return GreaterThanExpr.Compile();
  }

  static void Main()
  {
    int L = 7, R = 11;
    Console.WriteLine("{0} > {1} is {2}", L, R,
      CompileLambda()(L, R));
  }
}
```

The `CompileLambda()` method starts by creating two `ParameterExpression` objects: one for an integer named `Left`, and another for an integer named `Right`. Then the static `Lambda<TDelegate>` method in the `Expression` class is used to generate a strongly typed `Expression` for the delegate type you need. The `TDelegate` for the lambda expression is of type `Func<int,int,bool>` because you want the resulting expression to take two integer parameters and return a Boolean value based on the comparison of them. Notice that the root of the lambda expression is obtained from the `GreaterThan`property on the `Expression` class. The returned value is an `Expression` subclass known as a `BinaryExpression`, meaning it takes two parameters. The `Expression` type serves as a factory class for many `Expression`-derived types and other helper members. Here are a few of the other `Expression` subtypes you're likely to use when building expression trees programmatically:

- `BinaryExpression`—Add, Multiply, Modulo, GreaterThan, LessThan, and so on
- `BlockExpression`—Acts as a container for a sequence of other Expressions
- `ConditionalExpression`—IfThen, IfThenElse, and so on

- `GotoExpression`—For branching and returning to `LabelExpressions`
- `IndexExpression`—For array and property access
- `MethodCallExpression`—For invoking methods
- `NewExpression`—For calling constructors
- `SwitchExpression`—For testing object equivalence against a set of values
- `TryExpression`—For implementing exception handling
- `UnaryExpression`—Convert, Not, Negate, Increment, Decrement, and so on

The list goes on and on. In fact, there are more than 500 methods and properties returning dozens of expression types in that class. They cover about any coding construct you can imagine (and probably many more that you can't). Complex expression trees can be constructed entirely from `Expression`–derived objects instantiated directly from static properties and methods in this base class.

To round out this introductory section on the topic, let's look at one more interesting example. The manually assembled lambda expression shown earlier is nice, but it only provides predicates for integers. Moreover, it emits code only for greater-than operations. The following listing shows a more dynamic version of that code that can be used for any data type and a variety of ordering comparisons.

**Listing 1.9  A `DynamicPredicate` class using expression trees**

```
using System;
using System.Linq.Expressions;

class DynamicPredicate
{
  public static Expression<Func<T, T, bool>>
    Generate<T>(string op)
  {
    ParameterExpression x =
      Expression.Parameter(typeof(T), "x");
    ParameterExpression y =
      Expression.Parameter(typeof(T), "y");
    return Expression.Lambda<Func<T, T, bool>>
      (
        (op.Equals(">")) ? Expression.GreaterThan(x, y) :
          (op.Equals("<")) ? Expression.LessThan(x, y) :
          (op.Equals(">=")) ? Expression.GreaterThanOrEqual(x, y) :
          (op.Equals("<=")) ? Expression.LessThanOrEqual(x, y) :
          (op.Equals("!=")) ? Expression.NotEqual(x, y) :
          Expression.Equal(x, y),
        x, y
      );
  }
}
```

A generic function has been built to generate a type-safe expression based on the compared type and a comparison operation using a type parameter and a standard string parameter, respectively. The generator function is aptly named `Generate`. In the following listing, notice how predicates for different data types can now be defined and compiled dynamically.

**Listing 1.10  Invoking the `DynamicPredicate`**

```
static void Main()
{
  string op = ">=";
  var integerPredicate =
    DynamicPredicate.Generate<int>(op).Compile();
  var floatPredicate =
    DynamicPredicate.Generate<float>(op).Compile();

  int iA = 12, iB = 4;
  Console.WriteLine("{0} {1} {2} : {3}", iA, op, iB,
      integerPredicate(iA, iB));

  float fA = 867.0f, fB = 867.0f;
  Console.WriteLine("{0} {1} {2} : {3}", fA, op, fB,
      floatPredicate(fA, fB));

  Console.WriteLine("{0} {1} {2} : {3}", fA, ">", fB,
      DynamicPredicate.Generate<float>(">").Compile()(fA, fB));
}
```

The first predicate generated in this example uses the greater-than-or-equal-to operator on integer types. The next one is for the same operator comparing floating-point types. The predicates are then used to perform simple comparisons. In the last statement, a dynamic predicate is built for the greater-than operator on floating-point types, which is used to compare the same floating-point values from the last invocation. Figure 1.8 shows the result of running the code.

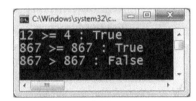

**Figure 1.8  Exercising the `DynamicPredicate` class**

We've only scratched the surface of what expression trees can do in .NET. The power of LINQ and the DLR wouldn't be possible without them. For example, LINQ's `IQueryable` interface can be used to consume dynamically assembled expressions, giving you a truly elegant way to make the search and query interfaces in your applications simple to extend over time. For that example and more, turn to chapter 6. In the meantime, let's take a look at one more way to do metaprogramming in .NET: dynamic typing.

### 1.2.4  *Metaprogramming via dynamic objects*

Statically typed languages rule the roost, as they say, in the .NET world. Even though Microsoft's IronPython implementation of the venerable Python programming language is impressive both in terms of performance and compatibility, programmers accustomed to working on the Microsoft stack don't seem to be as attracted to it as some of us had hoped. It's not just that old habits die hard. New skills are quite difficult to form, in particular when one believes that the tools they use are excellent for problem-solving. Asking C++ and Visual Basic 6 developers to upgrade their skills to learn C# and Visual Basic .NET was difficult enough. Asking those developers to invest time and energy to learn Python and Ruby has proven to be tougher still.

Dynamic languages like JavaScript, Python, and Ruby have a lot to offer. The languages themselves are all wonderfully expressive. Well-developed platforms and libraries like jQuery, Django, and Rails make it easy to get going. After working with these languages for a while, one discovers what seems to be endless depth in the included libraries. Almost anything you could ever want for building rich applications has been created and captured in the standard libraries. Pythonistas say about their language that it comes *batteries included.*

Alas, dynamic languages may never be as popular on the .NET Framework as our trustworthy, statically typed companions of old. But that doesn't mean that the dynamic programming language developers should have all the fun.

### A C# DYNAMIC TYPING BACKGROUNDER

On Jan. 25, 2008, Charlie Calvert of Microsoft Corporation posted a blog article titled "Future Focus I: Dynamic Lookup." In that post, he wrote, "The next version of Visual Studio will provide a common infrastructure that will enable all .NET languages, including C#, to optionally resolve names in a program at runtime instead of compile time. We call this technology dynamic lookup."

True to his word, version 4.0 of the C# programming language included great support for creating and handling dynamically typed objects. Charlie went on in the post to list the key scenarios for using this new capability. Years later, his list is still compelling. The list includes:

- Office automation and COM interop
- Consuming types written in dynamic languages
- Enhanced support for reflection

We look at the first two scenarios in detail in Part 3 (chapters 8-10) of this book. Because you've already gotten a taste of reflection in this chapter, let's build on that learning by examining Charlie's third scenario. We begin by taking a quick tour of so-called *duck typing.* This odd-sounding term traces its origins to James Whitcomb Riley, a 19th century poet: "When I see a bird that walks like a duck and swims like a duck and quacks like a duck, I call that bird a duck." The current phrase, specific to ensuring type-appropriateness in programming languages, is only a couple of decades old.

With respect to computer programming, you might translate Riley's "walk like a duck..." line into "If an object supports the methods and properties I expect, I can use them."

We use the word *expect* deliberately because the duck-typing concept is all about compile-time versus runtime expectations. If you expect an object to have a method named `CompareTo` in it, taking one `Object` parameter and returning an integer result, do you care how it got there? The answer depends somewhat on your worldview. More

## The L in SOLID

The programming acronym SOLID packs a lot of meaning into five little letters. The L stands for the Liskov substitution principle (LSP), which has a genuinely formidable sounding ring to it. Although it may sound a bit unnerving, the LSP isn't all that challenging to understand. It means that subtypes behave like the types from which they're derived. Inherent in the LSP is that the compiler gives the programmer support for enforcing type correctness at compile time.

Why is this significant to understand in a discussion about duck typing? Well, in statically typed languages like C#, classes behave like contracts. They make promises about their members, the count, order, and type of parameters that must be provided, and the return types. Truly dynamic languages don't enforce contracts this way, which makes them feel different to the programmer who's accustomed to getting LSP support from the compiler. This will be important to keep in mind as you learn about C#'s dynamic typing capabilities.

importantly, it depends on your tools. Examine the code in figure 1.9, which throws an exception at runtime while trying to perform a simple sort.

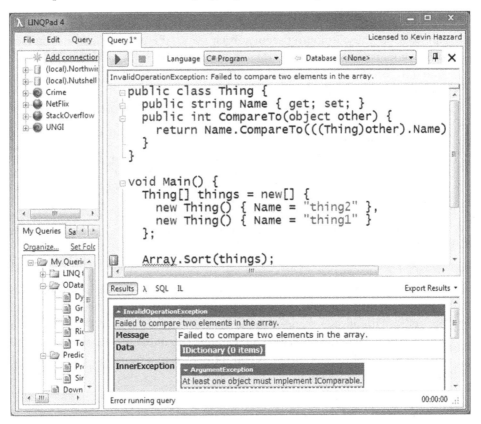

**Figure 1.9   Simple sorting that throws an exception**

The code looks okay, and indeed, it compiles perfectly. But an `ArgumentException` is thrown at runtime from the `Sort` function, indicating that "At least one object (in the comparison) must implement `IComparable`." If you were new to C#, having come from the Python or Ruby worlds, this error might cause real confusion. Having looked to other C# programs as examples, a dynamic-language programmer might have concluded that implementing a `CompareTo` function in a class with the expected method signature was all that's required to do sorting of arrays containing that type. The `Sort` function implementation is a bit more demanding than that, however. Not only must you include a `CompareTo` method in your class, it must specifically be of the type `IComparable.CompareTo`. Adding that one simple declaration to the `Thing` class solves the problem:

```
public class Thing : IComparable
{
  public string Name { get; set; }
  public int CompareTo(object other)
  {
    return Name.CompareTo(((Thing)other).Name);
  }
}
```

This kind of demand is foreign to programmers accustomed to working in dynamic languages because it doesn't seem substantive to them. In fact, to a dynamic-language programmer, this sort of demand feels downright offensive. Why should the `Array.Sort` function care how the `CompareTo` method got into the `Thing` class? To them, the existence of the function at runtime should be enough.

### No value in religious debate

This is the point in the discussion where we could spiral downward into a somewhat religious argument about the worth of various programming models, but we're going to resist the urge. The dynamic way of programming is no better or worse than the static way. It's different. Some problems are well-suited to one type of solution or another. The fact of the matter is that software developers get great work done in statically typed environments and dynamically typed ones, too. That makes both approaches worthy of study and respect.

The question that Charlie Calvert and the C# compiler team posed in 2008 is: "Can one modern programming language support both the static and dynamic typing models well?" With all due respect, the answer to that question is resoundingly no. C# is still a statically typed language. The dynamic capability in version 4.0 has been bolted on to the side of the language, as you'll discover in a moment. Declaring and using a dynamic object in C# could hardly be easier:

```
dynamic name = "Kevin";
System.Console.WriteLine("{0} ({1})",
  name, name.Length);
```

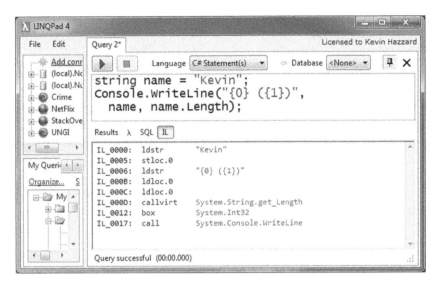

**Figure 1.10   The IL from writing a string to the console**

Run that code in LINQPad after selecting C# Statements from the Language drop-down list to see that it dutifully formats and prints the name and the length of the string as 'Kevin(5)' to the Results tab. Now change the declared type for the name variable to a string and run it again. You'll notice that the output in the Results tab is identical. What's the difference? While you have the name variable defined as a string, switch to LINQPad's IL tab. This will show you the compiled IL for the code, which will look something like figure 1.10.

Your introduction to IL is coming in chapter 2, but this code is so simple, you should be able to make out what's going on. The two literal strings you see in the C# code are pushed onto the stack before the get_Length method is called on the System .String class using the callvirt opcode. If you've never looked at IL, you may be surprised to find that the Length property accessor for a string is implemented with the name get_Length. The result of calling get_Length is of type System.Int32, but the Console.WriteLine method expects parameters of type of System.Object. The box opcode is used to box that integer value type as an object before calling System .WriteLine. All this was done with eight IL opcodes.

Now change the type of the name variable back to dynamic, rerun the code, and observe the IL it produces. We won't show that IL listing here because it would take up a couple of pages and require several more pages to fully describe. In chapter 8, we do a deeper investigation of the CallSite class and other metaprogramming-relevant classes from the System.Runtime.CompilerServices and Microsoft.CSharp namespaces. As you scroll through the IL on your own, take time to notice two literal strings that are pushed on the stack that weren't pushed in the previous example:

```
IL_0012:  ldstr       "WriteLine"
//... some code omitted ...
IL_0089:  ldstr       "Length"
```

You may also notice that the reference to the get_Length method is also missing from the IL. How could the get_Length method be invoked if it's not in the IL? The fact that it's missing is an interesting clue, as it turns out. Also, do you see literal strings for "WriteLine" and "Length" in the original C# code? No, so why do these literal strings appear in the IL now? When the type of the name variable was changed from string to dynamic, many changes happened under the covers, as you can see.

The outermost change involves the emission by the C# compiler of CallSite objects into the IL. A CallSite is literally the *site* in the code where something dynamic happens. It may surprise you that in this code, there are two CallSite objects. One is used to invoke the Length property accessor on the name, which happens through a call to the runtime binder's GetMember method:

```
IL_0089:  ldstr       "Length"
//... some code omitted ...
IL_00AA:  call        Microsoft.CSharp.RuntimeBinder.Binder.GetMember
```

That makes sense given that the name variable was marked as dynamic. Using the dot operator after the name variable to invoke the Length property ends up passing the literal string "Length" to the C# runtime binder to reflect against the object to get the value. Do you remember that Charlie said in his blog post how *dynamic lookup* would simplify reflection? The reflection that the C# runtime binder is doing for you also explains why the call to the get_Length function is conspicuously absent in this version of the code. There's no need to bind up a call to get_Length at compile time because the invocation is going to happen at the CallSite at runtime via reflection.

The remaining mysteries at this point are (a) that literal string "WriteLine" that you found in the IL, and (b) that second CallSite that was emitted into the site container. Could they be related? Indeed, they are related. The second CallSite is used to call InvokeMember on the C# runtime binder to dispatch a dynamic call to the static "WriteLine" method on the System.Console class. The question that might pop into your mind is: "Why on Earth is the WriteLine method being called dynamically?" After all, nothing about System.Console was declared to be dynamic.

This code highlights one of the biggest concerns that many developers have about dynamic typing in C#. When you pass a type declared as dynamic to a method, or if that method returns such a type, that method call will also be implemented dynamically through a CallSite that's emitted by the compiler. Most developers expect to pay a price for using the dynamic keyword in C#, but they don't expect that it will have a ripple effect, causing other nearby function calls and member accesses to become dynamically invoked as well. The best advice we can give is to be careful when using C#'s dynamic keyword.

Now that you have an appreciation for what's happening behind the scenes with dynamic typing in C#, let's turn our attention to a simple but useful class that can be used to implement dynamic property bags.

> ### No dynamic type in C#
> You may be surprised to find that there's no backing type for the `dynamic` keyword in C#. The functionality enabled by the `dynamic` keyword is a clever set of compiler actions that emit and use `CallSite` objects in the site container of the local execution scope. The compiler manages what programmers perceive as dynamic object references through those `CallSite` instances. The parameters, return types, fields, and properties that get dynamic treatment at compile time may be marked with some metadata to indicate that they were generated for dynamic use, but the underlying data type for them will always be `System.Object`.

### IMPLEMENTING METAOBJECTS IN C#

Many dynamic languages allow any object to be treated like a property bag. Members can be added to or removed from the bag at will. Some dynamic languages even let you modify the class definitions on the fly so that newly instantiated objects of those types will get the updated definition. Using Python, for example, it's simple to add properties to an instance on the fly using code like this:

```
>>> class PyExpandoObject():
...     pass
...
>>> container = PyExpandoObject()
>>> container.Name = 'Jenny'
>>> container.PhoneNumber = 8675309
>>> print container.Name, '-', container.PhoneNumber
Jenny - 8675309
```

In this code, The `PyExpandoObject` class is defined as an empty class using the `pass` keyword. Then an instance of the `PyExpandoObject` named `container` is allocated. What happens next may seem odd to a developer using statically typed languages, but it's common in many metaprogramming environments. Two new members called `Name` and `PhoneNumber` are added by assigning values to their names. A `print` statement is used to report the values of the new members back to the console. Python infers the types of the new members correctly, which you can test by using Python's `type()` function.

```
>>> type(container.Name)
<type 'str'>
>>> type(container.PhoneNumber)
<type 'int'>
```

Internally, Python manages a dictionary of its members, which it can modify on the fly, adding new members or redefining them as necessary. Python even allows the programmer to delete members programmatically. Adding new members to a class instance in C# 4.0 is similarly simple when using the `ExpandoObject` class:

```
dynamic container = new System.Dynamic.ExpandoObject();
container.Name = "Jenny";
container.PhoneNumber = 8675309;
```

```
Console.WriteLine("{0} - {1}",
  container.Name, container.PhoneNumber);
```

This C# code will write the same string to the console that the preceding Python code did. In Python, any object can act as a dynamic property bag. In C#, though, you must use an ExpandoObject or build that functionality into one of your own classes. Not surprisingly, the ExpandoObject uses a dictionary object internally to mimic the functionality that Python offers. What's unclear, however, is how the C# compiler understands how to interact with the ExpandoObject class to enable new name value pairs to get into the internally managed dictionary.

In the example shown earlier involving a dynamic string, the GetMember function from the C# runtime binder was invoked to reflect on the string to obtain the value of its Length property. The GetMember function was called because you were trying to get the value of the Length property to display on the console. In the previous C# code using ExpandoObject, the assignment to container.Name and container.Phone-Number are clearly not going to invoke GetMember in the binder, because you're attempting to mutate the values, not fetch them. As you can imagine, the DLR also includes a SetMember function in the C# runtime binder for this purpose. The IL that sets the value "Jenny" to the Name property follows this abbreviated flow:

```
IL_000E: ldstr       "Name"
//... some code omitted ...
IL_0039: call        Microsoft.CSharp.RuntimeBinder.Binder.SetMember
//... some code omitted ...
IL_0058: ldstr       "Jenny"
```

The C# compiler emits a call to SetMember for the "Name" property to set the value "Jenny." The C# compiler seems to have done its part well, but you still don't know how the name value pair "Name", "Jenny") is going to get into the ExpandoObject's internal dictionary. The answer to that comes by looking at the implementation of ExpandoObject, which implements six interfaces:

```
IDynamicMetaObjectProvider
IDictionary<string,object>
ICollection<KeyValuePair<string,object>>
IEnumerable<KeyValuePair<string,object>>
IEnumerable
INotifyPropertyChanged
```

The first interface in the list is the one that enables the standard C# runtime binder's SetMember function to call custom code to manage ExpandoObject's internal dictionary object. The definition of IDynamicMetaObjectProvider is deceptively simple looking:

```
public interface IDynamicMetaObjectProvider
{
  DynamicMetaObject GetMetaObject(Expression parameter);
}
```

In this interface, you're beginning to see common metaprogramming terms that you can recognize from examples in this chapter. You know what *dynamic* means. You know what `Expressions` are. Metaobjects aren't yet well-defined, but they're almost certainly some kind of type used in metaprogramming.

---

**Meta madness!**

The appearance of the prefix *meta* over and over again in metaprogramming jargon can be a bit overwhelming. It's not a prefix that we encounter on English words all that often, so it can be a bit confusing. Remember that in Greek, *meta* means *after* or *beside*. You might read the DLR term *metaobject* to mean *after-object* or *beside-object*. The way the DLR uses metaobjects in conjunction with the runtime binders, they fit the *beside-object* definition better. Metaobjects run alongside other types like the `ExpandoObject` to help the runtime binder in binding up specific methods like `SetMember` and `GetMember` when the code demands to set or get named values, respectively.

---

By implementing this interface, the `ExpandoObject` can interact with the C# runtime binder by providing handlers for specific events that occur in the lifecycle of those types. The `DynamicMetaObject` returned by the `GetMetaObject` function in the interface has many virtual methods that can be overridden to provide specific types of runtime binding functionality. We cover all of these methods in detail in chapter 8. For now, the two methods required to understand the interface between C#'s runtime binder and `ExpandoObject`'s internal dictionary are

```
BindGetMember
BindSetMember
```

When the runtime binder observes that the dynamic object it's operating on implements the `IDynamicMetaObjectProvider` interface, it defers the binding calls to the methods in the `DynamicMetaObject` that's provided through that interface rather than trying to resolve them with reflection. This multistep process is admittedly arcane sounding, but once you get the hang of using it, you'll understand that it's as simple as it needs to be and flexible enough to handle nearly any metaprogramming scenario.

To remove any remaining mystery, let's implement an expandable property bag called `MyExpandoObject`, providing custom implementations for `GetMember` and `SetMember` at runtime. Rather than implementing the entire `IDynamicMetaObject-Provider` contract, let's take a shortcut. A helper class has been included in the .NET Framework called `DynamicObject` that implements `IDynamicMetaObject-Provider` for you, hiding the somewhat complex `Bind*` methods and exposing a set of similarly named but simpler `Try*` methods instead. To implement the dynamic property bag, you'll need to derive your class from `DynamicObject` and override the `TryGetMember` and `TrySetMember` functions to provide your custom binding code. The following listing shows the definition of the `MyExpandoObject` type.

**Listing 1.11  `MyExpandoObject`: a DLR-based dynamic property bag**

```
using System;
using System.Collections.Generic;
using System.Dynamic;

public class MyExpandoObject : DynamicObject
{
  private Dictionary<string, object> _dict =
    new Dictionary<string, object>();

  public override bool TryGetMember(
    GetMemberBinder binder, out object result)
  {
    result = null;
    if (_dict.ContainsKey(binder.Name.ToUpper()))
    {
      result = _dict[binder.Name.ToUpper()];
      return true;
    }
    return false;
  }

  public override bool TrySetMember(
    SetMemberBinder binder, object value)
  {
    if (_dict.ContainsKey(binder.Name.ToUpper()))
      _dict[binder.Name.ToUpper()] = value;
    else
      _dict.Add(binder.Name.ToUpper(), value);
    return true;
  }
}
```

For this implementation, we've decided that the properties inserted into the bag shouldn't have case-sensitive names. Programmers should be able to save a value into the property bag named JABBERWOCKY and retrieve it later with the name jAbBeRwOcKy, for example. The ToUpper function on the string class is used whenever properties are set and fetched from an internally managed dictionary containing the name value pairs. The code in the following listing shows how the MyExpandoObject might be used.

**Listing 1.12  Exercising `MyExpandoObject`**

```
class TestMyExpandoObject
{
  static void Main()
  {
    dynamic vessel = new MyExpandoObject();
    vessel.Name = "Little Miss Understood";
    vessel.Age = 12;
    vessel.KeelLengthInFeet = 32;
    vessel.Longitude = 37.55f;
    vessel.Latitude = -76.34f;
    Console.WriteLine("The {0} year old vessel " +
```

```
            "named {1} has a keel length of {2} feet " +
            "and is currently located at {3} / {4}.",
            vessel.AGE, vessel.name,
            vessel.keelLengthINfeet,
            vessel.Longitude, vessel.Latitude);
    }
}
```

After instantiating a `MyExpandoObject` and assigning the reference to a dynamic variable named `vessel`, properties of different types are placed into the property bag. Each assignment will invoke the overridden `TrySetMember` implementation, which will place them into the internal dictionary object. At the end, the properties are fetched from the property bag by name. To exercise the case-insensitive handling of property names, they've been deliberately cased differently than they were in assignments beforehand. Figure 1.11 shows the result of running the code in listing 1.10 and listing 1.11 in LINQPad.

This little metaprogramming-enabled class does a great job of raising the abstraction level for managing name value pairs, making the code highly reusable. It also increases comprehension by providing a natural interface while reducing the perceived complexity.

## 1.3 Summary

In this chapter, we spent time trying to convey that metaprogramming might sometimes be a bit complex on the inside, but it can greatly reduce the perceived complexity on the outside of the classes that you provide to your team. You also learned how cohesion and abstraction relate to complexity and how metaprogramming can help to

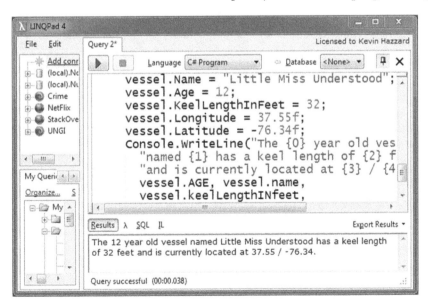

**Figure 1.11  The metaprogramming class called `MyExpandoObject` in action**

put them in balance. You discovered that you could use the synonyms *after-programming* and *beside-programming* to put the two basic ways in which metaprogramming is often implemented into contrast to enable future learning. Then you dove into common examples of metaprogramming that you may encounter working in and around the .NET Framework.

That's certainly a lot of material, but, to be honest, we've only been able to scratch the surface of the kinds of metaprogramming that can be done using the Microsoft .NET Framework. We made the examples in this chapter deliberately simple to get you started on the journey. We hope that these prototypes will serve you well as you continue your voyage through the remainder of the book.

# Exploring code and metadata with reflection

**This chapter covers**

- The need for reflection
- Reading metadata and executing code
- Practical uses of reflection

Metaprogramming in .NET can incorporate many different concepts and techniques. Some areas are fairly easy to grasp, others can be quite difficult. The best way to begin is to visit the Reflection API, which has been in .NET since version 1. It provides a fairly simplistic introduction to core concepts of metaprogramming (such as introspection) and it gives you a glimpse into the structure of .NET code.

To start the journey down the .NET metaprogramming road, you'll go through a couple of problems where reflection helps solve the issue. You'll walk through examples that demonstrate reading the contents of an assembly and running its code. Finally, you'll dissect real-world examples that we've used on projects in the past which illustrate how useful reflection can be in creating generalized, compact solutions. Let's start by looking at a couple metaprogramming-related issues you can solve with the power of the Reflection API.

## 2.1    *The need for reflection*

Reflection is a concept that has been around a long time in many programming languages, before .NET existed. *Reflection* is all about giving a developer the ability to read the contents of a program and execute its code. The depth of reflection that languages and platforms offer varies, but generally any system that allows you to inspect and invoke code at runtime uses some form of reflection.

Let's cover two scenarios that a .NET developer may run into where reflection can provide real value.

### 2.1.1   *Creating extensible applications*

It's not easy to write code that works well. Good developers review their designs with team members, write unit tests, use analyzers to review their work, and so on. And determining all the features that an application should have isn't the easiest endeavor. Users are always asking for new features, and understandably so. Markets and business vertical dynamics can (and do) change rapidly, so they want their applications to be flexible as well. If a developer creates tightly coupled applications, adding new features as time marches on can be difficult. But with a little bit of design and insight, your applications will be easier to extend.

Let's say you have an application that needs to display different reports based on a specific set of data. If you wrote the application such that it had explicit knowledge of all the reports it needs to show for version 1, adding new reports could require a complete redeployment of the application. Without reflection, your design is static and inflexible. But let's say you took this approach:

- You create an interface called `IReport` that developers can implement to create their own reports based on a common interface.
- You add code that looks at a specific directory for assemblies, loads them into memory, and looks for all the types that implement that interface.
- You create instances of those types and invoke members on those types as an `IReport` variable reference.

Now your application is extensible. You have a common way for other developers to add, or plug in, new reports to your application without having to recompile the entire application. All they need to do is put their custom reports in an assembly in a well-known directory, and the application will pick them up automatically. All this can easily be supported by the Reflection API. Figure 2.1 illustrates how this design works. Granted, there are a lot of details you need to be aware of to make such a system resilient and reliable, but the core concept is within reach via reflection.

### 2.1.2   *Manipulating code members at runtime*

If you're a developer who's used to working with dynamic languages, such as Ruby or JavaScript, you're comfortable working within a system where you can literally define the system as it runs by adding functions to objects. To seasoned C# or VB developers,

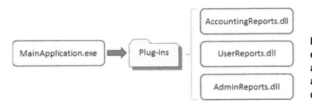

**Figure 2.1 High-level design of an extensible application. New assemblies are copied to a directory, which the main application monitors for changes to load desirable additions.**

this isn't a common activity; it may even seem unsafe. Why would you want to have such dynamic programs when they live within the comfort of the compiler that catches mistakes at compile time? In fact, only in .NET 4.0 was the `dynamic` type added to C# to support this kind of programming model.

So why would a C# or VB developer want to use dynamic language techniques? Simple: it makes it easier to create systems based on convention. Ruby on Rails (or RoR) is a common example cited by dynamic language aficionados as a framework that makes it easy to build web applications in Ruby. The classes in RoR create methods that a developer would expect to use to find, edit, and save objects by looking at a table in a database. This is an extremely simplistic view of RoR, but you get the point: you don't need to write all that boilerplate persistence code in RoR. The framework wires that up for you. Although you can't define new members with reflection, you can invoke members with reflection by knowing the name of the member as a string. At its core, this is what C#'s dynamic is doing for you. An open-ended system like this provides dynamic programming capabilities that can make system designs simpler.

> **Modern .NET frameworks based on dynamic programming**
> A number of projects have been created that make heavy use of dynamic programming techniques. Clay (http://clay.codeplex.com) lets you dynamically create the structure of an object at runtime. Massive (https://github.com/robconery/massive) is a library that makes it extremely simple to wire types to table definitions and perform ad-hoc queries against databases. You owe it to yourself to investigate these frameworks to see how they derive their power.

Now that you have a basic view of what's possible with reflection, let's start looking at the Reflection API and how you interact with it.

## 2.2 Reading metadata and executing code

This section is a whirlwind tour of `System.Reflection` and what's possible within its members. Our intent isn't to go through every possible class and method in this namespace, but rather to give a clear overview of the core concepts and functionality that reflection provides.

> **NOTE** Remember to add using `System.Reflection;` in any code file that uses reflection.

### 2.2.1  *Obtaining the starting point*

Depending on what you're looking for, there are two main entry points into the Reflection API: assembly or type. To get a reference to a type, all you need is its name. Here's how you get the Random type:

```
var type = Type.GetType("System.Random");
```

All you have to do to get a Type reference is provide the full name of the type. If you only use Random as the name, you'll get a null reference as the return value.

There are six overloaded versions of GetType() … and that's something you need to get used to when you're messing around with the Reflection API. Most of the Get methods you'll run across have a number of overloads. There's usually more than one way to solve a problem at hand, and seeing what overloads are available is worth the time. For example, GetType() won't throw an exception if it can't find the type in either the current assembly or any referenced assemblies, but you can change that by using an overload:

```
var type = Type.GetType("System.Random", true);
```

You can also get a type via the typeof keyword:

```
var type = typeof(Random);
```

Finally, every object has the GetType() method as it's defined in the Object class:

```
var type = new Random().GetType();
```

The last two approaches are safer than the string-based one. With typeof, you'll know at compile time if your code is correct, and calling GetType() on an object guarantees a non-null return value. Using strings provides a great deal of flexibility, but it's easy to make a typing mistake and not know about it until execution time. Good unit tests will weed out these sorts of errors, but don't fall into a false sense of security if your reflection-based code compiles. Make sure to test it!

Another approach is to load an assembly, then dig into its contents. The Assembly class has a number of load methods to do this. When you load an assembly, you're loading its contents into the current AppDomain so it can be used by your reflection-based code. When you reference an assembly in Visual Studio or in csc.exe, these references are baked into the assembly and are automatically loaded by the CLR.

> **Understanding AppDomains**
>
> You can think of an AppDomain as an isolated area where code executes. Most of the time, you don't have to deal with AppDomains because the runtime sets one up for you when an application starts. Creating multiple AppDomains in an application is possible, but that goes beyond the scope of what we're interested in here.

Here are three examples of loading assemblies that produce the same results (with slightly different implementation details):

```
var assembly = Assembly.Load(new AssemblyName()
  { Name = "mscorlib", Version = new Version(4, 0, 0, 0) });
var assembly2 = Assembly.Load("mscorlib, Version=4.0.0.0");
var assembly3 = Assembly.LoadFrom(
  @"file:///C:/Windows/Microsoft.NET/Framework/v4.0.30319/mscorlib.dll");
```

All the variables reference the same assembly. If the assembly is already loaded into the current `AppDomain`, it'll return the existing reference.

> **NOTE** Although all the `Load()` methods off of `Assembly` will get you a reference to an assembly, they do work differently under the hood.[1]

You can also get a reference to the assembly that's currently executing via `GetExecuting-Assembly()`, and the assembly that started everything up with an entry point method (for example, `Main()`) with `GetEntryAssembly()`. Finally, you can get a reference to the assembly that contains a given type with the `Assembly` property, and you can find a type within an assembly with `GetType()`:

```
var randomAssembly = typeof(Assembly).Assembly;
var randomType = randomAssembly.GetType("System.Random");
```

A nongeneric type like `Random` is easy to retrieve, but what about trying to find the `Lazy<T>` class in `mscorlib`?

```
var lazyType = randomAssembly.GetType("System.Lazy`1");
```

The names of generic classes and methods use this *tick format*, where the number after the tick specifies the number of generic parameters the class or method takes. You can also retrieve a generic type using the `typeof` keyword like this:

```
var lazyType = typeof(Lazy<>);
```

If the type had multiple generic arguments, you'd use a series of commas to specify the number of generic arguments. For example, the following code gets a `Tuple<T1,T2,T3>`:

```
var threeTupleType = typeof(Tuple<,,>);
```

---

### The infoof idea

The `typeof` keyword is the only one of its kind in C#. There's no *methodof, fieldof,* and so on. These other mythical operators are called *infoof* (a combination of *info* and *of*). There's a good article[2] that explains why they're not in C#; another article[3] demonstrates how you can use Expression trees (something we cover in chapter 6) to (almost) achieve the same effect.

---

[1] MSDN library, "Best Practices for Assembly Loading," http://mng.bz/kv4g.
[2] Eric Lippert (blog), "In Foof We Trust: A Dialogue," http://mng.bz/k0eQ.
[3] Patrick Smacchia (posted by), "Elegant infoof operators in C# (read Info Of)," June 28, 2010, http://mng.bz/YK8h.

### 2.2.2 *Finding member information*

As you saw in the last section, you can use GetType() on an Assembly object to retrieve a specific type. This pattern (for example, using a Get method) repeats itself throughout the Reflection API. Say you wanted to get the "Next" method off of a Random type. In that case, you'd use GetMethod():

```
var randomType = new Random().GetType();
var nextMethod = randomType.GetMethod("Next");
```

However, methods on a class definition can be overloaded, so you'll want to be more specific with GetMethod() to get a particular kind of method. In fact, if you don't supply enough criteria to GetMethod(), you'll get an AmbiguousMatchException. This piece of code gets the "Next" method that takes two arguments—a minimum and maximum value (both ints):

```
var nextWithTwoArguments = randomType.GetMethod("Next",
  new Type[] { typeof(int), typeof(int) });
```

You can also differentiate between methods by using a combination of BindingFlags:

```
var nextWithTwoArguments = randomType.GetMethod("Next",
  BindingFlags.Instance | BindingFlags.Public,
  null, new Type[] { typeof(int), typeof(int) }, null);
```

As you can see with BindingFlags, there's a Public value that you can use to look only for public members. There's also a NonPublic value, which means that you can see private and protected content via the Reflection API. Depending on your view, this may seem like a severe security breach when you consider that this allows arbitrary code to change the values of private fields in an object. But only privileged code can use the reflection calls. If you don't have this level of access, your use of reflection will fail. The article "Security Considerations for Reflection" at http://mng.bz/Gwau explains the security rules pertaining to reflection in detail.

Once you have a method, you can get all the parameters from it via GetParameters():

```
var nextParameter = nextWithTwoArguments.GetParameters();
```

This returns an array of ParameterInfo objects that contain the name, position, and type of parameter.

Similar methods exist for properties (GetProperty()), fields (GetField()), and events (GetEvent()). All of these also have plural versions to get a list of members—for example, GetFields() returns an array of FieldInfo objects. If you've also inferred that Info is in the class name for all the reflection query results, you'd be correct. There are MethodInfo, FieldInfo, EventInfo, and so on.

If the method or class is generic, things can get a little confusing in terms of how they're defined and retrieved with the Reflection API. As you saw in the preceding section, you use the bracket syntax to get the generic type in typeof. But if you know what type you want to specify for the generic in Lazy<T>, you can do that as well:

```
var openLazyType = typeof(Lazy<>);
var closedLazyType = typeof(Lazy<int>);
```

The first way gives you an *open* generic type, because not all the generic values have been specified. The second one specifies a value for T, so it's a *closed* generic type. If you have a type and you have no idea if it's generic, use `IsGenericType`. But if you want to know if it's open or closed, use `IsGenericTypeDefinition`—that returns `true` if the current type is generic and open. You can make a closed generic type from an open one by using `MakeGenericType()`:

```
var openLazyType = typeof(Lazy<>);
var closedLazyType = openLazyType.MakeGenericType(typeof(int));
```

There's also a method on a `Type` called `GetGenericArguments()` that returns an array of `Type` objects if you want to know about the generic values.

### 2.2.3 *Gathering attribute data*

It's one thing to be able to retrieve member information from an assembly, but the interesting reflection stuff comes in doing something with those discovered members, such as invoking a method or decorating a class with custom information. Performing these actions usually requires adding more information to a member so the reflection code knows to do something with that member. In a unit-testing framework like MSTest, you mark methods that should be run as a unit test with the `TestMethodAttribute`. In WCF, you can use the `KnownTypeAttribute` to specify which messages can be used in serialization scenarios for other message types. These custom attributes (which derive from the `Attribute` class) are stored as custom metadata in the assembly, and the Reflection API makes it easy to find this information.

Most every class in the Reflection API inherits from `MemberInfo`, which implements the `ICustomAttributeProvider` interface. This interface defines two overloaded `Get-CustomAttributes()` methods, which allow you to query a member to see if it contains the attribute you're looking for:

```
var testAttribute = someMethod.GetCustomAttributes(
  typeof(TestMethodAttribute), true);
```

Unfortunately, the result from `GetCustomAttributes()` is an object array, so you have to cast the results to the attribute type you're looking for. You can use `IsDefined()` to make sure the attribute is even there before you retrieve the attribute's data:

```
if(someMethod.IsDefined(typeof(TestMethodAttribute), true))
```

You could create a generic extension method to hide some of the type-casting mess you run into with `GetCustomAttributes()`, but there's also a method called `Get-CustomAttributeData()` that returns a list of `CustomAttributeData` objects. These objects contain the attribute data, separated between constructor and named arguments, and also the attribute type (via the `DeclaredType` property on the `Constructor` value), allowing you to get the attribute data and the attribute itself without any casts. The following LINQ statement gets all of the test methods from a specific assembly:

```
var tests = from type in assemblyWithTests.GetTypes()
            from method in type.GetMethods(
```

```
                        BindingFlags.Public | BindingFlags.Instance)
                     from attributeData in method.GetCustomAttributesData()
                     where attributeData.Constructor.DeclaringType ==
                         typeof(TestMethodAttribute)
                     select method;
```

### 2.2.4  *Executing code*

The last major aspect of reflection is code execution, which includes creating objects, invoking methods, and writing property values. Let's take a look at all three examples to see how they're done.

   If you have a type and you want to create an instance of it, look no further than `Activator.CreateInstance()`:

```
var lazyIntType = typeof(Lazy<int>);
var lazyInt = Activator.CreateInstance(lazyIntType);
```

In this case, `CreateInstance()` looks for a public, no-argument constructor on the type provided, invokes that constructor, and returns the object typed as an object. Unless you plan on using the result for other Reflection API calls, it's going to be pretty useless to you. You can typecast the return if you know what the type will be:

```
var lazyInt = Activator.CreateInstance(lazyIntType) as Lazy<int>;
```

If you're creating objects that you know implement a specific interface or have a base class somewhere in its inheritance hierarchy, this is a feasible approach. You can also use a generic version of `CreateInstance()`:

```
var lazyInt = Activator.CreateInstance<Lazy<int>>();
```

In this case, because you already know what the type is, there's no need to pass it into the method.

   You're not limited to calling only the no-argument public constructor on a type. In fact, it's not uncommon to find classes that don't have this kind of constructor defined for design reasons. If you wanted to create a `Lazy<int>` that has a value factory method, you can do this:

```
var lazyInt = Activator.CreateInstance(lazyIntType,
    new Func<int>(() => { return new Random().Next(); } )) as Lazy<int>;
```

There are other overloads that allow you to specify `AppDomains`, `ActivationContexts`, and so on—feel free to explore these other options.

   If you want to invoke a method on an object via reflection, all you need is a `Method-Base` object. This is the base class for both `ConstructorInfo` (returned by calling `Get-Constructor()`) and `MethodInfo` (returned by calling `GetMethod()`). `MethodBase` defines a method called `Invoke()` with a number of overrides, two of which we'll focus on. The first takes an object array, which maps to the arguments of the constructor. The following listing shows how you create a `Lazy<int>` via a `ConstructorInfo` object. The return value from `Invoke()` is the new object.

**Listing 2.1  Creating an object via `ConstructorInfo`**

```
var lazyIntType = typeof(Lazy<int>);
var lazyConstructor = lazyIntType.GetConstructor(
  new Type[] { typeof(Func<int>) });

var lazyInt = lazyConstructor.Invoke(new object[] {
  new Func<int>(
    () => { return new Random().Next(); } ) }) as Lazy<int>;

Console.Out.WriteLine(lazyInt.Value);
```

The other `Invoke()` is what you use to call a method on a class or object. The first argument is the object you want to invoke the method on (or null if the method is static). The second argument is an object array that contains all the arguments to the method. The following listing demonstrates how you'd dynamically call the `Next()` method on a `Random` object to get a value between 0 and 9.

**Listing 2.2  Invoking a method on an object**

```
var randomType = typeof(Random);
var nextMethod = randomType.GetMethod("Next",
  new [] { typeof(int), typeof(int) });
var random = Activator.CreateInstance(randomType);
Console.Out.WriteLine(nextMethod.Invoke(random,
  new object[] { 0, 10 }));
```

Now that you've seen what reflection lets you do as a developer, you may be conjuring up elegant, flexible architectures that will heavily involve the dynamic aspects that reflection provides. Although reflection can solve some problems in a concise manner, you should be aware of two of its pitfalls: performance and brittleness.

## 2.3   *Impractical uses of reflection*

Reflection is a powerful API that almost tempts you to use it liberally. Section 2.4 shows the effective use of reflection to solve some tricky problems, but we feel that covering some of the negative applications of reflection is necessary. Knowing reflection's potential issues will help you avoid common problems with this API. After reading this section, you'll understand why reflection shouldn't be used in large doses in your application.

### 2.3.1  *Performance concerns with reflection*

The first concern, performance, has to do with the work the Reflection API must perform. For example, calling a method like `Next()` on a `Random` object directly, like this:

```
var value = new Random().Next();
```

The compiler will know the tokens for the `Random` type reference and the `Next()` method reference, and this direct path is the speediest you can take. Granted, a fair amount of detail goes into the definition of a .NET object at runtime, but the call site is known, and getting that random value is a fairly simple process. But if all you knew was that there was a type called `System.Random` and a method called `Next` via their names, you'd need to use reflection to find those members and eventually invoke a method, which takes time. How much time? The following listing is a simplistic stress test to call `Next()` on a new `Random` object 500,000 times.

**Listing 2.3   Stress-testing a method invocation directly**

```
var stopwatch = Stopwatch.StartNew();

for(var x = 0; x < 500000; x++)
{
  var random = new Random().Next();
}

stopwatch.Stop();
Console.Out.WriteLine(stopwatch.Elapsed.ToString());
```

This isn't want you'd want to do to generate half a million new random values; you'd use the same `Random` object for each call. But the point is to compare object creation and method invocation with reflection. The following listing is conceptually the same as listing 2.3, except reflection is used.

**Listing 2.4   Stress-testing a method invocation via reflection**

```
var stopwatch = Stopwatch.StartNew();

for(var x = 0; x < 500000; x++)
{
  var randomType = Type.GetType("System.Random");
  var nextMethod = randomType.GetMethod("Next", Type.EmptyTypes);
  var random = nextMethod.Invoke(
    Activator.CreateInstance(randomType), null);
}

stopwatch.Stop();
Console.Out.WriteLine(stopwatch.Elapsed.ToString());
```

On average, we saw total times for the direct approach around 2 seconds, whereas the reflection approach took 7 seconds. As with any performance test, your mileage may vary, and depending on what an entire application is doing, the overhead of reflection may be acceptable compared to having some flexibility. You can also gain performance by moving the `Type.GetType()` lookup call outside of the `for` loop. For us, that reduced the total time for the reflection approach to 3.5 seconds. But in general, you'll always encounter slower execution time when using a reflection-based approach.

### 2.3.2  *Brittleness and reflection*

The other concern is brittleness. If you write code like this

```
var value = new Randon().Next();
```

the compiler will inform you about the incorrect type name (we assume you don't have a type called Randon). The error is caught right away when you compile the code.

Or, if this code worked before, but a new version of Random changes `Next()` to `Next-Value()`, you'll find out soon enough. But if you write code like

```
var value = Type.GetType("System.Randon");
```

you won't have any idea that you have a bug in the code by running the compiler. As we stressed in section 2.2.1, having good unit tests for any code base is critical, and this is true in particular for dynamic, reflection-based code. You need to ensure that the strings you're passing into calls like `GetMethod()` and `GetType()` are correct and resolve to members you're expecting.

Also, recall in section 2.2.2 where you saw that reflection gives you access to non-public members. Using these members in your code is *highly* discouraged because there's no guarantee that the names will stay the same, or that the members won't disappear entirely from version to version. For example, in the 4.0 version of .NET, the `Thread` class has a private field of type `IntPtr` called `DONT_USE_InternalThread`. That name alone should be a warning to you to not mess with it in any way, but let's say you did for some bizarre reason. What happens in a future version of .NET? You'd better have a lot of tests around your code to make sure nothing breaks, because a simple name change will break your assumptions in the future.

### Uses of non-public members

There are always exceptions to the rule, and that's true with the issue of using non-public members. An article by one of the authors[4] shows how to mock an `HttpContext` object with reflection. Another article[5] demonstrates how you can return exception information over the wire in WCF. A third article[6] illustrates how you can reverse a string via internal member manipulation. In some cases (like the `HttpContext` issue), changing hidden information is the only way to achieve a desired solution. In other cases (like the string reversing scenario), it's purely academic (and quite dangerous!). If you think you have no other choice but to use these private members, make sure you understand the potential dangers and guard your code accordingly (with strong unit tests, safe fallback paths in code when members can't be found, and so forth).

## 2.4   *Practical uses of reflection*

Now that you've seen what reflection can do, you may be wondering what some practical applications of the API are. In this section, we go through three scenarios using different Reflection APIs:

- Eliminating error-prone configuration
- Creating an informative string representation of an object
- Enabling a simplistic duck-typing system.

---

[4]  Jason Bock (blog), "Adding Session State to a Mock HttpContext Object," September 2005, http://mng.bz/V9r3.
[5]  Oleg Sych (posted by), "Simplifying WCF: Using Exceptions as Faults, July 2008," http://mng.bz/GC7R.
[6]  Jason Bock (blog), "Being Evil with a DynamicMethod, Class Internals, and Unsafe Code," July 2008, http://mng.bz/2i0t.

These examples illustrate how reflection provides elegant solutions to typical programming problems. We close out the chapter by reviewing all the examples together to find common patterns that will be useful for you to determine when reflection should be used.

Let's start by looking at WCF and the issues surrounding known types.

### 2.4.1   *Automatically registering known types in WCF*

In .NET, the common way of defining services is done through Windows Communication Foundation (WCF). These classes provide a number of classes and interfaces you can use to create services and pluggable behaviors to extend the request/response pipeline. Although WCF can reduce the amount of work needed to set up and call a service, it can also create subtle programming concept mismatches. Specifically, inheritance doesn't act like you think it should.

Here's a concrete example. Let's say you want to create a processor to handle different kinds of messages that you want to track in your application. You create a base type called `Message`:

```
[DataContract]
public class Message
{
  [DataMember]
  public string Data;

  public Message()
    : base()
  {
    this.Data = "Unknown";
  }
}
```

Then you start defining different messages, such as tracking when an application closes on a given machine:

```
[DataContract]
public sealed class ApplicationClosedMessage : Message
{
  [DataMember]
  public string MachineName;

  public ApplicationClosedMessage (string machineName)
    : base()
  {
    this.MachineName = machineName;
    this.Data = "Application has closed.";
  }
}
```

Here's the key point to take away from these two classes. Note that `Application-ClosedMessage` inherits from `Message`. Object-oriented developers are comfortable with inheritance and when its use is appropriate, and in this case it seems reasonable enough to design messages that use a common base class.

The problem with WCF is that it doesn't "know" anything about objects. Even though you create classes and objects in your WCF-based code, at the end of the day it's all about sending messages to services. If you define your contract like this

```
[ServiceContract]
public interface IMessageProcessor
{
  [OperationContract]
  string Process(Message fruit);
}
```

and then implement the contract like so

```
[ServiceBehavior]
public class MessageProcessor : IMessageProcessor
{
  [OperationBehavior]
  public string Process(Message message)
  {
    return message.Data;
  }
}
```

you're in trouble! Sure, the compiler will happily say all is well with the world, but things won't run. If you try to pass in a `Message` object to the processor like

```
var channel = new ChannelFactory<IMessageProcessor>(
  string.Empty).CreateChannel();
var result = channel.Process(new Message());
```

you'll get the right response. But try passing in an `ApplicationClosedMessage`:

```
var channel = new ChannelFactory<IMessageProcessor>(
  string.Empty).CreateChannel();
var result = channel.Process(
  new ApplicationClosedMessage("\\SomeMachine"));
```

This will fail miserably at runtime—you'll get a `CommunicationException`. Again, WCF is expecting a `Message` value to come through, so when it "sees" `Application-ClosedMessage`, it gets upset.

> **NOTE** The preceding example is a simplistic version of a real-world issue one of the authors ran into. The system had `Process()` defined as a one-way operation, which means that the operation invocation is "fire-and-forget"—the client doesn't have to wait for the service to finish. One-way operations don't return a value, but making `Process()` return a value makes it easier to create tests that you can read without having to know a lot about WCF.

There's a way around this via known types. A *known type* is self-explanatory: it's a way to tell WCF to "know" about a type. When you do this, it allows messages to come through even if they're subclasses. You can handle known types in WCF in a couple of different ways. One way is through configuration. You can define a known type in your .config file by adding a `<system.runtime.serialization>` element (which would go under the `<configuration>` element), like this:

```
<system.runtime.serialization>
  <dataContractSerializer>
    <declaredTypes>
      <add type="KnownTypes.Messages.Message, KnownTypes">
        <knownType
          type="KnownTypes.Messages.ApplicationClosedMessage,
          KnownTypes"/>
      </add>
    </declaredTypes>
  </dataContractSerializer>
</system.runtime.serialization>
```

That, however, can be a maintenance headache. The problem is when you add a new message to your application. If you forget to visit the .config file and add a new <known-Type> element, or if you have one character wrong, you'll get an error when that new message is passed to the service. Sure, good unit tests will catch that, but wouldn't it be even better if you could make known type registration automatic?

Fortunately, you can. WCF defines a ServiceKnownTypeAttribute that you can use to specify a method on a class that will provide a list of known types. Here's an updated version of IMessageProcessor with ServiceKnownTypeAttribute:

```
[ServiceContract]
[ServiceKnownType("GetMessageTypes",
  typeof(MessageProcessorKnownTypesProvider))]
public interface IMessageProcessor
{
  [OperationContract]
  string Process(Message fruit);
}
```

The first value is the name of the method to invoke on the type you specify in the second argument. This method has a couple of restrictions:

- It must be static.
- It must take one, and only one, argument that implements ICustomAttribute-Provider.
- It must return a list of known types.

**NOTE**  It's interesting to see that WCF is using reflection under the covers. It has to look for this attribute and, if the method exists, it must find a method on a given type. It would be interesting to see whether you can reproduce this functionality, given what you know about reflection.

By using some reflection goodness, you can easily make known type discovery a breeze. The following listing demonstrates how to find all the types that inherit from Message and register them as known types.

**Listing 2.5  Automatically discovering known types**

```
public static class MessageProcessorKnownTypesProvider
{
  private static Type[] knownTypes;
```

```
public static Type[] GetMessageTypes(
  ICustomAttributeProvider attributeTarget)
{
  if(MessageProcessorKnownTypesProvider.knownTypes == null)
  {
    var types = new List<Type>();
    var messageType = typeof(Message);

    foreach(var type in
      Assembly.GetAssembly(
        typeof(MessageProcessorKnownTypesProvider)).GetTypes())
    {
      if(messageType.IsAssignableFrom(type))
      {
        types.Add(type);
      }
    }

    MessageProcessorKnownTypesProvider.knownTypes =
      types.ToArray();
  }

  return MessageProcessorKnownTypesProvider.knownTypes;
}
```

**NOTE**  In the example in listing 2.5, all the messages are defined in the same assembly as the service contracts and services. We did this for simplicity; in real-world WCF applications, these entities are usually separated into different assemblies. But it's not hard to change the code in listing 2.5 to discover known types in different assemblies.

You look through all the types within the current assembly and see if they inherit from `Message` via `IsAssignableFrom()`. This method looks at the type given and checks to see whether it's a subclass of the current type. If it does, the method adds it to the list. The nice thing about this method is that it looks at the inheritance hierarchy. Looking to see if a type is equal to another type isn't sufficient. If the `if` statement looked like

```
if(typeof(Message).IsAssignableFrom(type))
```

it would fail. You can't use the `is` keyword either, because that checks an object to see whether it's a kind of type. In this case, you have two types, so that's not an option. But `IsAssignableFrom()` is exactly what you need. If you add a new message to this assembly, it'll automatically work when the updated service is deployed.

You now have seen how a little bit of reflection can eliminate manual configuration issues. Let's take a look at another example that handles `ToString()` for any object.

### 2.4.2 *Dynamic implementation of ToString*

Most .NET developers know that there's a method on the `Object` class called `ToString()`. There's no requirement to override it; you could theoretically spend all your time as a developer writing .NET code and never do anything with `ToString()`. But it can be a handy little method during debugging time.

Let's say you have a `Customer` class that looks like this:

```
public abstract class Customer : ICustomer
{
  protected Customer()
    : base()
  {
    this.Id = Guid.NewGuid();
  }

  public int Age { get; set; }
  public Guid Id { get; set; }
  public string FirstName { get; set; }
  public string LastName { get; set; }
}
```

And the `ICustomer` interface is defined as follows:

```
public interface ICustomer
{
  int Age { get; set; }
  Guid Id { get; set; }
  string FirstName { get; set; }
  string LastName { get; set; }
}
```

Now, let's say you've created an implementation of `Customer` in your application:

```
public sealed class CustomerReflection : Customer { }
```

As development continues on the code base, you run into a bug that requires you to crack open the debugger. During your debugging session, you hover over an instance of `CustomerReflection`. Figure 2.2 shows the information Visual Studio gives you about that object.

The debugger invokes `ToString()` on the object and displays it. The default implementation of `ToString()` is to return the name of the class, which isn't that helpful or informative most of the time. Sure, you can drill into the tree node to see more information, but sometimes it's helpful to get a quick indication that your object is in the correct state, or that it's the one you want to look at depending on the state of the object, which is usually the case when you're inspecting the contents of lists and dictionaries. Figure 2.3 shows what happens when you override `ToString()` with a descriptive implementation.

This approach takes all the properties and prints out their names and related values, separated by a double pipe (||). Here's what that code would look like if you did it by hand:

```
private static void RunToString(
    ICustomer customer)
{                         ⊞  ♦ customer  {Customers.CustomerReflection} ⇥
    Console.Out.WriteLine(customer.ToString());
}
```

Figure 2.2  Object description in the debugger. As you can see, you don't get a lot of information if you don't override it.

**Figure 2.3** Rich description of an object in the debugger. All the readable properties are listed with their names and values.

```
public static class Constants
{
  public const string Separator = " || ";
}

public sealed class CustomerHardCoded : Customer
{
  public override string ToString()
  {
    return new StringBuilder()
      .Append("Age: ").Append(this.Age)
      .Append(Constants.Separator)
      .Append("Id: ").Append(this.Id)
      .Append(Constants.Separator)
      .Append("FirstName: ").Append(this.FirstName)
      .Append(Constants.Separator)
      .Append("LastName: ").Append(this.LastName).ToString();
  }
}
```

It's not that hard to do, but doing it for every class you defined would get tedious. Plus, it's prone to error—you could easily forget a property or a separator. With reflection, you can create a generalized implementation of this idea with little effort. The following listing demonstrates code that combines reflection, an extension method, and some LINQ to create a description for any object.

**Listing 2.6  Using reflection to generate a description of an object**

```
public static class ObjectExtensions
{
  public static string ToStringReflection<T>(this T @this)
  {
    return string.Join(Constants.Separator,
      new List<string>(
        from prop in @this.GetType().GetProperties(
          BindingFlags.Instance | BindingFlags.Public)
        where prop.CanRead
        select string.Format("{0}: {1}",
          prop.Name,
          prop.GetValue(@this, null))).ToArray());
  }
}
```

There's a lot going on in those 14 lines of code, so let's start from the inside and work our way out. The LINQ query looks for all the public instance properties on the given object's type and filters for the ones you can read from. It takes those `PropertyInfo` objects and uses the `Name` property and `GetValue()` method to create a descriptive string for each object. The results of the LINQ query are then passed into `Join()` on the `string` class, which takes each descriptive string and joins them up, separating them with the || (double-pipe) separator.

With this in place, you can create a `CustomerReflection` class that uses the extension method:

```
public sealed class CustomerReflection : Customer
{
  public override string ToString()
  {
    return this.ToStringReflection();
  }
}
```

If you create an instance of this class

```
new CustomerReflection()
{
  FirstName = "Jason",
  LastName = "Reflection",
  Age = 20
}
```

you'll get the following value when you call `ToString()`:

```
@"Age: 20 || Id: e114900f-0257-48e0-8b1e-01453123a4bf ||
    FirstName: Jason || LastName: Reflection"
```

That's a nice application of reflection, but it's not perfect. The main issue is performance. Using some simple performance tests, we've found that the hard-coded approach is almost an order of magnitude faster than the reflection one. But let's face it—you probably won't call `ToString()` a lot in your application. In fact, it's uncommon to ever call `ToString()` in code. Therefore, even if the reflection approach takes a thousandth of a second, you'll never notice it. Later on in the book, we show you other dynamic techniques that are as fast as the hard-coded approach, yet are generalized like the reflection extension method.

Let's close out this section by seeing how reflection can support duck typing.

### 2.4.3 *Invoking arbitrary methods on objects*

If you've ever wanted different objects to support the same functionality (such as implementing a `Drive()` method), you created either a base class or an interface that defined the method, and subclasses would implement it appropriately. Therefore, if you have an `IDrive` interface like

```
public interface IDriver
{
  void Drive();
}
```

you could create a method that told any object to drive, so long as it implemented that interface:

```
public sealed class Golfer : IDriver
{
  public void Drive()
  {
    // Drive the ball.
  }
}
```

But there's a less type-safe yet more flexible version of this strategy: duck typing.[7] The key difference between duck typing and the previous approach is that duck typing doesn't rely on inheritance hierarchies. Instead, all you need is a method that matches what you're looking for. The existence of the method with the correct signature will make it work. Duck typing is also used to allow developers to create enumerable objects without implementing IEnumerable<T> and IEnumerator<T>.[8]

It may surprise you that duck typing already exists in some form or another in .NET. One example is operator overloading. When you overload an operator, the compiler ends up creating a method with a well-known name. That's what's used when you use the operator.

Here's a simplistic Range class that overloads the addition operator:

```
public sealed class Range
{
  public static Range operator +(Range a, Range b)
  {
    return new Range(Math.Min(a.Minimum, b.Minimum),
      Math.Max(a.Maximum, b.Maximum));
  }

  public Range(double minimum, double maximum)
  {
    this.Minimum = minimum;
    this.Maximum = maximum;
  }

  public override string ToString()
  {
    return string.Format("{0} : {1}",
      this.Minimum, this.Maximum);
  }

  public double Maximum { get; private set; }
  public double Minimum { get; private set; }
}
```

Adding two Range objects together like this

```
var rangeOne = new Range(-10d, 10d);
var rangeTwo = new Range(-5d, 15d);
Console.Out.WriteLine(rangeOne + rangeTwo);
```

---

[7]  "Duck typing," http://en.wikipedia.org/wiki/Duck_typing.

[8]  Krzysztof Cwalina (blog), "Duck Notation," July 2007, http://mng.bz/3lXH.

produces "-10:15" on the command line as expected. But what's going on behind the scenes?

When you overload the addition operation, the C# compiler names the method op_Addition and marks it with a special metadata flag called specialname. You can't merely name a static method op_Addition and use it for addition, because it doesn't have that flag. The compiler sprinkles that in for you. But it has to use the name op_Addition because that's the standard name for overloading + in .NET. Furthermore, it has to take two arguments. Therefore, if it quacks like a +, it must be an addition.

Let's see how you can implement duck typing with reflection. Let's say you had two classes that both had Drive() methods but didn't share a base class:

```
public sealed class Golfer
{
  public string Drive(string technique)
  {
    return technique + " - 300 yards";
  }
}

public sealed class RaceCarDriver
{
  public string Drive(string technique)
  {
    return technique + " - 200 miles an hour";
  }
}
```

Duck typing says, "Well, they both look like they Drive(), and they act like they Drive(), so let's make them Drive()." You don't care that there's no common class between them; the method definition itself is what makes them common.

With C# 4.0, the dynamic keyword gives you a somewhat limited version of duck typing out of the gate. For example, you can do this:

```
dynamic caller = new Golfer();
Console.Out.WriteLine(
  caller.Drive("Dynamic"));
```

That gets the job done. But let's take it another step by allowing the method name to be specified by the caller at runtime. The following listing shows an extension method that uses the capabilities of reflection to invoke a desired method.

**Listing 2.7  Invoking a method via its name**

```
public static class ObjectExtensions
{
  public static object Call(this object @this,
    string methodName,
    params object[] parameters)
  {
    var method = @this.GetType().GetMethod(methodName,
      BindingFlags.Instance | BindingFlags.Public, null,
      Array.ConvertAll<object, Type>(
```

```
        parameters, target => target.GetType()), null);
   return method.Invoke(@this, parameters);
 }
}
```

You look for the method based on the name and the types of the arguments given. In this case, the lookup is kept simple by only looking for public instance methods. You get the argument types via `Array.ConvertAll()`, which tells reflection which specific method to use in case the method is overloaded.

> ### Real-world use of run-time method invocation
> There's one well-known .NET framework that uses this idea of resolving a method call at runtime: CSLA (www.lhotka.net/cslanet/). It's primarily used for business object development and uses something called a `DataPortal` to manage object lifetime. The CSLA engine uses metaprogramming (to a degree) to determine which `Data-Portal_XYZ` method to invoke based on the type of criteria given.

Now, you can call any method you want with relative ease:

```
Console.Out.WriteLine(
  new Golfer().Call("Drive", "Reflection"));
Console.Out.WriteLine(
  new RaceCarDriver().Call("Drive", "Reflection"));
```

With this example, the name is specified in the code, but you could retrieve that name from myriad sources, such as an argument to the console window or a configuration file. If the method can't be found, an exception will be thrown, but for situations where you need the flexibility to invoke methods, reflection can easily provide that capability.

### 2.4.4 *Quick summary of reflection examples*

Before we close out this chapter, let's go over some of the commonalities of the examples in this section, focusing on stability and use.

The first thing to notice is that in two of the three examples, the code is resilient to name changes. For example, in the WCF example, it doesn't matter if a new known type is added to the assembly—the provider automatically picks up new subclasses without breaking at runtime. If you changed the name of the base message class, you'd know right away when you compiled the code. Similarly, the `ToString()` implementation doesn't error out if a new property is added to an object or one is removed; it'll work fine either way. The method invocation example *is* brittle because the name is hard-coded in a string, and the compiler won't help you out here in figuring out whether that name is correct. We hope your unit tests uncover the errors before you run the code in production.

The second aspect to notice is the size of the code that uses reflection. In all three examples, not many lines of code are needed to create some interesting (and useful) implementations. This is fairly typical when reflection is used in an application.

Having significant portions of the code base use reflection is uncommon. What's common is to see it used in small, effective portions where the flexibility outweighs any negative issues that reflection brings to the table. This isn't a hard-and-fast rule, because each problem you encounter as a developer can be solved in a number of ways. Sometimes using a liberal amount of reflection may be the best solution. But if you're using a lot of it all the time, you may want to rethink your result. A little reflection is usually all you need to attack a problem in an elegant manner.

## 2.5    Summary

In this chapter, you got a taste of metaprogramming via reflection. You discovered how to use the Reflection API to create dynamic, generic implementations. You also saw some potential pitfalls of reflection and a number of examples where reflection works best in an application. At this point, you should have a good understanding of how to use metaprogramming via the Reflection API to make your code flexible and adaptive to change within a system.

So far, we've restricted ourselves to working with code that already exists at runtime. In part 2, you'll expand your metaprogramming view by creating new code at runtime that you can use to solve all sorts of interesting problems. Hang on, the ride is about to get more interesting!

# Part 2

# Techniques for
# generating code

The next five chapters move into different tools and approaches to facilitate metaprogramming.

You'll focus on template-based metaprogramming using Microsoft's Text Template Transformation Toolkit (T4) and we'll emphasize the DRY approach. In chapter 4, attention is turned to the CodeDOM and underlying code probivers.

You'll emit code at runtime with the Emit API (chapter 5), providing a performance boost. You'll use expressions to create and modify existing expressions in chapter 6 and you'll learn how to modify assemblies to inject new code in the final chapter (chapter 7) in this middle part of *Metaprogramming in .NET*.

# The Text Template Transformation Toolkit (T4)

Pattern recognition and the beneficial repetition of proven patterns are considered to be excellent qualities in a software developer. Software developers and architects who have great *pattern vocabularies* are often the best among us. These are the developers who rarely try to reinvent complex solutions from scratch. Instead, they rely on well-known best practices, borrowing from the demonstrated success of others to produce their own great works. Code generation, which is viewed by many as a form of metaprogramming, is typically a key part of their successful development methodology. This chapter focuses on template-based metaprogramming using Microsoft's Text Template Transformation Toolkit (T4) to learn how these master developers think and work.

Among the SOLID object-oriented design principles we discuss in the opening chapter, the DRY (Don't Repeat Yourself) principle speaks plainly about the perils of repetition. According to DRY, repetition is bad because it decentralizes the authority for business logic in your code, leading to ambiguous, potentially conflicting implementations. That can lead to higher maintenance costs and potential errors as systems evolve. Pattern-based code generation based on templating is all about repetition, however. Is repetition a good thing or a bad thing? The answer is that it depends on how and why you're repeating the code.

Developers who are beginning to study the SOLID principles often misinterpret DRY to mean "don't repeat your code." It's true that manually duplicated code is bad practice, mainly because of the maintenance problems that flow from the practice. However, the DRY principle speaks to a higher-level set of concerns, namely: the authority, abstraction, and disambiguation of business logic. Pattern-based code generation systems that rely upon repetition by design don't typically violate the DRY principle because they reserve authority and abstraction to the templates. Beware of template-driven systems that allow or encourage developers to edit code that's emitted, however, because they will almost certainly force developers to violate the DRY principle.

Concerning DRY, the answers are uncomplicated. If feature authority stays with the template, all the variations that might be generated from it won't violate the DRY principle. This will be true even though there may be many similar versions of the same code floating about in your application.

You can refactor code in your templates into base classes to solve the code repetition problem. That's a good, old-fashioned, object-oriented design skill being brought to bear. You can also use compiler tricks like partial classes and partial methods to expose regeneration-safe extension points into your templates. But as long as you understand that the DRY principle is more concerned with where the authority for an application's features lies, you'll become comfortable with the art of doing code generation with templates. In cases where programmer comprehension can be enhanced by exposing domain-specific metadata as class features, we believe that you'll find template-based metaprogramming to be superior to more traditional specialization techniques like class inheritance and polymorphism. Type-safe, schema-specific classes generated from a database are perhaps the most common and most compelling examples of the power of template-based metaprogramming.

This chapter begins by examining how generics are a simple but powerful form of metaprogramming used by nearly every .NET developer today. We extend that line of thought into template-based metaprogramming, looking specifically at how you can use T4 to introduce flexibility into scenarios where generics present technical challenges. Then we dive into the some details of T4, helping you to understand the architecture as well as the way in which Visual Studio integrates features to simplify code generation.

## 3.1    *Thinking of generics as templates*

In the .NET languages, generics may be the most commonly used form of algorithmic standardization. To demonstrate the connection between generics and metaprogramming, think about a simple function that returns the larger of two values. In C#-like pseudo-code, the appropriately named max function might be written like this:

```
T max<T>(T left, T right)
{
  return left < right ? right : left;
}
```

Although that's a rather nice-looking concept for how the max function could be written, it won't compile as C# because the standard C# less-than operator (<) can't be applied to generic arguments. You could rewrite max as generic_max using a constraint like this:

```
T generic_max<T>(T left, T right)
  where T : IComparable<T>
{
  return (left.CompareTo(right) < 0) ? right : left;
}
```

The generic_max method will compile as C# and work for any parameterized type that implements the IComparable<T> interface because of the where constraint that was added. But what about those types that implement the older IComparable interface? Could you add another constraint to generic_max to solve the problem?

```
T generic_max<T>(T left, T right)
  where T : IComparable, IComparable<T>
{
  return (left.CompareTo(right) < 0) ? right : left;
}
```

Unfortunately, these constraints when specified together support only the parameterized types that implement *both* of the interfaces, not *one or the other*. You'll almost certainly encounter types that implement only one of the comparison interfaces, so this is something of an obstacle.

Some languages support *automatic generalization* and deep type inferencing to solve this problem in a much more straightforward way. Here's how a generic max function can be written in F#, along with some examples of its use:

```
let max left right = if left < right then right else left;;

max 1 2;;            // max of integers returns 2
max 3.0 4.0;;        // max of real numbers returns 4.0
max "hello" "world";; // max of strings returns "world"
```

This max function doesn't have any generic syntax markers in its definition, but it's definitely considered to be generic by the compiler. In fact, the signature for the function returned by the compiler reads like this:

```
'a -> 'a -> 'a
```

This is F#'s rather cryptic way of saying that the function, given two parameters of a to-be-determined type, will return a value of that same type. That sounds as generic as it truly is. Peeking back at the function definition, there are no indications of a required data type expressed or implied in the code. The F# compiler did a good job of keeping the intention of the algorithm intact without introducing any kinds of constraints or other limitations on the programmer. The magic of this, if there is any, lies in the generic implementation of F#'s standard less-than (<) operator. F#'s deep type inferencing also helps by allowing the generalization expressed in the operator to flow into functions that invoke it, like max.

As you ponder that, it may become apparent that the generic F# max function isn't a function in the ordinary sense. Instead, it's a kind of model or *template* that expresses the intent of some future functions that may be needed to deal with concrete types. As the constraint added to the C# generic_max method proves, the template is dependent only on the ability to rank two values of a known type. In C#, you could try to mimic the dynamism that you perceive in the F# implementation by using the Reflection API. In this way, you could try to get around the problem of needing to support the IComparable interface or the IComparable<T> interface as separate and equally sufficient constraints. The following listing shows an attempt to rewrite the generic_max function as dynamic_max to do that.

**Listing 3.1   dynamic_max as a dynamic, generic (and inefficient) max function**

```
public static T dynamic_max<T>(T left, T right)
{
  if (left is IComparable<T>)
    return ((left as IComparable<T>).CompareTo(right) < 0)
      ? right : left;

  if (left is IComparable)
    return ((left as IComparable).CompareTo(right) < 0)
      ? right : left;

  throw new ApplicationException(String.Format(
      "Type {0} must implement one of the IComparable or " +
    "IComparable<{0}> interfaces.", typeof(T).Name));
}
```

The generic dynamic_max function begins by testing the parameterized type for its implementation of IComparable<T>. If the left operand implements IComparable<T>, it's cast to that type, and the CompareTo member is invoked passing the right operand as the argument. This comparison yields the ranking required to determine which operand value is larger. If the first interface isn't implemented, the left operand is tested for implementing the nongeneric IComparable interface instead. If that second interface is implemented, its CompareTo function is invoked to rank the operands. An exception is thrown if neither required interface is supported by the parameterized type.

The dynamic_max function shown in listing 3.1 is admittedly inefficient. Can you imagine having to do all that reflection every time you needed to get the larger of two values? That's the kind of bad dynamic software design you may have been warned about when you began your journey to become a metaprogrammer. Writing code like that should be avoided at all cost.

To fix the performance problem with dynamic_max, you could try to implement some kind of dictionary that caches the comparison strategy for each type that's encountered at runtime. At least then the expensive reflection would be performed only once per parameterized type. But that's somewhat complex, too. This approach begs the question: "Do we need the max function to be completely dynamic at runtime?" After all, if the data types you're working with are well-known at compile time, why go to all that trouble of making the function dynamic at all?

If only there were a tool for capturing the comparison strategy at compile time for each of the data types you'll need to support at runtime. If such a tool existed, you could generate a class that contains highly optimized overloads of all of the max function variants that you'll need later on.

As it turns out, certain versions of Microsoft Visual Studio 2008 and Microsoft Visual Studio 2010 and 2012 contain such a tool—called the Text Template Transformation Toolkit, or T4 for short. In this chapter, we show you how to use T4 to generate C#, XML, T-SQL, and other kinds of code inside Visual Studio using templates similar to the generics in C# or Visual Basic you may already be familiar with. Let's start by taking a look at how to solve the problem of creating a set of max function variants at compile time using T4.

## 3.2    *Introducing T4*

You'll delve into the specifics of T4 syntax as we go along. Let's jump right in by examining listing 3.2, which contains a T4 template that creates a class called greater. The goal of the class is to provide strongly typed variants of the max function we toyed with in the opening section of this chapter. Each of those overloaded functions in the greater class is named of, which seems rather odd at first glance. But the naming is deliberate because, using that greater class, you'll be able to write code that reads smoothly like English text. Here's an example of using the greater class to obtain the *greater of* two integers:

```
int x = 7, y = 11;
Console.WriteLine(
   "The larger of {0} and {1} is {2}.", x, y, greater.of(x, y));
```

If you add the greater.tt template file to a Visual Studio project, it will automatically create the greater.cs file as a so-called *subordinate file* to be compiled within the same project. Using T4 in Visual Studio is that simple. We explore a few implementation details about the way in which T4 is integrated into Visual Studio later in the chapter.

**Listing 3.2   greater.tt as a T4 template for generating typed max functions**

```
<#@ template language="C#" #>
<#@ output extension=".cs" #>
<#@ assembly name="System.Core" #>
<#@ import namespace="System.Linq" #>
<#
  Type[] types_to_generate = new[]
  {
```

```
      typeof(object),    typeof(bool),     typeof(byte),
      typeof(char),      typeof(decimal),  typeof(double),
      typeof(float),     typeof(int),      typeof(long),
      typeof(sbyte),     typeof(short),    typeof(string),
      typeof(uint),      typeof(ulong),    typeof(ushort)
    };
#>
using System;
public static class greater
{
<#
  foreach (var type in types_to_generate)
  {
#>
  public static <#= type.Name #> of(
    <#= type.Name #> left, <#= type.Name #> right)
  {
<#
    Type icomparable =
      (from intf in type.GetInterfaces() where
        typeof(IComparable<>)
          .MakeGenericType(type)
          .IsAssignableFrom(intf)
        ||
        typeof(IComparable).IsAssignableFrom(intf)
      select intf).FirstOrDefault();
    if (icomparable != null)
    {
#>
    return left.CompareTo(right) < 0 ? right : left;
<#
    }
    else
    {
#>
    throw new ApplicationException(
      "Type <#= type.Name #> must implement one of the " +
      "IComparable or IComparable<<#= type.Name #>> interfaces.");
<#
    }
#>
  }
<#
  }
#>
}
```

## Naming of T4 template files

Take note of the fact that T4 templates like the one shown in listing 3.2 typically bear a file extension of TT (meaning Text Template). Why the extension T4 wasn't chosen for these files, who can say? Perhaps the T4 product moniker wasn't ascribed to the toolkit until after the TT file extension had already been established as a precedent.

### 3.2.1 *T4 syntax basics*

Most T4 template files begin with one or more directives bracketed by the <#@ and #> character sequences. If you think of T4 as a sort of compiler, these directives act like the command line options that you might use to control the compiler's behavior and output. You'll learn about several directives in this chapter, but the most common ones are:

- *Template*—Used to specify the language and compiler options
- *Output*—Used to control output file extension and encoding
- *Assembly*—Used to reference .NET assemblies during compilation
- *Import*—Used like an import (VB) or using (C#) directive

After the directives, the remaining lines in the greater.tt file are part of so-called control blocks and text blocks. Before diving into how control blocks and text blocks work, look at listing 3.3, which contains the abbreviated output of the greater.tt template file. As a learning exercise, try to correlate what appears in the template source code in listing 3.2 to the generated source code in listing 3.3. That exercise will give you an appreciation for the nuances in T4's syntax. The questions that pop into your mind while doing that will be answered shortly.

> **Listing 3.3  greater.cs as abbreviated output from the greater.tt template**

```
using System;
public static class greater
{
  public static Object of(Object left, Object right)
  {
    throw new ApplicationException(
      "Type Object must implement one of the " +
      "IComparable or IComparable<Object> interfaces.");
  }
  public static Boolean of(Boolean left, Boolean right)
  {
    return left.CompareTo(right) < 0 ? right : left;
  }
  public static Byte of(Byte left, Byte right)
  {
    return left.CompareTo(right) < 0 ? right : left;
  }
  // The remainder of the generated "of" functions have been
  // omitted for brevity. Each of them is implemented exactly
  // like the versions for the Boolean and Byte types shown
  // above, simply invoking CompareTo to rank the operands.
}
```

As you can see, the greater class contains a function named of for each of the types specified in the types_to_generate variable specified near the top of the template. There are 15 of those functions in the unabridged class because there are 15 types included in the types_to_generate array defined in the first control block below the directives.

### Comparing dynamic code to static, metadata-generated code

Compare the inefficient `dynamic_max` function shown in listing 3.1 to any one of the strongly typed `of` functions emitted into the `greater` class. The T4 approach generated a lot more code, that's for certain. The generated code may be bulkier, but (a) there's nothing dynamic about the code, so it will be more efficient at runtime, and (b) you didn't have to write all those functions anyway. We used metadata and T4 to write them for us, which makes T4 fit nicely into our metaprogramming bag of tools for solving the kinds of problems that benefit from code generation.

As you can see in listing 3.3, the first function in the output, which was emitted for the `System.Object` type, throws an exception because the template control code determined that the `System.Object` type doesn't implement either of the required `IComparable<Object>` or `IComparable` interfaces. The remaining 14 types included in the `types_to_generate` array implement one or both of the required comparison interfaces, so they have code emitted that looks like this:

```
return left.CompareTo(right) < 0 ? right : left;
```

That code is appropriate for invoking the generic `IComparable<T>` implementation of `CompareTo` or the loosely typed `IComparable` implementation. LINQ to Objects code in the third standard control block shown in the template in listing 3.2 makes this determination:

```
<#
    Type generic_icomparable =
      (from intf in type.GetInterfaces()
        let args = intf.GetGenericArguments()
        where intf.Name == "IComparable`1"
           && args != null
           && args[0].Equals(type)
        select intf).FirstOrDefault();
    if (generic_icomparable != null || type is IComparable)
    {
#>
    return left.CompareTo(right) < 0 ? right : left;
```

If the target class implements both of the interfaces, it doesn't matter to us which one is called, but the C# compiler's rules will select the strongly typed implementation because the emitted function's `left` and `right` parameters will be strongly typed. For now, all 14 `of` methods for the compliant types have the same exact implementation. Later in this chapter, when you customize the template to add other acceptable constraints to the template, you'll see some differentiation emerge in the `of` function implementations for the 15 built-in .NET types.

### 3.2.2 Understanding T4's block types

Now it's time to put the whole template into context to understand how the T4 engine works. Let's start with the control block that defines the types_to_generate variable. It immediately follows the directives at the top of Listing 3.2 and looks like this:

```
<#
  Type[] types_to_generate = new[]
  {
    typeof(object),  typeof(bool),     typeof(byte),
    typeof(char),    typeof(decimal),  typeof(double),
    typeof(float),   typeof(int),      typeof(long),
    typeof(sbyte),   typeof(short),    typeof(string),
    typeof(uint),    typeof(ulong),    typeof(ushort)
  };
#>
```

Note the <# and #> character sequences that demarcate the control block. All control code in a T4 template must appear in a control block and be written in the programming language specified in the language attribute of the template directive. In the case of the greater.tt template, the C# language was specified as the template's control language, so all its subsequently defined control blocks must be written in C#.

> **T4 Languages**
>
> At the time of this writing, C# and Visual Basic are the only other supported control languages allowed in T4 templates using the standard host. Output text can be generated by T4 for any language—for example, T-SQL, F#, Java, XML, and so on. After all, T4 isn't a code generator. It's a text generator, and as long as the target language uses text for its source code, T4 can emit it.

To understand how a unique of function was emitted into the generated class for each of the types defined in the types_to_generate array, locate the foreach statement within the second control block in the template in listing 3.2. It looks like this:

```
<#
  foreach (var type in types_to_generate)
  {
#>
```

The foreach statement iterates over the types defined in the types_to_generate array defined earlier. The key is that although T4 control blocks may be separated by text blocks and other control blocks, they're all part of the same control logic for the template. Processing from top to bottom, objects defined in a T4 control block can be referenced within subsequent control blocks, obeying the scoping rules of the selected control language.

### 3.2.3   *How T4 stitches together template blocks*

Perhaps the best way to understand how T4 connects all the blocks together during transformation is to visualize the first two control blocks at the top of listing 3.2 and shown again for convenience in listing 3.4. The following listing shows all three of those blocks together. Now compare it to listing 3.5 to see how T4 conceptually joins those three blocks during transformation.

**Listing 3.4   Two control blocks in T4 surrounding a block of raw text**

```
<#
  Type[] types_to_generate = new[]
  {
    typeof(object),  typeof(bool),    typeof(byte),
    typeof(char),    typeof(decimal), typeof(double),
    typeof(float),   typeof(int),     typeof(long),
    typeof(sbyte),   typeof(short),   typeof(string),
    typeof(uint),    typeof(ulong),   typeof(ushort)
  };
#>
using System;
public static class greater
{
<#
  foreach (var type in types_to_generate)
  {
#>
```

**Listing 3.5   How T4 conceptually joins control and text blocks**

```
Type[] types_to_generate = new[]
{
  typeof(object),  typeof(bool),    typeof(byte),
  typeof(char),    typeof(decimal), typeof(double),
  typeof(float),   typeof(int),     typeof(long),
  typeof(sbyte),   typeof(short),   typeof(string),
  typeof(uint),    typeof(ulong),   typeof(ushort)
};
WriteLine("using System; ");
WriteLine("public static class greater");
WriteLine("{");
foreach (var type in types_to_generate)
{
```

Did you notice how the lines of text between the control blocks were inserted as Write-Line statements in the conceptual, assembled control code? Comparing listings 3.4 and 3.5 should help you understand the inner workings of T4 host. T4 is a kind of *text compiler* that interleaves the code in the control blocks with WriteLine statements for each line in any text blocks encountered along the way. The result is a single class that can be compiled and executed to transform the template into an output file.

Understanding this *assembly process* will also help you to understand why the trailing opening brace ({) found at the end of second control block in listing 3.2 is perfectly acceptable. As long as the matching closing brace (}) is placed appropriately into a control block appearing later in the template, the resulting class that T4 generates will be well formed. In fact, for the foreach iteration in the template in listing 3.2, the matching closing brace appears as the last control block in the file, which looks like this:

```
<#
  }
#>
```

It may be odd to think of this single C# closing brace as the sole content within a T4 control block, but that's what it is. After T4 has assembled all the text and control blocks defined in the template together, that closing brace for the foreach statement won't seem so alone and out of place.

### 3.2.4    *T4's expression control block*

The last thing to explain about the greater.tt template is a syntax that appears multiple times near the second text block defined in the file. This type of control block, called an *expression code block*, uses the delimiters <#= and #> instead of the <# and #> delimiters used to define a *standard control block*. Here's how that section using expression control blocks looks in the template from listing 3.2:

```
public static <#= type.Name #> of(
  <#= type.Name #> left, <#= type.Name #> right)
{
```

Using the expression control block syntax, the type variable's Name property is emitted three times in between four bits of raw text. These expression control blocks are a convenient way to write the values of variables or the results of function calls into the output file without having to use bulky Write statements inside standard control blocks. The result is much cleaner looking and easier to read, leading to better overall comprehension of the template by programmers to need to understand what the template does.

When T4 *compiles* the template, all seven text and control blocks are reduced to a set of Write and WriteLine function calls within the internal class that T4 builds to handle the transformation. Understanding that T4 creates a simple class containing Write statements from the template's text and control blocks will go a long way in helping you understand the remaining material in this chapter.

Now, let's take a brain break and look at how T4 came into existence before we dig deeper into the details of putting text templating to work inside Visual Studio.

### 3.2.5    *A brief history of T4*

Understanding the decision-making processes behind the development of T4 can help you determine where it fits into your own projects. If you don't care about the history of T4 or if you want to focus on T4 implementation details right now, it's all right to skip to the next section and come back at a later time. For those interested in how T4 was developed, let's do a quick tour of the people and projects that have contributed to T4's success and popularity.

Several excellent third-party tools are available to do template-based code generation. Some provide integration with Microsoft Visual Studio. T4 has the advantage of shipping with certain versions of Microsoft Visual Studio 2008 and Microsoft Visual Studio 2010, so most of the software developers building commercial, Microsoft-based solutions have access to it without needing to install any extra tools.

T4 has become quite popular in recent years thanks to a number of factors, most importantly the adoption of T4 by various tool-building teams within Microsoft's developer division. Code generators for ASP.NET MVC, the ADO.NET Entity Framework, and other popular frameworks are based on T4, making it one of the most widely used tool-building frameworks around.

T4's pedigree as a toolkit for tool building is no wonder since it first appeared as part of Microsoft's Domain Specific Languages (DSL) Toolkit in 2005. The DSL team members are constantly experimenting with new programming languages and related concepts. They're tool builders by design. For that kind of work, you need a flexible, easily integrated code generator at your fingertips. Around the time that Gareth Jones of Microsoft's DSL team realized the need for something like T4 in 2004, the DSL team members were still doing a lot of their code generation work using old-fashioned `printf` statements in tools written in and around the C++ language. There's nothing wrong with C++, but the code-generation tools that the DSL team was using at the time lacked the flexibility and ease of integration that most of their projects demanded.

### An interview with Gareth Jones

To complete this chapter, Gareth Jones, the creator of T4, submitted to an interview with the authors of this book. The history of T4 outlined here comes with no citations. But Gareth's blog at http://blogs.msdn.com/b/garethj has many great articles and references to other sources that will corroborate what you learn from us about T4. As one of the most fascinating people working at Microsoft, we hope you'll follow Gareth's work closely and learn more about pattern-based software design.

Gareth looked at the code-generation technologies that other Microsoft software development teams had created and found that the ASP.NET page-processing engine had several of the key qualities his team was looking for. From a syntax perspective, the separation between the markup and control code was clear. Gareth's experience helped him understand that having a clear syntactical division between raw text and code could dramatically improve programmer comprehension in a general-purpose code-generation tool. More importantly perhaps, the architecture of the ASP.NET engine, performing its page transformation and HTML emission through assembly and execution, seemed to fit nicely with the needs of several of the DSL projects Gareth was involved in.

After reaching the conclusion that the ASP.NET page-processing engine was a good candidate for becoming a general-purpose code generation tool, Gareth used the ASP.NET engine as the basis for T4, combining it with other DSL team components in the lab. Although T4 has undergone a complete rewrite since Gareth used the ASP.NET engine as the basis for his toolkit in 2004, the similarities between the traditional ASP.NET page syntax and T4's syntax remain. Any developer who's worked in ASP or ASP.NET will recognize the patterns in T4 and take to them quickly. For that matter, any developer who has worked in PHP, JSP, and any number of other web page generators will also feel right at home in T4.

From the beginning, T4 has been available as both a standalone tool and as an add-in for Visual Studio. As you know, the first publicly available version of T4 appeared in 2005 as part of the DSL Toolkit. But because downloading the DSL Toolkit isn't something that average developers do, relatively few developers knew about that first version of T4. When Visual Studio 2008 shipped, the Professional and Ultimate versions of the product had T4 built right in. More developers began using the toolkit at that time, but adoption remained relatively low for a variety of reasons.

With the release of Visual Studio 2010, T4 finally stepped into the limelight. Better adaptation into the Integrated Development Environment (IDE), more thorough product documentation, and the emergence of several champions in the developer community helped T4 to earn the interest of thousands of programmers who had never before heard of the toolkit. Most importantly, several Microsoft Developer Division teams began using T4 to generate code from metadata for their frameworks around that same time.

## 3.3 *More useful T4 examples*

Imagine that you want to dynamically generate classes in C# to move data around. Given a list of property names and types, you could write code that generates the data class for you, as shown in the following listing.

**Listing 3.6  Chapter3Intro.cs dynamically generating a data class**

```csharp
using System;
using System.Collections.Generic;

class Chapter3Intro
{
  public static void GenerateDataClass(string className,
    List<Tuple<Type, string, bool>> properties,
    bool generateCtor = true)
  {
    Console.WriteLine("public class {0}", className);
    Console.WriteLine("{");
    foreach (var property in properties)
    {
      Console.WriteLine(
        "  public {0} {1} {{ get; {2}set; }}",
        property.Item1,
```

```
          property.Item2,
          property.Item3 ?  "" : "private ");
    }
    if (generateCtor)
    {
      Console.Write("  public {0}(", className);
      for (int ndx = 0; ndx < properties.Count; ndx++)
        Console.Write("{0}{1} {2}",
          (ndx > 0) ? ", " : "",
          properties[ndx].Item1,
          properties[ndx].Item2,
          properties[ndx].Item3);
      Console.WriteLine(")");
      Console.WriteLine("  {");
      foreach (var property in properties)
      {
        Console.WriteLine(
          "    this.{0} = {0};",
          property.Item2);
      }
      Console.WriteLine("  }");
    }
    Console.WriteLine("}");
  }
}
```

Notice that the function generator takes the name of the class to create, a flag indicating whether or not a constructor should be generated, and a list of properties including their names, types, and access modifiers. The code writes chunks of C# text to the console and uses control statements also written in C# to process the parameters and iterate over the property list.

To use the C#-based code generator shown in listing 3.1, let's assume you need to create a class called DynamicCar. The car should have properties for varying types for ordinary features like Make, Model, Year, and MPG (miles per gallon). Let's make one of the properties read-only for fun. Lastly, the DynamicCar needs a constructor, so that should be generated, too. The following listing shows how you might invoke the GenerateDataClass function shown previously to create the DynamicCar class.

**Listing 3.7   Chapter3IntroMain.cs generating a class dynamically**

```
using System;
using System.Collections.Generic;

class Demo
{
  static void Main()
  {
    string className = "DynamicCar";
    bool generateCtor = true;
    var properties = new List<Tuple<Type, string, bool>>()
      {
        Tuple.Create(typeof(string), "Make", true),
```

```
        Tuple.Create(typeof(string), "Model", true),
        Tuple.Create(typeof(int), "Year", true),
        Tuple.Create(typeof(int), "MPG", false)
    };

    Chapter3Intro.GenerateDataClass(className,
        properties, generateCtor);
    Console.ReadLine();
    }
}
```

Before the `GenerateDataClass` method is invoked, metadata for the class name, the flag to create the constructor, and a list of property descriptions for the `DynamicCar` are described. For simplicity, the output of this small program goes to the console window. When the program is run, the source code for the `DynamicCar` class shown in the following listing appears on the console window.

**Listing 3.8  The dynamically generated `DynamicCar` class**

```
public class DynamicCar
{
  public System.String Make { get; set; }
  public System.String Model { get; set; }
  public System.Int32 Year { get; set; }
  public System.Int32 MPG { get; private set; }
  public DynamicCar (System.String Make,
     System.String Model, System.Int32 Year,
     System.Int32 MPG)
  {
    this.Make = Make;
    this.Model = Model;
    this.Year = Year;
    this.MPG = MPG;
  }
}
```

Comparing the metadata to the class that was produced, everything seems to be in order. The `DynamicCar` class has the correct name. All the properties that were described are included, and each has the correct type. The `MPG` property, which was marked as read-only, correctly has a private mutator (setter), too. Lastly, notice that the constructor is correctly implemented, setting the value of each of the properties from the constructor's parameters.

Although the C#-based code generator works correctly, the approach demonstrates the pain that Microsoft's DSL team was dealing with in 2004. In many cases, they were using functions like `WriteLine` (rather than `printf` in C++) to generate code in this way. You can clearly see how cumbersome the model is, even when you abstract the code generator into a function like `GenerateDataClass`. There's no clear separation between the boilerplate text that needs to be emitted and the control code that runs *over* and *around* it. This lack of separation reduces comprehension, slows down development, and leads to otherwise avoidable errors. Templates that are marginally

more complex than the one shown in this example become difficult to implement
and maintain using this kind of code-generation approach. Moreover, the real benefits of metaprogramming have been lost.

Now look at how T4 can be used to solve this same problem (we get into how to do
this in Visual Studio in a bit). Examine the template shown in the next listing. This T4
template will create the same DynamicCar class shown in listing 3.3.

**Listing 3.9   GenerateDataClass.tt: a T4 template to generate data classes**

```
<#@ template language="C#" #>
<#@ import namespace="System.Collections.Generic" #>
<#@ output extension=".cs" #>
<#
  string className = "DynamicCar";
  bool generateCtor = true;
  var properties = new List<Tuple<Type, string, bool>>()
    {
      Tuple.Create(typeof(string), "Make", true),
      Tuple.Create(typeof(string), "Model", true),
      Tuple.Create(typeof(int), "Year", true),
      Tuple.Create(typeof(int), "MPG", false)
    };
#>
public class <#= className #>
{
<#
  foreach (var property in properties)
  {
#>
  public <#= property.Item1 #> <#=
    property.Item2 #> { get; <#=
    property.Item3 ? "" : "private " #>set; }
<#
  }

  if (generateCtor)
  {
#>
  public <#= className #>(<#
    for (int ndx = 0; ndx < properties.Count; ndx++)
      Write("{0}{1} {2}",
        (ndx > 0) ? ", " : "",
        properties[ndx].Item1,
        properties[ndx].Item2,
        properties[ndx].Item3);
#>)
  {
<#
    foreach (var property in properties)
    {
#>
    this.<#= property.Item2 #> = <#= property.Item2 #>;
<#
```

```
      }
    }
#>
    }
}
```

This template is straightforward to follow, but if you've never worked with T4, some syntactical concepts are worth explaining to make them clearer. First of all, the three lines at the beginning of the template delimited by `<#@` and `#>` are called *directives*. These are somewhat like command-line parameters to a compiler. In this case, the three directives tell the compiler the following:

1 This is a template, and the language you'll be using for your control code will be written in C#.
2 You want to import a namespace (like C#'s `using` directive) that will allow you to use the generic collection types like `List<T>`.
3 The code generator should output a file with a `.cs` extension.

After those directives comes a block containing the parameters defining the metadata of the class to be dynamically generated. These parameters are exactly like those shown in listing 3.2 used before invoking the C#-based code generator function. In the next chunk of the template, you see how T4 lets you *sprinkle* text between code and *sprinkle* code into text:

```
public class <#= className #>
{
```

Notice that there are no `<#` and `#>` delimiters on the outside of this section of the template. You can place raw text between control blocks without delimiters, making your boilerplate text much easier to read. Whenever T4 encounters text not delimited by special tags, it emits that text exactly as it's written to the output, whitespace and all.

In the tiny snippet from the template shown earlier are three separate T4 blocks. Embedded between two text blocks, notice there's an expression that emits the variable called `className`. Expression control blocks use the slightly modified delimiters `<#=` and `#>`, as you can see. The provided expression can be a variable, a literal, or a function call and must evaluate to a string. Expressions in T4 are most handy for inserting computed values or parameters into raw text as shown, without disrupting the flow of the text.

So far, you've seen that T4 lets you execute pure control code, emit raw text, and embed expressions within raw text. Next, let's look at some more interesting flow-control concepts.

T4 processes the template from top to bottom. In this top-down examination of the example template so far, all T4 would have emitted is the class declaration and the curly brace that follows it. The automatic properties will be generated next. If you look back at how property generation was done in the C#-based code generator in listing 3.1, you'll see a `foreach` loop that iterates over the metadata and outputs text using a `Console.WriteLine` statement. Here's how it was done in C#:

```
foreach (var property in properties)
   {
     Console.WriteLine(
        "  public {0} {1} {{ get; {2}set; }}",
        property.Item1,
        property.Item2,
        property.Item3 ? "" : "private ");
   }
```

You could use the same code in T4 by pasting it directly into a control block. But to demonstrate alternatives to that approach available in T4, we'll use a technique that mixes control code, boilerplate text, and expressions instead. It's not necessarily a better approach to do it that way, but it highlights some of the more interesting features of T4's syntax. Compare the following lines from the T4 template to its pure C# equivalent shown earlier:

```
<#
    foreach (var property in properties)
   {
#>
  public <#= property.Item1 #> <#=
    property.Item2 #> { get; <#=
    property.Item3 ? "" : "private " #>set; }
<#
   }
#>
```

The line that emits the code for the property begins with the `public` keyword. It would be even easier to understand if we could show it all on one line. When the `foreach` loop runs to iterate over the properties, this is the section of the template that will emit these four lines into the output file:

```
public System.String Make { get; set; }
public System.String Model { get; set; }
public System.Int32 Year { get; set; }
public System.Int32 MPG { get; private set; }
```

Did you notice in the template how two separate T4 control blocks have been used to *wrap* a mixed set of text blocks and expressions to produce this output? In fact, the closing curly brace of the `foreach` loop appears in a completely separate control block. That might seem odd, but in T4, it's perfectly acceptable. The first text block in between those control blocks emits the C# keyword `public`, then an expression is used that refers to the range variable defined in the `foreach` loop. The technique of mixing expressions and raw text continues to complete the declaration for each property.

When you begin working in T4, this kind of construction can be quite confusing. Your normal sense of scope in languages like C# or Visual Basic doesn't apply well. The key thing to remember is that the `<#` and `#>` delimiters used for control blocks in T4 do create scope for the template's control code. Syntactically, though, that scope isn't limited to a single pair of delimiters. You're free to split up the scope in your control language however you like, mixing in text, more control blocks, and expressions as you see fit.

The last section of the template shown in listing 3.9 generates the constructor for the class. The techniques you've seen so far are used again to iterate over the property list two more times. The first iteration produces the parameter list in the constructor's declaration; the other iteration produces the assignments of those parameters to their associated properties inside the constructor's body. The first of those loops introduces T4's `Write` utility function, which is a lot like `Console.WriteLine` used in the C#-based code generator. But T4's `Write` function emits text into the output file instead of sending it to the console device.

If you add the template file from listing 3.9 to a Visual Studio project, you'll observe that whenever you modify and save it, a C# source code file is generated containing the `DynamicCar` class. The output file will have the same name as the template and whatever extension is assigned in the `<#@output#>` directive.

There's a lot more to learn about T4's integration with Visual Studio. We'll get to that soon. For now, all we want you to understand is that T4 provides a clean syntax for separating control code from boilerplate text, some helpful utility functions, and effective, easy-to-use integration with Visual Studio.

### 3.3.1 *Templates should be beautiful*

The concept of mixing markup and code isn't new at all. In the web world, a small idea conceived in 1994 and initially known as the Personal Home Page (PHP) tools grew into a technological juggernaut that propelled names like Facebook, Joomla, Drupal, and Digg to fame and fortune. Active Server Pages (ASP), which Microsoft released in 1998, used the same technique of mixing markup and code to render its web pages. JavaServer Pages (JSP), released in 1999, and ASP.NET in 2002 followed the same basic pattern. It's no surprise that anyone who's coded in PHP, ASP, JSP, or ASP.NET will feel right at home in T4.

In recent years, many Microsoft developers have become critical of the ASP.NET syntax from which T4 was derived. Some complain that it's too *chunky* or too *decorative* for efficient web page layout, in particular when building large, complex pages. The separation between the markup and the control code is too heavy for the tastes of many modern web developers. Markup generators like HTML Abstraction Markup Language (HAML) and MVC view engines like Razor and Spark have appeared in recent years to appeal to an emerging sensibility that markup should be both *functional* and *beautiful.*

Where does this leave T4—which uses an older, arguably heavier syntax for separating control code and boilerplate text? Is T4 both functional and beautiful for what it's intended to do? Should T4 abandon the ASP-style syntax and adopt something more streamlined like Razor? The answer from Microsoft on that last question is no. What has proven to be desirable for web developers isn't always ideal in other cases. When you need to mix boilerplate code in C# or Visual Basic with metadata-driven control and expression code written in the same languages, having a bit more decoration in the templating syntax can be a good thing. If T4 had a Razor-like syntax, the separation between the template text and control code in the template would become nearly indistinguishable. That would reduce comprehension significantly. Even with good syntactic separation, there are places in listing 3.9, for example, where it's admittedly difficult to tell which curly braces belong to a text block or a control block. Try that in Razor syntax, and you would be scratching your head trying to figure it out.

Microsoft's other key reason for defending the syntax of T4 is that it isn't a code generator, as we've been telling you all along. T4 is a *text generator*. It can emit any kind of text-based output. View engines like Razor get some of their syntactical efficiency from the fact that the output type is well-known. Because Razor strictly emits web pages, its engine can make optimizing assumptions and provide domain-specific support for the parser that increases both comprehension and expressiveness. The Razor syntax takes full advantage of those engine optimizations to yield a *language* that makes web page design a truly joyful experience.

T4's engine, on the other hand, doesn't know or care what kind of output it generates. It's completely unaware of the output file type or any syntactical conventions of whatever you're trying to produce. Short of a handful of utility functions for handling indentation and emitting text, T4 syntax doesn't get much assistance from the engine upon which optimizations could be built. Does this mean that another syntax parser couldn't be adapted to T4? No. But without a good reason to support an alternative syntax, T4 is likely to continue using its arguably chunky, decorative syntax for the foreseeable future. It's a subjective assessment, but for a general-purpose text generator, T4's syntax may strike as good a balance between function and form as we can expect.

## 3.4    *T4 fundamentals*

Now that you've seen a simple example of T4 in action, let's dig a little deeper into some of the basics. To generate text, the T4 syntax offers three types of elements: directives, text blocks, and control blocks. The first element types we examine are the T4 directive and text block.

### 3.4.1    *Directives and text blocks*

Directives control the templating engine during the generation process, allowing you to specify parameters, the output file extension, the encoding of the generated file, referenced assemblies and imports, and the language you want to use in your control blocks. Directives are surrounded with the special delimiters <#@ and #>, as you saw in the example in the last section. It's helpful to think of T4 as a kind of compiler. If T4 were a compiler, most of the built-in directives would be the command-line switches that control the compilation and output processes. Here is a pair of directives that instruct T4 to load the System.Xml.dll assembly and output a file with a .sql extension:

```
<#@ assembly name="System.Xml" #>
<#@ output extension=".sql" #>
```

Now think about how the C# compiler that you might invoke from the command line handles assembly references and output file naming. For Microsoft's CSC.EXE compiler, you could use the /reference and /out command-line switches to control those options. For T4, the <#@assembly#> and <@#output#> directives allow you to do the same thing within the text of the template file.

The second type of T4 element to understand is the text block. *Text blocks* are lines of raw text that will be inserted into the transformed output. Unlike directives and control blocks, these blocks of raw text don't have any special delimiters surrounding them. In fact, what defines a text block in a T4 template is the *absence* of any T4 delimiters. The T4 engine doesn't evaluate the contents of a text block at all, so it could be anything: source code, MIME-encoded binary data, code comments, and so forth. T4 inserts the text block into the output whenever the transformation occurs.

> **Text blocks are like XML CDATA**
>
> If you're familiar with XML, you can think of T4 text blocks as the unparsed character data in an XML CDATA section. T4 text blocks allow you to insert raw, uninterpreted text directly into the output of the template, whitespace, and nonprintable characters included.

### 3.4.2 Control blocks

Control blocks come in several varieties. To get started, let's examine a standard control block, sometimes called a *statement block*.

#### STANDARD CONTROL BLOCK

Here's a small T4 template that writes the string "Hello, world!" to the output file:

```
<#@ template language="C#" #>
<#@ output extension=".txt" #>
Hello, <# WriteLine("world!"); #>
```

This simple template demonstrates all three types of blocks that you'll need to become familiar with to eventually master T4. The <#@ and #> delimiters on the first two lines indicate that they're directives. For this little template, the directives tell T4 that any control code in the template should be interpreted as C# and that the output file should have a .txt extension. The third line introduces both a text block, containing the word Hello, and a standard control block that calls the T4 host's built-in WriteLine utility function.

When you save the previously shown template file in Visual Studio, a few things will happen. First, a tool is invoked to compile the template into a .NET class and instantiate it. Then a method in the generated class called TransformText is invoked to produce the output, which is written to a file. Lastly, Visual Studio inserts or updates the generated file into the project as a so-called *subordinate file* that's associated with the template. You don't get to see the compilation and invocation steps when using the standard Visual Studio T4 host, but you can definitely see the newly created output file.

## T4's WriteLine != Console.WriteLine

The first time you see code in T4 that invokes the `WriteLine` function as shown previously, it's tempting to think that it's in some way related to the `WriteLine` method in the `System.Console` class. Although similarly named, T4's `WriteLine` method has an entirely different implementation. If you invoke `Console.WriteLine` by mistake in a T4 template, you won't get an error. You also won't get the expected output from the template because the generated text will be going to an invisible console window instead of your output file. This can be positively maddening until you figure out your mistake.

Assuming that the small template file shown earlier was named HelloWorld.tt, the resulting output file would be named HelloWorld.txt because of the `outputextension` directive specified within the template. Those two files will appear in Visual Studio's Solution Explorer view, as shown in Figure 3.1.

**Figure 3.1   The HelloWorld template and its output as shown in Visual Studio's Solution Explorer window.**

We get into the details of how that generation process works in a bit. For now, understand that adding a text template file to a Visual Studio project produces a single subordinate file whenever the template is modified and saved.

### MULTISTATEMENT STANDARD CONTROL BLOCKS

Calling T4's built-in utility functions like `WriteLine` in a standard control block is straightforward. Standard control blocks can have more than one statement in them, which is why you'll sometimes hear them called statement blocks. To generate the "Hello, world!" output with multiple statements, you might write the template in a slightly different way:

```
<#@ template language="C#" #>
<#@ output extension=".txt" #>
Hello,
<#
  Write("world");
  WriteLine("!");
#>
```

The two C# statements in the control block are easy enough to understand. The `Write` method doesn't emit a new line sequence into the output, but the `WriteLine` method does. However, when saved, this template doesn't produce "Hello, world!" on one line as you might expect. Instead, the text is on two lines like this:

```
Hello,
world!
```

What went wrong? Where's the extra new line coming from? A careful examination of the template shows that it's coming not from the control block but from the text block that precedes it. Within a text block, every character is interpreted literally, including invisible ones like carriage returns, line feeds, tabs, and spaces. To make this template produce the desired text on one line, you need to modify it slightly, like this:

```
<#@ template language="C#" #>
<#@ output extension=".txt" #>
Hello, <#
   Write("world");
   WriteLine("!");
#>
```

Did you notice that the new line at the end of the text block has now been replaced by the opening `<#` tag of the control block? It's a subtle change, but it makes a distinct difference in the output. This template will produce "Hello, world!" in the output file on one line.

### Line spacing in T4

When you first begin working in T4, line spacing can be a bit tricky if you're working in complex, multifile templates. Quite often, when examining the output of a template, you'll ask yourself, "Where are those extra lines coming from?" For source code generation, an extra line (or the absence of one) doesn't make a difference, depending on the language you're emitting. But if you're a Type A personality, these minor details might bother you. Moreover, poor line spacing can affect programmer comprehension when reading the code. After a bit of practice, you'll get a feel for how T4 line spacing works and establish some simple rules for making sure your generated code is consistently well formed.

It's also important to note that control characters and whitespace inside a T4 control block are only significant if the source language treats them that way. Everything inside a control block is treated purely as source code to be compiled into the template's class. If you were compiling a template using Visual Basic 9 or earlier as the control language, you'd need to use underscores as line-continuation characters whenever you split lines of code in your control blocks. Similarly, if you include a C# literal string beginning with the @ symbol in a T4 control block, the compiler will interpret every character inside the literal string exactly as it's expressed, including any invisible tabs or new line sequences expressed inside the literal string.

#### EXPRESSION CONTROL BLOCKS

Using the `Write` and `WriteLine` utility methods provided by T4 can be cumbersome when readability and comprehension are important. T4 offers expression control blocks to make your templates more fluent. To specify an inline expression, open a control block using a slightly different opening delimiter: `<#=` instead of `<#`. Inside the expression block, you're allowed to reference any field or property in the template class. You can also invoke a method in the expression block as long as it returns a value that can be converted to a string. The following template will output the string in the `planNumber` field:

```
<#@ template language="C#" #>
<#@ output extension=".txt" #>
```

```
<#
  int planNumber = 9;
#>
Plan <#= planNumber #> from Outer Space
```

The placement of the expression control block <#=planNumber#> between the two text blocks in this small example is certainly more readable than calling the Write utility method. The planNumber variable isn't a string, but T4 will invoke the ToString method to convert it for you. Passing an integer or any other type that has a properly overloaded ToString method is no problem in a T4 expression block.

> **Expression blocks may contain branching logic**
> When you write an expression control block in T4, it can be a reference to any single object that can be converted to a string. You might infer that a C# expression like <#= A ? B : C #> would work, too. After all, that expression will produce a reference to object B or object C, depending on the truth of the value A. The C# ternary operator used in an expression control block is a simple, compact way to create highly comprehensible T4 templates.

### 3.4.3   *Handling indentation*

Before talking about the last kind of control block in T4 basics, let's examine how indentation is handled. Software developers are typically picky about what nonprogrammers would think of as trivial—even meaningless details concerning our code. Formatting of source code is one of those topics that gets programmers into so-called *religious* arguments. We care so much about the nuances of formatting because we understand that readability directly affects human comprehension. Careful delimiter placement, line continuation, and indentation practices can make the difference between grasping a bit of complex source code and being completely lost in it. Furthermore, some languages like Python and F# are fundamentally dependent on indentation to reflect program structure.

The base class from which the standard T4 host derives includes a variety of utility functions. You've already used the Write and WriteLine utility functions in this chapter to format text being generated into the output file. Three other utility functions are available for managing indentation:

- voidPushIndent(stringindent);
- stringPopIndent();
- voidClearIndent();

There's also a read-only string property called CurrentIndent in the class containing the text that will be prefixed to each line generated by T4. When the transformation begins, CurrentIndent is an empty string, so each line that's emitted will have no characters prefixed to it.

Internally, the T4 generator class manages the indentation strings passed to Push-Indent on a stack-like structure. Calling PushIndent adds a string to the top of the stack. The `CurrentIndent` property accessor coalesces all the values on the stack into one long string. Calling `PopIndent` removes the indentation string last pushed so that `CurrentIndent` no longer includes it. The next listing demonstrates the basic concepts of how indentation works in T4.

> **Listing 3.10  BasicIndentation.tt**

```
<#@ template language="C#" #>
<#@ output extension=".txt" #>
<#
  PushIndent("L1 ");
#>
Item A
<#
  PushIndent("L2 ");
#>
SubItem A1
SubItem A2
SubItem A3
<#
  PopIndent();
#>
Item B
<#
  PushIndent("L2 ");
  for (int ndx = 1; ndx <= 3; ndx++)
    WriteLine("SubItem B" + ndx);
  ClearIndent();
#>
Done.
```

The output of the `BasicIndentation.tt` template looks like this:

```
L1 Item A
L1 L2 SubItem A1
L1 L2 SubItem A2
L1 L2 SubItem A3
L1 Item B
L1 L2 SubItem B1
L1 L2 SubItem B2
L1 L2 SubItem B3
Done.
```

We can make a few observations about the template code and its output. First, the current indentation applies to text that comes from both text blocks and control blocks. What we said about text blocks being interpreted literally before wasn't perfectly true. Each line that's emitted will be prefixed with the string value from `CurrentIndent`, whether it's hardcoded like the `SubItems` in the text block for `ItemA` or those dynamically generated using a `for` loop in a control block like the `SubItems` for `ItemB`.

Another thing to note from the example is that you don't have to indent strictly with whitespace. When you're generating source code for popular languages like C# or Visual Basic, whitespace for indentation is the norm. But as you can see in listing 3.10, any string can serve as indentation, even those like L1, L2, or anything else that makes sense for your output file type.

The last observation to make about listing 3.10 concerns the use of the Clear-Indent utility function. If you need to clear the stack of all the indentation strings that have been pushed so far, you could keep calling PopIndent until the CurrentIndent property returns an empty string. But that kind of code would be ugly and cumbersome to write when calling the ClearIndent utility function is available.

### CLASS FEATURE BLOCKS

As you learned earlier, T4 dynamically creates a new class that contains all the text and code defined in the template in executable form. It also contains class-level utility functions like Write and PushIndent that you can invoke anywhere inside the template's control code. If the template is a .NET class, why shouldn't you be able to add your own methods to it that can be invoked like the methods provided by the T4 base class? Class feature blocks let you do that. Appreciating that T4 uses metaprogramming internally will help you to understand how class feature blocks work.

Many times, when you're writing a T4 template, you want to organize your control code so that it can be invoked repeatedly. Even if your code isn't intended to be called repeatedly, you may find it useful to separate it into discrete methods and properties to make it more readable. The following listing shows a method named Expanded-TypeName implemented as a T4 class feature block. Given a .NET Type, this method formats a string containing the readable name of the type. That will be helpful in the next example when you want to output information about generic methods.

> **Listing 3.11   ExpandedTypeName functioning as a class feature block**

```
<#+
  private string ExpandedTypeName(Type t)
  {
    var result = new StringBuilder();
    if (!t.IsGenericType)
      result.Append(t.Name);
    else
    {
      result.Append(t.Name.Substring(0,
        t.Name.IndexOf('`')));
      result.Append("<");
      int ndx = 0;
      foreach (var tp in t.GetGenericArguments())
        result.AppendFormat(
          (ndx++ > 0) ? ", {0}" : "{0}", tp.Name);
      result.Append(">");
    }
    return result.ToString();
  }
#>
```

Did you notice the <#+ and #> sequences surrounding the function? Those are the special delimiters that surround a class feature block in T4. Think of the plus symbol as meaning *add this stuff* to the class. The `ExpandedTypeName` function defined here takes a `Type` object as the parameter and returns a string that looks like the C# definition for the type. If the supplied type isn't generic, the simple `Name` property is returned. But if the type is generic, its type arguments are formatted to resemble the C# declaration rather than the CLR notation that the `Name` property normally returns. The following listing shows the `ExpandedTypeName` method in action, being used to produce an interesting result.

**Listing 3.12   TemplateClassDiscovery.tt**

```
<#@ template language="C#" #>
<#@ output extension=".txt" #>
<#@ import namespace="System.Text" #>
<#= ExpandedTypeName(this.GetType())#> Information:
<#
  PushIndent("  ");
  WriteLine("Properties:");
  PushIndent("  ");

  foreach (var pi in this.GetType().GetProperties())
  {
    Write("{0} {1} {{",
      ExpandedTypeName(pi.PropertyType),
      pi.Name);
    WriteLine("{0}{1} }}",
      pi.CanRead ? " get;" : "",
      pi.CanWrite ? " set;" : "");
  }

  PopIndent();
  WriteLine("Methods:");
  PushIndent("  ");

  foreach (var mi in this.GetType().GetMethods())
  {
    Write("{0} {1}(",
      ExpandedTypeName(mi.ReturnType),
      mi.Name);
    var parms = mi.GetParameters();
    if (parms != null)
    {
      for (int ndx = 0; ndx < parms.Length; ndx++)
      {
        Write((ndx > 0) ? ", {0} {1}" : "{0} {1}",
          ExpandedTypeName(parms[ndx].ParameterType),
          parms[ndx].Name);
      }
    }
    WriteLine(");");
  }
#>
<#+
  private string ExpandedTypeName(Type t)
  {
```

```
    var result = new StringBuilder();
    if (!t.IsGenericType)
      result.Append(t.Name);
    else
    {
      result.Append(t.Name.Substring(0,
        t.Name.IndexOf('`')));
      result.Append("<");
      int ndx = 0;
      foreach (var tp in t.GetGenericArguments())
        result.AppendFormat(
          (ndx++ > 0) ? ", {0}" : "{0}", tp.Name);
      result.Append(">");
    }
    return result.ToString();
  }
#>
```

Reading from top to bottom, after an initial set of template directives, the Expanded-TypeName function is invoked in an expression control block passing this.GetType() as the parameter. Then the template iterates over the properties and methods to reflect some basic information about it. The question is, what does the this parameter (or Me in Visual Basic) refer to inside a T4 template? Running the template should make it clearer. The following listing shows the output from the template.

**Listing 3.13   The output of TemplateClassDiscovery.tt**

```
GeneratedTextTransformation Information:
  Properties:
    CompilerErrorCollection Errors { get; }
    String CurrentIndent { get; }
    IDictionary<String, Object> Session { get; set; }
  Methods:
    String TransformText();
    CompilerErrorCollection get_Errors();
    String get_CurrentIndent();
    IDictionary<String, Object> get_Session();
    Void set_Session(IDictionary<String, Object> value);
    Void Initialize();
    Void Dispose();
    Void Write(String textToAppend);
    Void WriteLine(String textToAppend);
    Void Write(String format, Object[] args);
    Void WriteLine(String format, Object[] args);
    Void Error(String message);
    Void Warning(String message);
    Void PushIndent(String indent);
    String PopIndent();
    Void ClearIndent();
    String ToString();
    Boolean Equals(Object obj);
    Int32 GetHashCode();
    Type GetType();
```

You can see from the output that the type of the this reference must be of a Type called GeneratedTextTransform. It has three properties and twenty methods as shown. You should recognize some of the other property and method names by now, too. For example:

- TransformText
- Write and WriteLine
- CurrentIndent, PushIndent, PopIndent, and ClearIndent

It's obvious now that inside a template, the this reference refers to the compiled class that's generated by T4. With a little reflection and a helper function defined in a class feature block, you discovered more about how T4 works internally. How cool is that?

---

**Where's the method you added?**

You may be wondering why the ExpandedTypeName function that was added in the class feature block didn't appear among the 20 methods shown in the output in listing 3.13. The reason is simple. The function was declared as private, and the Reflection API methods introspect for public members by default. Change the access modifier on the ExpandedTypeName function in the template to public, save it, and observe the output file again. This time, you'll see that 21 methods are reported, including ExpandedTypeName.

---

## 3.5    Using T4 inside Visual Studio

T4 integrates into Visual Studio without a lot of ceremony. If you add .tt files to nearly any project type, the output files are automatically generated back into the project. What could be simpler than that? This section examines how T4 and Visual Studio work together. In the process, you'll go beyond the basics you learned in the last section to understand how to use metaprogramming with T4 to solve some difficult problems.

### 3.5.1    How T4 uses the single file generator extension point

T4's relationship to Visual Studio isn't special from the Integrated Development Environment's (IDE's) perspective. The so-called *single file generator* extension point in the MSBUILD system is used to handle a variety of common code generation tasks, including T4 transformations. To support this feature generally, the project file format used by Visual Studio includes a source file property called CustomTool, shown in figure 3.2. Notice that the template file is marked not to build and not to be copied to the output directory. A custom tool called TextTemplatingFileGenerator will be run to process the file. That custom tool is the T4 host designed for Visual Studio.

Pay close attention to the value of the CustomTool property. The value was automatically set to TextTemplatingFileGenerator when the .tt file was added to the project.

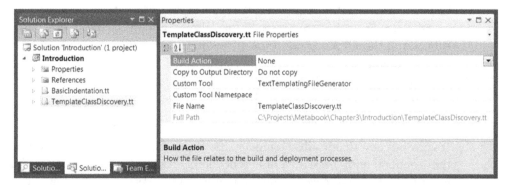

**Figure 3.2   The Solution Explorer and Properties windows in Visual Studio 2010 showing the file properties for a T4 template**

For other Visual Studio file types, a variety of `CustomTool` property values exist. Here's a short list of common code generators that you'll find if you scan the registry on a machine that has Visual Studio installed:

- `DataServiceClientGenerator`—Creates OData access clients
- `EntityModelCodeGenerator`—Creates classes from EF models
- `MSLinqToSQLGenerator`—Creates classes from LinqToSql models
- `ResXFileCodeGenerator`—Creates classes from .resx files
- `WCFProxyGenerator`—Creates web service proxy classes

If you've been doing .NET work for a while, you may have seen some of those values specified in the `CustomTool` property and wondered how they got there. Unfortunately, the answer isn't to be found in a nice, clean Visual Studio configuration dialog. It's buried in the registry near the generator names shown in the previous bullets. Files with an extension of .edmx are bound to the `EntityModelCode-Generator`, for example. And T4 template files with the extension.tt are bound to the `TextTemplatingFileGenerator` as shown in figure 3.2. These registered associations tell Visual Studio how to set the `CustomTool` property value whenever a file is added.

After the tool association has been set, other registry values help Visual Studio locate the assemblies that perform the code generation. For T4 transformations, the single file generator is in a class named `TemplatedCodeGenerator`. Each of the previously listed code generators follows this same pattern. They each have one or more file associations registered for them to ensure that the correct `CustomTool` property is set in the project file. And they each have an assembly registered that does the code generation step to produce subordinate files for each source file.

The point of understanding Visual Studio's single file code generator extension point is that T4 is integrated into Visual Studio using the same standard, single-file generator extensibility point that many other tools use. Other than that, Visual Studio doesn't know what goes on inside a T4 template. As of this writing, Visual Studio offers no customized IDE support or IntelliSense support for T4 templates. But a few excellent third-party tools do so.

### 3.5.2  *Creating a T4 template from Visual Studio*

Now that you know a bit about how T4 is connected to Visual Studio for design-time code generation, let's have some fun with it. Add a T4 design-time template to any project by right-clicking the project name in the Solution Explorer and selecting the Add New Item menu choice. The dialog shown in figure 3.3 will appear. Notice how the word `template` has been used in the search textbox to find the T4 item types. To add a design-time template, select the one called Text Template, name it, and click Add.

On the left side of the Add New Item dialog, note the Installed Templates list. These aren't T4 templates, although one can imagine that in some future release of Visual Studio, T4 could be used by the Add New Item function to create project files dynamically. There's certainly nothing stopping third parties from extending Visual Studio in that way.

Among the Visual Studio file templates are two T4-specific ones you can use to add text templates to your projects. Rather than hunting for them among all the Installed Templates categories in the list shown in figure 3.2, you can use Visual Studio 2010's template search function to find them instead. Type the word `template` into the search box on the Add New Item dialog and press Enter. Figure 3.3 shows the results of the query—two T4 choices that are available in Visual Studio 2010 today:

- *Preprocessed Text Template*—A run-time T4 template
- *Text Template*—A design-time T4 template

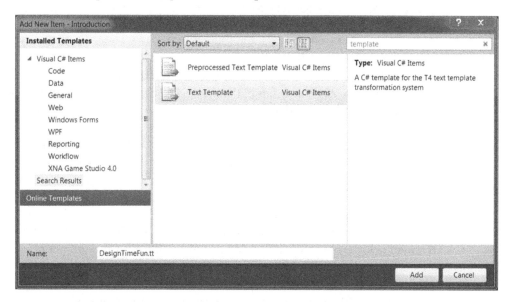

**Figure 3.3  Adding a design-time template to a project in Visual Studio 2010**

You can think of a Preprocessed Text Template as one that doesn't require Visual Studio to run. In fact, in the Visual Studio documentation, these are also called *Run-Time Text Templates*. We cover Preprocessed (run-time) Templates in detail in the next section. The other choice is the so-called Text Template, also called a *Design-Time Text Template* in the Visual Studio documentation. To create a template that's compiled and transformed during the build process for your solution, the Text Template is the right choice. In any open project, add a Text Template named DesignTimeFun.tt and click the Add button in the Add New Item dialog. When Visual Studio initially creates the new .tt file from its own template, it will contain only these two directives:

```
<#@ template debug="false"
    hostspecific="false" language="C#" #>
<#@ output extension=".txt" #>
```

Remember that all T4 directives are bounded by the <#@ and #> character sequences as shown earlier. If you're working in a Visual Basic project, the language attribute on the template directive will initially be set to "VB" instead of "C#" as shown. It's important to understand that the choice of language in the template directive determines the control language for the template, not the file type of the template's output.

> **T4 control language versus output**
> T4 is more generally a text generator than a code generator. You can use Visual Basic to produce C# or F#, Python or XML, for that matter. T4 transformations are also executed outside the context of normal, Visual Studio-controlled compilation, so if you're working in a C# project and want to use Visual Basic as the control language inside your templates, that's perfectly okay.

### 3.5.3   *More on the template directive*

All T4 templates must include a <#@template#> directive. For versions of T4 shipping with Visual Studio 2010 and later, the language attribute isn't required and will default to "C#" if not specified. Older implementations of T4 may require the language attribute on the template element, so check the documentation for the version you're using to be sure. Behind the scenes, the CodeDOM is used to compile T4 templates, so, depending on the installed CodeDOM providers on your computer, you may be able to select a specific version of your control language's compiler for T4 to use by setting the language attribute to a specific value—for example, "C#2.0." Check the documentation that comes with your version of Visual Studio to know exactly which languages are supported. In general, specifying "C#" or "VB" for the language attribute are safe choices because that will select the default compilers for those languages that are installed on your computer.

The debug and hostspecific attributes on the T4 template directive included by the Visual Studio file template are also not required. But because you're likely to want to make changes to these attributes from time to time, the Visual Studio file template that produces the initial .tt file includes them in the `template` element using their default values. You can leave the `debug` and `hostspecific` attributes in the `template` directive as they appear or remove them if you like.

This text isn't meant to be an exhaustive reference for all of the T4 directive options, but there are a couple of other attributes on the `template` directive worth mentioning. The first one is the `compilerOptions` attribute. We mentioned before that T4 uses the CodeDOM internally to create a class from the template, compile, and invoke it. During the compilation process, you can pass options to the compiler, as you would at the command line if you were invoking the compiler by hand. When the T4 control language is C#, any of the command line options for the CSC.EXE compiler can be passed using the `compilerOptions` attribute on the template directive like this:

```
<#@ template language="C#" compilerOptions="warnaserror+" #>
```

This example will elevate any warnings generated during the compilation to errors, causing it to fail. The Visual Basic compiler also supports the `warnaserror+` option, so the same `compilerOptions` value could be used when Visual Basic serves as the T4 control language.

The other `template` directive attribute worth mentioning is `culture`. When this attribute is specified, the thread that performs the transformation will be set to the designated culture beforehand. The string value that's provided must adhere to the standard of a two-character ISO 639 (culture) code followed by a hyphen and a two-character ISO 3166 (subculture) code. For example, to ensure that globalization settings for Brazilian Portuguese are used when generating a T4 template's output, the following template directive could be used:

```
<#@ template language="C#" culture="pt-BR" #>
```

If the culture is included in the template in this way, the standard T4 host used by Visual Studio sets the culture of the processing thread to the specified value before the transformation occurs. If the culture value isn't present, the transformation occurs using whatever the Windows default is for the machine.

### 3.5.4 *Using the output directive*

The output files from design-time templates are always named with the same root file-name as their associated template files. To set a different file extension, you must use an `<#@output#>` directive. Interestingly, if you fail to specify an `output` directive in a design-time template, the extension of the file that's emitted will always be .cs whether or not the including project type is C#.

Because a design-time template can generate any kind of text output at compile time, you must use an output directive to specify the extension of the file that's created. Programmers new to T4 sometimes assume that the extension that's specified affects the output in other ways. But that's not true. T4 doesn't do any special processing based on the designated `outputextension`. You could choose to emit a file with a traditional T-SQL file extension from a template by specifying the output directive, like this:

```
<#@outputextension=".sql"#>
```

But appending the .sql extension to the output filename doesn't invoke any special, T-SQL transformation logic during the process. T4 has no language-specific code for any kind of text that it might produce. What's emitted is purely a function of the control blocks and text blocks that are included in each template.

The output directive also allows you to set the encoding of the output file with using the optional encoding attribute. To create a Python file encoded as UTF-16, for example, the following output directive could be used in a T4 template:

```
<#@outputextension=".py"encoding="utf-16"#>
```

The default encoding is UTF-8, which is a Unicode encoding that's backward-compatible with ASCII. The only real problem with UTF-8 is that it's *multibyte*, meaning that some characters sequences are longer than others. This means that files using the UTF-8 encoding can't be randomly accessed like those encoded using fixed-width character formats, such as UTF-16 and UTF-32. If you're not working with huge input files, or if you plan to process the output files sequentially, UTF-8 is typically an excellent choice for file encoding because it's also independent of Byte Order Marking (BOM). In addition to the encodings mentioned so far, T4 also supports ASCII, UTF-16BE (Big-Endian), and UTF-7.

### 3.5.5   *Using T4 to generate Visual Basic dynamically*

Using what you know so far, let's have some fun. Let's create a console application using Visual Basic and include a T4 template that uses C# as the control language that produces a Visual Basic file to be compiled as the main module.

1   Create a Visual Basic console application and modify the Module1.vb file to write a string to the console, like this:

```
ModuleModule1
  SubMain()
    Console.WriteLine("Hello,world!")
  EndSub
EndModule
```

2   Compile and run the application to make sure it functions as you expect, outputting the phrase "Hello, world!" to the console window.

3   Replace the Module1.vb file with a template that produces it instead. Right-click the console project in the Solution Explorer and select Add New Item or select Add New Item from Visual Studio's Project menu. The Add New Item dialog shown earlier in figure 3.3 appears.

4   Search for the T4 templates by typing template in the search box in the upper right-hand corner and pressing Enter.

5 From the search results, select the Visual Studio file template called Text Template.

6 Name the new file DynamicModule1.tt and click the Add button to add the file to the project. Notice that a new T4 text template named DynamicModule1.tt has been added to the project.

7 Open the .tt file and enter the template code as shown in the next listing. Notice two things: the template control language is C# even though the project is of type Visual Basic and the file extension declared in the output directive is also for Visual Basic.

**Listing 3.14 DynamicModule1.tt**

```
<#@ template language="C#" #>
<#@ output extension=".vb" #>
<#
  string msg = "Hello, world!";
  int n = 0;
#>
Module Module1
  Sub Main()
    Console.WriteLine("<# while (n < msg.Length)
      Write(msg[n++].ToString());
    #>")
  End Sub
End Module
```

8 Save the DynamicModule1.tt file and look for any compilation errors in the Visual Studio output window. If you made a mistake that caused a compilation error, double-click the error in the output window—note that your cursor is taken to the offending spot in the template.

9 For Visual Basic projects, unlike C# projects, the output files for T4 text templates aren't shown in the Solution Explorer window by default. You have to click the Show All Files button at the top of the Solution Explorer window to be able to see the DynamicModule1.vb file that was produced by the template. Once you've done that, open the output file and look at it. Do you recognize it? Yes, it's exactly the same as the Visual Basic code shown in step 1 of this task.

10 Before you compile the whole project again though, there's one small problem that must be corrected. As it now stands, your project has two identical modules named Module1. The Visual Basic compiler isn't going to like that at all. Right-click the Moldule1.vb file in the Solution Explorer and choose Delete from the context menu.

11 Compile and run the project again. You should see that the output is identical to the output shown in step 2 of this task.

You've created a T4 text template using C# as the control language to dynamically generate a Visual Basic module into a Visual Basic project. You can use C# or Visual Basic as the template control language to emit any kind of file into any kind of project.

**NOTE**   Unfortunately, the version of T4 that ships with Visual Studio 2010 doesn't allow you to emit files based on the current project type, at least not without a bit of extra work. Perhaps a future version of T4 will make that much simpler.

The key learning point here is that T4 gives no special treatment to the output based on file type. Only the control blocks and text blocks in each template will determine what's in the resulting output files.

## 3.6   *Summary*

Microsoft's T4 is a highly addictive product. Then again, once your team starts benefitting from a code generator from any vendor, you'll find all sorts of opportunities to use it to speed up the work and reduce coding errors. To us, template-based code generation qualifies as metaprogramming because it requires all the same mental skills that the other forms of metaprogramming require and delivers many of the same benefits. To be a good template designer, you must learn to think in that same abstract, prototypical way about how code should behave in context and often later in time.

As compared to the many other template-based code generators on the market, the real advantage of T4 is its tight integration with Visual Studio. As you've discovered in this chapter, generating code with T4 is as simple as dropping a TT file into your Visual Studio solution and inserting the raw text and control blocks to emit the desired output. T4 and Visual Studio take care of all the rest at compile time.

# *Generating code*
# *with the CodeDOM*

**This chapter covers**

- Understanding the CodeDOM
- The code providers classes
- Adding objects to a code graph
- Metaprogramming with the CodeDOM

Web browsers have a Document Object Model (DOM) for creating windows and managing the navigation between pages. HTML has a DOM for describing the content and structure of those pages. JavaScript has a DOM for automating the others. These models are appropriately called DOMs because they're technologies for the World Wide Web, which is a largely document-oriented system.

Given the range of roles that a DOM can fill, what do you think Microsoft's CodeDOM does? It could be used to describe code. As you learned in chapters 1 and 2, .NET provides a rich metadata foundation for applications. Or perhaps it's used to define code as data in a sort of document outline fashion. An API so promisingly named might also be used to generate code. After all, JavaScript can generate HTML on the fly. Why shouldn't the CodeDOM be able to generate .NET code dynamically?

As you might have guessed by our hypothesizing about the nature of the API, the CodeDOM and the underlying code providers that you'll learn about in this chapter enable all these scenarios in .NET:

- Describing code in a mostly language-independent data structure
- Generating source code in a variety of languages
- Compiling code and code-as-data into .NET assemblies

The CodeDOM is a metaprogramming power tool that every serious developer on the .NET platform should take the time to understand. In this chapter, you'll start by learning about *code graphs*, a construct that the CodeDOM uses to express the logic and structure of code in terms of data. Then you'll take a tour of the various CodeDOM providers and the more important classes in the `System.CodeDom` and `System.CodeDom.Compiler` namespaces. After that, you'll study an example that will help you to grasp the range and flexibility of the CodeDOM's power.

## 4.1   *Understanding the CodeDOM*

The CodeDOM is a fairly complex collection of classes that can be found in the `System.CodeDom` and `System.CodeDom.Compiler` namespaces. Most of the types in these namespaces can be found in the mscorlib.dll and System.dll assemblies in the Global Assembly Cache (GAC). It's clear from that arrangement how essential the CodeDOM is in the .NET Framework Class Library (FCL).

One of the reasons that the CodeDOM is so prominently placed is that it's been in the .NET Framework since the beginning. The CodeDOM shipped with the original .NET 1.0 release in February 2002. It evolved quite a bit in the next two releases of the framework, mostly to support enhancements to the delegate model and the addition of generics.

Since 2005, though, the CodeDOM hasn't seen much growth, partly because the Code-DOM is already rich enough to support many kinds of metaprogramming scenarios without further modification. The other key reason is the emergence of expression trees.

---

### Code graph ≈ expression tree

The CodeDOM uses so-called code graphs to express code as data. A *code graph* is a hierarchical data structure that represents the logic and structure of an algorithm. It can be parsed from source code text or built one step at a time, like writing lines of code in your favorite language.

Code graphs can be turned into executable IL when it's time to use them. Expression trees, introduced in the 3.0 version of .NET, can represent code as data, too. They can also be built programmatically or parsed from source code and turned into IL for execution. Code graphs and expression trees seem alike at first glance. Under the covers, however, the implementations of these two metaprogramming systems couldn't be more dissimilar. As you study the CodeDOM in this chapter and expression trees in chapter 6, you'll learn to appreciate the differences and take advantage of them.

To enable Language Integrated Query (LINQ) in the CLR and the core .NET languages, something fundamentally different from the CodeDOM was needed. The CodeDOM has many of the metaprogramming capabilities that LINQ can use to build expressions dynamically, but it's packaged in a way that makes it difficult to use in a set of language extensions. For LINQ expressions, Microsoft decided to go a different way.

At this point, you may be asking yourself whether it's worthwhile to invest in learning the CodeDOM. Don't worry. The CodeDOM isn't going away, because it can still do some interesting things that expression trees can't, such as generate whole new types. Because of this, some popular tools have emerged from Microsoft since expression trees were introduced that use the CodeDOM for much of their metaprogramming work. For example, the T4 uses the CodeDOM under the covers to generate classes from templates and to compile them into assemblies. The ASP.NET MVC Framework and the Microsoft Entity Framework are two popular systems that use T4.

The CodeDOM is here to stay, and in some cases it's the preferred metaprogramming model where code generation and compilation are required. Investing time and energy to understand the CodeDOM is definitely worthwhile. The best way to start is by examining the CodeDOM namespaces, focusing on some of the key classes and how they're organized.

### 4.1.1   *CodeDOM organization and types*

The `System.CodeDOM` namespace is arranged into a hierarchical collection of classes. At the root is a class called the `CodeObject` that only provides a dictionary called `UserData`. Every derived object in the namespace has a dictionary that can be used to store bits of information. It's interesting to note that the dictionary type for the `UserData` property is a `ListDictionary` from the `System.Collections.Specialized` namespace, which is efficient for lists that will contain ten or fewer items. If you put a lot of data into the `UserData` list of a `CodeObject`, performance will suffer. The diagram shown in figure 4.1 depicts the `CodeObject` base class and several of its key derivatives.

From the `CodeObject`, several interesting classes are derived that represent the basic object model of a .NET program. The `CodeNamespace` type represents…well, namespaces in .NET. The `CodeNamespaceImport` is used to import one namespace into another so that references to types that aren't fully qualified in the resulting code can be found. The `CodeStatement` types represent statements in a .NET language. The `CodeExpression` types correspond to the bits of logic that make up statements. We discuss the distinction between statements and expressions in the next section.

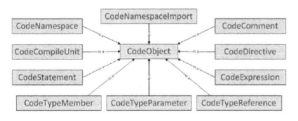

**Figure 4.1   The CodeDOM `CodeObject` base class and a partial list of derived types**

Most of the other type names shown in figure 4.1 are self-explanatory. They describe the remaining major components of a program: comments, directives, types (interfaces, classes, and structs), members (methods, fields, and properties), parameters, and references to other objects. The purpose of the `CodeCompileUnit` isn't so clear. For the most part, you can think of the `CodeCompileUnit` type as the CodeDOM concept for a .NET assembly. You can use a `CodeCompileUnit` to compile an assembly into memory for immediate use or to disk for loading the traditional way.

Let's go a bit deeper into the hierarchy and begin looking at some of the `Code-Expression` types depicted in figure 4.2.

It might make sense to look at how to construct statements or classes next because they're the way we think about coding in our favorite programming languages. But it's better to talk first about expressions because they represent the bricks in a CodeDOM building—the smallest units of program logic.

The `CodeExpression` class serves as the root for all the expression types in the CodeDOM. Figure 4.2 shows some of the more common expressions that you're likely to use in your code graphs. Program elements like arguments, binary operators (add, multiply, equality, and so on), cast operations, and method invocations can be used to construct an algorithm as data one expression at a time. The expression types with `Reference` in their names act as references to other CodeDOM types.

These reference expressions shouldn't be confused with the `CodeTypeReference` type shown in figure 4.1. The `CodeTypeReference` derived from `CodeObject` only serves as a placeholder for .NET types at runtime. For example, in a `CodeCatchClause`, which you'll learn about later, the type of exception that's caught is specified as a `CodeTypeReference`. The .NET CLR allows any type of object to be thrown during an exception, so the type used in the `CodeCatchClause` isn't specified as a `System.Exception` (as C# and Visual Basic programmers might expect). Instead, that parameter is typed as a `CodeTypeReference` so it's able to support languages that can handle throwing and catching types that aren't derived from `System.Exception`.

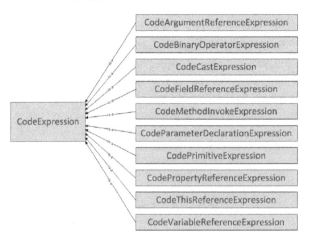

Figure 4.2  The `CodeExpression` base class and a partial list of derived types

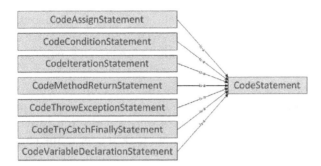

**Figure 4.3** The `CodeStatement` base class and a partial list of derived types

Now you're ready to look at the next level of abstraction: statements. Figure 4.3 shows some of the more common statements defined in the CodeDOM and their relationship to the `CodeStatement` base class.

### 4.1.2 How statements and expressions fit together

Statements use expressions. When you instantiate a CodeDOM statement object, you must specify the expressions that will be used to describe the constituent pieces. Consider the following statement written in C#:

```
R = fn(A + B) / C;
```

One way to visualize this is as a set of nested or chained function calls:

```
Assign(R, Divide(Invoke(fn, Add(A, B)), C))
```

This kind of functional breakdown is exactly how you must code it as a code graph using the CodeDOM.

At the outside is the assignment which you'd code using the `CodeAssignStatement` shown in figure 4.3. But you can't start there logically. Instead, you'd need to go to the *center* of the statement, which is the addition operation. For that, you must use an expression known as the `CodeBinaryOperationExpression`. To it you'd pass `Code-VariableReferenceExpression` objects for the variables A and B along with the operator type for doing addition. Moving outward, the next expression is the invocation of the fn function with the result of the addition expression. For that part, you use `CodeMethodInvokeExpression`, passing a method reference and the addition operation. Next comes another binary operation for dividing the function result by the variable C. Finally, after all of that work, you can build your `CodeAssignStatement` with a reference to the R variable and the result of the division expression.

Do you see how expressions can be chained and nested to produce statements? Learning to think this way, which is undeniably inside-out, isn't easy for everyone. The process is related to the concepts in functional programming which some developers find difficult, in particular those who've coded only in imperative, object-oriented languages for many years. On the bright side, because the CodeDOM gives you such rich classes for describing code as data, learning to build algorithms by hand can make it easier for you to transition into *functional thought*. Forcing yourself to break down statements and expressions in your mind's eye, the way that a language and a compiler would do it for you, creates new prototypes upon which functional programming constructs fit cleanly.

Now that you've learned a bit about the classes that make up the CodeDOM and the logical assembly of an algorithm, let's turn our attention to the code providers. They interpret code graphs, translating them into source code in a variety of languages. They also provide compiler services, which we look at later in the chapter.

## 4.2    *The code provider classes*

Most developers write code on the .NET platform using C# and Visual Basic. It's not surprising, then, that the only two CodeDOM code providers that are defined inside the System.dll assembly are for these popular languages. The code providers for C++, Jscript, and Visual J# are also in the Global Assembly Cache (GAC), but they're implemented in separate assemblies. Several third-party code providers are available on CodePlex.com and other source code repositories, but only the ones for the five languages just mentioned are supported by Microsoft.

> **The Boo CodeDOM provider**
>
> If you want to understand how a CodeDOM provider is implemented on the inside, check out how it's done for the Boo language.[1] Dissecting a CodeDOM provider is a great way to learn the CodeDOM from the inside-out.

### 4.2.1    *Code provider instantiation*

When the CodeDOM classes are initially loaded, the constructor for the `CodeDom-CompilationConfiguration` class loads up the configuration data for all five code providers (mentioned in the preceding section) by name. During this process, the configuration handler class also loads the data associated with any other user-configured code providers from the application's configuration files or from the machine .config file. This configuration section is located along the path shown in the following listing.

**Listing 4.1   Configuring the CodeDOM via XML**

```
<configuration>
  <system.codedom>
    <compilers>
      <compiler
        language="languageName[;...;...]"
        extension="fileExtension[;...;...]"
```

---

[1]  "Boo.Lang.CodeDom.booproj," posted 2010, http://mng.bz/Gqq9.

```
        type="typeName, assemblyName"
        warningLevel="number"
        compilerOptions="option1 option2 [...]">
     </compilers>
   </system.codedom>
</configuration>
```

You can configure code providers by specifying <compiler/> rows in the configuration file with the type, extension, and language attributes properly specified. The other attributes are optional. For example, the <compiler/> element for a mythical language named K# might appear in a configuration file as

```
<compiler
  language="k#;ks;ksharp"
  extension=".ks;ks"
  type="KSharp.KSharpCodeProvider, KSharpCodeProvider">
```

This would allow the language provider class defined in the KSharp.KSharpCodeProvider.dll assembly to be instantiated using any of the language strings associated with it, like this:

```
var ksharpProv = CodeDomProvider.CreateProvider("k#");
```

Internally, when the CodeDOM loads the configuration data for a language, it's stored in a CompilerInfo class instance in an internal dictionary maintained by the CodeDOM. You can query that dictionary to find out which languages are supported by calling the static method GetAllCompilerInfo on the CodeDomProvider class to retrieve all those CompilerInfo objects. Here's an example:

```
foreach (System.CodeDom.Compiler.CompilerInfo ci in
    System.CodeDom.Compiler.CodeDomProvider.GetAllCompilerInfo())
{
  foreach (string language in ci.GetLanguages())
    System.Console.Write("{0}      ", language);
  System.Console.WriteLine();
}
```

This code will yield a list that looks something like this:

```
c#      cs       csharp
vb      vbs      visualbasic   vbscript
js      jscript  javascript
vj#     vjs      vjsharp
c++     mc       cpp
```

You can see the five preconfigured code providers in this list reporting their various language synonyms to the console. If you have more language providers configured, you'll see more lines in the output.

There are a couple of ways to instantiate a CodeDOM code provider. You can use the static CreateProvider method on the CodeDomProvider class, as shown previously, as a kind of class factory to find a preconfigured provider by one of its synonyms. You can also instantiate a code provider directly if you have a reference to the assembly

**Configured code providers**

Just because a CodeDOM code provider is configured doesn't mean it's available. Some code providers, like Visual J#, are hardcoded to be configured during CodeDOM construction. But if you don't have the Visual J# redistributable package installed, locating that code provider at runtime will fail. Wrap calls to the `CreateProvider` factory in the `CodeDomProvider` class in a `try` block; be prepared to catch an exception if you attempt to instantiate a missing code provider.

and the desired `CodeDomProvider`-derived type. The following two lines of code, demonstrating those two approaches, are roughly equivalent:

```
var csProv1 = System.CodeDom.Compiler
  .CodeDomProvider.CreateProvider("c#");

var csProv2 = new Microsoft.CSharp
  .CSharpCodeProvider();
```

The key difference between these two methods is that the first one, which uses the `CreateProvider` factory, picks up all the provider settings that were configured during construction of the CodeDOM. Using the second method, instantiating the code provider directly, doesn't use any externally configured values.

Both methods for creating a CodeDOM code provider allow for various options to be specified. For example, the C# and Visual Basic providers support an optional parameter named `CompilerVersion`, which, as you may guess, you can use to select the version of the compiler to use. Internally, this works by searching for installed compilers on the local system. In the next listing, a small program is shown that will compile another program from source code in a string. The program selects the `"v4.0"` version of the compiler by passing a dictionary containing that option keyed as the `"CompilerVersion"` to the provider's constructor.

**Listing 4.2   InstantiatingCodeProviders.cs**

```
using Microsoft.CSharp;
using System.CodeDom.Compiler;
using System.Collections.Generic;

class IntantiatingCodeProviders
{
  static void Main()
  {
    var providerOptions = new Dictionary<string, string>();
    providerOptions.Add("CompilerVersion", "v4.0");
    var csProv = new CSharpCodeProvider(providerOptions);
    var compilerParameters =
      new CompilerParameters(new string[] { });

    CompilerResults results =
      csProv.CompileAssemblyFromSource(compilerParameters,
@"namespace V3Features
{
```

```
    class Program {
      static void Main() {
        var name = ""Kevin"";
        System.Console.WriteLine(name);
      }
    }
}");
    }
}
```

If you execute the program created from the InstantiatingCodeProviders.cs file on a system that has the C# 4.0 compiler installed, it will run to completion without errors, compiling the small program with the V3Features namespace passed as a string to the CompileAssemblyFromSource method. But if you change the CompilerVersion value in the providerOptions dictionary to "v2.0" instead, you may get an exception that reads like the one shown in the following listing.

**Listing 4.3    Possible exception output from InstantiatingCodeProviders.cs**

```
"Compiler executable file csc.exe cannot be found."

Stack Trace:
  at System.CodeDom.Compiler.RedistVersionInfo
    .GetCompilerPath(...)
  <... some stack frames omitted ...>
  at System.CodeDom.Compiler.CodeDomProvider
    .CompileAssemblyFromSource(...)
  at IntantiatingCodeProviders
    .Main() in C:\...\InstantiatingCodeProviders.cs:line 17
```

You'll get such an exception if the version of the C# compiler you requested isn't installed on the computer running the program. Notice, though, that you won't get this exception when you instantiate the provider. Instead, you'll see that the exception comes later when the CodeDOM needs the compiler to do some real work—for example, when you invoke a method like CompileAssemblyFromSource.

You can see in the exception message in listing 4.3 that the CodeDOM is searching for the compiler executable named csc.exe. That's the executable filename for the standalone C# compiler. The stack trace further shows that the CodeDOM is trying to get the path to a specific redistributable version of the compiler, in this case the "v2.0" version. Because all C# compilers have been named csc.exe since .NET 1.0, the folder containing the 2.0 version needs to be located.

If you have the 2.0 version of the C# compiler installed on your machine, and the CodeDOM can find it, you won't get a CodeDOM exception when you run the program. Instead, you'll get an exception from the C# 2.0 compiler itself. Can you guess what the error will be? (Hint: the program passed as a string to be compiled included a namespace called V3Features.)

**More on the CompilerVersion option**

Interestingly, the code provider for the version of Visual Basic that ships in the .NET Framework 4.0 isn't `"v10.0"` as you might expect given that the language product is at version 10 in that release. For now, the code provider version for both C# and VB matches the version of the Framework, so you'll have to specify `"v4.0"` instead. Better yet, if you want the latest version of either compiler, you can omit the `Compiler-Version` option altogether. The Visual J#, C++, and JScript code providers don't support the `CompilerVersion` option as of this writing.

### 4.2.2   *Code generator supportable options*

Each language generator can support a variety of features. Some languages support try/catch blocks, and some don't. As of this writing, the CodeDOM allows language generators to register 26 supportable features. Source code case sensitivity can also be registered, but in a different way, as you can see in the next listing. The example shown in this listing enumerates each of the installed CodeDOM code providers and records which language and generator features are supported.

**Listing 4.4   ShowCompilerFeatures.cs**

```csharp
using System;
using System.Text;
using System.CodeDom.Compiler;

class ShowCompilerFeatures
{
  static void Main()
  {
    foreach (CompilerInfo ci in
      CodeDomProvider.GetAllCompilerInfo())
    {
      StringBuilder output = new StringBuilder();
      string language = ci.GetLanguages()[0];
      output.AppendFormat("{0} features:\r\n", language);
      CodeDomProvider provider = CodeDomProvider
        .CreateProvider(language);
      output.AppendFormat("CaseInsensitive = {0}\r\n",
        provider.LanguageOptions.HasFlag(
          LanguageOptions.CaseInsensitive));
      foreach (GeneratorSupport supportableFeature
        in Enum.GetValues(typeof(GeneratorSupport)))
      {
        output.AppendFormat("{0} = {1}\r\n",
          supportableFeature,
          provider.Supports(supportableFeature));
      }
      Console.WriteLine(output.ToString());
    }
  }
}
```

Running the program in listing 4.4 shows that the C# and Visual Basic languages report `True` for all 26 supportable code generator features. We've achieved good language parity between C# and VB in recent years, so that makes sense. The provider's `LanguageOption` property for the enumerated type value `LanguageOption.Case-Insensitive` reports `False` for C# and `True` for Visual Basic. This report is correct because VB is case insensitive, and C# isn't.

Here are some of the more interesting findings about supported language features in the output from the program in listing 4.4:

- JScript doesn't support 17 of the language characteristics that C# and VB have, including generics, nested types, and various features concerning metadata.
- C++ reports that it doesn't support several features:
  - `ArraysOfArrays`
  - `ChainedConstructorArguments`
  - `Resources`
  - `PartialTypes`
  - `GenericTypeDeclarations`

When you're building a CodeDOM code graph to generate code, avoid adding objects to the code graph for language features that aren't supported in the target language. Using C# and Visual Basic for output is typically a good bet because they support all the language features.

The requirement to match structural abstractions about code to a provider that may or may not support them is one of the unfortunate realities that you must deal with when trying to develop a language-independent way of describing code as data. Using the CodeDOM approach, it can't be done cleanly in every case. Expression trees, which we look at in depth in chapter 6, don't suffer from this problem as much because they were developed from the more pure abstraction of lambda expressions, which were developed in the realm of mathematics, not computer science.

### The history of lambda expressions

As a software developer, you might be forgiven for thinking that lambda expressions were conceived as a computer science construct. But they come from mathematics and predate modern computer science by a couple of decades. Although *lambdas* (for short) have more mathematical origins, computers as we know them wouldn't have come into existence without certain portions of what's known as the *lambda calculus*. Lambdas were initially created as a notation for proving certain parts of the lambda calculus and eventually made their way into functional programming languages like Scheme, Haskell, and F# for creating functions. Nowadays, we can enjoy the expressiveness that lambdas provide for writing LINQ queries in object-oriented languages like C# and Visual Basic. The .NET implementation of expression trees was also heavily influenced by lambdas, making rich interlanguage support through the Dynamic Language Runtime (DLR) possible, too.

### 4.2.3   *Code provider services*

Each CodeDOM code provider is derived from a base class called `CodeDomProvider`. You've seen static invocations on that class to get configured provider information or to instantiate providers for specific languages. But you haven't seen the other interesting services available. Some of the other useful static methods in the `CodeDomProvider` class are:

- `GetCompilerInfo`
- `GetLanguageFromExtension`
- `IsDefinedExtension`
- `IsDefinedLanguage`

These are all helper methods for searching in the dictionary of configured code providers and finding information about them.

Here are some of the more interesting instance methods you can call once you have a `CodeDomProvider`-derived class in hand:

- `CompileAssemblyFromDom`
- `CompileAssemblyFromFile`
- `CompileAssemblyFromSource`
- `CreateCompiler`
- `GenerateCodeFromCompileUnit`
- `GenerateCodeFromNamespace`
- `GenerateCodeFromType`
- `Parse`

As you can see, these methods all involve compilation, code generation, or parsing. Each could be collected into one of three groups that represent the three forms that your application code can be in. In the first form, source code exists, written in popular programming languages like C# or C++. That source code could be compiled into the second form, known as a .NET assembly. It could also be parsed into the third form, called a code graph. You may also build code graphs by hand using statement and expression objects. Forms two and three can be generated back into form one anytime you want.

> **CodeDomProvider implementations**
>
> Not all code providers implement all the compilation, generation, and parsing methods shown previously. Some code providers will implement code generation from one source but not from another. As of this writing, none of Microsoft's code providers implements the `Parse` method, which is intended to convert source code directly into a code graph. Future versions of Microsoft languages and tools may support something even better than parsing code into a CodeDOM code graph. Turn to chapter 10 to find out more.

As you can see, the CodeDOM provides a versatile framework, not merely for source code generation, but for the manipulation of programs into and out of all of the forms they might take during their lifetimes. We'll look at parsing into code graphs and generating assemblies from them later. For now, let's examine how to build up a code graph programmatically. Constructing a program by hand will help you understand how the CodeDOM and the various code providers work internally.

## 4.3 Adding objects to a code graph

Once you've instantiated a CodeDOM code provider, you can begin to build so-called code graphs. In CodeDOM-speak, a *code graph* is a hierarchical data structure that can describe a program. This concept of code-as-data is common in metaprogramming. You'll see it over and over again throughout this book, because when code can be articulated in terms of data, it can reduce the mismatch between human expression and machine interpretation.

Source code in a high-level language like C# is pretty far removed from the machine. That kind of abstraction is good for most kinds of application development. But when you're metaprogramming, having abstractions that represent the logic of an application in a way that's purer, unencumbered by language ceremony and syntax, is much more useful.

Let's begin our voyage into CodeDOM code graphs by exploring some of the key data types that are used for describing code as data.

### What's a Jubjub?

Throughout this section, we'll be examining various CodeDOM features by building a class called Jubjub. Author Kevin Hazzard chose this name and some of the others in the examples from the 19th century poems "Jabberwocky" and "The Hunting of the Snark" by Lewis Carroll. Teaching instruments named Jubjub, Mimsy, Vorpal, and Wabe are guaranteed not to conflict with other concepts that we're trying to convey as we move along. Their oddness also makes them striking and memorable. When you're learning to metaprogram, the names and classifications for things can start to stumble all over each other in your mind. This is the essence of metaprogramming and one of the things that makes it challenging. Writing code that creates code is a recursive experience, somewhat like standing between two mirrors. Choosing odd names for your subjects can help you sort out what's real and what's merely a reflection. Through the looking glass we go, one Jubjub at a time.

### 4.3.1 Creating a namespace with imports

Namespaces in .NET are a somewhat artificial construct. They're useful for dealing with potential clashes between types by giving you a way to add uniqueness to names. They're also useful for organizing large collections of types into smaller groups with meaningful, often hierarchical names. Namespaces are convenient but not strictly necessary. Most C# code you see nowadays starts with a set of using declarations to import namespaces for the entire file, followed by a namespace declaration that contains one or more type definitions. Maybe you've seen code that's organized this way instead:

```
namespace Whatever {
  using System;

  class Program {
    static void Main() {
      Console.WriteLine("Hi!");
    }
  }
}
```

Notice how the using declaration is inside the namespace declaration? This kind of import style was seen more commonly when .NET was new and produces some subtle differences in the compilation process. Over time and for whatever reasons, many developers have chosen to place their import declarations outside of their namespace declarations. Using the CodeDOM, when you build a code graph, you'll often create a CodeNamespace first and then insert some CodeNamespaceImport objects into it, reflecting the kind of code organization shown previously:

```
CodeNamespace mimsyNamespace = new CodeNamespace("Mimsy");
mimsyNamespace.Imports.AddRange(new[]
{
  new CodeNamespaceImport("System"),
  new CodeNamespaceImport("System.Text"),
  new CodeNamespaceImport("System.Collections")
});
```

The preceding code creates a namespace in the resulting code called Mimsy, with three imports for the System, System.Text, and System.Collections namespaces declared inside it. Notice that the Imports property on the namespace, which is of the type CodeNamespaceImportCollection, supports an AddRange function for adding an array of imports to a namespace all at once. There's also an Add function on the collection that allows imports to be added one at a time.

If you were to generate C# code for the namespace named mimsyNamspace, it would appear as follows:

```
namespace Mimsy
{
  using System;
  using System.Text;
  using System.Collections;
}
```

As you can see, the using declarations have been emitted inside the namespace declaration, mirroring the way that the Imports collection is defined as a property within the CodeDOM's CodeNamespace type. Now that you can create a basic container for your dynamically generated program structure, let's add a type declaration.

### 4.3.2  Adding a class to a namespace

At this point, you want to be able to generate some C# code so you can visualize your code graphs at each step. The function `GenerateCSharpCodeFromNamespace`, shown in the following listing, will be referenced from time to time in the remainder of this section to do that.

**Listing 4.5  The `GenerateCSharpCodeFromNamespace` helper function**

```
static string GenerateCSharpCodeFromNamespace(CodeNamespace ns)
{
  CodeGeneratorOptions genOpts = new CodeGeneratorOptions
  {
    BracingStyle = "C",
    IndentString = "  ",
    BlankLinesBetweenMembers = false
  };
  StringBuilder gennedCode = new StringBuilder();
  using (StringWriter sw = new StringWriter(gennedCode))
  {
    CodeDomProvider.CreateProvider("c#")
      .GenerateCodeFromNamespace(ns, sw, genOpts);
  }
  return gennedCode.ToString();
}
```

This helper function calls `GenerateCodeFromNamespace` on the C# code provider with some popular options. The source code that's generated is streamed into a `String-Builder` using a `StringWriter` and returned to the caller as a `String`.

You can add a type to a code graph with `CodeTypeDeclaration`. The following lines of code add a class to the code graph named `Jubjub`:

```
CodeTypeDeclaration jubjubClass =
  new CodeTypeDeclaration("Jubjub")
{
  TypeAttributes = TypeAttributes.NotPublic
};
```

Setting the `TypeAttribute` to `NotPublic` will cause the `Jubjub` type to be marked as an `internal` class in C#. If you wanted to expose the class as `public`, you could use `Public TypeAttribute` instead. It's important to note that unlike many of the other types highlighted in this chapter, the `TypeAttribute` enumerated type isn't in one of the CodeDOM namespaces. It's defined in the `System.Reflection` namespace. As you dig deeper into the CodeDOM, more references to the Reflection API will surface.

Now you're ready to add a member field to the `Jubjub` class. You do that by creating a `CodeMemberField` object, setting its name and type, then adding it to the `Jubjub` class `Members` collection:

```
CodeMemberField wabeCountFld =
  new CodeMemberField(typeof(int), "_wabeCount")
{
```

```
        Attributes = MemberAttributes.Private
};
```

```
jubjubClass.Members.Add(wabeCountFld);
mimsyNamespace.Types.Add(jubjubClass);
```

Note that after creating the member field object and adding it to the `Members` of the class, the `Jubjub` class was also added to the namespace's `Types` collection. The `JubJub` class was constructed independently of the namespace and then inserted into it. Some other DOMs you may have used operate differently by providing factory functions within each container, which create and then attach child objects in the hierarchy. The CodeDOM however, uses a more free form, disconnected create-then-attach model.

Let's look at the code that would be generated from what's been constructed so far. Calling the `GenerateCSharpCodeFromNamespace` function shown earlier and passing a reference to the `mimsyNamespace` yields the following output:

```
namespace Mimsy
{
  using System;
  using System.Text;
  using System.Collections;

  internal class Jubjub
  {
    private int _wabeCount;
  }
}
```

### 4.3.3 *Adding a constructor to a class*

Our code graph now has a namespace with imports and an internal class named `Jubjub` containing a private field. But to do some work, you need to add other members like methods and properties. Before you add those, however, let's add a constructor to the `Jubjub` class with the `CodeConstructor` type:

```
CodeConstructor jubjubCtor = new CodeConstructor()
{
  Attributes = MemberAttributes.Public
};
```

By using a `MemberAttribute` of `Public`, this constructor object will be marked as `Public` in the code graph. The code provider will use that metadata to generate the constructor as `public` in the source code that's emitted. Another similar-looking type in the CodeDOM called `CodeTypeConstructor` may also be used to add constructors to classes. But that kind of constructor will be marked as `static` in C# (or `Shared` in Visual Basic). The nomenclature here is significant. The word `Type` appearing in the class name between `Code` and `Constructor` means that it creates a constructor for the type (the class) that's emitted, not for instances of a class. Not all .NET languages support static constructors, though, so be aware of your target language before attempting to generate them into a specific language.

Before attaching the constructor to the `Jubjub` class, you need to add a parameter to it using `CodeParameterDeclarationExpression`. As we showed earlier when adding a member field to the class, parameters also need to declare a type and a name. For the on-going example, the code that adds an integer parameter called `wabeCount` to the `Jubjub` constructor looks like this:

```
var jubjubCtorParam =
  new CodeParameterDeclarationExpression(
    typeof(int), "wabeCount");
```

Note that when CodeDOM type names get long, we sometimes use the `var` keyword to make the code more readable. We're not doing that to be lazy, and we only do it when it increases comprehension. You need to add the parameter expression to the constructor next. To do that, add the expression to the `Parameters` collection on the constructor object:

```
jubjubCtor.Parameters.Add(jubjubCtorParam);
```

### 4.3.4   *Adding statements to a member*

To make the newly added constructor do something, you need to add statements to its `Statements` collection. All the statement types in the CodeDOM derive from a base class named `CodeStatement`. Some of the more common statement types are shown in figure 4.3. Statements use expressions to refer to objects and to provide other basic building blocks for a program. CodeDOM expressions share a base class called `Code-Expression`. Some of the more common expression types are shown in figure 4.2. You can recognize statement and expression classes quickly in the CodeDOM because their type names conveniently end in `Statement` and `Expression`, respectively.

To do the work of assigning the `wabeCount` constructor parameter to the `_wabeCount` member field, use the following `CodeStatement` and `CodeExpression` derivatives:

- `CodeFieldReferenceExpression`—To refer to the `_wabeCount` field
- `CodeThisReferenceExpression`—To include a `this` reference
- `CodeArgumentReferenceExpression`—To refer to the `wabeCount` parameter
- `CodeAssignStatement`—To perform the assignment

Let's begin by creating reference expressions for the `_wabeCount` member field and the `wabeCount` constructor argument. Using one type to create objects and another type to reference them is a common pattern in the CodeDOM. For example, the `_wabeCount` integer was defined as a member of the `Jubjub` class using the `Code-MemberField` type, which is a subclass of the `CodeTypeMember` class (shown in figure 4.1). But to refer to that member in a statement, we use a `CodeFieldReferenceExpression`, which is, as its name implies, derived from `CodeExpression`.

The following code snippet builds an assignment expression using the argument and member references to assign the value of the constructor argument to the member field.

**Generating explicit this references**

When people write code by hand, including unnecessary references to the `this` parameter (or the `Me` parameter in VB) is sometimes considered bad form because it clutters up the code. But when you automate the generation of source code, you may want to be more explicit and include `this` references for safety. Who knows when a local variable or parameter will get introduced in the future that inadvertently obscures a class member by name? But if your machine-generated code uses sufficiently unique names or is intended to be edited by developers, you might want to omit the `this` references, because doing so can increase comprehension. You can do that by passing null whenever you might have included a `CodeThisReference-Expression` in the construction of an expression.

The assignment statement will then be added to the `Statements` collection of the constructor. The code to perform all of these steps looks like this:

```
var refWabeCountFld =
  new CodeFieldReferenceExpression(
    new CodeThisReferenceExpression(), "_wabeCount");

var refWabeCountArg =
  new CodeArgumentReferenceExpression("wabeCount");

var assignWabeCount =
  new CodeAssignStatement(refWabeCountFld, refWabeCountArg);

jubjubCtor.Statements.Add(assignWabeCount);
```

After you've been writing code graphs for a while, your brain will be able to see this sequence of steps more functionally as:

```
jubjubCtor.Statements.Add(
  new CodeAssignStatement(
    new CodeFieldReferenceExpression(
      new CodeThisReferenceExpression (),
      "_wabeCount"),
    new CodeArgumentReferenceExpression(
      "wabeCount")));
```

When you see code written by CodeDOM experts, it will often have this more compact, fluent look to it. For now, let's stick to the step-by-step model until you get the hang of it. If you generated the C# code for what we've shown so far, you might be surprised. The `Jubjub` class would still be devoid of statements. What did you miss? Let's take inventory for your actions so far. You:

- Created a namespace
- Added two imports to the namespace
- Created a class
- Added a member field to the class
- Attached the class to the namespace
- Created a constructor

- Created an assignment expression
- Added the assignment expression to the constructor

Aha! We forgot to have you add the constructor to the Members collection on the Jubjub class! Our omission was deliberate, because we wanted to demonstrate that you don't have to attach complete objects to a CodeDOM code graph. You could, for example, attach a container object like a CodeTypeDeclaration to a namespace before you add members to it. It's perfectly acceptable to do that, even when the order of attachment would cause the graph to produce an invalid object.

The CodeDOM doesn't perform any kind of verification on the graph until you attempt to generate something from it using one of the code providers. The Code-DOM's style of creating objects and then attaching them promotes reusability, as you'll see, but it can lead to errors of omission as you try to keep track of what you're doing in a complex code graph.

### New respect for your tools

Building expressions by hand forces you to think like a programming language and a compiler all at once. Many developers have never tried to understand how their tools work, so the transition into that kind of metaprogramming mindset can be challenging. As you gain respect for what your software tools have been doing for you behind the scenes, you'll also become a better software craftsperson. By understanding how computations are expressed inside the machine, useful patterns will begin to emerge in everyday code that you couldn't perceive before.

The other reason for failing to attach the constructor in the preceding sequence of steps is to give you some encouragement about the mistakes you'll invariably make when you begin constructing your own code graphs. Building code by hand is confusing at times. Don't worry about slipping up. Those kinds of mistakes can be great learning experiences. Correcting the problem is simple enough. You can attach the constructor to the class like this:

```
jubjubClass.Members.Add(jubjubCtor);
```

If you generate the code for this example now, you'll see the C# code shown in the following listing on the console.

### Listing 4.6 Code-graph-generated class with a field and a constructor

```
namespace Mimsy
{
    using System;
    using System.Text;
    using System.Collections;

    internal class Jubjub
    {
        private int _wabeCount;
```

```
    public Jubjub(int wabeCount)
    {
      this._wabeCount = wabeCount;
    }
  }
}
```

### 4.3.5   *Adding a property to a class*

Our little `Jubjub` class is shaping up nicely, but it doesn't do much yet. Let's add a property to get access to the private member field from outside the class. The following listing shows how you can add a simple integer type property named `WabeCount` to the class.

**Listing 4.7   Adding a property to the code graph**

```
CodeMemberProperty wabeCountProp =
  new CodeMemberProperty() {
  Attributes = MemberAttributes.Public
    | MemberAttributes.Final,
  Type = new CodeTypeReference(typeof(int)),
  Name = "WabeCount"
};

wabeCountProp.GetStatements.Add(
  new CodeMethodReturnStatement(refWabeCountFld));

jubjubClass.Members.Add(wabeCountProp);
```

Generating the code from the graph now produces a property that looks like this in C#:

```
public int WabeCount
{
  get
  {
    return this._wabeCount;
  }
}
```

In listing 4.7, a `CodeMemberProperty` was created, marked with the `Public` and `Final` attributes, given the integer type, and named `WabeCount`. Marking a type as `Public` is familiar enough, but what does marking it as `Final` mean? In the CLR, marking a class as *final* makes it nonvirtual. You saw references to this metadata marker in IL code in chapter 2. If you removed the `Final` attribute from the code in listing 4.7 and ran it again, the property would be generated like this instead:

```
public virtual int WabeCount
{
  get
  {
    return this._wabeCount;
  }
}
```

Method and property members of a CodeDOM-generated type are marked as virtual (or not Final) by default. You want the WabeCount property to be nonvirtual, so you've explicitly marked it as Final.

A CodeDOM class called CodeTypeReference is used to mark the type of the property as an integer. So far you've only needed references to .NET's built-in types for things like this, but what if you needed to reference a type in a private assembly instead? You could load the type into the generator program and use the built-in typeof function as you did for integers. But the CodeTypeReference class has an overloaded constructor that lets you pass a string instead. This is handy when you don't want to load the dependencies that the generated code will need later during code generation. For example, if you had a type called Vorpal that you wanted to designate to the generated property, you could set its Type property in the code graph by using a literal string containing the type name:

```
Type = new CodeTypeReference("Vorpal"),
```

By doing so, the compiled assembly containing the Vorpal type wouldn't need to be loaded during code generation to obtain a reference to it. Using *magic strings* like this can lead to errors, so be aware that the chances for making mistakes will go up if you decide not to load and reference the assemblies during code generation upon which the generated code will depend later on.

Unlike method and constructor member types in the CodeDOM, the CodeMember-Property used in listing 4.7 has no Statements property at all. Instead, it has two properties named GetStatements and SetStatements that are used to define the bodies of the generated property's get (accessor) and set (mutator), respectively. Notice that we've added a flow control statement of type CodeMethodReturnStatement to the GetStatements property that uses the same reference to the _wabeCount member field that we used earlier in the constructor statements. In general, once you've created a reference object in the CodeDOM, using it over and over again wherever you need that referenced object in the code graph is appropriate.

## 4.4    Metaprogramming with the CodeDOM

Beyond simple classes with fields and properties, almost any kind of CLR type programming construct can be generated into a CodeDOM code graph. This section examines how to add branching logic, reference class members, invoke methods, and more.

### 4.4.1   Using branching logic

To demonstrate the addition of branching logic to a code graph, let's modify the WabeCount property by adding a mutator (setter). Adding a simple assignment from the property's value to the member field would be straightforward with code like this:

```
wabeCountProp.SetStatements.Add(
  new CodeAssignStatement(
    refWabeCountFld,
    new CodePropertySetValueReferenceExpression()));
```

After adding this assignment statement to the property's mutator, the generated code for the entire property would look like this:

```
public int WabeCount
{
  get
  {
    return this._wabeCount;
  }
  set
  {
    this._wabeCount = value;
  }
}
```

That's nice, but what if you wanted to add business logic to the class so that the _wabeCount member field can never have a negative value set into it? The easiest way to do that is to test the value assigned to the property's mutator, assigning a zero value when the supplied value is out of the valid range. Later in this chapter we show you how to do something even more useful when exceptional conditions occur.

Adding flow control statements to a code graph can be tricky, so let's do this in a few steps. First, you need a comparison operation that produces a Boolean result, which tells you if the value supplied to the mutator is less than the boundary value you want to test for. The two parts you want to compare can be coded as CodeDOM objects like this:

```
var suppliedPropertyValue =
  new CodePropertySetValueReferenceExpression();
var zero = new CodePrimitiveExpression(0);
```

The names suppliedPropertyValue and zero refer to the value keyword in the mutator and the literal integer value 0, respectively. These names will make the code that follows easier to read and understand.

It's interesting to note that there's a specific CodeDOM expression type for referring to the value in a property setter, sometimes called a mutator. For the zero value you need to compare to, the CodePrimitiveExpression type is used. The CodeDOM doesn't have specific classes to represent the .NET Common Type System (CTS) types (as some other expression-oriented metaprogramming interfaces do). Whenever you need to express literal values in the CodeDOM, a CodePrimitiveExpression will typically work fine.

Now that you have a way to refer to the two values to compare, you need to perform a less-than comparison operation on them. Standard operators that take two parameters are described in the CodeBinaryOperatorType enumerated type in the CodeDOM. These operators fall into several logical groups.

- *Math*—Add, subtract, multiply, divide, and modulus
- *Identity*—IdentityInequality and IndentityEquality
- *Bitwise*—BitwiseOr and BitwiseAnd

- *Boolean*—BooleanOr and BooleanAnd
- *Rank*—ValueEquality, LessThan, LessThanOrEqual, GreaterThan, and Greater-ThanOrEqual

We're interested in using the CodeBinaryOperatorType.LessThan to compare the supplied property value to zero, so create a CodeBinaryOperatorExpression that does that. Read it from top to bottom to get a feel for the expression's meaning:

```
var suppliedPropValIsLessThanZero =
  new CodeBinaryOperatorExpression(
    suppliedPropertyValue,
    CodeBinaryOperatorType.LessThan,
    zero);
```

Do you agree that the descriptive variable names for the value keyword object and the literal value 0 make the preceding code more readable? You're ultimately seeking to create a statement for the property's SetStatements that looks like this when emitted as C#:

```
if (value < 0)
{
  this._wabeCount = 0;
}
else
{
  this._wabeCount = value;
}
```

It's important to understand that the suppliedPropValueIsLessThanZero expression represents only the Boolean test of the whole expression—the part that reads (value < 0). To create the if and else parts of the statement, you need to use that test in a CodeConditionStatement, as shown in the following listing.

**Listing 4.8  Creating an if/else construct with a CodeConditionStatement**

```
var testSuppliedPropValAndAssign =
  new CodeConditionStatement(
    suppliedPropValIsLessThanZero,
    new CodeStatement[]
    {
      new CodeAssignStatement(
      refWabeCountFld,
      zero)
    },
    new CodeStatement[]
    {
      new CodeAssignStatement(
        refWabeCountFld,
        suppliedPropertyValue)
    });

wabeCountProp.SetStatements.Add(
  testSuppliedPropValAndAssign);
```

The binary operator expression `suppliedPropValueIsLessThanZero` shown earlier is used as the first parameter when building the condition. The `(value < 0)` test will follow the `if` in the code that gets generated. The other two parameters are the groups of statements that will become the blocks following the `if` part and the `else` part in the resulting code. An overload for the `CodeConditionStatement` constructor exists that takes one less parameter. As you might have guessed, you can use that constructor whenever you need to generate an `if` code condition statement for which you want no associated `else` branch to be defined in the code graph.

After adding the condition expression as the `SetStatements` on the `WabeCount` property, the generated code for the property's mutator now becomes the following:

```
set
{
    if ((value < 0))
    {
        this._wabeCount = 0;
    }
    else
    {
        this._wabeCount = value;
    }
}
```

This looks correct. The only potential annoyance is the extraneous pair of parentheses following the `if` keyword. This is unavoidable using the CodeDOM for a good reason. If you were chaining together multiple expressions using arithmetic or Boolean logic, and the C# code provider didn't emit parentheses around each binary expression individually, elusive operator precedence bugs could be introduced into the generated code. The C# code provider could perform look-behind and look-ahead parsing logic in the code graph to optimize the parentheses away, but that would add another kind of complexity you don't want. Besides, the extra parentheses are benign and in some cases can add real clarity to the code that's emitted.

### Beware the CodeSnippetExpression

Although the `CodeSnippetExpression` type comes in handy from time to time, you should avoid it for the most part. It works by inserting a literal code fragment into the generated code. But if a code fragment inserted this way uses a C++ specific feature, for example, you'll never be able to generate C# or VB code from code graphs that include it. On the other hand, if you want to use a particular language feature for which the CodeDOM has no support, and you know that the target language will never change, code snippet types provide useful flexibility.

### 4.4.2   *Referencing a member*

To enforce the new business logic used in the `WabeCount` property mutator completely, you need to revisit the `Jubjub` constructor you created at the beginning of this example and fix it. Remember that the constructor assigned its argument value to the private `_wabeCount` member field directly. What if the valued supplied during construction is less than zero? That assignment should be done through the `WabeCount` property so that disallowed values can be dealt with, keeping all your precious `Jubjub` objects in pristine condition. To do this, define a `CodePropertyReferenceExpression` and use it instead of the member field reference that was used to initially build the `CodeAssignStatement` that will serve as the constructor's body. The property reference and the modified assignment statement follow:

```
var refWabeCountProp =
  new CodePropertyReferenceExpression(
    new CodeThisReferenceExpression(),
    "WabeCount");

var assignWabeCount =
  new CodeAssignStatement(
    refWabeCountProp, refWabeCountArg);
```

Generating the code for the example at this point yields the beautifully formatted and highly functional `Jubjub` class containing a private, instance integer member field, a property for accessing the field that enforces a simple bit of range-checking logic, and a constructor that allows the type to be instantiated safely by invoking the property's setter. This class is shown in listing 4.9.

Listing 4.9 A more complete CodeDOM-generated `Jubjub` class

```
namespace Mimsy
{
  using System;
  using System.Text;
  using System.Collections;

  internal class Jubjub
  {
    private int _wabeCount;
    public Jubjub(int wabeCount)
    {
      this.WabeCount = wabeCount;
    }
    public int WabeCount
    {
      get
      {
        return this._wabeCount;
      }
      set
      {
        if ((value < 0))
        {
          this._wabeCount = 0;
        }
        else
        {
```

```
        this._wabeCount = value;
      }
    }
  }
}
```

You can find the source code for the `Jubjub` code generator to this point in the sample code for the book as the TypeDeclarations project.

C++ and C# developers reading this may be wondering why you didn't attempt to emit the body of the `WabeCount` property setter using the ternary operator. After all, the following single line of code is much more succinct:

```
this._wabeCount = (value < 0) ? 0 : value;
```

Indeed, many C++ and C# developers prefer this syntax for simple option-based testing over `if/else` and `switch/case` language constructs, which are a bit bulkier and potentially reduce the reader's comprehension. Unfortunately, the CodeDOM has no expression type that supports simple test-and-branch-to-value logic like this. Interestingly, though, expression trees, examined in detail in chapter 6, support ternary operations very well.

### 4.4.3 *Invoking methods*

Suppose you'd like the `Jubjub` class developed so far to be able to track all the values set by calling the `WabeCount` property mutator. To do that, you need some sort of array to track the changed values. First, you'll create a `CodeTypeReference` to an `ArrayList` from the `System.Collections` namespace. Then you'll create another `CodeMember-Field` and add it to the `Members` collection of the `Jubjub` class:

```
var typrefArrayList =
  new CodeTypeReference("ArrayList");
CodeMemberField updatesFld =
  new CodeMemberField(typrefArrayList, "_updates");
jubjubClass.Members.Add(updatesFld);
```

If you generated the code for the `mimsyNamespace` now, a new line would appear inside the `Jubjub` class definition:

```
private ArrayList _updates;
```

Had you built the `CodeTypeReference` using `typeof(ArrayList)` instead of a string, that new line would have appeared differently as:

```
private System.Collections.ArrayList _updates;
```

Using the `typeof` function is definitely the preferred method. But even though you can insert import statements into a CodeDOM namespace, the CodeDOM itself has no concept of imports. It's a machine, so it doesn't need such pleasantries.

When you use a type like `typeof(ArrayList)`, the CodeDOM will always emit it as a fully qualified type name into the generated source code. When you expect humans to read the code that's produced, those long names can detract from the readability. We used a string to make it friendlier to the eyes. Besides, you already inserted an import into the code graph namespace for the System.Collections namespace. Any generated code that refers to classes defined in that namespace (such as the Array-List) in a non-fully qualified way will resolve correctly.

Next, you need to update the constructor to instantiate an ArrayList. For this, use a CodeObjectCreateExpression, which you can use whenever you need to instantiate a class. Think of it as the new operator for the CodeDOM:

```
var refUpdatesFld =
  new CodeFieldReferenceExpression(
    new CodeThisReferenceExpression(), "_updates");
var newArrayList =
  new CodeObjectCreateExpression(typrefArrayList);
var assignUpdates =
  new CodeAssignStatement(
    refUpdatesFld, newArrayList);
jubjubCtor.Statements.Add(assignUpdates);
```

Before instantiating the ArrayList, a CodeFieldReferenceExpression that refers to the new _updates field is created. It's used here and again throughout the remaining example code shown in this section. A CodeAssignStatement is built to do the assignment and then added to the Jubjub class constructor's Statements. The constructor now emits as

```
public Jubjub(int wabeCount)
{
  this._updates = new ArrayList();
  this.WabeCount = wabeCount;
}
```

Notice that we deliberately inserted the construction of the ArrayList before the use of the WabeCount property mutator. This was intentional because that property mutator will be updated in a moment to add an item to the ArrayList whenever the value is changed. If the ArrayList hadn't been allocated when you tried to add an item to it, a NullReferenceException would be thrown. The order of statements in the constructor is important. To modify the WabeCount property to perform the update, you need to add a CodeMethodInvokeExpression to its SetStatements property, like this:

```
wabeCountProp.SetStatements.Add(
  new CodeMethodInvokeExpression(
    new CodeMethodReferenceExpression(
      refUpdatesFld,
      "Add"),
    refWabeCountFld));
```

Now the mutator for the WabeCount property in the Jubjub class will be generated like this:

```
set
{
```

```
  if ((value < 0))
    this._wabeCount = 0;
  else
    this._wabeCount = value;
  this._updates.Add(this._wabeCount);
}
```

Every time the property mutator is invoked, it will store the new value in the Array-
List. Now all you need is some sort of history function that can report out all the pre-
viously set values for the property. Before diving into the code graph construction of
that function, however, let's look at how the function should look when you're done.
The following listing shows the source code you'd like to generate for a method in the
Jubjub class named GetWabeCountHistory.

**Listing 4.10   A function you'd like to generate into the Jubjub class**

```
public string GetWabeCountHistory()
{
  StringBuilder result = new StringBuilder();
  for (int ndx = 0; ndx < this._updates.Count; ndx++)
  {
    if ((ndx == 0))
      result.AppendFormat("{0}", this._updates[ndx]);
    else
      result.AppendFormat(", {0}", this._updates[ndx]);
  }
  return result.ToString();
}
```

This is a fairly simple function expressed in C#, but to code this into a CodeDOM code
graph will take a bit of mental tenacity on your part. We'll go step by step to help you
think through this. To begin, you need to create a CodeDOM object for the method
and add it to the Jubjub class. Remember how you used a CodeMemberProperty earlier in this chapter to create the WabeCount property? Creating a method with the
CodeMemberMethod type is done similarly:

```
CodeMemberMethod methGetWabeCountHistory =
  new CodeMemberMethod
  {
    Attributes = MemberAttributes.Public
      | MemberAttributes.Final,
    Name = "GetWabeCountHistory",
    ReturnType = new CodeTypeReference(typeof(String))
  };
jubjubClass.Members.Add(methGetWabeCountHistory);
```

The new method, called GetWabeHistory, will be public and non-virtual and return
a String. We've also added it to the Jubjub class to make sure you don't forget to do it
later. Remember: it's okay to add the method to the code graph even though you
haven't added any statements to it yet. Looking back at listing 4.10, the next steps are
instantiating a StringBuilder object and assigning its reference to a local variable
named result. Here's how it's done:

```
methGetWabeCountHistory.Statements.Add(
  new CodeVariableDeclarationStatement(
    "StringBuilder", "result"));
var refResultVar =
  new CodeVariableReferenceExpression("result");
methGetWabeCountHistory.Statements.Add(
  new CodeAssignStatement(
    refResultVar,
    new CodeObjectCreateExpression(
      "StringBuilder")));
```

This code block begins by using a CodeVariableDeclarationStatement to create a StringBuilder local variable called result. Then a reference to the result variable is created for use here and later on when you need to invoke methods on it. Lastly, an assignment statement is added to the new method's Statements property to invoke the new operator on a StringBuilder and assign the reference to the result variable.

Referring to listing 4.10 again, the next thing you need to do is build a for loop to iterate over each of the items in the _updates ArrayList and add formatted strings to the StringBuilder you created. But the C# syntax shown in listing 4.10 can't be created exactly that way in a CodeDOM code graph. The C# compiler exposes certain bits of syntactical sugar that make code more readable. One of those sugary treats is the ability to instantiate a local variable like the ndx variable inside the for expression, like this:

```
for (int ndx = 0; ndx < this._updates.Count; ndx++)
```

In the CodeDOM however, you must construct it this way:

```
int ndx;
for (ndx = 0; ndx < this._updates.Count; ndx++)
```

Before you create the for loop, let's create that local integer variable called ndx and a reference to it. The ndx variable is used several times within the loop shown in listing 4.10. Having the reference handy will make the coding work inside the loop a lot less wordy:

```
methGetWabeCountHistory.Statements.Add(
  new CodeVariableDeclarationStatement(
    typeof(int), "ndx"));
var refNdxVar =
  new CodeVariableReferenceExpression("ndx");
```

Now you're ready to create the for loop. This one's a doozy, as the saying goes. Before you look at the code that will create and insert this construct that looks so simple in C#, you need to think about how a for loop is constructed. It has an initialization part, a test part, an increment part, and a block of statements. The CodeIterationStatement type in the CodeDOM takes four parameters to its constructor. They map to the for loop parts perfectly. You'll perform a simple CodeAssignStatement for the initialization part of the constructor to assign zero to the local variable ndx:

```
new CodeAssignStatement(
  refNdxVar,
  new CodePrimitiveExpression(0))
```

The next part is the test to see if the loop block should execute or not. You can do this with a CodeBinaryOperatorExpression of type LessThan comparing the reference to the ndx local variable to the value of the Count property for the _updates ArrayList. You'll also use the reference to the _updates field you built earlier to make the code a bit easier to read:

```
new CodeBinaryOperatorExpression(
  refNdxVar,
  CodeBinaryOperatorType.LessThan,
  new CodePropertyReferenceExpression(
    refUpdatesFld,
    "Count"))
```

Now you're ready to tackle the increment expression. The CodeDOM doesn't have a way to express the ndx++ statement as it's shown in listing 4.10, but you could write it as ndx = ndx + 1. That's how you'll build it into the code graph. You'll need another CodeBinaryOperatorExpression for that. This one will be of type Add. You'll also need another CodeAssignStatement to assign the result of the addition operator back to the local ndx variable:

```
new CodeAssignStatement(
  refNdxVar,
  new CodeBinaryOperatorExpression(
    refNdxVar,
    CodeBinaryOperatorType.Add,
    new CodePrimitiveExpression(1)))
```

The body of the for iterator comes next, and at the top of the graph is an if/else statement, which you learned about when building the setter on the WabeCount property. As you did back then, use a CodeConditionStatement to express the logic shown in listing 4.10. As you recall, the first part of a CodeConditionStatement is a test. Your test in this case is (ndx == 0), which looks like another CodeBinaryOperatorExpression. This one will be of type ValueEquality, comparing the reference to the ndx local variable to zero:

```
  new CodeBinaryOperatorExpression(
    refNdxVar,
    CodeBinaryOperatorType.ValueEquality,
    new CodePrimitiveExpression(0))
```

The block following the if in listing 4.10 is a method invocation, so code that into the graph as a CodeMethodInvokeExpression. To insert that into a CodeStatement array as the CodeConditionStatement requires, you must wrap it in a CodeExpression-Statement. This is a condition of the CodeDOM that must be met when CodeStatement derivatives are required:

```
new CodeExpressionStatement(
  new CodeMethodInvokeExpression(
    new CodeMethodReferenceExpression(
      refResultVar,
      "AppendFormat"),
```

```
new CodePrimitiveExpression("{0}"),
new CodeArrayIndexerExpression(
  refUpdatesFld,
  refNdxVar)))
```

Note how you're invoking the `AppendFormat` method using the reference to the
results variable that you saved earlier, passing the `"{0}"` format string argument and
an indexed value from the `_updates` `ArrayList` at the index specified by the reference to the local `ndx` variable.

The `else` block looks similar, so we won't show the CodeDOM code for it here. The
only difference is that the format string passed to the `AppendFormat` method on the
`StringBuilder` is slightly different. It prefixes commas to the output for the second and
subsequent items during the iteration to make the output a well-formatted comma-
separated list. Stringing together all of the blocks concerning the `CodeIteration-`
`Statement` so far creates the one large fluent expression shown in the following listing.

**Listing 4.11  Creating an iterator using the CodeDOM**

```
methGetWabeCountHistory.Statements.Add(
  new CodeIterationStatement(
    new CodeAssignStatement(
      refNdxVar,
      new CodePrimitiveExpression(0)),
    new CodeBinaryOperatorExpression(
      refNdxVar,
      CodeBinaryOperatorType.LessThan,
      new CodePropertyReferenceExpression(
        refUpdatesFld,
        "Count")),
    new CodeAssignStatement(
      refNdxVar,
      new CodeBinaryOperatorExpression (
        refNdxVar,
        CodeBinaryOperatorType.Add,
        new CodePrimitiveExpression(1))),
    new CodeConditionStatement(
      new CodeBinaryOperatorExpression(
        refNdxVar,
        CodeBinaryOperatorType.ValueEquality,
        new CodePrimitiveExpression(0)),
      new CodeStatement[] {
        new CodeExpressionStatement(
          new CodeMethodInvokeExpression(
            new CodeMethodReferenceExpression(
              refResultVar,
              "AppendFormat"),
            new CodePrimitiveExpression("{0}"),
            new CodeArrayIndexerExpression(
              refUpdatesFld,
              refNdxVar)))},
      new CodeStatement[] {
        new CodeExpressionStatement(
```

```
          new CodeMethodInvokeExpression(
            new CodeMethodReferenceExpression(
              refResultVar,
              "AppendFormat"),
            new CodePrimitiveExpression(", {0}"),
            new CodeArrayIndexerExpression(
              refUpdatesFld,
              refNdxVar))})));
```

Although the code is somewhat difficult to read all at once, breaking it down one constructor parameter at a time as we did earlier makes it much easier to understand. We recommend that, when you're building complex code graphs by hand, you break down each piece of the program structure and logic into smaller parts. Then you can reassemble them into larger, more fluent expressions to whatever depth suits you and other potential readers of the code generator.

The last thing you must do to complete the `GetWabeHistory` method is return a value. You can do this by building a `CodeMethodReturnStatement` that invokes the `ToString` method on the reference to the `result` local variable that you saved early on:

```
methGetWabeCountHistory.Statements.Add(
  new CodeMethodReturnStatement(
    new CodeMethodInvokeExpression(
      new CodeMethodReferenceExpression(
        refResultVar, "ToString"))));
```

The complete example code for this section can be found in the book's source code repository in a project named AddingAndInvokingMethods in chapter 4. The output of the metaprogram shown in the next listing has a `GetWabeHistory` method that closely matches the goal that was shown in listing 4.10.

**Listing 4.12  The `Jubjub` class with its new `GetWabeHistory` method**

```
namespace Mimsy
{
  using System;
  using System.Text;
  using System.Collections;

  public class Jubjub
  {
    private int _wabeCount;
    private ArrayList _updates;
    public Jubjub(int wabeCount)
    {
      this._updates = new ArrayList();
      this.WabeCount = wabeCount;
    }
    public int WabeCount
    {
      get
      {
        return this._wabeCount;
      }
```

```
    set
    {
      if ((value < 0))
      {
        this._wabeCount = 0;
      }
      else
      {
        this._wabeCount = value;
      }
      this._updates.Add(this._wabeCount);
    }
  }
  public string GetWabeCountHistory()
  {
    StringBuilder result;
    result = new StringBuilder();
    int ndx;
    for (ndx = 0; (ndx < this._updates.Count); ndx = (ndx + 1))
    {
      if ((ndx == 0))
      {
        result.AppendFormat("{0}", this._updates[ndx]);
      }
      else
      {
        result.AppendFormat(", {0}", this._updates[ndx]);
      }
    }
    return result.ToString();
  }
 }
}
```

We coded method invocations into the code graph in this section, but not to methods defined in our dynamically generated Jubjub class. In the next couple of sections, we place the namespace into a CodeCompileUnit, compile it to memory, instantiate the Mimsy.Jubjub class dynamically, change the WabeCount property value a few times, and inspect the history of our changes by calling the GetWabeCountHistory method that we added.

### 4.4.4 *Compiling assemblies*

Before you can generate an assembly from a namespace, you must place it into Code-CompileUnit. This class is rather oddly named and seems even stranger given that the compilation process, which is done through a CodeDomProvider derived type, is performed through a method named CompileAssemblyFromDom. You might have expected that method to be called something like CompileAssemblyFromCompile-Unit. Is the CodeCompileUnit what the progenitors of the CodeDOM at Microsoft thought of as the pinnacle DOM type for code graphs? The naming seems to imply that, but we don't know.

The code shown in the following listing is a useful helper function called Compile-NamespaceToAssembly. It's helpful because it combines a few of the steps that must be performed when a CodeNamespace needs to be compiled into in-memory assembly.

**Listing 4.13    The helper function** CompileNamespaceToAssembly

```
static Assembly CompileNamespaceToAssembly(
  CodeNamespace ns)
{
  var ccu = new CodeCompileUnit();
  ccu.Namespaces.Add(ns);
  CompilerParameters cp =
    new CompilerParameters()
    {
      OutputAssembly = "dummy",
      GenerateInMemory = true
    };
  CompilerResults cr =
    CodeDomProvider.CreateProvider("c#")
    .CompileAssemblyFromDom(cp, ccu);
  return cr.CompiledAssembly;
}
```

The function begins by creating a CodeCompileUnit and adding the CodeNamespace passed in as a parameter to the Namespaces collection. Then a CompilerParameters object is constructed for which two properties are set:

- OutputAssembly—The name of the assembly in memory or on disk.
- GenerateInMemory—A flag that indicates whether the assembly should be made available immediately as an in-memory object.

The OutputAssembly is given the name "dummy" here because you don't care what it's called. The GenerateInMemory flag is set to true because you don't intend for the compiled assembly to be written to disk. You're going to consume it right away in the running application. Understand, though, that in-memory compilation could lead to what amounts to a memory leak in your programs due to the way that the CodeDOM marks the newly compiled assembly. If you're loading assemblies once at the start of an application, and expect them to stay in memory until the program completes, this shouldn't be an issue. But if you're creating new assemblies again and again throughout the lifetime of the application, you shouldn't use the simple, in-memory compilation approach.

Finally, the CompileAssemblyFromDom method on the CSharpCodeProvider is called, passing the CompilerParameters and the CodeCompileUnit as parameters. The result is a CompilerResults object that has a CompiledAssembly property referencing the dynamically compiled assembly.

There are a few things that this helper function should be doing but isn't. Exceptions that can be thrown throughout the process aren't being caught. And the compiler may encounter errors in the code graph. For your production applications, you

> **Always set the OutputAssembly**
>
> If you fail to set some value for the `OutputAssembly` property of the `Compiler-Parameters`, the compiler will pick a random assembly name that's guaranteed not to clash with others. You might think that because you're generating the assembly for in-memory use, a randomly selected name would be okay. But if you allow the compiler to select a random name, you won't be able to use the assembly reference in the `CompilerResults` object that's returned. Always name your `OutputAssembly` when calling one of the `Compile` methods on a CodeDOM code provider.

should use the `CompileNamespaceToAssembly` method shown in listing 4.13 as a starting point. But you should add the appropriate exception handling and inspect the `Errors` collection on the `CompilerResults` before returning to the caller.

### 4.4.5 *Dynamic invocation*

To create a `Mimsy.Jubjub` object from a dynamically compiled assembly, we'll use the helper function named `InstantiateDynamicType` shown in the following listing. It fetches the `Type` metadata for a named class and uses the `Activator` class to create an instance of the specified type, passing a variable number of constructor parameters. The `CreateInstance` method on Microsoft's `Activator` class will attempt to find the correct constructor based on the type and order of the parameters.

**Listing 4.14  The helper function `InstantiateDynamicType`**

```
static dynamic InstantiateDynamicType(Assembly asm,
  string typeName, params object[] ctorParams)
{
  Type targetType = asm.GetType(typeName);
  return Activator.CreateInstance(
    targetType, ctorParams);
}
```

Notice also that the `InstantiateDynamicType` method returns a C# 4.0 dynamic type. As you learned in chapter 1, there is no such thing as a dynamic type in C#, even though the existence of the keyword implies otherwise. Under the covers, dynamic objects are `System.Object` instances given special treatment by the compiler. They also have a special `DynamicAttribute` applied to them to allow post-compilation tooling to continue the process of treating them in special, dynamic ways. If you want to use the code shown here using an older C# compiler, change the dynamic keywords to `object`. Then you can perform your own reflection against those `object` instances to invoke the methods and properties dynamically the old-fashioned way.

With the helper functions shown in listings 4.12 and 4.13, you're ready to compile your `mimsyNamespace` and exercise the `Jubjub` class a bit. We've also bundled this up as a method called `CompileAndExerciseJubjub` shown in the following listing.

**Listing 4.15   Compiling and instantiating CodeDOM-generated classes**

```
static string CompileAndExerciseJubjub(
  CodeNamespace theNamespace, params int[] wabes)
{
  if (wabes == null || wabes.Length == 0)
    return string.Empty;

  Assembly compiledAssembly =
    CompileNamespaceToAssembly(theNamespace);

  dynamic bird = InstantiateDynamicType(
    compiledAssembly, "Mimsy.Jubjub",
    new object[] { wabes[0] });

  for (int ndx = 1; ndx < wabes.Length; ndx++)
    bird.WabeCount = wabes[ndx];

  return bird.GetWabeCountHistory();
}
```

This test method accepts a CodeNamespace to be compiled and a list of wabes to pass to the Mimsy.Jubjub object that will be dynamically instantiated. The first wabe is passed to the constructor, and any remaining ones are set via the WabeCount property. Finally, the history of all your WabeCount changes is fetched via the GetWabeCountHistory method and returned to the caller as a string.

The code for this example can be found in the book's sample code repository as the DynamicInvocation project. In that project, you'll also find a method called CreateMimsyNamespace that pulls all the code concerning the creation of the Mimsy.Jubjub code graph into one concise package. You can now invoke the test function like this:

```
CodeNamespace mimsyNamespace =
  CreateMimsyNamespace();
Console.WriteLine(
  CompileAndExerciseJubjub(
    mimsyNamespace,
    8, 6, 7, 5, 3, -1, 9));
```

The console output will appear something like figure 4.4.

You can see from comparing the output in figure 4.4 with the code above that the -1 wabe that was passed to the WabeCount property mutator was coerced to the value 0.

In this section, you built a code graph dynamically to produce a fairly sophisticated little class. Then you dynamically assembled the code graph in memory. An instance

**Figure 4.4   The result of dynamically invoking a dynamically generated and dynamically assembled class**

**The InternalsVisibleToAttribute**

When you run the code in the DynamicInvocation project in the chapter 3 sample source code, it'll work. But if you've been modifying the code along the way rather than using the samples provided, you'll get an interesting failure. Remember at the beginning of the `Mimsy.Jubjub` example when you marked the `Jubjub` class with the `MemberAttribute` of `NonPublic`? That caused the `Jubjub` class to be generated as an `internal` class, if you recall. When you try to instantiate an object from a dynamically loaded assembly that's marked `internal`, the call will fail. That makes sense, doesn't it? Why should the running assembly have access to an `internal` class in another assembly? It shouldn't. You have a choice to correct this problem. You can mark the class as `public` instead. Or you can set the assembly level attribute known as `InternalsVisibleTo` on the dynamic assembly, fully qualifying the name of another assembly that should have access to types marked as `internal` within it. This second method isn't practical, so we chose instead to mark the class as `public` in the DynamicInvocation project sample source.

of the class was dynamically created then dynamically invoked to get the object into the state which produced the output shown previously.

Everything about this example is dynamic. Although it's a simple example, it's important because it highlights a range of tools and techniques that you can use in your own application to add flexibility and reusability to your applications. You probably won't use them all in a single application, but you could if you needed to.

As a parting exercise, think about the modifications that would be necessary to make the `Jubjub` class operate on data types other than integers. Here's a hint: it can be done by changing two lines of sample code. With the introduction of a `CodeType-Reference`, that change could be reduced to one line. Do you see the connection between metaprogramming and generic types? Generics are all about reusability, and metaprogramming provides lots of opportunities for creating reusable data structures of your own design.

## 4.5   Summary

This chapter isn't meant to be an exhaustive reference of the CodeDOM. To be exhaustive would require an entire book—or two. Instead, our goal here is to open your mind to the flexibility and richness of the CodeDOM by highlighting a handful of scenarios you're likely to face when you begin to generate code and compile assemblies dynamically.

Microsoft has excellent reference materials in the MSDN Library concerning the CodeDOM. They contain good examples that you can pick up quickly once you've learned the basic skills taught in this chapter. You can also find many excellent examples of CodeDOM use on the Internet.

What we've done in this chapter however is fundamentally different from all those examples. Our approach is to teach you systematically how the CodeDOM works and why it's constructed as it is. Now that you've established a strong foundation for learning about metaprogramming by implementing code as data, those examples provided by Microsoft and others should be much easier to digest. Furthermore, the prototypes you established here will serve you well as you study the other metaprogramming facilities that .NET has to offer in the remainder of this book.

# Generating code
# with Reflection.Emit

In chapter 4, you saw how you can generate code via the CodeDOM. Another option in .NET lets you do the same thing, except it uses IL directly to create the code at runtime. This provides a substantial performance boost and access to any feature supported by the CLR. All the supporting classes exist in the `System .Reflection.Emit` namespace, and that's where you'll spend your time in this chapter. We cover how the common opcodes work, and then you'll see examples that generate dynamic assemblies and methods.

The first thing you need to understand is why one would ever bother diving into the Emitter classes to solve particular problems. That's what the next section discusses.

## 5.1    Why Emitter classes?

It's probably a safe bet to assume that most of the code you've written in .NET has followed the same general workflow:

- Write code in your favorite language
- Compile it
- Run the results

But what if you were able to write and compile code while your code was executing?
Let's cover some scenarios where the Emitter classes may come in handy in solving
particular programming problems at runtime.

### 5.1.1    Support for DSLs

If you've ever had to do a lot of text parsing and
processing (whether or not using a .NET-based
language), you probably used something called a
regular expression. *Regular expressions* are these
somewhat cryptic-looking strings that contain a
wealth of power to get specific textural patterns
in a sea of characters. For example, figure 5.1
shows a regular expression to find phone numbers.

`((\(\d{3}\) ?)|(\d{3}-))?\d{3}-\d{4}`

3 digits in    OR    3 digits    3 digits,
parentheses                     dash,
                                4 digits

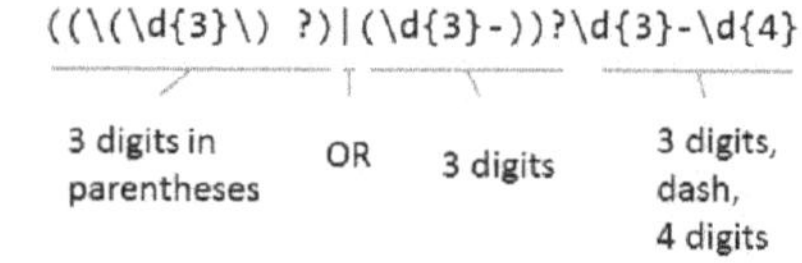

**Figure 5.1   A simple regular expression
to find phone numbers**

This may not look like much, but this expression can find a U.S. phone number in
text, so long as it uses hyphens to separate the digits, like this: 123-555-1212. If you
spend time digging into regular expressions, you can do amazing things to pull information out of a text file.

So what does this have to do with emitting opcodes? .NET provides a class called
`Regex` that provides regular expression support. Here's how you'd use the previous
expression in .NET to find a phone number:

```
var phone =
  "Find this: 123-555-1212. Or this: 123-555-9999.";
var matches = Regex.Match(phone,
  @"((\(\d{3}\) ?)|(\d{3}-))?\d{3}-\d{4}");

while(matches.Success)
{
  Console.Out.WriteLine(matches.Value);
  matches = matches.NextMatch();
}
```

A regular expression is an example of a DSL. DSLs, as you learned in chapter 1, are typically smaller, lightweight languages that are tailored to a specific problem. They're
usually embedded within other languages and frameworks. Regular expressions aren't
suited to creating complex applications by themselves, but they can easily find URLs in
text from a file an application has loaded into memory.

The issue in using regular expressions in .NET is that `Regex` has to parse the expression to translate it into executable code. That's where the Emitter classes come into

play. Regex uses Reflection.Emit to create a fast implementation of the given regular expression to perform the operations defined in the expression. If you're creating your own DSL and want to use it in your code, you can use Reflection.Emit to compile the code into IL, which can run as fast as any code written in C# or VB.

> **NOTE** Regular expressions aren't specific to .NET. They've been around since way before opcodes saw the light of day, so there's a lot of information out there you can find to learn more about these amazing expressions. One good site to start with is www.regular-expressions.info. You can also check out *DSL in Action* by Debasish Ghosh (Manning, 2010) at http://manning .com/ghosh/.

### 5.1.2 *Moving reflection code into IL*

There are times where you need to perform a bit of processing that may not happen at runtime. The ToString() example in chapter 2 demonstrates why you'd want to use metaprogramming to reduce to amount of code you write and defer that processing until it's needed. You also saw this with the Lazy<T> class in chapter 2. Lazy<T> provides you with the ability to defer the loading of a value until the user calls the Value property—at that time, Lazy<T> will create the value. If you never call Value, Lazy<T> won't do anything. A similar case happens with serialization. *Serialization* is the process where the contents of an object are saved into some kind of persistent storage, like memory or a file. You can deserialize the object later if needed. Some serialization strategies can be quite complex, and it's best to defer execution until you know you need it.

Such is the case with XML serialization via the XmlSerializer class. If you've never seen how the XmlSerializer works, it's pretty simple. Let's say you had a simple object with a couple of properties:

```
public sealed class DataBucket
{
  public Guid Id { get; set; }
  public string Value { get; set; }
}
```

Serializing an instance of DataBucket takes only a few lines of code:

```
var target = new DataBucket
{
  Id = Guid.NewGuid(),
  Value = Guid.NewGuid().ToString("N")
};

using(var stream = new StringWriter())
{
  var serializer = new XmlSerializer(typeof(DataBucket));
  serializer.Serialize(stream, target);
  Console.Out.WriteLine(
    stream.GetStringBuilder().ToString());
}
```

This would print the following XML information to the console window:

```
<?xml version="1.0" encoding="utf-16"?>
<DataBucket xmlns:xsi="http://www.w3.org/2001/XMLSchema-instance"
  xmlns:xsd="http://www.w3.org/2001/XMLSchema">
  <Id>b3a14833-7fbc-4e09-86b0-0d878055c1e9</Id>
  <Value>ee77b2ea4c664ec798e67ce74fa9eb9f</Value>
</DataBucket>
```

The `XmlSerializer` uses a fair amount of reflection to figure out what data is in a given object to perform the necessary serialization operations on it. Because it's possible to write code that uses `Serialize()` and `Deserialize()`, but isn't executed when the application runs, `XmlSerializer` defers the creation of the serialization logic until it's needed.

This approach has two advantages. The first is easy to see: you perform a lazy computation for serialization, which is nice if the serialization never occurs. The second may not be so easy to see (though because you've read chapter 2 you probably know what it is!). It's the ability to persist and reuse dynamic logic for future usage. Finding out all the information about an object via its metadata takes time—remember, reflection is slower than comparable compiled code. Furthermore, once you figure out what needs to be serialized in an object, that logic won't change for the lifetime of the application because the type definition won't change. `XmlSerializer` uses Reflection.Emit to generate an assembly at runtime that contains all the serialization logic necessary for a given object.

This is another use for Reflection.Emit. If you're writing code that uses reflection, it's fairly common to run into the case where you're performing logic based on a given type or assembly. By using some Emitter API magic (as you'll see in section 5.5), you can compile your logic into executable code that you can cache. As you'll see in section 5.5.3, this technique can yield substantial performance benefits.

### 5.1.3 Using .NET functionality not supported in your language

Most .NET developers are familiar with exceptions handlers. In the following code snippet, the code in the `catch` block will run if any code in the `try` block throws a `NotImplementedException`:

```
try
{
  // logic goes here...
}
catch(NotImplementedException)
{
  // Exception handling logic goes here...
}
```

You can also use a `finally` block, which will always run no matter what goes on in the `try` block:

```
try
{
  // logic goes here...
}
finally
{
  // Clean-up logic usually goes here...
}
```

**NOTE** This is what the using statement turns your code into, more or less. `Dispose()` is called on the object in the using statement within the `finally` block, which guarantees that `Dispose()` will be called.

However, did you know there's another kind of handler block in .NET that C# and VB don't expose? It's called the `fault` block, and, if it *were* in C#, it might look something like this:

```
try
{
  // logic goes here...
}
fault
{
  // Exception handling logic goes here before it's rethrown...
}
```

Code within a `fault` block will execute *only* if an exception is thrown in the `try` block. Then the exception is rethrown. This would come in handy with transactions as you call a `Rollback()` method in the `fault` block—but alas, the `fault` keyword isn't exposed in C# or VB.

With the Emitter classes, you could easily write code that will wrap code in a try...`fault` block, because Reflection.Emit supports all of the functionality that .NET allows, not the stuff that you see in your favorite .NET language. Other esoteric functionalities are possible at the IL level, such as:

- Calling overloaded methods that differ only by their return types
- Throwing exceptions that don't inherit from the `Exception` class
- Creating method calls known as *tail calls*, which eliminate the stack before calling a method (quite handy for preventing stack overflows in recursive call scenarios)

Granted, the need to use some of these additional features is rare (or nonexistent), but it's nice to know that you have the full power of .NET available to you via the Emitter classes. If you want to know everything that's available within .NET, you can find a set of.

**NOTE** There's an exception-specific CLR feature that VB supports but C# doesn't. It's called the `filter` block, and it's like a `catch` block with an additional Boolean expression. If that expression evaluates to true, the code in the block executes; otherwise, the exception continues unwinding the stack. This simple feature makes VB a bit more expressive with respect to exception handling than C#.

Now that you've seen a couple scenarios where dynamic code is desirable, let's go through a brief description of how code is transformed into an assembly, and what this transformation looks like behind the scenes.

## 5.2 *An overview of assembly internals*

Before you can start manipulating opcodes, understanding how assemblies are structured is essential. This information will make creating dynamic assemblies easier to understand. Let's start by looking at what happens when you compile your code.

### 5.2.1 *Transforming high-level languages*

When you compile your programs, the compiler transforms your code into a format that the CLR can understand. This format is somewhat dense and harder to understand than what you use with a higher-level language like C#, so we'll spend some time examining the details slowly.

Let's start with the simple example shown in the following listing. This code creates a random number that's retrieved by using the lazy-loading class, Lazy<T>. The number is then shown to the user via the console window.

**Listing 5.1  Lazy-loading a random number**

```
using System;

namespace LazyIntegers
{
  internal static class Program
  {
    private static void Main(string[] args)
    {
      var lazyInteger = new Lazy<int>(() =>
      {
        return new Random().Next();
      });

      Console.Out.WriteLine(lazyInteger.Value);
    }
  }
}
```

When you compile this code, the compiler transforms it into an assembly. An *assembly* is a file that contains all the contents you give the compiler, like classes and resource files. The code in listing 5.1 is intended to be a console application, so you'll get an executable (EXE) file, like LazyIntegers.exe, when compilation is complete. If you were creating a

An overview of assembly internals

class library, the compiler would create a dynamic link library (DLL). Both of these files are in the format of a portable executable (PE) file, but for your purposes it's sufficient to know that the compiler produces a file that the CLR can take and execute.

If you saw the code snippet in listing 5.1 online, figuring out what it did would be pretty easy. The following listing shows code that does the same thing as the Main() method in listing 5.1, but it's in the format that's stored in the assembly once the compiler has done its job.

**Listing 5.2   C# code transformed into the .NET assembly format**

```
.method private hidebysig static void Main(string[] args) cil managed
{
  .entrypoint
  .maxstack  3
  .locals init ([0] class
    [mscorlib]System.Lazy`1<int32> lazyInteger)
  IL_0000:  ldsfld      class [mscorlib]System.Func`1<int32>
    LazyIntegers.Program::'CS$<>9__CachedAnonymousMethodDelegate1'
  IL_0005:  brtrue.s    IL_0018
  IL_0007:  ldnull
  IL_0008:  ldftn       int32 LazyIntegers.Program::'<Main>b__0'()
  IL_000e:  newobj      instance void class
    [mscorlib]System.Func`1<int32>::..ctor(object, native int)
  IL_0013:  stsfld      class [mscorlib]System.Func`1<int32>
    LazyIntegers.Program::'CS$<>9__CachedAnonymousMethodDelegate1'
  IL_0018:  ldsfld      class [mscorlib]System.Func`1<int32>
    LazyIntegers.Program::'CS$<>9__CachedAnonymousMethodDelegate1'
  IL_001d:  newobj      instance void class
    [mscorlib]System.Lazy`1<int32>::..ctor(class
      [mscorlib]System.Func`1<!0>)
  IL_0022:  stloc.0
  IL_0023:  call        class [mscorlib]System.IO.TextWriter
    [mscorlib]System.Console::get_Out()
  IL_0028:  ldloc.0
  IL_0029:  callvirt    instance !0 class
    [mscorlib]System.Lazy`1<int32>::get_Value()
  IL_002e:  callvirt    instance void
    [mscorlib]System.IO.TextWriter::WriteLine(int32)
  IL_0033:  ret
}
```

This format comes from the Intermediate Language Disassembler tool, or ILDasm. This is a .NET framework tool that lets you see all of the internal parts and figures of an assembly. You can run it from the Visual Studio command prompt by typing *ildasm*. Figure 5.2 shows what ILDasm looks like when the console application is loaded that contains the code from listing 5.1.

**NOTE**   Depending on how you have your environment set up, you may not have the correct path information such that typing ildasm at the command line works. VS installs the Visual Studio command prompt tool, which you can find in the Visual Studio Tools folder. Run this batch file, and you'll be able to use ILDasm.

**Figure 5.2    An assembly opened in ILDasm. You can see the contents of the assembly in a tree view format.**

To load an assembly in ILDasm, you use the File > Open menu option. You can drill into any member of the assembly and inspect its contents. Figure 5.3 is the code window that's shown when you double-click the Main() method.

If you've never seen .NET-level assembly code, trying to figure out what's going on can be confusing the first time you encounter it. This is the intermediate language of .NET. Every language must transform its syntax into this format if it wants to have its code execute on the CLR. It may look like assembly code, but it's not quite that powerful. It's a layer between higher-level languages and assembly code. The CLR understands this language and converts it into assembly code for the target processor.

Even after you've spent some time trying to understand this format, it can still throw you for a loop or two (which, after all, is why we as .NET developers don't

**Figure 5.3    Code in ILDasm. This is the code behind the Main() method.**

often—if ever—program program in this format). But this base language of .NET isn't too hard to comprehend once you understand the structure of .NET assemblies. Furthermore, having this foundational knowledge is crucial in understanding and applying the concepts in later chapters.

### 5.2.2 *Member layouts in assemblies and keywords*

Let's focus on the first line of code from listing 5.2. For now, we won't spend time on those lines that start with IL. That's the method implementation—what you're seeing are the opcodes. We'll come back to opcodes in section 5.3; right now we're more interested in member definitions and assembly layouts.

Most of this first line is fairly easy to interpret. The first piece is .method, which defines that the content within the curly braces is a method. As you can imagine, you can have members scoped within other members. The next listing shows that this method is a member of the Program class. Any time you encounter something with a dot in front of it, it's called a directive. There are many other directives, and most map to members you're familiar with in .NET, such as .assembly, .field, and .event.

**Listing 5.3  Scoping the Main() method in the Program class**

```
.class private abstract auto ansi sealed beforefieldinit
  LazyIntegers.Program
  extends [mscorlib]System.Object
{
  .method private hidebysig static void Main(string[] args) cil managed
  {
    // ...
  }
}
```

You can also see other keywords within the method definition. For example, private defines the visibility of the method, and static specifies that the method is defined on the class (it's not an instance method). Some of the other ones may not be so obvious with their mapping to the original C# code, such as managed and hidebysig. Furthermore, some of the combinations may even seem contradictory. In the case of the class definition of LazyIntegers.Program, the keywords abstract and sealed are used at the same time. How, you may wonder, can a class be both at the same time?

> **NOTE**  The reason ILDasm shows the class name as LazyIntegers.Program is because that *is* the class name. C# and VB allows you to split the full class name into a namespace and a class name. You can also reference namespaces via the using (C#) or Imports (VB) keywords, but that's all syntactic sugar and organizational aids over what is the true name of the class.

There are many more directives and keywords you can use than we have time to cover in this book. How can you determine all the keywords you could possibly run into when you look at .NET code in this format? Fortunately, a number of specification documents, called the Partition documents, contain detailed information about .NET. You can always reference those documents in case you run into a directive or a keyword you've never seen before. You can find them at http://mng.bz/qu5U. We refer to the ECMA standards documents from time to time to clarify certain concepts, so we strongly recommend downloading them. Perusing their contents to see what can go on within a .NET assembly is also educational.

---

**Keyword definitions**

If you're curious, `managed` means that the method contains IL opcodes only (which is different from a `P/Invoke` method).

`hidebysig` defines how the method "hides" other methods from a base class and itself.

`Program` is defined as both `sealed` and `abstract` because it's a C# static class.

There's no notion of a static class at the CLR level, but you can make a class both `sealed` (you can't inherit from it) and `abstract` (you can never create an instance of it).

---

So far, you've seen how the contents of an assembly are laid out. Now let's focus in on the opcodes and how they work.

## 5.3    *A lightning tour of opcodes*

Listing 5.2 showed the implementation of a method in IL form. At that point, the discussion focused on metadata and directives; the implementation was deferred because explaining those details at that time wasn't necessary. Now it's time to cover that information. To be proficient with metaprogramming using Reflection.Emit, you must first understand opcodes, as they're part of virtually every method call you'll make with that API. This section gives you a summary of how opcodes are named and the various functions you can do with them. In the next section, you'll use this new-found knowledge as you work with Reflection.Emit.

### 5.3.1    *The mnemonic patterns for opcodes*

For developers to see similarities between opcodes in IL and assembly language instructions isn't uncommon. In some ways, this comparison is valid. They're both terse and not as friendly to use as a higher-level language is. However, writing code in IL doesn't mean your code will execute any faster than what the C# compiler will produce. That's why you don't see inline IL as an option in C# or VB—because there's really no value-added in allowing a developer access to opcodes in a method. But as we've stated before, emitting code via Reflection.Emit means you need to understand opcodes. As it turns out, it's not too hard to see what the opcodes are doing. Here's a line of code from listing 5.2:

```
IL_0022:  stloc.0
```

All the opcodes have a mnemonic pattern to them. If the opcode name starts with st, it means *store*. loc means *local*. Therefore, this opcode stores a local value. The .0 determines where a value will be stored—we cover that in the next section.

Table 5.1 contains a list of common patterns you'll see in opcodes. The list isn't complete, but it will help you in deciphering most of the opcodes you'll see.

**Table 5.1   Common mnemonic phrases used in opcodes**

| Mnemonic | Meaning |
|----------|---------|
| ld | Load a value. |
| ldc | Load a constant value. |
| st | Store a value. |
| loc | Do something with a local value. |
| br | Break to a specified point in a method. |
| arg | Reference an argument. |
| loc | Use a local variable. |
| ovf | Overflow detection. |
| conv | Perform a conversion. |
| elem | Use an element in an array. |
| fld | Use a field. |
| call | Call a method. |

Some opcodes, like castclass, are fairly easy to read and don't require a lot of translation. You can easily guess that this casts an object to a specified type. Other opcodes may not seem so obvious, like conv.ovf.i4. But by looking at table 5.1, you know that the opcode has something to do with converting a value with overflow detection. We discuss what the i4 part means in a bit.

Whether or not a name is easy to understand at first glance, we strongly recommend you have the third Partition document handy as you dive into the opcode names. It covers all the details about every opcode available in .NET. For now, let's cover the opcodes you'll probably use heavily in Emitter-based code.

**NOTE**   Those IL_statements are labels generated by ILDasm. The names have no formatting requirements, nor do you need to use them all the time. The only opcodes that need them are opcodes that relocate the control flow to a new opcode. The format ILDasm uses to generate labels is to specify how far in the opcode stream you are via a hexadecimal value. Therefore, IL_0022 means you're currently at the 34th byte in the method. This is good to know

when you're doing branching because you can use special opcodes to minimize the size of the method. We cover branching and how labels are used in
more detail in section 5.3.6.

### 5.3.2   *Using local variables*

Before we continue, let's rewrite the code you saw in listing 5.2 to something that's a
little friendlier to read. The C# compiler has to create some nasty names for anonymous members, so this listing is a cleaner version for you to use.

**Listing 5.4   A cleaner version of the `Main()` method from listing 5.2**

```
.method private hidebysig static void Main(string[] args) cil managed
{
  .entrypoint
  .maxstack 3
  .locals init (
    [0] class [mscorlib]System.Lazy`1<int32> lazyInteger)

  ldnull
  ldftn int32
    LazyIntegersInIL.Program::LazyIntegerValueFactory()
  newobj instance void class
    [mscorlib]System.Func`1<int32>::.ctor(object, native int)
  stsfld class [mscorlib]System.Func`1<int32>
    LazyIntegersInIL.Program::LazyIntegerValueFactoryDelegate

  ldsfld class [mscorlib]System.Func`1<int32>
    LazyIntegersInIL.Program::LazyIntegerValueFactoryDelegate
  newobj instance void class
    [mscorlib]System.Lazy`1<int32>::.ctor(
  class [mscorlib]System.Func`1<!0>)
  stloc.0

  call class [mscorlib]System.IO.TextWriter
    [mscorlib]System.Console::get_Out()
  ldloc.0
  callvirt instance !0 class
    [mscorlib]System.Lazy`1<int32>::get_Value()
  callvirt instance void
    [mscorlib]System.IO.TextWriter::WriteLine(int32)
  ret
}
```

If you want to create a local variable in your method, you need to do two things. First,
you declare them via the `.locals` directive:

```
.locals init (
  [0] class [mscorlib]System.Lazy`1<int32> lazyInteger)
```

In this case, a local variable named `lazyInteger` is used, which is of type Lazy<int>.
Note that this local variable is in slot 0. You don't have to specify the slot location (via
the [0] syntax) if you don't want to; the compiler will put the variable in the next
available slot if you don't say where it should go. You can reference variables either by
slot location or name. Using variables requires the `ldloc` and `stloc` opcodes:

```
stloc.0
call class [mscorlib]System.IO.TextWriter
   [mscorlib]System.Console::get_Out()ldloc.0
```

Remember that we said in the last section that we'd address those .0 parts of the opcodes? Those mean that you want to store a value in the 0th local variable or fetch one from that location. You could also use a variable name to load and store values:

```
stloc lazyInteger
call class [mscorlib]System.IO.TextWriter
   [mscorlib]System.Console::get_Out()ldloc lazyInteger
```

At this point, you may be wondering where these values go. IL is a stack-based language, which means you push and pop values on a stack. Therefore, if you issue the ldloc.0 instruction, the runtime takes the 0th local variable and pushes it onto the stack. Using stloc.0 would pop that value and store it back into the 0th local variable.

Here's a simple example using the stack with some other "loading" opcodes. Push two values on the stack, a double and a long, and then pop the value into a local variable:

```
.locals init (
   [0] class [mscorlib]System.Int64 value)
ldc.r8 35.5
ldc.i8 234
stloc.0
```

Figure 5.4 shows what the stack looks after the second value is pushed to the stack, then what's left on the stack after stloc.0 executes. Leaving that last value on the stack is something you shouldn't do because it's an IL rule that you can't leave a method with something still on the stack. It's extremely important to keep track of what's on the stack as you define methods with opcodes. It's quite easy to accidentally misuse the stack with disastrous results—another good reason for not exposing inline IL in C# or VB.

**Figure 5.4 Using the IL stack. After storing the long value into the variable, one double value remains on the stack.**

> **NOTE** We talk about a tool you can use to uncover opcode mistakes in section 5.4.3.

### 5.3.3 Accessing fields

In listing 5.4, you can see that an anonymous method is passed into the constructor for Lazy<int>. The C# compiler ends up creating a method with a complicated name to store that method's implementation, which is called LazyIntegerValueFactory in listing 5.1. That method is turned into a delegate (which is eventually passed into Lazy<int>), and that delegate is stored in a field. To create a field, use the .field directive:

```
.field private static class
   [mscorlib]System.Func`1<int32> LazyIntegerValueFactoryDelegate
```

Depending on its accessibility and access needs, you'll use keywords like private and static. To use the field, you use the ldfld, ldsfld, stfld, and stsfld opcodes:

```
stsfld class [mscorlib]System.Func`1<int32>
  LazyIntegersInIL.Program::LazyIntegerValueFactoryDelegate

ldsfld class [mscorlib]System.Func`1<int32>
  LazyIntegersInIL.Program::LazyIntegerValueFactoryDelegate
```

The extra s in two of the opcodes (ldsfld and stsfld) means you're trying to use a static field. If you were using an instance-level field, you'd use ldfld and stfld. Note that with instance fields, you need to have the object that has the field on the stack—you'll see how to create objects in the next section.

### 5.3.4 Creating objects

To create your Lazy<int> with a factory method, you need to call a constructor on the class. You do that with the newobj opcode:

```
ldnull
ldftn int32
  LazyIntegersInIL.Program::LazyIntegerValueFactory()
newobj instance void class
  [mscorlib]System.Func`1<int32>::.ctor(object, native int)
```

Remember, when you're using IL, you're pushing and popping values on a stack. To call any method in IL, the first thing you have to do is push all the values onto the stack that will be passed into the target method (in this case, a constructor). Things look a little odd. You're passing in a method—why do you need to pass in an object and a native int? To make a long story short, when you're working with delegates, you need to provide the object that the target method is defined on and a function pointer to the delegate. In your case, your method is static, so you have no object to reference when you need to call it. Therefore, the first thing you do is push a null value onto the stack with ldnull. Then, you get the function pointer via ldftn. Finally, you can create your Lazy<int> via newobj.

To summarize, you need to do two things when you create an object:

- Push the argument values on the stack in the order that the constructor needs them.
- Use newobj to call the constructor.

When newobj is done, all the argument values are popped off the stack, and the new object is on the stack. That's why stsfld was called to store the new Lazy<int> into your static field.

### 5.3.5 Calling methods

Now that you know how to create an object, understanding how to call a method should be fairly easy. To be sure, there are some differences, but the process is the same: push the argument values on the stack and call the method:

```
ldloc.0
callvirt instance !0 class
  [mscorlib]System.Lazy`1<int32>::get_Value()
```

Wait, you might say. Why is the Lazy<int> local variable (the 0th one) pushed on the stack to call get_Value(), which takes no arguments? And the C# code that generated this IL used a Value property, not get_Value(), so where did this method come from? And what's with that strange-looking !0 syntax? So many questions!

Let's start with the first question. When you call an instance method, the CLR needs to know which object you're targeting to call the method on. That's why you push the target object onto the stack first. Every instance method takes an object reference as its first argument that specifies the target. You don't see this in languages like C# or VB (nor do you see it in the method definition in IL either), but it's there. If you were calling a static method, you wouldn't push an object on the stack first because there's no need to specify a target with a static method.

The next issue is get_Value(). Properties in C# and VB are syntactic sugar around method calls. The C# compiler generates get_[PropertyName] and set_[Property-Name] methods for the getters and setters of a property. Therefore, when you use a property, you're really calling its methods, and that's why you see a call to get_Value() in the IL in this example.

Finally, the !0 text. Whenever you call a method in IL, you must include the return type in the signature of the method. This is probably different from most languages you've used because you don't explicitly provide the return type. But that's the way it is in IL. What's interesting about this rule is that you can overload methods based on a difference in return type alone—mentioned in section 5.1.3. With most methods, you'd provide the type name for the return value, like [mscorlib]::System.Int32. But Lazy<T> is a generic, and get_Value() returns a type of T. To specify that type, you use the !n syntax, where the n value is equal to the position of the generic type parameter in the type or method declaration. In this case, there's only one generic type declaration, T, so that's why 0 was used.

There are a couple of method invocation opcodes you should be aware of. In the example, you're using callvirt because you're calling a virtual method. You use the call opcode if you're calling a nonvirtual or static method. There's also calli, which allows you to call functions when you have a function pointer. calli is used with delegates or native method (a P/Invoke).

> **NOTE** You can call a virtual method with call if you want. Reference sections 3.19 and 4.2 of Partition III (http://mng.bz/qu5U) for details on when call and callvirt can and should be used.

### 5.3.6  *Controlling code flow*

There aren't any if or while statements in the code from listing 5.2, but these control flow keywords are common in most languages. Branching is supported in IL via the *break* opcodes. For example, if you wanted to break to a label in a method based on whether the first argument was null, you'd do this:

```
ldarg.1
brtrue ArgumentWasNotNull
```

```
// More IL goes here...
ArgumentWasNotNull: // ...
```

Like traditional assembly languages, IL also lets you branch based on the results of value comparisons. The following code snippet will break to the label if the first argument is greater than the second:

```
ldarg.1
ldarg.2
bge OneIsBiggerThanTwo:
// More IL code goes here...
OneIsBiggerThanTwo: // ...
```

A bunch of these control flow opcodes are available—we encourage you to visit section 3 in Partition III to learn more about these opcodes.

### 5.3.7   *Exception handling*

If you need to handle exceptions, you can do so in IL with a syntax that looks similar to what you'd see in C#. Here's how you'd catch a DivideByZeroException in IL with a finally block:

```
.try
{
  .try
  {
    // Math code goes here...
  }
  catch [mscorlib] System.DivideByZeroException
  {
    // Exception handling code goes here...
  }
}
finally
{
  // Finally handling code goes here...
}
```

It may surprise you to learn that you can't add a finally block directly to a try-catch block. That doesn't work in IL. You need to wrap the try-catch with a try-finally. Other than that, the rules you're used to in C# or VB work here as well—for example, you can have multiple catch blocks with a try block.

You can also catch types that don't derive from the Exception type. Because the CLR has to support executing code from languages that were written with the ability catch any type (like C++), in IL it's possible to write a catch block that catches a string or a Guid. But you don't want to do that unless you're writing a compiler for C++ to target .NET. Catching types that don't derive from Exception isn't CLS-compliant code.

> **NOTE**   CLS stands for Common Language Specification, which defines a basic set of features that all .NET languages must support. You can find more information at http://mng.bz/nz4x.

This concludes our lightning tour of IL. You can do a *lot* more in IL than what we had time for in this section, but this introduction is sufficient for now. Let's move from understanding what IL is to using it to generate dynamic code at runtime.

## 5.4 Creating dynamic assemblies

Now that you've had a brief dive into the world of opcodes, you're ready to tackle Reflection.Emit. By the end of this section, you'll know how to create a dynamic assembly. We revisit the `ToString()` example from section 2.4.2 and implement it with the Reflection.Emit API so you can see how it all works.

### 5.4.1 Building a dynamic version of ToString()

This section goes over the common tasks you'll use whenever you create dynamic code with Reflection.Emit. This boils down to three steps:

- Create an assembly.
- Create one or more types.
- Implement one or more methods on that type.

Let's break down each part into the necessary details.

#### CREATING THE ASSEMBLY

The first building block you need is a dynamic assembly. Technically, this means you need to create two things: an assembly and a module. Modules aren't talked about all that much in .NET, but they're important when emitting code using Reflection.Emit. Each assembly contains one or more modules, and the modules are what you use to build your types. It's possible to create multimodule assemblies, but we'll stick to the "one module per assembly" approach for simplicity's sake.

Anyway, let's see some code. The following listing demonstrates what you need to do to get started in Reflection.Emit by creating an assembly and a module. This code is contained in a class called `ReflectionEmitMethodGenerator`—later on, you'll see how to call this from a `ToString()` method. There's a lot to this class, so we'll go over it in small chunks, starting with the constructor that creates the dynamic assembly.

**Listing 5.5  Creating a dynamic assembly and module**

```
public sealed class ReflectionEmitMethodGenerator
{
  private AssemblyBuilder Assembly { get; set; }
  private ModuleBuilder Module { get; set; }
  private AssemblyName Name { get; set; }

  public ReflectionEmitMethodGenerator()
    : base()
  {
    this.Name = new AssemblyName()
    {
      Name = Guid.NewGuid().ToString("N")
    };
```

 **①** **Define assembly name**

```
this.Assembly = AppDomain.CurrentDomain.DefineDynamicAssembly(
  this.Name, AssemblyBuilderAccess.Run);
this.Module = this.Assembly.DefineDynamicModule(
  this.Name.Name);
```

First, you define a name for the assembly with the `AssemblyName` class ❶. Next, you create a new `AssemblyBuilder` object with this name via `DefineDynamicAssembly()` on an `AppDomain` object ❷—we'll stick with the default one in the example. Finally, you create your dynamic `ModuleBuilder` object by calling `DefineDynamicModule()` ❸. As mentioned in section 2.2.1, there are a number of overloads in the reflection world, and this holds true in the Reflection.Emit namespace as well. Feel free to explore the method options available to you.

You should also note that there a number of values for `AssemblyBuilderAccess`, like `RunAndSave`, `Save`, and so on. Using `Run` means the assembly will exist only in memory and won't be persisted to disk. That suits your needs for now; in section 5.4.3 you'll see where having the ability to save the assembly to disk lets you perform verification operations.

### CREATING THE TYPE

In the following code snippet, you can see how a dynamic type is created by calling `DefineType()` on our `ModuleBuilder`—this gives you a `TypeBuilder`. This `Generate<T>` method exists in the `ReflectionEmitMethodGenerator` class so it has access to all the fields defined in listing 5.5

```
public Func<T, string> Generate<T>()
{
  var target = typeof(T);
  var type = this.Module.DefineType(
    target.Namespace + "." + target.Name);
```

If you haven't picked up on the pattern yet, all the Emitter classes end with the word *Builder*. This reinforces the notion that you're building code on the fly.

### ADDING OPCODES

Finally, you arrive at the code that creates and implements the dynamic `ToString()` method. The first thing you have to do is create a method, shown in the next code snippet. This code, which is a continuation of the method from the previous code snippet, calls `DefineMethod()` on your `TypeBuilder`, specifying its argument types and visibility as arguments:

```
var method = type.DefineMethod(methodName,
  MethodAttributes.Static | MethodAttributes.Public,
  typeof(string), new Type[] { target });

method.GetILGenerator().Generate(target);
```

Your new method is a public, static method that takes one argument (typed as `T`—the object that wants a dynamic `ToString()` implementation) and returns a string.

Don't be fooled by that last line of code, though—there's a *lot* going on there. `GetILGenerator()` returns an `ILGenerator`, and that's what you'll use to define your method with opcodes. As you can guess, it takes a fair amount of code to implement on-the-fly methods, so we created an extension method, Generate(), to do this for you. The following listing shows the implementation of Generate().

**Listing 5.6  Using `ILGenerate` to emit code**

```
internal static void Generate(this ILGenerator @this, Type target)
{
  var properties = target.GetProperties(          ❶ Obtain public
    BindingFlags.Public | BindingFlags.Instance);     property list

  if(properties.Length > 0)
  {
    var stringBuilderType = typeof(StringBuilder);

    var toStringLocal = @this.DeclareLocal(        ❷ Declare local
      typeof(StringBuilder));                          StringBuilder

    @this.Emit(OpCodes.Newobj,
      stringBuilderType.GetConstructor(Type.EmptyTypes));  ❸ Create new
    @this.Emit(OpCodes.Stloc_0);                       StringBuilder
    @this.Emit(OpCodes.Ldloc_0);

    var appendMethod = stringBuilderType.GetMethod(   ❹ Get Append()
      "Append", new Type[] { typeof(string) });          method
    var toStringMethod = typeof(StringBuilder).GetMethod(
      "ToString", Type.EmptyTypes);

    for(var i = 0; i < properties.Length; i++)
    {                                              ❺ Print
      ToStringILGenerator.CreatePropertyForToString(    property
        @this, properties[i], appendMethod,             values
        i < properties.Length - 1);
    }

    @this.Emit(OpCodes.Pop);                       ❻ Return concatenated
    @this.Emit(OpCodes.Ldloc_0);                      property values
    @this.Emit(OpCodes.Callvirt, toStringMethod);
  }
  else
  {
    @this.Emit(OpCodes.Ldstr, string.Empty);
  }

  @this.Emit(OpCodes.Ret);
}
```

As before, you need to get a list of public properties on the target object ❶. If there are any, you create a local StringBuilder variable via DeclareLocal() ❷. Then you create a new StringBuilder via newobj and store that with stloc.0 ❸. Every time you want to add an opcode to your method, you call Emit(). It has a bunch of overloads to let you specify certain values, such as which constructor you want to call on StringBuilder.

Next, you get a reference to the Append() method on StringBuilder. This MethodInfo object ❹ is used every time you want to specify a call to Append() in the IL stream. That's handled in CreatePropertyForToString()—we'll come back to this method. Once you've created all the code to print the properties and their values ⑤, you clear the stack via the pop opcode. Finally, you load the local `StringBuilder`, call `ToString()` on that, and return with a `ret` opcode ⑥.

The following listing shows how the property information is added to the dynamic method.

---

**Listing 5.7   Adding property information to a dynamic method**

```
private static void CreatePropertyForToString(ILGenerator generator,
  PropertyInfo property, MethodInfo appendMethod,
  bool needsSeparator)
{
  if(property.CanRead)
  {
    generator.Emit(OpCodes.Ldstr, property.Name + ": ");          ❶ Get property name
    generator.Emit(OpCodes.Callvirt, appendMethod);               ❷ Append property name
    generator.Emit(OpCodes.Ldarg_0);                              ❸ Load object reference

    var propertyGet = property.GetGetMethod();

    generator.Emit(propertyGet.IsVirtual ?                        ❹ Call getter correctly
      OpCodes.Callvirt : OpCodes.Call,
      propertyGet);

    var appendTyped = typeof(StringBuilder).GetMethod("Append",
      new Type[] { propertyGet.ReturnType });

    if(appendTyped.GetParameters()[0].ParameterType !=
      propertyGet.ReturnType)
    {
      if(propertyGet.ReturnType.IsValueType)
      {                                                           ❺ Add property value
        generator.Emit(OpCodes.Box, propertyGet.ReturnType);
      }
    }

    generator.Emit(OpCodes.Callvirt, appendTyped);

    if(needsSeparator)
    {                                                             ❻ Add value separator
      generator.Emit(OpCodes.Ldstr, Constants.Separator);
      generator.Emit(OpCodes.Callvirt, appendMethod);
    }
  }
}
```

---

For each readable property, you get its name and put that on the stack via `ldstr` ❶. Then you append it to the `StringBuilder` by invoking `Append()`—this is what the `callvirt` opcode is for ❷. Now you need to get the property's value. Recall that if you ever call a method on an object, you need to push the object on the stack first—that's what `ldarg.0` does ❸. Then you either invoke the getter via a `callvirt` or `call` opcode depending on whether the method is virtual or not ❹. Now you put the property's value in the `StringBuilder`. Figure out what the best `Append()` overload match is for the property's type (emitting a `box` opcode if the property is a value type) and

use `callvirt` on that specific `Append()` call ❺. If you need to add a double-pipe separator between one property value and the next property name, you emit two opcodes:
`ldstr` and `callvirt` ❻.

**INVOKING THE NEW METHOD**

Now that the method implementation is done, you need to "bake" the `TypeBuilder` to
make it a full-fledged type and then get the method you created off the new type. The
following code snippet (which finishes the class definition from listing 5.3 and the code
snippets in the "Creating a type" and "Adding opcodes" subsections in section 5.4.1)
shows how you do this:

```
var createdType = type.CreateType();

var createdMethod = createdType.GetMethod(methodName);
return (Func<T, string>)Delegate.CreateDelegate(
  typeof(Func<T, string>), createdMethod);
}
}
```

You call `CreateType()` and then find the method with the familiar `GetMethod()` call.
The last line of code may seem a bit odd—what's this `Delegate.CreateDelegate()`
call for? That allows you to use the method you created as a `Func<T, string>`, which is
somewhat easier than trying to use a `MethodInfo`. Furthermore, it gives you an easy
way to cache the method for future invocations. The following listing closes out the
discussion by showing the extension method that creates the dynamic code and
caches the resulting `Func<T, string>`.

**Listing 5.8 Extension method to create the dynamic method**

```
public static class ToStringViaReflectionEmitExtensions
{
  private static Lazy<ReflectionEmitMethodGenerator> generator =
    new Lazy<ReflectionEmitMethodGenerator>();
  private static Dictionary<Type, Delegate> methods =
    new Dictionary<Type, Delegate>();

  internal static string ToStringReflectionEmit<T>(this T @this)
  {
    var targetType = @this.GetType();

    if(!ToStringViaReflectionEmitExtensions.methods.ContainsKey(
      targetType))
    {
      ToStringViaReflectionEmitExtensions.methods.Add(
        targetType,
        ToStringViaReflectionEmitExtensions.generator
          .Value.Generate<T>());
    }

    return (ToStringViaReflectionEmitExtensions.methods[
      targetType] as Func<T, string>)(@this);
  }
}
```

At this point, everything is in place. To implement the `ToString()` method dynamically, all you need to do is this:

```
public override string ToString()
{
  return this.ToStringReflectionEmit();
}
```

That's it! You've created dynamic code on the fly that's adaptive to any object's structure. Although it's not a trivial amount of code to write, once you have it in place, all it takes is one method call to create a rich yet terse description of any object with code that will execute quickly.

Living this close to the CLR metal has its pitfalls. It's easy to create incorrect code that will fail in bizarre ways or cause an exception to be thrown. Let's see how you can debug your code so you can handle the first pitfall.

### 5.4.2   *Adding debugging support*

One nice feature about Reflection.Emit is that it can create debugging information on the fly, allowing you to step into the debugger and see how your dynamic code is working. The code samples for this book have a modified version of `ReflectionEmitMethod-Generator` called `ReflectionEmitWithDebuggingMethodGenerator`—the only difference between these two classes is how debugging is enabled in the second one. Let's focus on these differences so you can see what it takes to create the necessary debugging data.

The first thing to do is add an attribute to your dynamic assembly so the CLR knows that your assembly has been created with debugging symbols. The following listing contains this attribute code—it creates a `DebuggableAttribute` with the necessary values and adds it to the new assembly.

> **Listing 5.9   Adding a debugging attribute to your dynamic assembly**

```
private void AddDebuggingAttribute(AssemblyBuilder assembly)
{
  var debugAttribute = typeof(DebuggableAttribute);
  var debugConstructor = debugAttribute.GetConstructor(
    new Type[] { typeof(DebuggableAttribute.DebuggingModes) });
  var debugBuilder = new CustomAttributeBuilder(
    debugConstructor, new object[] {
      DebuggableAttribute.DebuggingModes.DisableOptimizations |
      DebuggableAttribute.DebuggingModes.Default });
  assembly.SetCustomAttribute(debugBuilder);
}
```

> **NOTE**   You can learn more about the technical reasons why you need this attribute at http://mng.bz/18Q7 and http://mng.bz/aSg7.

Now you need to create your module such that it'll create debugging information. This is as simple as calling a different version of `DefineDynamicModule()`:

```
this.Module = this.Assembly.DefineDynamicModule(
  this.Name.Name + ".dll", true);
```

The key part is the second parameter, which is a Boolean value. By passing in `true`, you're telling the `ModuleBuilder` to emit symbol information.

Next, tell the `ModuleBuilder` of the files you'll use to associate debug symbol information for. These files are code files, like .cs files. Unfortunately, there's nothing in Reflection.Emit that will create an .il file for you that matches the opcodes you emit, so you have to handle this manually. That's not as hard as it seems—you'll see how to do it on the fly shortly. For now, here's how you create that dynamic document:

```
var fileName = target.Name + "ToString.il";
var document = this.Module.DefineDocument(fileName,
    SymDocumentType.Text, SymLanguageType.ILAssembly,
    SymLanguageVendor.Microsoft);
```

This doesn't create the file; you're making your module aware that you're going to use this file for debugging. The three enumeration values have different options depending on the code you've created, or you call an overload of `DefineDocument()` that takes the filename if you don't care about these options.

Now comes the fun part. You need to align specific areas within a code file with the opcodes you emit in your method. In this example, you create that file and pass it into the helper `Generate()` method:

```
using(var file = File.CreateText(fileName))
{
    method.GetILGenerator().Generate(target, document, file);
}
```

There are three things that you can do with methods and debugging. The first is you can add descriptive information to your parameters, like a name. You do that by calling `DefineParameter()` on your `MethodBuilder`:

```
method.DefineParameter(1, ParameterAttributes.In, "target");
```

The second thing is adding descriptive information to your local variables. Do that by calling `SetLocalSymInfo()` on the `LocalBuilder` you get after calling `DeclareLocal()`:

```
toStringLocal.SetLocalSymInfo("builder");
```

The third thing is the interesting part. You can mark points in your code file to match a corresponding set of opcodes. You do that by calling `MarkSequencePoint()` on your `ILGenerator`. Again, there's no .il file to speak of when you create code on the fly with Reflection.Emit, but it's pretty easy to create a pseudo-.il code file based on the opcode you're emitting. The next listing shows an extension method in the sample code that handles the sequence point details. This extension method is for opcodes that do something with a string (like `ldstr`)—the sample code has other extension methods to handle opcodes that call methods and use types.

**Listing 5.10  Marking sequence points in a dynamic code file**

```
internal static void Emit(this ILGenerator @this,
    OpCode opcode, string value,
```

```
    ISymbolDocumentWriter document,
    StreamWriter file, int lineNumber)
{
    var line = opcode.Name + " \"" + value + "\"";
    file.WriteLine(line);
    @this.MarkSequencePoint(document, lineNumber,
        1, lineNumber, line.Length + 1);
    @this.Emit(opcode, value);
}
```

You create a line of IL and add it to the text file. Then, you inform the `ILGenerator` that a debugger should highlight that new code line for any following opcodes added by an `Emit()` call with `MarkSequencePoint()`.

Once you've emitted all your debugging content, you now have the ability to step into the code you generated to see how it works. Figure 5.5 is a screen shot of Visual Studio with the new .il file loaded.

You can see that the code is highlighted correctly. You can also see that the name of the argument and the local variable is displayed as well. Being able to debug IL like this is extremely powerful. The more you use Reflection.Emit, the more you'll be thankful that you can do something like this.

Debugging isn't the only tool you can use to ensure your code is correct. In the next section, you'll see how verification comes in handy with dynamic code.

### 5.4.3   *Verifying results with peverify*

It's one thing to have a logical error in your code, such as incrementing a value instead of decrementing it. Those can lead to odd errors, but generally they're not too hard to track down. What happens if you emit a set of opcodes that leads to a method implementation that, well, doesn't make any sense? Let's say you had the following two opcodes in a static method that didn't take any arguments and returned a string:

```
ldstr "Some value"
ret
```

That makes sense. A string is pushed onto the stack and then it's popped off as it becomes the return value. But what happens if you forget the `ldstr` opcode? Now all you have is this:

```
ret
```

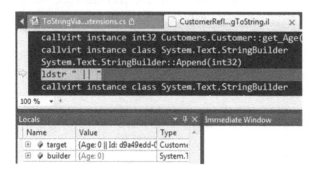

Figure 5.5   Debugging dynamic code in .NET. By creating an IL file on the fly with debug information, you can step into your newly created code.

**Figure 5.6 Using peverify on an assembly with errors. Any metadata and opcode error will show up from its analysis.**

What does your code do in this case? The Emitter classes will happily create a method like that, but when you try to execute that method, you'll get an `InvalidProgram-Exception`. Sometimes you may get some really strange results, depending on what's wrong with the method implementation. No matter what the results are, you'd really like to know as soon as possible that your code is incorrect.

There is hope. .NET comes with a tool called peverify.exe that can verify the metadata and implementation of the code within an assembly. It's a command-line tool that can take in a number of arguments, though you'll usually stick with two: `/md`, which tells peverify to look for metadata errors, and `/il`, which asks peverify to find implementation problems. Peverify can't find logical errors in your code, but it can find that nasty IL error you saw earlier in this section. Figure 5.6 shows what the results of peverify look like. You can see that it reports an IL error—here's the specific text of the issue: `Return value missing on the stack`.

The problem with peverify is that it's a command-line tool. You can't reference a peverify.dll assembly in your code and tell it to verify an assembly you created. But we've created an assembly that executes peverify.exe for you underneath the scenes. It's called AssemblyVerifier, and all you need to do is reference this assembly and add the following lines of code:

```
assembly.Save(name.Name + ".dll");
AssemblyVerification.Verify(assembly);
```

You have to save your dynamic assembly to disk for this to work, so you also need to make sure you define the dynamic assembly with the `AssemblyBuilderAccess.RunAnd-Save` value. If peverify finds any issues with your code, `AssemblyVerification` parses the console output and transforms the information into a `VerificationException`, where you can see all the scific errors in the `Errors` property.

**NOTE** You can get AssemblyVerifier via NuGet. To get the source code, visit http://assemblyverifier.codeplex.com.

Before we move on to another dynamic code generation option, let's go over ways to make using the Emit APIs a bit easier for you.

### 5.4.4   *Using ILDasm to cheat*

Unless you write .il files on a day-to-day basis, or you're deep into the Reflection.Emit API all the time, using opcodes isn't going to be high on your skills list. As much as we love metaprogramming and generating code, emitting opcodes can be tricky, even if you're good at it. But you really don't have to be good at all—you need to know how to cheat.

Recall in section 2.4.2 that there was a hard-coded version created of `ToString()` in C#. To emulate that code in Reflection.Emit, you can use the tools already at your disposal. First, compile the code as you normally would. Then, load the assembly with ILDasm and navigate to the code you'd like to reproduce. For example, this is what some of the IL looks like for the C# version of `ToString()`:

```
IL_0000:  newobj  instance void
  [mscorlib]System.Text.StringBuilder::.ctor()
IL_0005:  ldstr "Age: "
IL_000a:  call instance class
  [mscorlib]System.Text.StringBuilder
  [mscorlib]System.Text.StringBuilder::Append(string)
IL_000f:  ldarg.0
IL_0010:  call instance int32 Customers.Customer::get_Age()
IL_0015:  callvirt instance class
  [mscorlib]System.Text.StringBuilder
  [mscorlib]System.Text.StringBuilder::Append(int32)
IL_001a:  ldstr " || "
IL_001f:  callvirt instance class
  [mscorlib]System.Text.StringBuilder
  [mscorlib]System.Text.StringBuilder::Append(string)
```

In listings 5.6 and 5.7, you should be able to see the similarities. That's because we based our Emit-based code on the IL we saw in ILDasm. It's much easier to implement what you want to do in a language like C# or VB. By stealing what the compilers are already creating for you, you can minimize the amount of time it takes to write verifiable dynamic code that works the way you expect it to.

> **NOTE**  Sometimes the compiler will emit nop, or no operation, opcodes. This is usually done by a compiler for debugging purposes when it wants to align breakpoints in your code. There's no need for you to reproduce those in Emit-based code—you can happily ignore them when you following this cheating technique.

You now know how to create code on the fly with the classes in Reflection.Emit. But that's not the only option available. The next section covers another dynamic option that has certain advantages over Reflection.Emit.

> **Creating dynamic proxies**
>
> If you want to explore deeper into what the Emit API can provide, please check out the DynamicProxies (http://dynamicproxies.codeplex.com) and EmitDebugger (http://emitdebugger.codeplex.com) projects. EmitDebugger wraps the Emit classes to automatically create an IL file with breakpoints for dynamic code. DynamicProxies create proxy classes on the fly so you can intercept virtual method calls on a class (visit http://en.wikipedia.org/wiki/Proxy_pattern for more information on the proxy pattern).
>
> As you can imagine, this isn't a simple thing to do because you have to be concerned about a number of issues, such as by-reference arguments, generics, and interface implementation on a class.
>
> Note that DynamicProxies uses EmitDebugger to give you the ability to debug your proxy classes—quite a nice feature to have.

## 5.5 *Lightweight code generation with dynamic methods*

Another IL-based code emitting technique uses a class called `DynamicMethod`. This class generates methods for you at runtime. Let's cover the reasons why you'd use this over Reflection.Emit and then demonstrate how you'd use it by revisiting the `ToString()` example from section 2.4.2 using `DynamicMethod`.

### 5.5.1 *When creating an assembly is too much*

There are two disadvantages to Reflection.Emit when it comes to generating code at runtime. The first issue is the complexity, or *heaviness* of the Emit approach. If all you need is to create a small piece of code, you have to create a dynamic assembly, module, and type to create a method. For most of the dynamic code we've seen, most only need a method created, making this approach somewhat cumbersome. Granted, there are times where you need to generate a complete assembly (or at least a type, as in the case of creating a dynamic proxy), but otherwise a more lightweight approach is what you want.

The other (more concerning) issue is memory pressure. When you create a dynamic assembly, that assembly is loaded into the domain you created it from, which is usually the default `AppDomain`. The problem is that you can't unload assemblies directly; the only way to unload an assembly from memory is to call `Unload()` on the `AppDomain` the assembly is in. This is probably something you don't want to do on your default `AppDomain`! You can circumvent this by creating dynamic assemblies in other `AppDomains` you create, but that's not a trivial task. As you create more and more dynamic assemblies, your memory will grow and grow, and if you're not careful, you'll run into memory issues.

> **NOTE**  With 4.0, it's possible to mark a dynamic assembly as unloadable by using the AssemblyBuilderAccess.RunAndCollect value when you create the assembly. This will unload the assembly if needed, which is a big benefit from a memory pressure perspective. This isn't a foolproof solution, as you must

adhere to a number of restrictions to ensure that the associated memory with the dynamic assembly is released, although these restrictions probably won't affect most of the scenarios you'll run into as a developer. Visit http://mng.bz/mK5M for more information on these restrictions.

With a `DynamicMethod`, you don't incur the entire API overhead to create dynamic code. All you have, once `DynamicMethod` is done, is a method that you can invoke like any other method (more or less). And the nice thing about a `DynamicMethod` is that it's garbage collectable by default. Therefore, once you're done using a `Dynamic-Method`, you don't have to worry about memory piling up. The GC will happily get rid of it for you once it's determined that it's no longer used.

Now that you know what the basic differences between Reflection.Emit and `Dynamic-Method` are, let's see how you can use this class to create a method at runtime.

### 5.5.2  *Creating shim methods*

Let's revisit the `ToString()` example you saw in section 2.4.2. Instead of using reflection, let's generate a method that will create the descriptive string for you at runtime. Remember that the goal is to take all of the public, instance-level, readable properties on an object and concatenate them together. As with the `CustomerReflection` class, let's create a `CustomerDynamicMethod` class that will defer the implementation of `ToString()` to a helper extension method:

```
public sealed class CustomerDynamicMethod : Customer
{
  public override string ToString()
  {
    return this.ToStringDynamicMethod();
  }
}
```

The implementation of `ToStringDynamicMethod()` is similar to the code in listing 5.6. If the `DynamicMethod` doesn't exist for a given type, it's created and added to a `Dictionary<Type, Delegate>` field. The method creation is in a method called `Create-ToStringViaDynamicMethod()`—its implementation is shown in the following listing. As you can see, there's really not much to it: you create your dynamic method, add opcodes, and create a delegate.

**Listing 5.11  Creating dynamic code with `DynamicMethod`**

```
private static Func<T, string> CreateToStringViaDynamicMethod<T>()
{
  var target = typeof(T);

  var toString = new DynamicMethod(
    "ToString" + target.GetHashCode().ToString(),
    typeof(string), new Type[] { target });

  toString.GetILGenerator().Generate(target);
  return (Func<T, string>)toString.CreateDelegate(
```

```
        typeof(Func<T, string>));
}
```

The `DynamicMethod` constructor is similar to the `DefineMethod()` method on a `Type-Builder`. You provide a method name, the type of the return value, and the types of the parameters (if you have any). Once you have the `DynamicMethod`, you get an `ILGenerator` via `GetILGenerator()`. Hey, guess what? You can reuse the `Generate()` extension method from the code snippet in the "Creating the type" subsection of section 5.4.1, because it's the *exact* same opcode generation. The final step is to turn the method into a delegate, and then you're done.

As you can see, when all you need to create is a method, the `DynamicMethod` approach is the way to go over Reflection.Emit. You still need to emit the opcodes, but you don't have to create the builder classes to get there.

### 5.5.3  *Using caching for performance*

In both the Reflection.Emit and `DynamicMethod` implementations, a collection (specifically, a dictionary) was used to store the dynamic code artifacts once they were created. This is an extremely important technique to use when you create dynamic code if you can. Once you've created the necessary `ToString()` code, you don't need to keep recreating it because the type definition won't change for the lifetime of the application. In fact, if you don't cache the dynamic code, your performance will suffer greatly. Figure 5.7 is a chart that shows the relative performance of all the techniques you've seen in this chapter and chapter 2 to implement `ToString()` in a reusable fashion.

The performance among all five approaches is relative. The Reflection.Emit is the fastest of them all (even faster than the hard-coded approach!). Reflection is more than 10 times worse than Reflection.Emit. But if you turn off caching by removing the collection, things get really, really bad for dynamic code. Figure 5.8 shows the adjusted

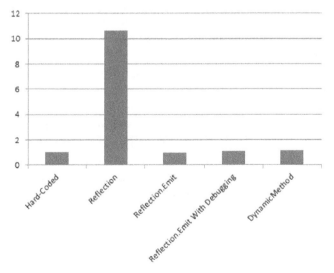

**Figure 5.7   Relative performance of dynamic coding techniques. As expected, reflection is the slowest of them all.**

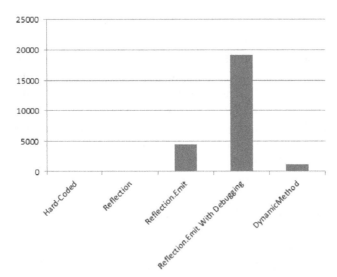

**Figure 5.8    Removing caching from dynamic code. Without caching, your solution may have performance issues, so cache dynamic results whenever possible.**

values with no caching, and it's painfully clear that you must have a caching strategy in place when you create dynamic code.

Without caching, Reflection.Emit becomes 4000 times worse than the hard-coded approach. Add debugging information, and performance dive-bombs. The message is clear: cache your dynamic code results whenever possible.

### 5.5.4    Disadvantages of DynamicMethod

There are disadvantages to `DynamicMethod`: debugging and verifiability. With `Dynamic-Method`, there's no way to generate debug information on the fly like you can with the Reflection.Emit classes. Therefore, you can't *step into* the code you generate in `Dynamic-icMethod`. The other problem is verification of code. Section 5.4.3 mentions a tool called peverify.exe to ensure that the code you generate with Reflection.Emit is correct. But peverify only works with assemblies, not specific methods. This means you don't have a way to ensure the code in the dynamic method is verifiable.

There's one way around this using dependency injection. Here's how it works. You create an interface that will have two implementations: one that uses `DynamicMethod` and one that uses Reflection.Emit. The interface defines a method that will return a `Func` or an `Action` that's dynamically created by the concrete class. During debugging and testing, you can use the version that uses Reflection.Emit, so you can verify the code and debug it using the techniques described in this chapter. Once you're confident things are working as expected, you can move over to the `DynamicMethod` implementation. Either way, you don't care how the dynamic code was created.

Let's use real code to crystalize this approach. First, here's the interface:

```
public interface IToStringBuilder
{
    string ToString<T>(T target);
}
```

Now, create two implementations of this interface. The following listing shows the two concrete classes. They use the examples from sections 5.4.1 and 5.5.2, so there's not much to them.

**Listing 5.12  Concrete implementations of `IToStringBuilder`**

```
public sealed class ToStringDynamicMethodBuilder
  : IToStringBuilder
{
  public string ToString<T>(T target)
  {
    return target.ToStringDynamicMethod();
  }
}
public sealed class ToStringReflectionEmitBuilder
  : IToStringBuilder
{
  public string ToString<T>(T target)
  {
    return target.ToStringReflectionEmit();
  }
}
```

Here's where the flexibility of this approach becomes apparent. You create a version of `Customer` that takes a reference to an `IToStringBuilder` on construction:

```
public sealed class CustomerDependencyInjected
  : Customer
{
  public CustomerDependencyInjected(IToStringBuilder builder)
    : base()
  {
    this.Builder = builder;
  }
  public override string ToString()
  {
    return this.Builder.ToString(this);
  }

    private IToStringBuilder Builder { get; set; }
}
```

The `ToString()` method gets its return value from the builder injected into it. This gives you an easy way to swap out your two approaches. When you create this version of a customer, you specify which dynamic code builder you want to use:

```
new CustomerDependencyInjected(
  new ToStringDynamicMethodBuilder())
```

If you started to run into problems with your code generation, you swap out the concrete class for one that you can debug and verify:

```
new CustomerDependencyInjected(
  new ToStringReflectionEmitBuilder())
```

**NOTE** There's one way to see what the IL is that you generate in a `Dynamic-Method` via a debugging visualizer. Visit http://mng.bz/j4s9 for more on how to do this. You can also debug `DynamicMethod` via WinDBG, but that's not a trivial endeavor. All the details you need to know to get this to work can be found at http://mng.bz/1s3m.

## 5.6   *Summary*

In this chapter, you saw the strength behind the Reflection.Emit APIs to generate code at runtime. You learned about the opcodes that are the foundation for every .NET language and how they're used to define and structure your implementations. You found powerful techniques to debug your dynamic code to ensure its correctness. You discovered two different options in this API and the situations where one should be used over the other. With this newfound information, you now have a number of tools available to you to generate code at runtime for scenarios mentioned in section 5.2. Need a new type to act as an intermediary of an object, or a mock of a type? Generate one with the Emitter classes. Want to optimize a call path that's determined at runtime? Build a dynamic method. Want to create a compiler for a language you've created? You can use the Emitter classes for that. Any time you have the need to generate code at runtime, System.Reflection.Emit is your friend.

Although generating code using opcodes is extremely powerful, there's yet another way in .NET to perform such creations using a higher-level API that's arguably easier to comprehend, yet as powerful as raw opcode usage. This technique uses something called *expressions*, and that's what the next chapter is all about.

# Generating code
# with expressions

**This chapter covers**

- Using code as data
- Using the power of expression trees
- Improving code with expressions

As you saw in chapter 5, you can use the Reflection.Emit APIs to create dynamic code that you can execute at runtime. This requires intimate knowledge of IL. Let's be honest: learning IL isn't a skill set that most .NET developers have, nor is it one they necessarily want to acquire, even if they're interested in metaprogramming techniques. The reason is simple: writing code in IL can easily lead to incorrect implementations and requires a mental model of code execution in .NET that's not as intuitive as the one a high-level language provides.

Fortunately, there's another API in .NET that lets you create code without having to know anything about IL. This is the Expression API that exists within the LINQ world. In this chapter, you'll see how you can view your code as data in a way that will make metaprogramming much easier to do in .NET. When something is easier to accomplish, you end up using it more, which is why learning about expressions to generate dynamic code is advantageous. You'll end up seeing scenarios in your code where you can use expressions to handle certain problems elegantly. Let's start by looking at how expressions work at a higher level.

## 6.1     Expression-oriented programming

This section covers how expressions work and why they're so desirable in the world of metaprogramming. In essence, *expressions* are a representation of code via a data structure, and you'll see how you can use this representation (coding structures as data) effectively and the flexibility you gain with this view.

### 6.1.1   Understanding code as data

In chapter 1 we spent a fair amount of time defining metaprogramming. You may recall that section "Creating IL at runtime using expression trees" (a part of section 1.2.3) gave a high-level overview of expressions. After that overview, you saw metaprogramming techniques in action that were at the lower level of IL. That gave you a solid (and we think necessary) understanding of the inner workings of .NET, but more often than not, you don't need to write code in IL. You're finally going to come back to expressions, the focus of this chapter. Although that section gave a good overview of expressions, it's time to narrow the discussion to a discrete example that you'll use as a starting point into how expressions work in .NET.

Consider the following function:

```
public int Add(int x, int y)
{
    return x + y;
}
```

Writing this as an expression in .NET isn't too hard—you'll see an example of this momentarily. But consider this nomenclature:

```
(+ x y)
```

If you've spent any time even glossing over the Lisp language, you know where this line of code comes from. Even if you've never seen Lisp before, you probably could guess that this code is taking two variables and adding them together. There's a big reason why you're seeing a little bit of Lisp at this point, because at its core Lisp is all about expressions. For example:

```
(1 2 add)
```

This is a list in Lisp that contains three atoms: 1, 2, and *add*. Note that there's no difference in the formatting between a list and how the add operator works. They're both expressions. Code and data are both expressed the same way. This arrangement allows you to handle a function as if it were a data structure, which allows tremendous flexibility for a developer to modify and alter code in a fairly natural way. If you write your code in IL, there's no natural way to modify that code in the same way you'd modify a list of items. If you can treat your code like data, it becomes more natural to modify code as you would modify data. That's why a concept like expressions has been around for so long. This flexibility can also give rise to some mind-bending implementations, but we'll keep our dive into Lisp at this more moderate level for now.

**NOTE** Lisp is one of the oldest programming languages and is considered to be the source and inspiration for many ideas you probably take for granted in many languages, such as trees and self-hosted compilers, among other things. We don't expect you to become proficient in Lisp in any fashion—we're not even remotely close to being Lisp experts ourselves—but spending some time learning a little about Lisp is always a good thing. You can find out more about Lisp from http://landoflisp.com. Also, *The Joy of Clojure* by Amit Rathore (Manning, 2011) covers a fairly recent language called Clojure that's heavily influenced by Lisp. Check out http://manning.com/rathore/.

How would you take the add C# function you saw in the beginning of this section and turn it into an expression? Like this:

```
Expression<Func<int, int, int>> add = (x, y) => x + y;
```

That's not as concise as the Lisp syntax, but that's how it works in C#. The add variable after this point is a lambda expression. It's not a function you can execute. In fact, if you tried to write this

```
Expression<Func<int, int, int>> add = (x, y) => x + y;
var result = add(2, 3);
```

you'd get a compiler error stating that you're trying to use add, which is a variable, like a method, which it isn't. It's an expression tree at this point. To execute this code, you need to do this:

```
Expression<Func<int, int, int>> add = (x, y) => x + y;
var result = add.Compile()(2, 3);
```

The Compile() method takes the expression tree and turns it into something that the runtime can execute—namely, IL. Figure 6.1 shows what the tree looks like from a logical perspective.

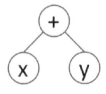

**Figure 6.1  A logical representation of an expression that adds two parameters. As you can see, IL is nowhere to be found because you're focusing on the structure of the implementation, not the opcodes to do it.**

Notice that you don't ever see any IL when you use an expression, and frankly, that's a good thing. Knowing intimate details of IL isn't necessarily bad because it can yield great insight into the inner workings of .NET. However, coding in IL can lead to some unintended results if you're not extremely careful. Using expressions is much more natural.

Unfortunately, you can't create an expression at runtime using the "fat arrow" syntax: =>. You'll see more details on the Expression API in this chapter, but the following is a code snippet that does the same thing as the lambda expression syntax—the only difference is it uses the Expression API explicitly:

```
var x = Expression.Parameter(typeof(int));
var y = Expression.Parameter(typeof(int));

return (Expression.Lambda(
   Expression.Add(x, y), x, y)
      .Compile() as Func<int, int, int>)(2, 3);
```

This may seem a little verbose, but look at the next code snippet that does the same thing in IL:

```
var method = new DynamicMethod("m",
    typeof(int), new Type[] { typeof(int), typeof(int) });
var x = method.DefineParameter(
    1, ParameterAttributes.In, "x");
var y = method.DefineParameter(
    1, ParameterAttributes.In, "y");
var generator = method.GetILGenerator();
generator.Emit(OpCodes.Ldarg_0);
generator.Emit(OpCodes.Ldarg_1);
generator.Emit(OpCodes.Add);
generator.Emit(OpCodes.Ret);
return (method.CreateDelegate(
    typeof(Func<int, int, int>))
    as Func<int, int, int>)(2, 3);
```

In our opinion, the first approach is easier to read and more succinct. Imagine if you had to write all your dynamic code this way. Yes, you could do it, but using less code that does the same thing seems like a better approach.

Later in this chapter you'll use this API extensively to create code that will create different code based on that code at runtime. The next section gives an example of a popular .NET assembly that uses expressions to simplify method resolution.

### Why can't I use var for my expressions?

You may have noticed that the code snippets in this section use an explicit type declaration for the lambda expression. Here's why. If you typed this

```
var expression = (x, y) => x + y;
```

did you mean this?

```
Func<int, int, int> expression = (x, y) => x + y;
```

or this?

```
Expression<Func<int, int, int>> expression =
    (x, y) => x + y;
```

Without explicit typing, the compiler can't tell which one you mean, and there's a difference. A Func or an Action type turns into an anonymous method in your code once the compiler is done, but an expression resolves into API calls that you'll see in section 6.2.

To find out more gory details about when the var keyword can't be used in C# check out the two articles at http://mng.bz/1OD0 and http://mng.bz/56bw.

### 6.1.2  *Expressions take metaprogramming mainstream*

You may be thinking, "Great, expressions are awesome and expressive and wonderful, but where in the world would I use this in my code?" At first glance, it may seem like you'd never use expressions in your code base (though if you're reading this book, you might). But a lot of .NET-based frameworks out there use expressions to some degree or another. One in particular is Component-based Scalable Logical Architecture (CSLA), which is a business object framework. Our intent isn't to go over every aspect of CSLA in this section; rather, you're going to see how CSLA uses expressions under the hood.

If you've ever used CSLA, you're familiar with the object creation convention through the `DataPortal` class. You don't make an instance of an object directly; you let the portal create it for you. The following code listing demonstrates how you could fetch data for a `Person` object via an identifier typed as a `Guid`.

**Listing 6.1  Fetching data for an object in CSLA**

```
[Serializable]
public sealed class Person
  : BusinessBase<Person>
{
  private Person()
    : base() { }

  public static Person Fetch(Guid id)
  {
    return DataPortal.Fetch<Person>(id);
  }

  private void DataPortal_Fetch(Guid id)
  {
    // ...
  }
}
```

You usually create a static `Fetch()` method that takes all the values it needs for a successful lookup. You pass those values into the `Fetch()` method from the `DataPortal`. The `DataPortal` creates an instance of the target specified by the generic parameter value and then looks for a `DataPortal_Fetch` method that has a parameter with the right type. In this case, there's a method that takes a `Guid`, so everything will work out.

> **NOTE** If your static `Fetch()` method takes multiple parameters, you have to pack those up into one criteria object. Using a `Tuple` makes that relatively painless.

CSLA is using a bit of reflection to resolve the call. It's going to do something like this:

```
var method = typeof(T).GetMethod(
  "DataPortal_Fetch",
  BindingFlags.Public | BindingFlags.NonPublic |
    BindingFlags.DeclaredOnly | BindingFlags.Instance,
  null,
  new Type[] { criteria.GetType() }, null)
```

The exact implementation in CSLA is more involved than this, but it boils down to a method lookup via reflection. Once CSLA knows the method exists, it then creates a method dynamically at runtime to figure out the call flow and caches this in memory. In chapter 5 (section 5.5.3), you saw the benefit of keeping dynamic methods around once they're created, which is why CSLA does this. But CSLA doesn't use `DynamicMethod`; it uses the Expression API to create this new method. When CSLA was first created for .NET, it initially used reflection exclusively, and once `DynamicMethod` was introduced, CSLA switched over to that for performance reasons. But the Expressions API produces code with the same performance characteristics without requiring the developer to understand IL, which is why CSLA uses the Expression API for method invocation scenarios like `DataPortal_Fetch`.

> **TIP**  CSLA is available in Nuget. Download the source code from www.lhotka
> .net/cslanet/Download.aspx. If you're interested in seeing how CSLA uses the
> Expression API, take a look at the `DynamicMethodHandlerFactory` class.

Now that you've had a high-level overview of expressions and where they exist in the .NET world, let's take a look at the mechanics of expressions. You'll start by seeing why expressions exist in a sub-namespace of LINQ.

## 6.2    *Making dynamic methods with LINQ Expressions*

As you've already seen in this chapter, you can use expressions to create methods on the fly. In this section, you'll dive deeper into this API to see what's possible with expression creation in .NET, including the following:

- Creating and calling methods
- Using mathematical operations
- Adding exception handlers
- Controlling the flow of code

Before we do that, let's start by looking at why LINQ is even in the picture with expressions.

### 6.2.1    *Understanding LINQ Expressions*

At first glance, for the Expression API to reside in the `System.Linq.Expressions` namespace may seem odd. What does LINQ have to do with expressions anyway? The best way to see how expressions are used in .NET is to write some LINQ, decompile it, and look at the results.

The following listing shows a simple LINQ query that finds objects with property values that contain the character a.

**Listing 6.2  Using LINQ to filter a list of objects**

```
public sealed class Container
{
  public string Value { get; set; }
}

// ...
```

```
var containers = new Container[]
{
  new Container { Value = "bag" },
  new Container { Value = "bed" },
  new Container { Value = "car" }
};

var filteredResults =
  from container in containers
  where container.Value.Contains("a")
  select container;
```

There's nothing fancy going on here—you're using a where clause to filter the list. Let's say your filtering was more complex and dynamic based on a user's choices in the application. The user may want, for example, to find the Container objects where the Value property contains a and is between 3 and 10 characters long. You could write this LINQ statement with no issues, but that would be hardcoded at compile-time. There's no way for you to change that query with the familiar LINQ techniques most .NET developers are aware of. But if you're knowledgeable with expressions, you can change the filter on the fly. Let's change the filter from listing 6.2 to use an expression, shown in the following listing.

**Listing 6.3  Using a LINQ expression to create the filter**

```
var argument = Expression.Parameter(typeof(Container));
var valueProperty = Expression.Property(argument, "Value");
var containsCall = Expression.Call(valueProperty,
  typeof(string).GetMethod(
    "Contains", new Type[] { typeof(string) }),
  Expression.Constant("a", typeof(string)));
var wherePredicate = Expression.Lambda<Func<Container, bool>>(
  containsCall, argument);
var whereCall = Expression.Call(typeof(Queryable), "Where",
  new Type[] { typeof(Container) },
  containers.AsQueryable().Expression, wherePredicate);

var expressionResults = containers.AsQueryable()
  .Provider.CreateQuery<Container>(whereCall);
```

You need an IQueryable object reference to start out, which is what the AsQueryable() extension method is for. Then, you use the Provider property to call the CreateQuery() method. That method takes an expression that can do pretty much whatever you want it to do to the queryable object. The next section explains the details about the creation of this expression in detail, but for now it's sufficient to take away the fact that you can create dynamic LINQ queries at runtime via the Expression API.

At this point, it's time (finally!) to go over the API within System.Linq.Expression. You'll start by going over the expression created in listing 6.3, one part at a time.

**Using DynamicQueryable**

Buried within the sample that comes with an installation of Visual Studio lies a hidden namespace gem called `System.Linq.Dynamic`, which contains a class called `DynamicQueryable` (among many other interesting classes). This class allows you to write your dynamic query via a small piece of code rather than explicitly using the Expression API. The code in listing 6.3 is reduced to one line of code with `DynamicQueryable`:

```
var dynamicResults = containers.AsQueryable()
  .Where("Value.Contains(\"a\")");
```

For more information on how to use this cool API, see http://mng.bz/KN7v.

### 6.2.2  *Generating expressions at runtime*

This section examines the classes and methods you use to create dynamic expressions. The API surface is quite extensive, so we focus on the common activities you'll do when creating an expression. You'll also see how you can use other features in the Expression API to create rich implementations in your expressions.

#### CREATING A SIMPLE LAMBDA EXPRESSION

Listing 6.3 created an expression to perform a dynamic query on a simple data set. The query was the same as writing this line of code:

```
where container.Value.Contains("a")
```

This is the same as writing the following line of code (which is what the C# compiler will do with the previous LINQ statement, more or less):

```
containers.Where(value => value.Value.Contains("a"))
```

Let's go through each line of code in listing 6.3 to see how the expression translates into the exact same line of code that invokes the `Where()` method on the list.

The first thing you need is a parameter to the lambda expression—that's what the `value` parameter is. You do that by creating a `ParameterExpression`:

```
var argument = Expression.Parameter(typeof(Container));
```

You can give an explicit name to the parameter via an override of `Parameter()`, but in this case you only need to specify the type, which is a `Container` type. Note that creating the `ParameterExpression` object requires a static call on the `Expression` class. That's how you'll create all the expression pieces you need. You go through a static factory method on `Expression`.

Now that you have a parameter of type `Container`, you need to use the `Value` property on that parameter. To get it, use the `Property()` method, which returns a `MemberExpression`:

```
var valueProperty = Expression.Property(argument, "Value");
```

As with the Reflection API, there are numerous overloads with many of these factory methods. You can get a `MemberExpression` object for a property by passing a

`PropertyInfo` object into the `Property()` method, rather than using a string, for example.

The next step is calling `Contains()` on that property. That's what the following line of code does:

```
var containsCall = Expression.Call(valueProperty,
  typeof(string).GetMethod(
    "Contains", new Type[] { typeof(string) }),
  Expression.Constant("a", typeof(string)));
```

The `Call()` method returns a `MethodCallExpression`. You can invoke a method in numerous ways, so you can imagine there are a lot of overloads to `Call()`. In your case, you need to call the method on the `Value` property, which is why that `MemberExpression` is passed in first. Then you specify the method you want to call on the property. Here, the code uses a bit of reflection via `GetMethod()` to look up the `Contains()` method on a `string` with the right signature. The last things `Call()` needs are any argument values. You only need to pass in the literal `"a"` string value, which is what a `ConstantExpression` provides.

You're close to done at this point. You now need a lambda expression that you'll pass into a `Where()` invocation:

```
var wherePredicate = Expression.Lambda<Func<Container, bool>>(
  containsCall, argument);
```

The `Lambda()` call takes an expression to represent the body of the lambda and any arguments the lambda needs.

Finally, you need to invoke the `Where()` method on the queryable object itself:

```
var whereCall = Expression.Call(typeof(Queryable), "Where",
  new Type[] { typeof(Container) },
  containers.AsQueryable().Expression, wherePredicate);
```

That's it. You now have an expression that will invoke the correct method when `Create-Query()` is invoked.

Let's move on to look at APIs that can help you with adding mathematical capabilities.

**INCLUDING MATHEMATICAL OPERATIONS**

Let's revisit the code snippet in section 6.1.1. In that expression, you saw how you could create a method that would add two numbers. You did that via the `Add()` method, which returns a `BinaryExpression`. Numerous Expression APIs return a `Binary-Expression`. For example, you can make the code in section 6.1.1 perform a subtraction with one change:

```
Expression.Subtract(x, y)
```

If you need the remainder of x divided by y:

```
Expression.Modulo(x, y)
```

You can also raise the power of x by y via the `Power()` call:

```
Expression.Power(x, y)
```

What's nice about this function is that you don't have to make a `MethodCallExpression` to `Math.Pow()`. Use this static method. But you do need to make sure that the types of x and y are defined to be a double type. `Expression.Power()` ends up making a call to `Math.Pow()` for you, so you can't use the `int` type.

You also have the ability to use checked mathematical operators that will raise an `OverflowException`. For example, `AddChecked()` will handle this scenario. Speaking of exceptions, you may wonder whether you can add exception handlers to your expressions. The answer is yes, you can, and that's what the next section is about.

### USING EXCEPTION HANDLERS

Let's say you created a dynamic method that uses a checked addition via `Add-Checked()`. If someone passes in two values that would cause an overflow, you'd get an exception. Although it may seem odd to catch the `OverflowException` that you want to have raised with `AddChecked()`, let's see how you can do this with expressions in the following listing.

**Listing 6.4   Adding a `try-catch` block to an expression**

```
var x = Expression.Parameter(typeof(int));
var y = Expression.Parameter(typeof(int));

var lambda = Expression.Lambda(
  Expression.TryCatch(
    Expression.Block(
      Expression.AddChecked(x, y)),
    Expression.Catch(
      typeof(OverflowException),
      Expression.Constant(0))), x, y);
```

Before 4.0, the Expressions API was limited in what it could do. One of its limitations was in the area of exception handling. There was no way to add a `try...catch` block to your expression body. But in the 4.0 version, you now have that support.

The first thing you need to do is add the exception handler. In listing 6.4, `Try-Catch()` is called, which returns a `TryExpression`. Next, take the code that you want in the `try` block and wrap it in a `BlockExpression`. That's what the `Block()` call does. Finally, with a `try...catch` block, you need to define the code block that will run if an exception occurs, which is what the `Catch()` call performs. Note that in listing 6.4, the catch block is defined to catch exceptions of type `OverflowException`.

With this `try...catch` block in place, the following code would return 5:

```
return (lambda.Compile() as Func<int, int, int>)
  (2, 3);
```

But this code will return 0:

```
return (lambda.Compile() as Func<int, int, int>)
  (int.MaxValue, int.MaxValue);
```

What's nice about the exception handling support in the Expression API is that it's not limited to what you've seen here. You can create `try-finally` handlers, multiple catch handlers—in fact, there's a `TryFault()` call that will create a fault handler. Recall from chapter 5's section 5.1.3 that there's a fault handler that isn't supported in either C# or VB. With the Expression API, you can add that support if you want, with relative ease.

### ADDING CONTROL FLOW

The Expression API also has numerous ways to support branching and control flow in your code. Let's look at a simple example of a function that takes a `bool` and returns a 1 if the argument is `true`, and 0 if the argument is `false`.

As before, the first thing you need is an argument:

```
var @switch = Expression.Parameter(typeof(bool));
```

Next, call the `Condition()` method:

```
var conditional = Expression.Condition(@switch,
  Expression.Constant(1),
  Expression.Constant(0));
```

It's pretty simple. The first expression has to return a `bool` value, which is your argument. If it evaluates to `true`, the expression specified by the second argument is executed. Otherwise, the last expression is run. If you saw this code in C#, it would look something like this:

```
public void AFunction(bool @switch)
{
  if(@switch)
  {
    return 1;
  }
  else
  {
    return 0;
  }
}
```

Finally, you compile the expression stuffed into a lambda expression:

```
var function = (Expression.Lambda(conditional, @switch)
  .Compile() as Func<bool, int>);
var result = function(true);
```

The value of the result would be 1 in this case. You can also use `Break()` to move to a specific label in the expression body. There's even a `Goto()` method if you want "goto" semantics in your expression.

That covers the basics of expressions in .NET. There's so much more in the Expression API that we haven't covered—we've barely scratched the surface of what you can do with expressions. In fact, you're not limited by the Expression API compared to what you can do in IL with `DynamicMethod`. Is there any disadvantage to using expressions compared to using a `DynamicMethod`? Why would you use expressions over a `DynamicMethod`? In the next section you'll see how the two approaches compare.

### 6.2.3  *Comparison with dynamic methods*

Chapter 5 introduced you to the `DynamicMethod` class, which was an IL-based way to generate a method at runtime. As you've seen in this chapter, the Expression API provides the same functionality, so the inevitable question is which one should you choose? We'll take two views on this question: abstraction and performance.

Abstraction is all about using an API that's easy to understand, such that a developer can start using it with a minimal learning curve. Both approaches have an API that's consistent, but in our opinion avoiding IL is the preferred approach. Being able to use `Expression.Call()` to invoke a method is easier than trying to figure out the right opcodes to move local variables or arguments on the stack (along with the object for instance methods). Again, at the end of the day, this is a subjective metric, but we've used both approaches, and our preference is the Expression API.

Another thing to take into consideration is whether or not there is overhead in using one over the other. The code samples for this book contain code that compares the performance of the `DynamicMethod` way of creating a generic `ToString()` implementation to using the Expression API. We won't show that code here in the book, as you've already seen how the `DynamicMethod` version works, and the Expression API version is as lengthy. What's far more interesting is to see the comparison between the execution times, which is illustrated in figure 6.2.

As you can see, there's not much difference between the two. There's a slight benefit in execution time with `DynamicMethod`, but the difference is trivial. On average, executing the Expression-based method took about 1.48623 microseconds. The `DynamicMethod` approach was 1.48601 microseconds. Both implementations effectively execute at the same speed. The key difference is that with the Expression API, you don't have to learn IL to use it.

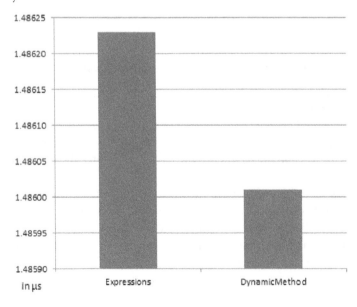

Figure 6.2  Comparing the execution time between an expression and `DynamicMethod`. The difference between the two is virtually the same.

However, the graph in figure 6.2 is a little misleading. The data was gathered using a cached version of both approaches; it doesn't take into consideration the time it takes to create the method.

Let's see how much time it takes to create a method that performs the following calculation:

```
f(x) = ((3 * x) / 2) + 4
```

Here's how it's done with expressions:

```
var parameter = Expression.Parameter(typeof(double));
var method = Expression.Lambda(
  Expression.Add(
    Expression.Divide(
      Expression.Multiply(
        Expression.Constant(3d), parameter),
      Expression.Constant(2d)),
    Expression.Constant(4d)),
  parameter).Compile() as Func<double, double>;
```

Here's how you can do it with DynamicMethod:

```
var method = new DynamicMethod("m",
  typeof(double), new Type[] { typeof(double) });
var parameter = method.DefineParameter(
  1, ParameterAttributes.In, "x");
var generator = method.GetILGenerator();
generator.Emit(OpCodes.Ldc_R8, 3d);
generator.Emit(OpCodes.Ldarg_0);
generator.Emit(OpCodes.Mul);
generator.Emit(OpCodes.Ldc_R8, 2d);
generator.Emit(OpCodes.Div);
generator.Emit(OpCodes.Ldc_R8, 4d);
generator.Emit(OpCodes.Add);
generator.Emit(OpCodes.Ret);
var compiledMethod = method.CreateDelegate(
  typeof(Func<double, double>)) as Func<double, double>;
```

If you create 10,000 of each of these and figure out the averages, you get a graph like figure 6.3.

It took 6.8 times longer to use expressions than to use DynamicMethod. Keep in mind, though, that creating the method using an expression took, on average, under 1 ms. That may be a performance bottleneck for your application, depending on how fast you need it to execute, but once you create the method, you'll probably cache it so you won't incur any time recreating it. Furthermore, once the method is created, there's no difference in execution time between an expression and a DynamicMethod. Although expressions are slower, that creation time may be acceptable for your application. As with any performance results, make sure you do your own evaluation and use your data to come to a conclusion that's right for your code base.

You now have a solid, basic understanding of expressions in .NET. But there's more to expressions than creating methods. You can debug them, use them in Reflection.Emit,

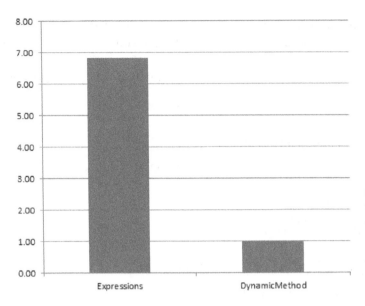

Figure 6.3   Comparing
the time it takes to create
an expression versus a
DynamicMethod.
The DynamicMethod
approach is clearly quicker,
but requires intimate
knowledge of IL.

and mutate them (sort of!). In the next section, you'll see how you can accomplish all three tasks.

## 6.3   *Using expressions effectively*

Now that you've seen how expressions are created, let's get into areas that will make your expression life easier with debugging, emitting, and mutating. Learning these techniques is important so that you know your expressions do what you think they should do. Let's start by seeing how to add debug information to your expression.

### 6.3.1   *Debugging expressions*

Using the Expression API is a simpler, cleaner experience than trying to work with IL. That said, any time a developer writes a piece of code, something can go wrong. Fortunately, there are a couple of techniques you can use to debug your expressions. Let's start with the first one: visualizing your expression in the debugger.

#### VISUALIZING AN EXPRESSION IN VISUAL STUDIO

Whenever you create an expression of any type, you can get a textural visualization of that node in Visual Studio when you run your code under the debugger. You move your mouse pointer over the variable in code, drill down to the Debug View option, and select Text Visualizer. Figure 6.4 shows what the expression from section 6.1 looks like in this visualizer.

You may wonder why the language used in the visualizer doesn't use C# or VB. Expressions can support options that a language may not be able to express (like a fault block), so the designers of the visualizer came up with a different language to show the expression. It's not that hard to follow, and it's a quick and easy way to get a good idea for what your expression looks like at a particular point in its construction.

**Figure 6.4** **Visualizing an expression in Visual Studio. The language may not look like anything you've seen before, but the intent is clear.**

**NOTE** For more information on the visualizer, see http://mng.bz/E6Q7.

In the next section, you'll see how you can step into an expression at runtime.

### USING REFLECTION.EMIT TO DEBUG EXPRESSIONS

Although a visual representation of an expression is a nice tool to have, sometimes you want to have the debugger dive right into the code. Unfortunately, an expression is a tree that represents your code structure. Or is it? When you compile your method, it's emitting IL for you, like the code you emitted in chapter 5 that used Reflection .Emit. Surprisingly, there's a connection between expressions and Reflection.Emit that lets you create debug information for an expression. Let's see how you can get it to work.

Similar to the exception handler example, you're going to start with the simple "add two numbers together" code snippet from section 6.1.1. The first thing you need to do is create a bunch of dynamic members from the Reflection.Emit API. Don't worry, you won't need to write any IL for debugging purposes; these members act as a host to your expression, as you'll see in a moment:

```
var name = Guid.NewGuid().ToString("N");
var assembly = AppDomain.CurrentDomain.DefineDynamicAssembly(
  new AssemblyName(name), AssemblyBuilderAccess.Run);
var module = assembly.DefineDynamicModule(name, true);
var type = module.DefineType(
  Guid.NewGuid().ToString("N"), TypeAttributes.Public);
var methodName = Guid.NewGuid().ToString("N");
var method = type.DefineMethod(methodName,
  MethodAttributes.Public | MethodAttributes.Static,
  typeof(int), new Type[] { typeof(int), typeof(int) });
```

All this code is doing is getting an in-memory dynamic assembly set up along with dynamic type and method. As you can see, the names of these members don't matter in this case—what does matter is the debugging support. For that, you need a Debug-InfoGenerator:

```
var generator = DebugInfoGenerator.CreatePdbGenerator();
var document = Expression.SymbolDocument("AddDebug.txt");
```

The generator created from CreatePdbGenerator() will be used when the expression is compiled. You also need to create a symbol document based on a text file. The Add-Debug.txt file in this example is the expression expressed in the language used in the expression visualizer demonstrated in the previous section. We won't show the code here, but you'll see what some of it looks like in a figure near the end of this section.

To create debug symbols for sections of the code, you need to wrap a specific node in the expression tree with a DebugInfoExpression:

```
var addDebugInfo = Expression.DebugInfo(document,
  6, 9, 6, 22);
var add = Expression.Add(x, y);
var addBlock = Expression.Block(addDebugInfo, add);
```

The section in the document that maps to the expression node being wrapped is defined in the DebugInfo() call. This DebugInfoExpression object is used in a Block() call to wrap the BinaryExpression that represents the addition functionality of this expression.

Once you're done defining your expression, save the expression's implementation into the dynamic assembly:

```
var lambda = Expression.Lambda(addBlock, x, y);
lambda.CompileToMethod(method, generator);

var bakedType = type.CreateType();
return (int)bakedType.GetMethod(methodName)
  .Invoke(null, new object[] { a, b });
```

In this case, you use CompileToMethod() to specify which method you're implementing in the dynamic assembly along with the debug information related to this method. At this point, when you step into the Invoke() call in a debugger, you'll get into the file specified in the SymbolDocumentInfo object. Figure 6.5 shows what this looks like when you step into the "expression" language copied to the text file.

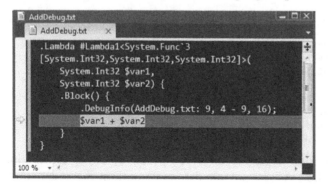

**Figure 6.5  Debugging an expression. Even though the language may look a little odd, it's clear that you've stopped at the point where addition occurs in the method.**

> **CAVEAT**  Using expressions to implement your methods in Reflection.Emit is a nice alternative to IL. But there's one major limitation to this approach: you can only use expressions to define static methods. You can't use an expression for an instance method. For more information on why this is the case, see http://mng.bz/U254.

You now know how you can debug your expression.

Let's move on to another topic: immutability. It will definitely affect your design, and that's what the next section is all about.

### 6.3.2  *Mutating expression trees*

Section 6.2 contained an overview of the Expression API to create dynamic methods at runtime. In this section, you'll look at expressions, immutability, and how you can create new expressions based on existing ones via the `ExpressionVisitor` class. Let's start by looking at the reasoning behind having immutable trees.

#### IMMUTABILITY OF EXPRESSION TREES

To frame the conversation on immutable expressions, let's go back to the expression in section 6.1 that added two integers together:

```
Expression<Func<int, int, int>> add = (x, y) => x + y;
```

Let's say someone wanted to change that expression to make it subtract the two arguments rather than add them. Because `Expression<T>` is a reference type, the expression you were referencing will now perform a subtraction, not an addition. That's not at all what you want! Immutable data structures are easier to reason about because you know that once the structure is created, it won't change. This also has benefits from a concurrency perspective because these structures are automatically thread-safe.

> **NOTE**  For more information on the benefits (and some shortcomings) of programming using immutable values see http://en.wikipedia.org/wiki/Immutability and http://mng.bz/AId8.

Being able to use a structure as the basis for future changes isn't a bad thing. In the next section, you'll see how you can create a new expression based on an existing one.

#### CREATING VARIATIONS OF EXPRESSIONS

You now know that expressions are immutable. Let's see how to create a new expression from the contents of an existing expression.

The key class you need is `ExpressionVisitor`. As the name implies, this class is based on the visitor pattern, which is designed to allow you to traverse complex object structures in a simplistic way by "visiting" specific methods that you care about.

> **NOTE**  For more on the visitor pattern, see http://en.wikipedia.org/wiki/Visitor_pattern.

You feed a subclass of `ExpressionVisitor` the expression that's your baseline and then you overwrite the `VisitXYZ()` methods you're interested in to create a new expression. Let's create a custom visitor that will change an add operation to a subtract operation. The following code listing demonstrates what it takes to write such a visitor.

**Listing 6.5  Creating an expression visitor**

```
internal sealed class AddToSubtractExpressionVisitor
  : ExpressionVisitor
{
  internal Expression Change(Expression expression)
  {
    return this.Visit(expression);
  }

  protected override Expression VisitBinary(BinaryExpression node)
  {
    return node.NodeType == ExpressionType.Add ?
      Expression.Subtract(
        this.Visit(node.Left), this.Visit(node.Right)) :
      node;
  }
}
```

As you can see, it doesn't take that much code to change an expression. In this case, you override VisitBinary() because you're trying to find the mathematical expression node Add. If you find one, then you create a new node that subtracts the child nodes. Note that you need to keep visiting the Left and Right nodes from the given node because they may also contain addition operations. For example, if you didn't do that, an expression like this

```
(x, y) => ((((32 * x) / 4) + y) + (x + 4))
```

would turn into this:

```
(x, y) => ((((32 * x) / 4) + y) - (x + 4))
```

That's not what you want, because there are still two addition operations in the expression. Visiting the child nodes gives you the right result:

```
(x, y) => ((((32 * x) / 4) - y) - (x - 4))
```

> **NOTE**  Before .NET 4.0, there wasn't a way in the .NET Framework to visit an expression. The ExpressionVisitor class existed in System.Linq.Expressions, but it was marked as internal, so you couldn't use it. There are a couple of ways to support this technique in .NET 3.5—see http://mng.bz/09bP and http://mng.bz/a3N3 for details on these approaches.

You now know how to debug and change expressions in .NET. In the last main section of this chapter, you'll tie everything together to create programs that better themselves through evolutionary techniques.

## 6.4 Evolving expression trees

Throughout this chapter, you've seen how to create expressions as well as debug them. Most of the time, the reasons to use expressions are similar to reasons you'd create a `DynamicMethod`. But because of its expressiveness and mutability via the `Expression-Visitor` class, you can use expressions in some amazing programming scenarios. In this section, you'll see how powerful metaprogramming and expressions can be when it comes to creating new programs on the fly. The topic of conversation is genetic programming. Next is an overview of genetic programming.

### 6.4.1 The essence of genetic programming

Before you start writing code that makes code better by rewriting it, let's start with a definition of what genetic programming is. *Genetic programming* is a technique that uses ideas and operations from the theory of evolution to create new programs based on existing ones. A genetic algorithm (GA) is a more general version of genetic programming. You create a pool of programs, or a population, that changes via an iterative approach. At each step in the process, you evaluate and/or change members of the population based on various rules and conditions. If a program in the population (called a *chromosome*) meets some kind of acceptable criteria, the process stops and that chromosome is selected as the answer.

> **TIP** There's a vast amount of information on genetic programming. We recommend starting with John Koza's web site: www.genetic-programming.com. Koza is considered a pioneer in the world of genetic programming. The problem in section 6.4 is based on one of Koza's first forays into genetic programming. He used Lisp; we use expressions in .NET.

Let's go through an example you'll use in this chapter to create functions that match a given data set. Let's say you were given a data set that looked something like that in figure 6.6. In the real world, the data set would be larger than this, but you get the idea. You're given two columns: the input to a function and the result of that input to the function.

| x | f(x) |
|---|------|
| 1 | 1 |
| 2 | 8 |
| 3 | 27 |
| 4 | 64 |
| 5 | 125 |

**Figure 6.6 Inputs and outputs to a function. Keep in mind that you don't know what the function is.**

Looking at the data in figure 6.6, you may be able to figure out that the underlying function is this:

```
f(x) = x ^ 3
```

This means *x raised to the power of three*. You'd be right, but the pattern behind the data values you're given may be much harder to find an underlying function. Let's look at how you could use genetic programming to evolve functions that try to produce outputs that match (or are close to) the data set values you're given.

## POPULATION

The first step is to create a population of functions to use for your first iteration. How you create those functions is up to you. They could be a best-guess by someone or generated randomly by a computer. However you do it, let's say you come up with the following set of functions:

```
f(x) = x ^ 2
f(x) = x + 3
f(x) = (x ^ 3) + 1
f(x) = 3 * x
```

Note that your population size will probably be bigger than this, but for our purposes this will suffice. One of these functions is a decent fit for your target data set, and that's okay. You're starting with a bunch of guesses, and you'll improve on them as you move along. The next step is to pick "good" candidates.

## SELECTION

Now that you have a population of chromosomes, you need to find those that are a good fit. To determine what a "good fit" is create a fitness function that gives a score for a given chromosome. How you define that fitness function is completely up to you, but hopefully it's a good indicator for how well the chromosome solves the given problem. In this case, we'll use the mean-squared error (MSE) to determine how fit a function is. The smaller the error, the better the function is at matching the given data set.

> **NOTE** For more on MSE, see http://mng.bz/x12Q and http://en.wikipedia .org/wiki/Mean_squared_error.

Figure 6.7 shows the average MSE for each of the four functions in the population and an indicator that shows which functions were selected for the next operation.

You may wonder why the third one wasn't selected because it's clearly the best choice. In genetic programming, there are different methods to select the "best" chromosome (such as tournament and roulette), but all the methods have a degree of randomness built in. Therefore, by random selection, you may not get what appears to be the best choice. But this randomness keeps the gene pool (so to speak)

| f(x) | MSE Average | Selected |
|------|-------------|----------|
| x ^ 2 | 2528.8 | ✔ |
| x + 3 | 3479.4 | |
| x ^ 3 + 1 | 1 | |
| 3 * x | 3027.2 | ✔ |

**Figure 6.7  Selecting functions in genetic programming. You want to select good candidates, but you won't always select the best ones.**

dynamic. As you'll see in the next section, it's possible to make something good out of some not-so-good chromosomes.

## CROSSOVER

Once you select chromosomes, you'll determine (via random chance) whether you'll perform crossover on the chromosomes. This means you'll take a piece (or pieces) of one chromosome and swap them with a piece (or pieces) from another. Figure 6.8 shows what happens when you swap the constant nodes between the selected functions.

Sometimes crossover may lead to better solutions, and sometimes it may make things worse. As you see in figure 6.8, the first function now matches perfectly to the data set you started with. But you're not done yet—there's one more operation to cover that can throw new material in the mix.

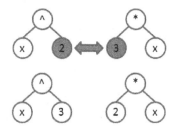

**Figure 6.8  Performing crossover on two functions. Note how the first function has changed and how much "better" it is.**

**MUTATION**

After crossover is done, you may perform mutation on a given chromosome. Usually the chance of mutation happening in a GA run is low, but it can occur to keep the population dynamic. A mutation may be a good or a bad thing for a chromosome—you never know. Figure 6.9 shows what the fourth function looks like after crossover occurred and the constant value changed into a whole new operation.

Is this "better" or "worse"? We'll leave that calculation up to the interested reader. The point is you now have new genetic material in your population that may (or may not) make things better.

**Figure 6.9 The results of mutating a function. The constant has been replaced with a whole new subtree.**

**ITERATION**

Selection, crossover, and mutation—those are the three key operations that drive genetic programming. You keep iterating over the population with these three operations until one of two things occurs:

- You find a chromosome that exceeds some kind of threshold value (for example, the MSE is under 0.5 percent).
- You exceed the maximum number of iterations that you specified at the beginning of the run.

Hopefully you find a good enough solution before the second condition happens. Fortunately, you can let a GA run go on for hours on a computer and let it find all sorts of interesting solutions. In fact, people who have used GAs on a number of diverse problems have found solutions that they would have never thought of, and that can take them into new areas of research. The searching power of GAs is quite impressive, and the more you take a look into how GAs work...well, you may end up using them on a project of your own in the future to solve a problem in a unique way.

Now that you have an overview of how GAs work, let's see how you can do this in .NET using expression trees.

### 6.4.2  Applying GAs to expressions

It's one thing to see how GAs work using pictures. But getting them to work and seeing the results are the fun parts. In this section, you'll see how to evolve expressions to find a function to match a given data set. To do this, you'll get code snippets for a program we've written called ExpressionEvolver, which is included with the online code. The code base is quite vast, so we'll focus on the aspects that deal with the GA operators and .NET expressions. Let's start with how you can create random expressions in .NET.

### CREATING RANDOM EXPRESSIONS

The first section of code you'll see is the class (RandomExpressionGenerator) that handles the creation of expressions. You need this when you create an initial population, or when a mutation occurs. For this example, you'll stick with the basic mathematical operations defined in the Operators enum:

```
private enum Operators
{
  Add,
  Subtract,
  Multiply,
  Divide,
  Power
}
```

You'll also need to be able to create constant values, which is handled in the GetConstant() method:

```
private ConstantExpression GetConstant()
{
  var value = this.Random.NextDouble() * this.ConstantLimit;
  var constant = value * (this.Random.NextBoolean() ? -1d : 1d);
  return Expression.Constant(constant);
}
```

The value for the ConstantLimit property is passed into the constructor—it's a best guess to limit the size of constant values created during a GA run.

Creating a random expression is a bit involved. It's done with the GetRandom-Operation() method, shown in the following listing.

**Listing 6.6   Creating a random operation**

```
private void GetRandomOperation(Operators @operator)
{
  var isLeftConstant = this.Random.NextDouble() <
    this.InjectConstantProbabilityValue;
  var isRightConstant = this.Random.NextDouble() <
    this.InjectConstantProbabilityValue;
  var isLeftBody = true;
  var isRightBody = true;

  if(!isLeftConstant && !isRightConstant)
  {
    isLeftBody = this.Random.NextDouble() < 0.5;
    isRightBody = !isLeftBody;
  }
  else if(isLeftConstant && isRightConstant)
  {
    isLeftConstant = this.Random.NextDouble() <
```

```
  this.InjectConstantProbabilityValue;
    isRightConstant = !isLeftConstant;
  }
  else if(@operator == Operators.Divide &&
    !isLeftConstant && !isRightConstant)
  {
    isLeftConstant = this.Random.NextBoolean();
    isRightConstant = !isLeftConstant;
  }

  this.Body = RandomExpressionGenerator.GetExpressionFunction(
    @operator)(
    isLeftConstant ? this.GetConstant() :
  (isLeftBody ? this.Body : this.Parameter),
    isRightConstant ? this.GetConstant() :
  (isRightBody ? this.Body : this.Parameter));
}
```

Most of the function ends up trying to make sure a good mix of constants and parameters are used during the creation of the random expression. The GetExpression-Function() gets a reference to the right function from the Expression class based on the value of the operation parameter:

```
private static Func<Expression, Expression, Expression>
  GetExpressionFunction(Operators @operator)
{
  Func<Expression, Expression, Expression> selectedOperation = null;

  switch(@operator)
  {
    case Operators.Add:
      selectedOperation = Expression.Add;
      break;
    case Operators.Subtract:
      selectedOperation = Expression.Subtract;
      break;
    case Operators.Multiply:
      selectedOperation = Expression.Multiply;
      break;
    case Operators.Divide:
      selectedOperation = Expression.Divide;
      break;
    case Operators.Power:
      selectedOperation = Expression.Power;
      break;
    default:
      throw new NotSupportedException(
      string.Format(CultureInfo.CurrentCulture,
        "Unexpected operator type: {0}", @operator));
  }

  return selectedOperation;
}
```

To create a random expression, the GetRandomOperation() method is called in a for loop that builds up the Body property to a desired size for the expression tree:

```
private void GenerateBody(int maximumOperationCount)
{
  for(var i = 0; i < maximumOperationCount; i++)
  {
    this.GetRandomOperation(
      (Operators)this.Random.Next((int)Operators.Power + 1));
  }
}
```

Here's how you would use `RandomExpressionGenerator` to create a random expression:

```
var parameter = Expression.Parameter(typeof(double), "a");
var body = new RandomExpressionGenerator(10,
  0.5, 100d, parameter, new SecureRandom()).Body.Compress();
```

You've now seen how to generate random expressions in .NET. Let's move on to the crossover function in a GA and see how to use the `ExpressionVisitor` class to handle that.

#### HANDLING CROSSOVER WITH EXPRESSIONS

As you saw in the "Creating variations of expressions" subsection, you can use the `ExpressionVisitor` class to create new expressions based on the structure of an existing expression. You'll use this class to handle crossover. You pick a node in two expressions and find where that node exists in the other expression, swapping it for the node in the other expression. You do that with the `ReplacementVisitor` class, which has `ExpressionVisitor` as its base class. Here's how it does a transform:

```
public Expression Transform(Expression source,
  ReadOnlyCollection<ParameterExpression> sourceParameters,
  Expression find, Expression replacement)
{
  this.Find = find;

  if(sourceParameters != null)
  {
    this.Replacement = new ParameterReplacementVisitor()
      .Transform(sourceParameters, replacement);
  }
  else
  {
    this.Replacement = replacement;
  }

  return this.Visit(source);
}
```

The thing you need to keep in mind when you swap components between expressions is that you can't swap parameters. If you move a `ParameterExpression` node from one expression to another, you'll get an exception when you try to use that new expression. That's why the `ParameterReplacementVisitor` class is used. It's a nested class of `ReplacementVisitor`, and all it does is replace any parameters in the target node with the given source parameters.

ReplacementVisitor overrides VisitBinary(), VisitConstant(), and Visit-Parameter(), all of which call ReplaceNode(), which determines whether the swap should occur:

```
private Expression ReplaceNode(Expression node)
{
  if(node == this.Find)
  {
    return this.Replacement;
  }
  else
  {
    return node;
  }
}
```

You now have implementations in place to generate expressions, along with being able to do crossover on two expressions. The last part is being able to create a data set to test the GA. In the next section, you'll see how you can use a bit of reflection magic to make data generation easy.

### GENERATING DATA SETS

When you're evolving expressions, you need a set of data that the GA can use as its target. But nobody likes to create a data set by hand. You'd like to parse an expression in a string like this:

```
"a => a + 3 * Math.Pow(a, 2.5)"
```

Once you have the lambda expression, you could compile it and feed it random input values, capturing the results in the process. Then you'd have your data set that you could give the GA. Unfortunately, there's no parsing functionality in System.Linq .Expressions, but a parser already exists with the C# compiler!

In the ExpressionEvolver solution is a project called ExpressionBaker. This contains a class called Baker, which takes a string and "bakes" it such that an expression is created. This is done in the Bake() method:

```
public Expression<TDelegate> Bake()
{
  var name = string.Format(CultureInfo.CurrentCulture,
    BakerConstants.Name, Guid.NewGuid().ToString("N"));
  var cscFileName = name + ".cs";
  File.WriteAllText(cscFileName,
    string.Format(CultureInfo.CurrentCulture,
      BakerConstants.Program, name, this.GetDelegateType(),
      this.Expression));

  this.CreateAssembly(name, cscFileName);

  return Assembly.LoadFrom(name + ".dll").GetType(name)
    .GetField("func").GetValue(null) as Expression<TDelegate>;
}
```

This method takes the given expression (stored in the Expression property) and puts it into a .cs file, which contains code that looks like this:

```
public const string Program =
  @"using System;using System.Linq.Expressions;
  public static class {0}{{
  public static readonly Expression<{1}> func = {2};}}";
```

Once the file is saved to disk, `CreateAssembly()` creates a new DLL via the C# compiler:

```
private void CreateAssembly(string name, string cscFileName)
{
  var startInformation = new ProcessStartInfo("csc");
  startInformation.CreateNoWindow = true;
  startInformation.Arguments = string.Format(
    CultureInfo.CurrentCulture,
    BakerConstants.CscArguments, name, cscFileName);
  startInformation.RedirectStandardOutput = true;
  startInformation.UseShellExecute = false;

  var csc = Process.Start(startInformation);
  csc.WaitForExit();
}
```

Now that you have an assembly, you can easily find the expression in the read-only field with a little bit of reflection magic, which is what the last line of code in `Bake()` does. It's a little bit of a hack, but hey, if the compiler already has all the logic to parse an expression, why not reuse that code?

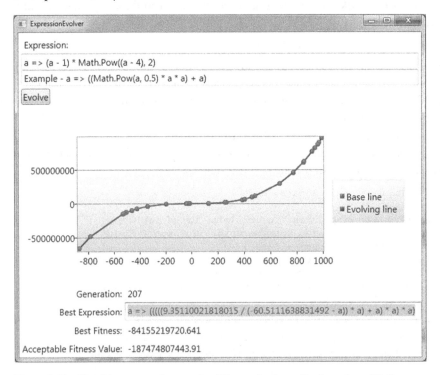

**Figure 6.10   Watching expressions evolve. The graph shows the base line with the current best-evolved expression. In this case, you can't see a difference, and that's a good thing!**

**NOTE** Admittedly, although the `Baker` class provides the functionality needed to compile an expression at runtime, it's clunky and feels hackish. In chapter 10, you'll see how Project Roslyn makes the compiler easily accessible at runtime. You may want to come back to this section and rewrite the `Baker` class using Project Roslyn's compiler API once you're done with chapter 10.

Again, there's more code to `ExpressionEvolver` than what's shown in this chapter. But let's see what happens when you run the code.

### RUNNING THE CODE

You have everything in place. Mutating expressions, parsing expressions and so on. Now it's time to run the application. Figure 6.10 shows what the application looks like when it runs. You can see two lines: one is the target, and the other is the best-evolved expression in the current generation.

The resulting expression doesn't look much like the given expression, but that's exactly the point. The GA doesn't know what that original expression is, but it's still able to come up with an expression that matches the original line well.

---

### Reducing expressions

One artifact of using tree-based structures in a GA is the notion of *bloat*. Bloat is when the trees start growing out of hand during the evolutionary process. This is something that we've seen in ExpressionEvolver. For example, starting with a data set that was generated from this expression

```
a => (2 * Math.Pow(a, 4)) - (11 * Math.Pow(a, 3)) -
  (6 * Math.Pow(a, 2)) + (64 * a) + 32
```

yielded the following acceptable result:

```
a => (((((-1 * a) - a) * ((-1 * a) - a)) *
  (((-1 * a) - a) - a)) +
  (((((-1 * a) - a) * (-1 * a)) *
  (-1 * a)) * (-1 * a)))
```

Even though the graphs are similar, the expressions don't look anything alike, until you do some symbolic reduction on the result:

```
a => (2 * Math.Pow(a, 4)) - (12 * Math.Pow(a, 3))
```

Having an expression that's smaller would help in reducing some of the memory consumption we've seen while executing `ExpressionEvolver`.

There's a `Reduce()` method in the `Expression` class, but that has nothing to do with mathematical symbolic reduction. It would be nice if there were a library out there to do this kind of reduction on .NET expressions. The closest we've found is WolframAlpha (http://alpha.wolfram.com), which is what we used to reduce the previous result. But although an API is available, finding the result would require a web service call. That's not too bad, but we'd have to be careful not to reduce every expression after every generation. Having an engine in-process would be a better alternative.

You've now seen how to use expressions that can create programs better than existing programs. That's quite a powerful example of metaprogramming in action!

## 6.5   *Summary*

In this chapter, you learned how to create and modify expressions, the differences between expressions and dynamic methods, and how to use expressions to evolve code.

In the next chapter, you'll see how to write succinct code that's augmented after the compiler process. Rather than waiting until runtime to generate code, a parser is used to examine an assembly and change its contents based on the existence of metadata or a coding convention.

# Generating code
# with IL rewriting

**This chapter covers**

- The benefits of code rewriting
- Using libraries to rewrite assemblies
- Debugging injected code

Throughout part 2 (beginning in chapter 3) you've seen a number of techniques and frameworks that you can use to generate code at various stages of execution. But there's one area of code execution that we've not yet addressed. It's after compilation, when your code has been turned into IL that's stored in an assembly. At that point, your code is in a format that the CLR uses to run your code, and most developers think the assembly is *frozen* at that point—that it can't be changed. But that's not the case!

In this chapter, you'll see how to rewrite assemblies to inject common code aspects or to add instrumentation to code. You'll understand the benefits of code injection and what libraries you'll need to use to pull off this technique. By the end, you'll have a powerful tool in your metaprogramming toolkit that will allow you to parcel small, reusable code concepts across multiple applications. The result is code that looks lean, yet contains all the implementations you want.

As always, we start with an explanation of the benefits of injecting code.

## 7.1    *The case for code injection*

Before we dive into the details of IL rewriting, let's start with a couple of examples that illustrate the need to rewrite assemblies: reducing recurring implementations and restructuring code flow.

### 7.1.1    *Repeated implementations of coding patterns*

It's common in software development to run across implementations in code that are repeated in the application, yet don't follow common idioms to support that duplication. The `ToString()` example, used in numerous places in this book to demonstrate metaprogramming ideas, is an easy example. You could copy-and-paste a hard-coded example into each class that you want to have the same `ToString()` pattern results. You could also use reflection, Reflection.Emit, or expressions to create this implementation at runtime. But getting the best of both worlds would be the way to go. The following code snippet is a hint of things to come in section 7.2. You add an attribute to your code, and the implementation is injected into the assembly:

```
[ToString]
public sealed class AttributedCustomer : Customer
{
  // ...
}
```

You don't have to be concerned about how `ToString()` is created, nor do you have to wait until execution time for this code to be created. All you care about is that something during the compilation process implements it in a standardized way.

Another well-known example is tracing. Let's say you wanted to trace a method when it was invoked, when it was finished, and when an exception was thrown. You'd probably want to include method arguments as well to give you more information when you went through the tracing logs. The following code listing shows a hard-coded example of tracing a method with these patterns in place.

**Listing 7.1    Tracing the execution of a method**

```
public static int Divide(int x, int y)
{
  Console.Out.WriteLine("Divide started");

  Console.Out.WriteLine("x = " + x);
  Console.Out.WriteLine("y = " + y);

  if(y == 0)
  {
    Console.Out.WriteLine("Divide threw an ArgumentException");
    throw new ArgumentException();
  }

  var result = x / y;
  Console.Out.WriteLine("Divide finished - return = " + result);

  return result;
}
```

This is verbose and provides a lot of detail, but there are a couple of issues with this approach. For one, you need to manually include this pattern in every method you want to have it. It's not hard to do, but it's easy to make a small mistake. What if the parameters were reference types and not value types? Or what if you forget to include a parameter value? You'd also have to make a check to make sure tracing their values wouldn't cause an exception, which would be a possibility with reference types.

Another issue is code bloat. This code is always compiled into your assembly, whether or not you need the tracing. Typically, you only need tracing to debug problematic issues—you don't want to include it in production builds. But unless you're willing to add numerous conditional compilation statements, you're stuck with keeping the code in.

Wouldn't it be nice to have code like this?

```
[Trace]
public static int Divide(int x, int y)
{
  if(y == 0)
  {
    throw new ArgumentException();
  }

  return x / y;
}
```

That's much cleaner. You let a dynamic code injection process figure out what to add in the method to trace it based on the existence of the attribute (or some other configuration-based approach), and you can focus on your implementation.

### 7.1.2 *Code restructuring (Code Contracts)*

Another trick you can do with rewriting is moving the code around to support a specific coding approach. This is illustrated with the introduction of design-by-contract into the .NET framework via Code Contracts. Design-by-contract is a way for developers to specify pre- and postconditions in methods along with object invariants in objects. The following code snippet shows a method that requires that the given id can't be zero and that the return value is non-null:

```
public static Customer Create(uint id)
{
  Contract.Requires(
    id > 0, "The ID must be greater than zero.");
  Contract.Ensures(Contract.Result<Customer>() != null);

  return new Customer(id);
}
```

The Contract.Requires() call handles the precondition (the id parameter must be non-zero) and the Contract.Ensures() enforces the postcondition that the return value will be non-null. What may seem a bit odd is that the postcondition comes before the return call. How is this code going to make that guarantee?

It's done through a bit of code rewriting magic. Because Code Contracts is only an API and isn't supported in languages like C# or VB via keywords, you must install a tool in Visual Studio to rewrite the IL flow in the method after the compiler has done its job. Once that's done, the code flow changes (if you'd follow it in the debugger) from

- Opening curly brace
- Return
- Closing curly brace

to

- Contract.Requires
- Opening curly brace
- Return
- Closing curly brace
- Contract.Ensures

Even though this still seems like the method "returns" a value before the postcondition is evaluated, it doesn't. You need to ensure the postcondition is correct *before* the method returns. But you can't put any code after the return statement—the C# compiler won't allow it. Therefore, the Code Contract developers wrote their tool to rewrite the execution of code such that the code executes correctly, but it looks like the return statement is "evaluated" first, and then the postcondition is executed. As you can guess, the care it takes to rewrite code flow without disrupting the developer's original intentions isn't trivial.

Thankfully, all the code rewriting is handled for you by the Code Contracts tools. You don't have to think about how it's done; you write your code and let the tools do their post-compilation magic. This rewriting magic, done correctly, can give a developer a powerful piece of machinery to revamp implementations to his or her liking, and you'll see in the next section how you can pull it off.

> **TIP** If you've never run into the concept of design-by-contract before and you'd like to learn more, there are two places you should visit. One is the official site from Microsoft: http://research.microsoft.com/en-us/projects/contracts/. The Code Contracts are built into the 4.0 version of the .NET Framework (under System.Diagnostics.Contracts), but you need the rewriting tools from that site to get the full effect. The other resource is a series of articles written by one of us (Kevin). You can find those at http://mng.bz/04zB.

Now that you've seen a couple of scenarios where code modification in an assembly is useful, let's see how you can do this yourself. It's not going to be an easy ride because there's nothing in the stock set of tools and libraries that you get in the .NET 4.0 Framework that handles this, so you're going to have to roll your own. As you'll see, though, there are libraries out there to make the task easier to achieve.

## 7.2 Creating an injection framework

It may sound like an appealing, powerful idea—having the ability to restructure your code once the compiler is done. But there's a catch. The .NET Framework doesn't ship with the ability to support this endeavor. Therefore, you need to come up with a way on your own. Although it won't be easy, a framework called Cecil has the functionality you need. This section covers Cecil and shows how you can use it to rewrite assemblies.

### 7.2.1 What's Cecil?

Throughout this book, you've seen powerful examples of metaprogramming that use various classes in .NET. But reflection in .NET doesn't have enough power to modify existing code. Here's why. First, reflection reads the contents of an assembly and allows you to invoke assembly members. But you can't *change* the contents of a method or a class; you can only use it as is. The Emitter API gets you one step closer by giving you the ability to create code on-the-fly, but you can't edit existing code in assemblies. What you need is a combination of both: to read the contents of an assembly and modify it. Fortunately, there's another way to pull this off.

Cecil is an assembly that's part of the Mono project (www.mono-project.com). It allows you to read and write assemblies and debug files. You can get the source code for Cecil at www.mono-project.com/Cecil. Cecil is also available on NuGet, so you can easily reference it in your projects. Cecil is used on a number of Mono-related projects, such as Gendarme (www.mono-project.com/Gendarme), a static analysis tool.

The next section delves deep into the Cecil API to reveal how Cecil enables code weaving.

### 7.2.2 Weaving code with Cecil

To see how Cecil works, we're going to use the Injectors project, which was created by one of the authors (Jason). You can find the source code at http://injectors.codeplex.com. This project uses Cecil to read the contents of an assembly and change specific parts based on the existence of metadata. Once all the changes have been made, the assembly is saved back to disk. Figure 7.1 gives a high-level picture of the process Injectors takes to change an assembly.

Because Cecil isn't an assembly that comes with .NET, you'll have to spend time getting familiar with a new API. But as you'll discover, Cecil isn't too hard to pick up once you get past some of the initial steps. Let's start by looking at how assemblies are loaded and saved in Cecil.

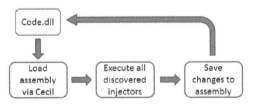

**Figure 7.1  Modifying an assembly with the Injectors framework. All changes to a loaded assembly are saved back to the same assembly.**

**NOTE** It would be somewhat easier if we could point you to an API that already exists in .NET that handles assembly parsing and code rewriting, but we can't. Thankfully, the .NET developer community has a number of options you can choose from to do this. We've picked Cecil for this book, but we highly encourage you to look at CCI (http:// ccimetadata.codeplex.com), IKVM (www.ikvm.net), and Tao (https://github.com/philiplaureano/Tao), to name a few.

### LOADING AND SAVING ASSEMBLIES WITH CECIL

To run any code that will change the contents of an assembly, first you must load the target assembly, change it, and save the alterations back to disk. This is pretty easy to do in Cecil:

```
public static class InjectorRunner
{
  public static void Run(FileSystemInfo assemblyLocation)
  {
    var assembly = AssemblyDefinition.ReadAssembly(
      assemblyLocation.FullName);
    assembly.Inject();
    assembly.Write(assemblyLocation.FullName);
  }
}
```

The `AssemblyDefinition` class provides a `ReadAssembly()` method, which you use to load the contents of that assembly. The `Inject()` method is an extension method provided by the Injectors framework—you'll see how it works in the next section. Once the changes are done, you call `Write()` on that assembly.

As you can see, loading and saving assemblies in Cecil is pretty straightforward. The challenge is changing the contents. You'll see how to do that in the next section.

### VISITING ASSEMBLY CONTENTS

Cecil doesn't provide a mechanism to visit the entire contents of an assembly, so you have to create your own. The Injectors framework has a number of extension methods to visit a specific member and inject it with code modifications if needed. Here's what the `Inject()` method looks like for an `AssemblyDefinition`:

```
internal static class AssemblyDefinitionExtensions
{
  internal static void Inject(
    this AssemblyDefinition @this)
  {
    @this.RunInjectors();

    foreach(var module in @this.Modules)
    {
      module.Inject();
    }
  }
}
```

The RunInjectors() extension method examines the current member to see if it's marked with any injector attributes that will modify the assembly. You'll see the definition of InjectorAttribute in the "Executing injectors" section. The key point is that once the AssemblyDefinition has been examined, all the modules in the assembly are injected. In each module, all the types are injected—and so on all the way down to a parameter in a method. All the other extension methods for the other members follow this pattern.

With these extension methods in place, the entire assembly is visited and injected with modifications. You need a way to mark code with attributes that will change the content. In the next section, you'll see how you can use a bit of IL to create a generic attribute that'll be useful in not only defining metadata but also in being extensible for other Cecil members.

### DEFINING THE INJECTORATTRIBUTE

In languages like C# and VB, you can define attributes that inherit from the Attribute class. But you can't make your custom attributes generic. You can't write code like this:

```
public sealed class MyCustomAttribute<T> : Attribute
```

This is purely a language restriction. The CLR supports generic attributes, but C# and VB don't allow it—much as you can overload methods by return type only in IL, but not in C# and VB. This would be beneficial because you could make a custom generic attribute that could be used for any Cecil-based member, such as TypeDefinition or MethodDefinition. But if you're willing to write a little IL, you can define a generic attribute.

It's not as hard as you think. The trick is to write your attribute in your favorite .NET language, then tweak it in IL. Start by writing the attribute:

```
public class InjectorAttribute : Attribute
{
  public InjectorAttribute
    : base() { }
  public void Inject(object target)
  {
    if(target == null)
    {
      throw new ArgumentNullException("target");
    }
    this.OnInject(target);
  }
  protected abstract void Inject(object target);
}
```

Then compile the code, open up the assembly in ILDasm, and dump the contents to a text file. In the text file, you can then make the attribute generic. Three spots need to be changed. The first is the class definition:

```
.class public abstract auto ansi beforefieldinit
  Injectors.Core.Attributes.Generic.InjectorAttribute`1<class T>
    extends [mscorlib]System.Attribute
```

Now that the class is generic, you can use T in Inject() and OnInject():

```
.method public hidebysig instance void
  Inject(!T target) cil managed

.method family hidebysig newslot abstract virtual
  instance void OnInject(!T target) cil managed { }
```

Note how the parameters are now generic, so you can pass in whatever specific type you want. In the next section, you'll see how this attribute is discovered and executed.

### EXECUTING INJECTORS

In the "Visiting assembly contents" section, you saw RunInjectors() called in the Inject() extension method. Now that you have the custom attribute defined, you can see how these attributes are handled:

```
internal static void RunInjectors<T>(this T @this)
  where T : class, ICustomAttributeProvider
{
  var injectors = @this.GetInjectors();

  foreach(var injector in injectors)
  {
    injector.Inject(@this);
  }
}
```

In Cecil, each definition class (like AssemblyDefinition and MethodReturnType-Extensions) implements the ICustomAttributeProvider interface, which defines the CustomAttributes property. This is a collection of attributes on the given member, which is what you need to use to find InjectorAttribute-based attributes. But InjectorAttribute doesn't have a generic constraint on T for ICustomAttribute-Provider, so that's why the constraint is done here.

GetInjectors() returns a list of InjectorAttribute-based objects. The following listing shows what that method does.

### Listing 7.2  Getting a list of injectors from a member

```
internal static ReadOnlyCollection<InjectorAttribute<T>>
  GetInjectors<T>(this T @this)
  where T : class, ICustomAttributeProvider
{
  var injectors = new List<InjectorAttribute<T>>();

  foreach(var attribute in @this.CustomAttributes)
  {
    var baseAttributeType =
      attribute.AttributeType.Resolve().BaseType.Resolve();

    while(baseAttributeType != null &&
      baseAttributeType.BaseType != null)
```

```
  {
    if(baseAttributeType.FullName ==
         ICustomAttributeProviderExtensions.baseFullName &&
       baseAttributeType.Scope.Name ==
            ICustomAttributeProviderExtensions.baseScopeName)
    {
      var injectorAttribute =
            attribute.Create<InjectorAttribute<T>>();
      injectors.Add(injectorAttribute);
      break;
    }

    baseAttributeType = baseAttributeType.BaseType.Resolve();
  }
}

  return injectors.AsReadOnly();
}
```

In Cecil, there's no IsAssignableFrom method like you get in the Reflection API. You'd like that so you could find the specific attributes in the CustomAttribute property that derive from InjectorAttribute<T>. But you're left with writing a while loop and looking at the BaseType to see if it matches the name for InjectorAttribute<T>. If it does, you create an instance of the attribute and add it to the collection. The Create() extension method is provided in the following listing.

**Listing 7.3  Creating an attribute in Cecil**

```
internal static T Create<T>(this CustomAttribute @this)
  where T : class
{
  var type = @this.AttributeType.Resolve();
  var attributeTypeName = type.FullName + ", " +
    type.Module.Assembly.Name.Name;
  var attributeType = Type.GetType(attributeTypeName);

  object[] arguments = null;

  if(@this.HasConstructorArguments)
  {
    arguments = new object[@this.ConstructorArguments.Count];

    for(var i = 0; i < @this.ConstructorArguments.Count; i++)   ❶ Get
    {                                                             constructor
      arguments[i] = @this.ConstructorArguments[i].Value;        arguments
    }
  }

  T value = Activator.CreateInstance(                           ❷ Create attribute
    attributeType, arguments) as T;

  if(@this.HasProperties)
  {                                                             ❸ Set
    foreach(var attributeProperty in @this.Properties)           attribute's
    {                                                             properties
      attributeType.GetProperty(attributeProperty.Name)
```

```
        .SetValue(value,
        attributeProperty.Argument.Value, null);
    }
}

return value;
}
```

❸ Set attribute's properties

It's not the easiest thing in the world to create the attribute object either; you can't use `Activator.CreateInstance()`. The first thing you need to do is find the constructor arguments, if any exist ❶. These values need to be provided to `CreateInstance()` to ensure you're creating the object in the correct state ❷. You also need to set any property values if the attribute was defined using named properties. Each of those values needs to be set via a `GetProperty()` call ❸. Once the attribute object is in the correct state with the right data, it's returned, where the `Inject()` method is called in `RunInjectors()`.

At this point, you've seen the core architecture of injectors. Although some of Cecil's API may be unfamiliar to you, if you've used the Reflection API, you'll see a fair amount of analogies between classes in terms of their logical use (for example, `Method-Info` and `MethodDefinition`). To close the discussion, let's go through a simple injector to see how you can add null checks to argument methods.

### CREATING THE NOTNULLATTRIBUTE

Checking reference-based method arguments to see if they're null is a common idiom in .NET. Good code should throw an `ArgumentNullException` if an argument was provided as null, rather than waiting for the .NET runtime to throw the `NullReference-Exception` for you if you try to use it in any way. `ArgumentNullException` can provide more information (such as the parameter name), whereas `NullReferenceException` isn't related to a parameter in any way.

Now, making the null check involves straightforward, boilerplate code:

```
public void AMethod(string value)
{
  if(value == null)
  {
    throw new ArgumentNullException("value");
  }
}
```

As you can see, it's pretty easy to do. The point is that it's simple, yet tedious code. You have to write the `if` block that throws the exception with the right parameter name every single time. It would be far easier if you could let something else—like an injector—write that for you. The following listing demonstrates the `NotNullAttribute` and how it injects the IL to handle this check.

Listing 7.4   Adding a non-null check

```
[AttributeUsage(AttributeTargets.Parameter,
  AllowMultiple = false, Inherited = true)]
[Serializable]
public sealed class NotNullAttribute :
```

```
                  InjectorAttribute<ParameterDefinition>                      ❶ Verify
                  {                                                             parameter's
                    protected override void OnInject(ParameterDefinition target)  type
                    {
                      if(!target.ParameterType.IsValueType)                  ◄───┘
                      {
    Get reference to ❷   var method = (target.Method as MethodDefinition);
       Argument-          var argumentNullExceptionCtor =
      NullException          method.DeclaringType.Module.Assembly.MainModule.Import(
      constructor            typeof(ArgumentNullException).GetConstructor(
                                   new Type[] { typeof(string) }));

                        var processor = method.Body.GetILProcessor();        ❸ Get list of
                        var first = processor.Body.Instructions[0];            instructions

                        processor.InsertBefore(first,
                            processor.Create(OpCodes.Ldarg, target));
                        processor.InsertBefore(first,
                            processor.Create(OpCodes.Brtrue_S, first));
                        processor.InsertBefore(first,                        ❹ Add
                            processor.Create(OpCodes.Ldstr, target.Name));     opcodes for
                        processor.InsertBefore(first,                          null check
                            processor.Create(OpCodes.Newobj,
                            argumentNullExceptionCtor));
                        processor.InsertBefore(first,
                            processor.Create(OpCodes.Throw));
                      }
                    }
                  }
```

The first thing you need to do is make sure that the parameter the attribute is on is a reference type and not a valid type via the `IsValueType` property, because there's no way to specify via an attribute that it can only be on one or the other ❶. This is valid code:

```
public void AMethod([NotNull] string value1, [NotNull] Guid value2)
```

There's no reason to emit code for `value2` because it will always be non-null.

Once you know the parameter is a reference type, you can start emitting the non-null check. You need to get a reference to the `ArgumentNullException`'s constructor that takes one argument because you'll use that in the IL you're going to emit, which is what the `Import()` call is for ❷. Next, you get an `ILProcessor` reference, which is similar to the `ILGenerator` class in Reflection.Emit in that you can add opcodes to the method ❸. But it's more flexible because you can pick an instruction and add new instructions before or after it, which isn't possible with `ILGenerator`. In this case, you need to make sure the non-null check occurs before any other code in the method happens, so you find the first instruction and insert all of opcodes before it ❹.

The five opcodes you use work this way:

- `Ldarg`—Put the target parameter on the stack.
- `Brtrue_S`—If it's non-null, skip to the rest of the code in the method.
- `Ldstr`—Put the parameter name on the stack.

- Newobj—Create a new ArgumentNullException, which will use the parameter on the stack to construct it.
- Throw—Throw the exception.

That's it. You now have a way to add an attribute to your code that will make this non-null check for you the same way every time (and it'll always get the parameter name right!).

Attributes don't do anything on their own. You need something to kick-start the injection process on your assembly. In the next section, you'll see how you can get the Injectors framework executed in your projects via a custom MSBuild task.

### 7.2.3 Creating an MSBuild task

MSBuild is an XML-based build platform that's used to orchestrate numerous tasks that occur in a build process. There are a number of predefined tasks that you can use in an MSBuild file, such as <Exec> (to run an executable). You can also create your own custom tasks. Interestingly, the

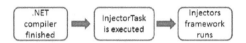

Figure 7.2 At some point in an MSBuild file, a compiler is run. Once that task is finished, the InjectorTask runs to modify the new assembly via Injectors.

Visual Studio project files for C# and VB use the MSBuild format as well, which makes it ideal to create a custom injector task that you could use to add post-build assembly modification to a VS project. Figure 7.2 illustrates where the task comes into play in an MSBuild file.

First, create the custom task. As the following listing shows, doing so is quite simple.

Listing 7.5 Creating a custom MSBuild task for injection

```
using Injectors.Core;
using Microsoft.Build.Framework;
using Microsoft.Build.Utilities;
using System.Diagnostics;
using System.IO;

namespace Injectors.Task
{
  public sealed class InjectorTask : AppDomainIsolatedTask
  {
    public override bool Execute()
    {
      Log.LogMessage("Injecting assembly {0}...",
        this.AssemblyLocation);
      var stopwatch = Stopwatch.StartNew();
      InjectorRunner.Run(new FileInfo(this.AssemblyLocation));
      stopwatch.Stop();
      Log.LogMessage(
        "Assembly injection for {0} complete - total time: {1}.",
        this.AssemblyLocation, stopwatch.Elapsed.ToString());
      return true;
    }
```

```
    [Required]
    public string AssemblyLocation { get; set; }
  }
}
```

To create a custom task, you need your class to derive from `ITask`. The helper class `AppDomainIsolatedTask` does this for you; the only method you need to handle is `Execute()`, which is where you'll define your custom task's logic. Note that you can also create properties, such as `AssemblyLocation`, that users of the custom task can set to specify pieces of information your task will need (you'll see shortly how to use this task in an MSBuild file).

> **NOTE** You need to reference the `Microsoft.Build.Framework` and `Microsoft.Build.Utilities.v4.0` assemblies to create custom tasks.

As you can see in `InjectorTask`, all `Execute()` does is call `Run()` on `InjectorRunner`, sprinkling in debugging statements before and after the call. Add this task to your MSBuild file so it will execute it correctly:

```
<?xml version="1.0" encoding="utf-8"?>
<Project ToolsVersion="4.0" DefaultTargets="Build"
  xmlns="http://schemas.microsoft.com/developer/msbuild/2003">
  <UsingTask TaskName="Injectors.Task.InjectorTask"
    AssemblyFile="Injectors.Task.dll"/>
  <!-- Other build elements go here... -->
</Project>
```

The `<UsingTask>` element lets you specify an assembly that contains a custom MSBuild task. Once you add this element, you can reference the task anywhere in the MSBuild file:

```
<InjectorTask AssemblyLocation="Injectors.SampleTarget.exe" />
```

Set the `AssemblyLocation` property in the `<InjectorTask>` element, which will be done before `Execute()` is called on the custom task.

Getting this set up with a simple MSBuild file is pretty easy. Because C# and VB project files are MSBuild files, you can add this custom injection task to your own projects. You do that by either editing the project file manually outside of VS or unloading the project within VS and doing it there. To edit the file in VS, right-click the project and select Unload Project from the context menu. Then, right-click the project again and select Edit {project name}.{project file}. That will show the file contents in VS. (Remember to right-click and Reload Project to get the project loaded again in the solution). Whatever approach you use to edit the project file, you want to find this section of XML:

```
<Target Name="AfterBuild">
</Target>
```

Put the `<InjectorTask>` element within the `<Target>` element. If you can't find it in the project file, add the element within the `<Project>` element. Also, this element may be wrapped in an XML comment, so remove the comment first. Once you've done that, your code modifications will occur after the project is built.

Up to this point, you've seen how to use Cecil to modify an assembly. In the next section, you'll see how you can enhance these modifications by adding debugging symbols. This enhancement will give the developer an indication during a debugging session that code has been changed.

## 7.3    *Debugging injected code*

Cecil gives you a lot of power to change assemblies in all sorts of ways. But some of these changes can leave developers scratching their heads, wondering why they're getting the behaviors they're seeing. In this section, you'll see how you can add debugging support to your modified assemblies.

### 7.3.1    *Clearing up debugging confusion*

To see how the simple `NotNullAttribute` can raise a developer's eyebrows, look at the following code:

```
public class SomeClass
{
  public SomeClass([NotNull] string data)
  {
    this.Data = data;
  }

  public string Data { get; set; }
}
```

Now, let's say a developer was using this code like this:

```
var data = new SomeClass(null);
```

Nowhere in the code is there any explicit "throw new ArgumentNullException" line of code. Sure, there's a `[NotNull]` attribute next to the data argument, but when users try to debug this code, all they're going to get is a dialog box telling them that the exception has been thrown. But from where? Where did it come from?

What would be better is to alter the program debug file (.pdb) and change the assembly such that the developer would see that the `NotNullAttribute` did something. For example, having the "NotNull" text be highlighted in the debugger when the five opcodes are executed would be a great visual indicator during a debugging session.

Fortunately, Cecil has support to read debug information along with letting you edit it as well. Let's see how you can add debugging support for the `NotNullAttribute`.

### 7.3.2    *Loading and saving debug information*

The first thing you need to find is the PDB file that contains all the debugging symbol information. Keep in mind that you may not always have this. It's perfectly legal for a compiler to not create any debugging information during compilation, or maybe the PDB wasn't shipped with the assembly you're trying to modify. Therefore, the techniques shown in section 7.3 have to be defensive, because you may not have any debugging information available. To load the debug symbols, you need to change your code that loads the assembly:

```
var assembly = AssemblyDefinition.ReadAssembly(assemblyLocation.FullName,
    new ReaderParameters { ReadSymbols = true });
```

Include a `ReaderParameters` object to `ReadAssembly()`, with the `ReadSymbols` property set to `true`. Note that if you try to load an assembly this way, and Cecil can't find a PDB file, you'll get a `FileNotFoundException`, so you need to include a `try-catch` block to handle this expected exception.

You also need to save the file with debugging information if you want to preserve any changes you've made during the assembly modification process:

```
assembly.Write(assemblyLocation.FullName,
  new WriterParameters() { WriteSymbols = true });
```

### 7.3.3 *Issues with adding debugging information*

Once you have debug symbols loaded, you can read existing symbol information as well as add new symbols. But before you start adding debugging information, knowing when it's possible to add it is important.

One issue is performing a code modification where there was no code to begin with. PDB files only contain information that relates to code that executes. Specifically, a PDB file doesn't contain full assembly information, like type names. It only knows that a particular opcode relates to some chunk of text in a code file. Therefore, if you add code to an assembly, you may not be able to add the symbols because you'll never know where the code file is.

Let's look at a specific example. In the Injectors project, there's another attribute called `ToStringAttribute`, which adds a `ToString()` method to a class that follows the format convention shown in chapters 2 and 4. You add it to a class like this:

```
[ToString]
public class MyClass { }
```

If `ToString` has not been defined on `MyClass`, the attribute will inject a new `ToString` method into the class. But note that `MyClass` never had `ToString()` overridden. Therefore, if a PDB was created at runtime, there won't be any information about a MyClass.cs file that you can find. It's possible that you could extend a code weaver like Injectors to get code file information during its execution, in particular if you're running it in VS after every project is run, but in general a PDB file doesn't always have the code file information you're looking for.

Another issue is parsing code. As you'll see in the next section, you need to find the exact section in code where the "NotNull" or "NotNullAttribute" text shows up for the parameter you found that has this metadata associated with it. At first glance, this may not seem that hard, but there are always the edge cases that bite you. Usually when you add an attribute to a property in C#, you'll see it like this:

```
public void AMethod([NotNull] string value)
```

However, the following chunk of code is perfectly valid C# as well:

```
public void AMethod([NotNull]
  string value)
```

Surprisingly, this is legal too:

```
public void AMethod([
  NotNull
  ] string value)
```

Also, remember multiple properties may have `NotNullAttribute` on them, and the parameters may have other custom attribute defined on them as well:

```
public void AMethod([NotNull, MoreInformation] string value,
  [NotNull] string data)
```

Again, PDB files are all about the executable code parts in an assembly. It may know what file contains the code you're looking for, but you're on your own trying to figure out any more information in the code file. Fortunately, there's a way out of this parsing mess such that you don't have to write a parser.

There's an OSS IDE tool in the .NET community called SharpDevelop (www.sharpdevelop.com). Because it's an IDE to develop .NET-based applications, it needs to be able to parse code in the IDE to provide features like IntelliSense. Fortunately, this parsing code is shipped as a separate assembly with Sharp-Develop, called ICSharpCode.NRefactory.dll. In the next section, you'll see how you can use this assembly to make finding the code you're looking for in a given file painless.

**TIP** You can get NRefactory from Nuget: www.nuget.org/packages/ICSharp-Code.NRefactory.

### 7.3.4  *Adding debugging information for injected code*

Now that you've seen why modifying the PDB file with new information will aid a developer during the debugging process and how you can address the parsing issue, let's see how you can do it.

#### DEFINING A PARSING CLASS

First, find out if you can add debugging information. Let's change the IL weaving code in `OnInject()` for `NotNullAttribute` a bit:

```
var processor = method.Body.GetILProcessor();
var first = processor.Body.Instructions[0];
var ldArgInstruction = processor.Create(OpCodes.Ldarg, target);
ldArgInstruction.SequencePoint =
  new NotNullAttributeParser(method, target).SequencePoint;
processor.InsertBefore(first, ldArgInstruction);
```

You need to handle the first instruction differently than the other four. You set its `SequencePoint` property to a `SequencePoint` object, which contains debugging information, such as the starting and ending lines that the debugger should highlight when this opcode is hit.

The `NotNullAttributeDebugger` is a class that contains the code needed to add debugging information. The following listing shows how the constructor sets its `SequencePoint` property.

**Listing 7.6  Creating an NRefactory parser**

```
internal sealed class NotNullAttributeDebugger
{
  internal NotNullAttributeDebugger(
    MethodDefinition method, ParameterDefinition target)
  {
    this.SetPoint(method, target);
  }
  private void SetPoint(
    MethodDefinition method, ParameterDefinition target)
  {
    var point = method.FindSequencePoint();

    if(point != null)
    {
      using(var parser = ParserFactory.CreateParser(
        point.Document.Url))
      {
        parser.Parse();

        if(parser.Errors.Count <= 0)
        {
          var visitor = new NotNullAttributeVisitor(
            point.Document, method, target);
          parser.CompilationUnit.AcceptVisitor(
            visitor, null);
          this.SequencePoint = visitor.SequencePoint;
        }
      }
    }
  }

  internal SequencePoint SequencePoint { get; private set; }
```

The `FindSequencePoint()` extension method will return the first `SequencePoint` object it found in the `MethodDefinition`'s `Instruction` collection. You need a `SequencePoint` because it contains information about the location of the code file related to this method. If you find a `SequencePoint` object, then an `IParser`-based object is created via the `CreateParser()` method from the NRefactory `ParserFactory` class. The code file is contained in the `Uri` property of the `SequencePoint`'s `Document` property. If the `Parse()` call didn't find any errors, a `NotNullAttributeVisitor` object is created, which is passed to the parser. This is a nested class defined within `NotNullAttributeDebugger`, which is why there isn't a closing curly brace in this code snippet. (You'll see how this visitor objects works in the next section.) The SetPoint() method will either set the SequencePoint property on the NotNullAttributeDebugger object with a new SequencePoint object or a null reference. In the next section, you'll see how the right portion of "non-null" code is found.

In the last section, you saw that a visitor object was passed to AcceptVisitor(). The NotNullAttributeVisitor derives from an abstract class called AbstractAst-Visitor. This class contains a bunch of "VisitXYZ" methods that you can override to find specific parts in a code file, like a type or method definition. In this case, you need to find a method with the same name as the method you're currently looking at in the Injectors framework and then find the parameter with the same name that has the NotNullAttribute defined on it. NRefactory makes this simple. Let's look at the definition of this class and the two methods you need to override to look for methods. The following code listing defines the definition of this custom visitor.

**Listing 7.7   Creating an NRefactory Visitor**

```
using NR = ICSharpCode.NRefactory.Ast;

// ...

private sealed class NotNullAttributeVisitor : AbstractAstVisitor
{
  internal NotNullAttributeVisitor(
    Document document, MethodDefinition method,
      ParameterDefinition target)
  {
    this.Document = document;
    this.Method = method;
    this.Parameter = target;
  }

  public override object VisitConstructorDeclaration(
    NR.ConstructorDeclaration constructorDeclaration,
      object data)
  {
    this.VisitParametrizedNode(constructorDeclaration, true);
    return base.VisitConstructorDeclaration(
      constructorDeclaration, data);
  }

  public override object VisitMethodDeclaration(
    NR.MethodDeclaration methodDeclaration, object data)
  {
    this.VisitParametrizedNode(methodDeclaration, false);
    return base.VisitMethodDeclaration(
      methodDeclaration, data);
  }

  private Document Document { get; set; }
  private MethodDefinition Method { get; set; }
```

```
private ParameterDefinition Parameter { get; set; }
internal SequencePoint SequencePoint { get; private set; }
```

One unfortunate aspect of using NRefactory and Cecil together is that they use the same type names in a number of cases, such as `MethodDeclaration`.

Therefore, add a using statement to qualify when you're using a class defined from either the NRefactory or Cecil assembly. As you can see, you only need to override two methods, `VisitConstructorDeclaration()` and `VisitMethodDeclaration()`. Because `ConstructorDeclaration` and `MethodDeclaration` both inherit from a base class called `ParametrizedNode` that defines the members you need, that parsing code is defined in a common method called `VisitParametrizedNode()`. The following code listing shows how `VisitParametrizedNode()` creates the `SequencePoint` you need.

---

**Listing 7.8 Creating a `SequencePoint` for the `NotNullAttribute`**

```
private void VisitParametrizedNode(
  NR.ParametrizedNode node, bool isConstructor)
{
  if(((isConstructor && this.Method.IsConstructor) ||              ❶ Determine if this
    (node.Name == this.Method.Name)) &&                               is correct method
    node.Parameters.Count == this.Method.Parameters.Count)            by name
  {
    var doParametersMatch = true;
    NR.ParameterDeclarationExpression matchingParameter
      = null;

    for(var i = 0; i < node.Parameters.Count; i++)
    {
      var parsedParameter = node.Parameters[i];

      if(parsedParameter.ParameterName !=
          this.Method.Parameters[i].Name)                           ❷ Verify
      {                                                                parameters
        doParametersMatch = false;
        break;
      }
      else if(parsedParameter.ParameterName ==
        this.Parameter.Name)
      {
        matchingParameter = parsedParameter;
      }
    }

    if(doParametersMatch && matchingParameter != null)
    {
      this.SequencePoint =
        (from attributeSection in matchingParameter.Attributes
        from attribute in attributeSection.Attributes           ❸
        where (attribute.Name == "NotNullAttribute" ||
          attribute.Name == "NotNull")                          Find right
        select new SequencePoint(this.Document)                 NotNullAttribute
          {                                                     within the
            EndColumn = attribute.EndLocation.Column,           parameters
            EndLine = attribute.EndLocation.Line,
```

```
            StartColumn = attribute.StartLocation.Column,
            StartLine = attribute.StartLocation.Line
        }).Single();
    }
  }
}
```

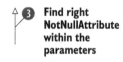

**③ Find right
NotNullAttribute
within the
parameters**

Check to see if the current method in the code file AST is the one Cecil found. You
have to do this verification by name, but if the method is a constructor, that name
won't match what Cecil will call a constructor: .ctor. That's why the name check is a little convoluted ❶.

Once you verify the method name, the next step is to check the parameter names ❷.
Again, all you have is a code file—you don't have type information at that point. The
best check is to see whether the number of parameters is the same and if the names
are in the same order as what Cecil found in the assembly. If that's true, finding the
attribute is only a LINQ statement away ❸. You traverse the attribute information in
the matched parameter to find the location where the "NotNull" or "NotNullAttribute"
text is. You can use that attribute's StartLocation and EndLocation properties to create a SequencePoint marked with the right text locations.

### OBSERVING THE RESULTS

Now that you've added debugging support for the NotNullAttribute, what happens when you run code that uses the attribute in the debugger? Figure 7.3 shows
the results. This screenshot was taken when the method was stepped into. The
debugger correctly highlights the "NotNull" text, and now the developer has a
much better indicator that something has added code to the method that's related
to the presence of the attribute.

You now know how to weave code into an assembly and provide debugging support. It's definitely not a trivial endeavor, but thankfully, due to the hard work of indi-
viduals that created and maintain Cecil and NRefactory, it's relatively painless.

## 7.4    Summary

In this chapter, you learned about the need to alter implementations post-build, how
to use the Cecil framework to edit assemblies based on the existence of metadata, and
how to add debugging support for injected code with Cecil and NRefactory.

```
namespace Injectors.SampleTarget
{
    [ToString(FlattenHierarchy = true)]
    public sealed class AttributedCustomer : Customer
    {
        private AttributedCustomer()
            : base() { }

        [Trace]
        public AttributedCustomer(Guid id, [NotNull] int age,
            [NotNull]string firstName, [NotNull]string lastName,
            : this()
```

**Figure 7.3  Adding highlighting
to attributes. You can clearly
see that code is associated
with the NotNullAttribute.**

Up to this point, you've seen numerous metaprogramming techniques that focused mostly on static languages, like C#. In part 3, we switch gears and introduce frameworks and concepts that are targeted for dynamic languages like Ruby and Python. You'll also see how you can use other languages that have metaprogramming techniques built in. Hang on—the ride's going to get even more interesting!

# Part 3

## Languages and tools

Learning about advanced techniques to build the supporting foundations of metaprogramming in your code is fun, but it's also beneficial to use the hard work of others.

In chapter 8 you'll see how you can use the Dynamic Language Runtime to support dynamic programming.

Discovering tools and languages that already have metaprogramming as a primary focus of its feature set is the focus of chapter 9.

In chapter 10, you'll get a tour of a new compiler API from Microsoft called Project Roslyn and what it brings to the table for developers.

# The Dynamic
# Language Runtime

**This chapter covers**

- The simplest dynamic classes: the
  `ExpandoObject` class, the `DynamicObject`
  class, and parsing the Open Data Protocol
  dynamically
- The DLR hosting model: runtimes, engines,
  and scopes
- Adding a rules engine to your application

Ask a group of Python or JavaScript programmers what they enjoy about their languages and they'll probably mention the term *dynamic*. Then ask the group what the word means, and there will undoubtedly be a range of responses, mostly centered on the theme of flexibility. These lovers of dynamic languages typically value flexibility and rapid development over type-safety. These priorities lead to an even deeper question: should the classification and access of data be the responsibility of compilers or a privilege reserved for programmers? The answer depends entirely on the kind of problem you're trying to solve.

If you need extremely high performance, dynamic typing may not be the smart choice. But if your program can decrease rigidity while increasing developer comprehension at the cost of a few more milliseconds here and there, dynamic typing can be helpful. Good software architects know how to balance these kinds of concerns. The desire for balance is why statically typed programming languages like C# offer dynamic typing as an option these days: static typing for safety and performance, and dynamic typing for when you need a bit of flexibility.

This chapter focuses on understanding when dynamic typing might be appropriate in an otherwise statically typed application. This isn't a chapter on learning Python or Ruby. In fact, we only touch on those languages to show how they can be integrated into a C# program to provide scripting capabilities. We begin by studying some of the most useful classes for creating dynamic objects in the Dynamic Language Runtime (DLR). One skill-building example shows how to add and remove methods and properties to a class at runtime. Then we put those new skills to work, showing how you can use the DLR to handle semistructured documents gracefully at runtime. We demonstrate how to use the DLR's hosting capabilities to embed a user-callable rules engine into your application with a few lines of code. Finally, we go behind the scenes to help you understand that the magic of dynamic programming isn't magic at all—by exploring the architecture of the DLR.

## 8.1    The simplest dynamic classes

There aren't many public classes in the System.Dynamic namespace, but there are 13 classes in that namespace with the term Binder in them. Near the end of this chapter, we look at binders and their crucial role in what the DLR calls *dynamic dispatch*. Of the five remaining classes in the namespace, only two are likely to be used by the average developer: the ExpandoObject and the DynamicObject. Both classes are useful for metaprogramming and for writing more flexible code in general.

### 8.1.1    The ExpandoObject class

The DLR's ExpandoObject has one of the funniest-sounding names in the .NET Framework. For English speakers, the name of this class connotes elasticity. What kind of stretchiness might be implied by such a name? Could the ExpandoObject be a collection class that grows automatically as you insert new items into it? In fact, the ExpandoObject is a collection. If you examine the documentation for the class, you'll notice that the ExpandoObject implements the interface IDictionary<string, Object>. Code like this should be possible:

```
ExpandoObject elastic = new ExpandoObject();
elastic["phrase"] = "Hello, world";
```

But when you compile that tiny bit of code, you get an error saying that the indexer isn't available. Why isn't the ExpandoObject behaving like a dictionary if it's declared as one? Because the ExpandoObject has implemented the dictionary interface explicitly. Therefore, the following modified snippet will compile:

```
IDictionary<string, object> flex = new ExpandoObject();
flex["phrase"] = "Hello, world!";
```

As it turns out, for an explicitly declared interface, you must declare the variables by which you intend to access the members as the specific interface type. This peculiarity of the C# language is used most often by not-so-inventive job interviewers looking for ways to fluster their candidates. It also happens to be a nice way to *conceal* an interface implementation to a certain degree as Microsoft has done in this case. The reason for implementing a dictionary interface at all might become apparent after studying this next bit of code:

```
IDictionary<string, object> flex = new ExpandoObject();
flex["phrase"] = "Hello, world!";
Console.WriteLine(((dynamic)flex).phrase);
```

You may be surprised that this will compile and successfully run to emit the venerable expression "Hello, world!" on the console window. Did you notice that in the last line of the code snippet, there were no quotes around the word *phrase*? It's being used like a property name. How can the C# compiler allow access to a property that doesn't exist? The answer lies in the casting of the `flex` variable as `dynamic` and C#'s handling of variables marked that way.

> **NOTE** Dynamic types in C# are a bit like the bending spoon in the movie *The Matrix*. As the child explains to the character Neo in that famous scene, "Do not try to bend the spoon—that's impossible. Instead, only try to realize the truth: there is no spoon." Similarly, there is no underlying type in C# that represents the `dynamic` keyword. If you disassemble a bit of compiled C# code using dynamic types, you'll see that the dynamic things are declared as `System.Object`. It's the C# compiler's treatment of those plain old objects that makes them behave dynamically. Don't try to understand dynamic as a type. Only realize the truth: there's no dynamic type.

By now, we hope you're beginning to grasp the connection between the `Expando-Object`'s implementation of `IDictionary<string, object>` and the ability to access elements of that collection as dynamic properties. This is possible because of C#'s `dynamic` keyword and another DLR interface called `IDynamicMetaObjectProvider`. We cover that interface and the concept of so-called *metaobjects* in detail later in this chapter. For now, we'll refer to the capability provided by that interface as *dynamic binding*. It's what adds the dynamic *feeling* to the C# programming language that Python, Ruby, and JavaScript programmers have enjoyed for many years.

The bit of code shown earlier is admittedly more awkward than it needs to be. After all, the folks at Microsoft made it easy to get ad hoc properties out of an `Expando-Object`. It should be as simple to get them into a dynamic object. The trick is to declare the `ExpandoObject` as dynamic from the start, like this:

```
dynamic flex = new ExpandoObject();
flex.phrase = "Hello, world!";
Console.WriteLine(flex.phrase);
```

That's much simpler, isn't it? This new snippet will compile and run to produce the same output as the last example. You no longer have to put the property name `phrase` in quotes or use the dictionary's indexer to set the string "Hello, world!" into it. Because the ExpandoObject is declared as dynamic, it gets dynamic treatment from the C# compiler instead of static treatment, doing that work for you using C#'s familiar syntax for accessing properties.

This also holds true when passing objects as parameters to functions. For example, listing 8.1 shows a function called TestBag that exercises a parameter named bag by adding data and code to it dynamically. The bag parameter is declared using the dynamic keyword, giving it special treatment by the C# compiler throughout the function.

**Listing 8.1  The TestBag function**

```
static void TestBag(dynamic bag)
{
  bag.Listen =
    new Func<string>(() => Console.ReadLine());
  bag.Say =
    new Action<string>(s => Console.Write(s));

  bag.Say("What's your ID? ");
  bag.ID = bag.Listen();
  bag.Say("Hello, " + bag.ID + "." +
    Environment.NewLine);
}
```

**NOTE**  The parameter in the TestBag function in listing 8.1 is named bag for a reason. Classes like ExpandoObject are sometimes called *property bags* because you can toss values into them and retrieve them later by name. Property bags need no formal declaration to contain data of any shape. They provide ad hoc access to variably shaped data, so they're called bags to cement the metaphor in your mind.

Note in listing 8.1 that not only can you toss properties into the bag but functions, too. The Listen and Say functions are assigned to the bag parameter as easily as the ID property. The Listen method as shown reads a line of text from the console. But you could easily modify that code at runtime by assigning a different function that invokes a web service to get the required input. Similarly, the Say function, which writes to the console, could also be replaced with another that writes the string elsewhere. With that kind of flexibility, perhaps you can begin to see how the DLR can enable simple yet compelling metaprogramming scenarios in your own code.

Invoking the functions that were added dynamically to the TestBag method is also quite natural, as you can see in listing 8.1. To call one of the newly added methods, you use the member access (dot) operator on the dynamic object, name the function to call, and pass required parameters between parentheses. This is the standard C# syntax for any function invocation operation. Because the bag parameter was declared as dynamic, C# includes all the necessary code to access ExpandoObject's dynamic binding capability for invoking member functions by name.

**NOTE** Among the so-called SOLID object-oriented programming principles, the "L" stands for the Liskov substitution principle (LSP). The simple idea of the LSP is that replacing an object with an instance of one of its subtypes shouldn't break the program. At the heart of the LSP is the idea that types implement contracts. For example, if consuming code expects a function named Listen to exist in an object, it must be there or the program could crash. But when a function can be injected dynamically as demonstrated with ExpandoObject, are traditional subtypes needed to violate or satisfy the LSP?

### 8.1.2   *The DynamicObject class*

The ExpandoObject is quite useful, but it's marked as sealed in the .NET Framework Class Library. You can't use it as a base class to enable other data types with dynamic binding. You could use the ExpandoObject as a model, implementing the somewhat complex IDynamicMetaObjectProvider interface to produce similar dynamic behavior, but that requires a fairly deep understanding of expression trees and other complex concepts.

Thankfully, the DLR provides another class in the System.Dynamic namespace that isn't sealed and provides a nice set of methods for selectively implementing dynamic binding on your own classes. The DynamicObject base class provides the following 12 public, virtual methods which can be overridden selectively to enable specific kinds of behaviors when working in a DLR-compliant language:

- TryBinaryOperation—Enables binary operators like addition (+), subtraction (-), and so on
- TryConvert—Enables the conversion to statically known types
- TryCreateInstance—Enables the instantiation of underlying data types that may be needed to support a dynamic object
- TryDeleteIndex—Enables the deletion of an indexed collection element (not supported by C# or Visual Basic syntax)
- TryDeleteMember—Enables the deletion of a member property or member function (not supported by C# or Visual Basic syntax)
- TryGetIndex—Enables fetching the value of an indexed collection element
- TryGetMember—Enables fetching the value of a property
- TryInvoke—Enables the invocation of the dynamic object itself as a function
- TryInvokeMember—Enables the invocation of a member as a function
- TrySetIndex—Enables the mutation of an indexed collection element
- TrySetMember—Enables the mutation of a member property or the assignment of a member function's implementation
- TryUnaryOperation—Enables the unary operators like increment (++) and decrement (–)

The two words repeated throughout this list are *try* and *enables*. Those words are important because they define the spirit of the DynamicObject class. When you use the `DynamicObject` class as a base class, you choose to enable various dynamic binding features by overriding as many or as few of these virtual methods as necessary. The so-called metaobject within the `DynamicObject` will invoke your overridden methods when the runtime binder dispatches calls into it.

If, for example you don't intend for your dynamic type to be treated as an array—using C#'s index operator (`[]`)—you don't need to override the `TryGetIndex` and `TrySetIndex` methods in your class. But if at some later time, a consumer of your class attempts to use the index operator when accessing your dynamic objects, the base class will throw an exception at runtime because it can't find an implementation for the requested operation.

To put this into context, let's create your own version of the `ExpandoObject` aptly named `ElastoObject`, as shown in the following listing.

**Listing 8.2  `ElastoObject` Source Code**

```
class ElastoObject : DynamicObject
{
  Dictionary<string, object> members =
    new Dictionary<string, object>();

  public override bool TrySetMember(
    SetMemberBinder binder, object value)
  {
    if (value != null)
      members[binder.Name] = value;
    else if (members.ContainsKey(binder.Name))
      members.Remove(binder.Name);
    return true;
  }

  public override bool TryGetMember(
    GetMemberBinder binder, out object result)
  {
    if (members.ContainsKey(binder.Name))
    {
      result = members[binder.Name];
      return true;
    }
    return base.TryGetMember(binder, out result);
  }

  public override bool TryInvokeMember(
    InvokeMemberBinder binder, object[] args,
    out object result)
  {
    if (members.ContainsKey(binder.Name))
    {
      Delegate d = members[binder.Name] as Delegate;
      if (d != null)
      {
        result = d.DynamicInvoke(args);
        return true;
```

```
      }
    }
    return base.TryInvokeMember(binder, args,
      out result);
  }
}
```

The `ElastoObject` shown in listing 8.2 behaves much like the DLR's `ExpandoObject`. In fact, using the test function shown in listing 8.1, the following two lines of code will behave identically:

```
TestBag(new ExpandoObject());
TestBag(new ElastoObject());
```

The key to the `ElastoObject`'s dynamic binding capability starts with deriving from the DLR's `DynamicObject` base class. Internally, the `ElastoObject` creates a `Dictionary <string, object>` for storing name-value pairs, but it doesn't implement any interfaces specific to that capability, as `ExpandoObject` does. We'll use that difference to show how you can expose dictionary-like functionality without interfaces in the next section. To handle calls from the runtime binder and the `DynamicObject`'s metaobject, three overrides are provided in the `ElastoObject`:

- `TrySetMember`
- `TryGetMember`
- `TryInvokeMember`

The remaining nine virtual functions in the `DynamicObject` base class aren't overridden in the `ElastoObject` because you don't need those kinds of dynamic binding capabilities to mimic the behavior of `ExpandoObject`. Each of the three implemented overrides takes an operation-specific binder class as its first parameter. The `TrySet-Member` method takes a `SetMemberBinder` type parameter, the `TryGetMember` takes a `GetMemberBinder` type parameter, and so on. Twelve of these binder types are defined in the `System.Dynamic` namespace, one for each of the twelve binding operations supported by DLR-compliant languages. Each binder class can have properties and methods specific to the type of binding operation to be performed.

The `TrySetMember` override handles the setting of new properties and methods into the dynamic object. The name of the property or method to set is passed in the `Set-MemberBinder`'s `Name` property. The value to be set is passed as a separate parameter and assigned to the internal dictionary class by name for future use. Returning `true` from `TrySetMember` signals the metaobject that invoked it that the member was successfully set.

Even though the C# language doesn't syntactically support the concept of deleting class members at runtime, the `TrySetMember` function in the `ElastoObject` provides a way to do that. Consider the following line of code:

```
bag.Say = null;
```

If you were to add that line near the end of the test function shown in listing 8.1, you'd effectively delete the `Say` function from the class at runtime. The `TrySetMember`

---

**The DLR binders as the "language of languages"**

If you started a cleanroom exercise to define the discrete operations necessary to make any two programming languages communicate with each other, the chances are good that you would end up with something resembling the 12 binding methods defined in the DLR's `DynamicMetaObject` class.

The 12 virtual methods in the `DynamicObject` class beginning with `Try` reflect these binding operations nicely. With them, you can create new dynamic objects, convert them, assign property values and new functions, fetch property values, and invoke functions. You can even use them to treat your dynamic objects as arrays or to perform unary and binary operations on them in the syntax of your favorite DLR-compliant language.

The DLR provides a robust *language of languages* that could be considered not a metaprogramming tool but a generalized Inter-Process Communication (IPC) framework.

---

method considers null to be a sentinel value for signaling the removal of members from the internal dictionary—even functions that have been added to the dynamic class. Any attempt to invoke the `Say` function after removing it would result in a run-time error.

The `TryGetMember` override handles the fetching of property values. The `Get-MemberBinder`'s `Name` property is used to find the desired dictionary entry and return it to the caller through the `result` output parameter. If the named member isn't found in the dictionary, the base class implementation of `TryGetMember` is allowed to run, which will throw a meaningful, DLR-specific exception if it can't find the named member. Again, returning `true` from this method signals to the metaobject that fetching the member was successful.

Lastly, there's `TryInvokeMember`, which handles the calling of functions on the dynamic `ElastoObject` class. Like `TryGetMember`, this method attempts to find the member named within the binder parameter. But rather than returning what it finds, the `TryInvokeMember` method casts it to a `Delegate` and calls its `DynamicInvoke` function, passing whatever parameters were provided by the caller.

One of the key differences between the DLR's `ExpandoObject` and the `ElastoObject` is in the exposure of the dictionary implementation used to manage the member properties and methods. The `ExpandoObject` explicitly implements the interface `IDictionary <string, object>`, whereas the `ElastoObject` hides its internal use of a generic `Dictionary<string, object>` class. You may be asking yourself that because both `ExpandoObject` and `ElastoObject` are always meant to be used dynamically, why does the `ExpandoObject` expose its dictionary via interface implementation at all? Why not use dynamic dispatch methods like the one shown in the following listing instead?

---

**Listing 8.3  Adding Indexing to `ElastoObject`**

```
public override bool TryGetIndex(
  GetIndexBinder binder, object[] indexes,
  out object result)
```

```
{
  string name = indexes[0] as string;
  if (members.ContainsKey(name))
  {
    result = members[name];
    return true;
  }
  return base.TryGetIndex(binder, indexes,
    out result);
}
```

If the `TryGetIndex` method shown in listing 8.3 were added to the `ElastoObject` shown in listing 8.2, an interesting new dynamic capability would be added. Specifically, you could write code like this, using the listings provided so far in this chapter:

```
dynamic squishy = new ElastoObject();
TestBag(squishy);
Delegate shout = squishy["Say"];
string id = squishy["ID"];
shout.DynamicInvoke("Howdy, " + id + ".");
```

This is ugly code, we admit. But it does demonstrate how DLR binding can be used to expose collection-like functionality from a dynamic type without implementing any collection-specific contracts. There's nothing wrong with implementing interfaces, but for classes that are always meant to be used dynamically, what's the value in doing so?

If you disassemble the DLR's `ExpandoObject`, you'll see that it provides a much more robust implementation of a property and function bag than the `ElastoObject` shown here. We encourage you to do your own disassembly and inspection. Dissecting Microsoft's code in the .NET Framework Class Library is a great way to learn. But even without that sort of investment, you should recognize from the simple `ElastoObject` class shown here that writing your own dynamic types using the DLR's `DynamicObject` as a base class isn't difficult.

Now that we've successfully mimicked the `ExpandoObject` to a certain extent, let's take a look at a real-world example of dynamic types in action.

### 8.1.3 *Parsing the Open Data Protocol dynamically*

The 2011 Digital Universe Study by IDC (sponsored by EMC) estimated that 1.2 zettabytes of data was created. In 2011, the estimate was 1.8 zettabytes. That's almost two trillion gigabytes of information. Anyone working in a data-rich business environment nowadays understands that a lot of this data is unstructured or semistructured in nature. That study also showed that the growth of data in the coming decade will exceed 7,500 percent, whereas the growth in the available IT staff will grow by a comparatively modest 150 percent.

One of the ways to meet the challenge is through extensible systems like the Open Data Protocol (OData). The excellent depth of expression in OData lies in the Common Schema Definition Language (CSDL) and its Entity Data Model (EDM). The OData Atom format allows for metadata-rich, highly extensible property sets to be exposed on nearly any type of schema. One of the most popular internet services supporting OData is Netflix. To query the Atom (XML) document for the movie *The Terminator*, the following query might be used:

```
http://odata.netflix.com/Catalog/Titles
  ?$filter=Name eq 'The Terminator'
```

Key that web address into your browser to see the Atom document describing the movie. The XML clipping in the following listing shows an interesting chunk of the document that could be returned.

**Listing 8.4  Fragment of Netflix OData describing a movie**

```
<m:properties>
  <d:Name>The Terminator</d:Name>
  <d:Synopsis>In the post-apocalyptic ...</d:Synopsis>
  <d:AverageRating m:type="Edm.Double">3.9</d:AverageRating>
  <d:ReleaseYear m:type="Edm.Int32">1984</d:ReleaseYear>
  <d:Runtime m:type="Edm.Int32">6420</d:Runtime>
  <d:Rating>R</d:Rating>
  <d:Dvd>
    <d:Available m:type="Edm.Boolean">true</d:Available>
  </d:Dvd>
  <d:BluRay>
    <d:Available m:type="Edm.Boolean">true</d:Available>
  </d:BluRay>
  <d:Instant>
    <d:Available m:type="Edm.Boolean">true</d:Available>
  </d:Instant>
  <d:BoxArt>
    <d:SmallUrl>http://cdn-1.nflximg.com/...</d:SmallUrl>
  </d:BoxArt>
</m:properties>
```

In Atom documents like the one shown in listing 8.4, the "m:" prefix denotes the Atom metadata namespace, whereas "d:" signifies an Atom data property. Notice that some of the properties in the Netflix feed are tagged with a data type attribute. For example, the AverageRating property is declared as the type Edm.Double. This is a well-known, primitive data type from the CSDL EDM for double-precision floating point numbers. Also in the Netflix document fragment, observe the use of the primitive data types Edm.Int32 and Edm.Boolean. This is valuable metadata that any code designed to parse OData feeds should take full advantage of.

Now look at another example. The following URL will retrieve the OData feed from ebay.com for items related to *The Terminator*. Realize that because ebay.com can sell items of any type, such a search term may return many items:

```
http://ebayodata.cloudapp.net/Items?search=The Terminator
```

The following listing shows a subset of the properties returned by the ebay.com OData service for such a search term.

**Listing 8.5   Fragment of ebay.com OData feed for a search term**

```
<m:properties>
  <d:Title>Terminator 3: Rise of the Machines (DVD)</d:Title>
  <d:TimeLeft>P0DT0H9M42S</d:TimeLeft>
  <d:Currency>USD</d:Currency>
  <d:CurrentPrice m:type="Edm.Double">
    2.5</d:CurrentPrice>
  <d:Country>US</d:Country>
  <d:GalleryUrl>http://thumbs...</d:GalleryUrl>
  <d:Condition>
    <d:Name>Like New</d:Name>
  </d:Condition>
  <d:ListingInfo>
    <d:ListingType>Auction</d:ListingType>
  </d:ListingInfo>
  <d:ShippingInformation>
    <d:ShippingServiceCost m:type="Edm.Double">
      3</d:ShippingServiceCost>
  </d:ShippingInformation>
</m:properties>
```

Saying that the schema of Netflix OData and ebay.com OData differ would not be accurate. After all, they both adhere to the same CSDL specification and they're both Atom-compliant. But in looking at them, they're clearly structured differently using the extensible data properties available via Atom. The code to parse these two different feeds obviously needs to be specialized—in particular, because one of them will return at most one item and the other may return many. Or does it? A dynamic data type may help to solve this problem generically by exposing a natural, language-integrated syntax for parsing any kind of OData.

#### ESTABLISHING THE FRAMEWORK OF THE DYNAMICODATA CLASS

Because OData sources can be slow and aren't suitable for synchronous consumption from UI code, let's begin by adding a delegate called `DataReady` that can pass a dynamically typed object to event subscribers. This will allow the asynchronous feed fetching methods to signal callers when OData documents become ready:

```
public delegate void DataReady(dynamic obj);
```

Next let's define a couple of XML namespaces commonly used in the publication of OData feeds via Atom. These are for the metadata properties collection and the data properties contained therein, as shown in listings 8.4 and 8.5. An event of the `DataReady` delegate type will also be exposed from the class:

```
public class DynamicOData
{
  public event DataReady OnDataReady;

  private const string odataNamespace =
    "http://schemas.microsoft.com/ado/" +
    "2007/08/dataservices";
```

```
private const string metadataNamespace =
   odataNamespace + "/metadata";
}
```

Now, let's add to the class the means for storing a reference to an XML node within the feed:

```
private IEnumerable<XElement> _current = null;
```

To complete the basic setup, you need a few constructors for the class. A default constructor that sets no _current XML element will come in handy. The other two constructors will help handle two specific cases during XML as you move through the document hierarchy: one where a single XML node needs to be wrapped as a new DynamicOData object and another when a sequence of nodes needs to be presented that way:

```
public DynamicOData() { }

protected DynamicOData(XElement current)
{
  _current = new List<XElement> { current };
}

protected DynamicOData(
  IEnumerable<XElement> current)
{
  _current = new List<XElement>(current);
}
```

### FETCHING AND PARSING AN ODATA FEED ASYNCHRONOUSLY

Now that you have the basic framework for the DynamicOData class in place, let's add a method to fetch data from a query string:

```
public void FetchAsync(string queryUrl)
{
  WebClient client = new WebClient();
  client.DownloadStringCompleted +=
    OnDownloadCompleted;
  client.DownloadStringAsync(
    new Uri(queryUrl));
}
```

The class must also include a method to be called when the WebClient's Download-StringCompleted event fires:

```
private void OnDownloadCompleted(object sender,
  DownloadStringCompletedEventArgs e)
{
  string xml = (e != null || e.Error == null)
      ? e.Result : String.Empty;
  if (xml != null)
  {
    var document = XDocument.Parse(xml);
    XNamespace ns = metadataNamespace;
    _current = document.Descendants(
```

```
          ns + "properties");
  }
  if (OnDataReady != null)
    OnDataReady(this);
}
```

The `OnDownloadCompleted` method parses the XML string from the OData server and assigns the descendent nodes matching the Atom metadata properties namespace to the `_current` enumeration. Finally, the `OnDataReady` event is fired for any subscribers to let them know that the data is ready.

### ADDING DYNAMIC TRYGETMEMBER FUNCTIONALITY TO THE CLASS

So far, there's no dynamic capability in the `DynamicOData` class. It doesn't even derive from the DLR's `DynamicObject` class as we've constructed it so far. Let's add that declaration to the class:

```
public class DynamicOData, DynamicObject
```

To make the OData Atom data properties available in DLR-compliant languages as properties on the dynamic class, override the `TryGetMember` method as shown in the next listing. This method exposes a pseudoproperty called `Value` that can be used to obtain the text value at a given XML node. The code works by fetching the `Value` property of the first `XElement` on the `_current` collection.

**Listing 8.6   Adding `TryGetMember` to the `DynamicOData` class**

```
public override bool TryGetMember(
  GetMemberBinder binder, out object result)
{
  result = null;
  if (binder.Name == "Value")
  {
    XElement element = _current.ElementAt(0);
    result = _current.ElementAt(0).Value;
  }
  else
  {
    var items = _current.Descendants(
      XName.Get(binder.Name,
        odataNamespace));
    if (items == null || items.Count() == 0)
      return false;
    result = new DynamicOData(items);
  }
  return true;
}
```

If the property named in the `GetMemberBinder` parameter isn't the special pseudoproperty, the code gathers up the XML descendants of the `_current` node, packages them as a new `DynamicOData` object using one the constructors described earlier, and returns it. By returning a new `DynamicOData` object for the newly discovered nodes, you can chain dynamic accesses one after the other to traverse the XML hierarchy.

Peek at the fragment of the Netflix OData feed in listing 8.4, examining how DVD availability is encoded. With the simple `TryGetMember` function in place, you can write simple code like this to access such an element:

```
DynamicOData movie = new DynamicOData();
movie.OnDataReady += title => {
  Console.WriteLine(title.Dvd.Available.Value); };
movie.FetchAsync(
  "http://odata.netflix.com/Catalog/Titles" +
  "?$filter=Name eq 'The Terminator'");
```

This will write the string `"true"` to the console window if the requested movie is available at Netflix. Observe how the lambda expression assigned to the `OnDataReady` event chains together XML elements in the feed. Because of the way the delegate was declared, the `title` parameter is treated dynamically by the compiler. Therefore, the call to `title.Dvd` invokes the `TryGetMember` method, which wraps the XML nodes there as a new `DynamicOData` object and returns it. From there, the treatment continues dynamically, so the `Available` node is similarly accessed via `TryGetMember` and wrapped as another new `DynamicOData` object. Finally, the special `Value` pseudoproperty is requested, so the `TryGetMember` implementation obtains the `Value` of the DVD availability node and returns it to the caller. This doesn't look like XML parsing at all, does it? Instead, it appears as though we're accessing well-known properties within the OData using plain old C# syntax.

One of the refinements that would be nice at this point is to take advantage of the CSDL EDM type data that's embedded in the Atom feed. Observe in listing 8.4 that the Netflix feed includes type information for DVD availability. Specifically, a `type` attribute is included like this:

```
<d:Dvd>
  <d:Available m:type="Edm.Boolean">true</d:Available>
</d:Dvd>
```

Rather than return a string of the XML node value, why not have the dynamic type coerce the value into its declared type and return it to the caller? You can do that by adding a bit of parsing code to the `TryGetMember` method where it handles the `Value` pseudoproperty, as shown in the following listing.

#### Listing 8.7  Coercing to various OData CSDL EDM data types

```
XAttribute typeAttr = element.Attribute(
  XName.Get("type", metadataNamespace));
if (typeAttr != null)
{
  string type = typeAttr.Value;
  if (type != null)
  {
    switch (type)
    {
      default:
        break;
```

```
      case "Null":
        result = null;
        break;
      case "Edm.Boolean":
        result = Convert.ToBoolean(result);
        break;
      case "Edm.Byte":
        result = Convert.ToByte(result);
        break;
      case "Edm.DateTime":
        result = Convert.ToDateTime(result);
        break;
      case "Edm.Decimal":
        result = Convert.ToDecimal(result);
        break;
      case "Edm.Double":
        result = Convert.ToDouble(result);
        break;
      case "Edm.Single":
        result = Convert.ToSingle(result);
        break;
      case "Edm.Guid":
        result = Guid.ParseExact(
          (string)result, "D");
        break;
      case "Edm.Int16":
        result = Convert.ToInt16(result);
        break;
      case "Edm.Int32":
        result = Convert.ToInt32(result);
        break;
      case "Edm.Int64":
        result = Convert.ToInt64(result);
        break;
      case "Edm.SByte":
        result = Convert.ToSByte(result);
        break;
      case "Edm.DateTimeOffset":
        result = DateTimeOffset.Parse(
          (string)result);
        break;
    }
  }
}
```

With the code from listing 8.7 inside the TryGetMember's Value pseudoproperty handler, try running the preceding small exercise to get the DVD availability for a movie. You'll notice that now what appears on the console are the words "True" or "False" instead of "true" or "false," respectively. Visually, it's a small difference, but under the covers the change is significant. When the words "true" or "false" were being displayed on the console, it was because the literal string within the XML was being written. But after adding code to coerce the property value to .NET data types, depending on the EDM data types declared in the underlying XML, the outputs "True" and

"False" indicate that you're working with the return values from the `ToString` method on a `System.Boolean` object instead.

### ADDING DYNAMIC TRYGETMEMBER FUNCTIONALITY TO THE CLASS

Reading XML from an OData feed using fluent C# syntax is great, but you may want to modify the document, too. That's simple: override the `TrySetMember` method in the `DynamicOData` class, as shown in the following listing.

**Listing 8.8   Adding `TrySetMember` to the `DynamicOData` class**

```
public override bool TrySetMember(
  SetMemberBinder binder, object value)
{
  if (binder.Name == "Value")
  {
    _current.ElementAt(0).Value =
      value.ToString();
    return true;
  }
  return false;
}
```

Notice in listing 8.8 that only the `Value` pseudoproperty is assignable. We stopped there for simplicity, but you can certainly add more functionality to the `TrySetMember` method if good reasons to do so exist. With this simple, new method in place, you could now add the following lines of code to the lambda expression shown earlier to modify the movie obtained from the Netflix service:

```
title.Dvd.Available.Value = false;
title.AverageRating.Value = 4.1;
```

This will set the DVD availability and average rating in the underlying XML document. Querying those values later will prove that the change has been recorded. Not that Netflix would allow us to change those values by posting back to its OData service, but if it did, the modified document in hand would be a good starting point.

### ADDING DYNAMIC TRYGETINDEX FUNCTIONALITY TO THE CLASS

Not all OData queries will produce a single object as the Netflix query does. In fact, because individual properties within a node can themselves be collections of other properties and can be wrapped as new `DynamicOData` objects, having the class behave as an array from time to time is important. To do that, add the following method:

```
public override bool TryGetIndex(
  GetIndexBinder binder, object[] indexes,
  out object result)
{
  int ndx = (int)indexes[0];
  result = new DynamicOData(
    _current.ElementAt(ndx));
  return true;
}
```

For simplicity, only a single, numeric index will be accepted. You could add as many index dimensions as you like, and those could be of any data type. Notice that you're using the other custom constructor described at the beginning of this example, wrapping the single XElement at the specified index as a new DynamicOData object. That allows the returned object to be used to continue the chain of resolution like this:

```
DynamicOData ebayItem = new DynamicOData();
ebayItem.OnDataReady += item => {
  Console.WriteLine(
    item[3].ShippingInformation
      .ShippingServiceCost.Value); };
ebayItem.FetchAsync(
  "http://ebayodata.cloudapp.net/ +
  "Items?search=The Terminator ");
```

This small bit of code will display the shipping service cost of the fourth item on the console window. Observe the similarities between the code used to query Netflix and this code that queries ebay.com. The DynamicOData class makes it possible to treat all OData feeds in a similar fashion, greatly increasing programmer comprehension by reducing code complexity. If you recall, this was a key goal for the application of metaprogramming techniques that we declared at the beginning of the book.

## 8.2 *The DLR hosting model*

Thinking back to the goals of metaprogramming stated in the beginning of the book, remember that *meta* can mean *after* or *beside*. Many types of metaprogramming we've explored so far are the after kind, realized by modifying types and classes after they've been created to alter their behavior. Other types of metaprogramming you've seen are the beside varieties, creating types on the fly to suit your needs at runtime. Scripting fits nicely into the beside style of metaprogramming because it involves running code alongside another system, often acting as its controller.

There are many reasons for wanting to integrate your application's main programming language, say C#, with a scripting language like Python or Ruby. To highlight one of the more interesting examples of this type, take a look at the pseudocode in the next listing. Don't worry about syntax and such for now. Read through the listing and imagine that the business users of an e-commerce application wrote this pseudocode to express the basic rules that govern the discounting of products based on their advertising promotions.

**Listing 8.9  A script for discounting items by type in a shopping cart**

```
totalItems = 0
clothingItems = 0

for line in cart.LineItems:
  line.Discount = 0.0
  totalItems = totalItems + line.Quantity
  if line.Product.Category == 'Clothing':
    clothingItems = clothingItems + line.Quantity
```

```python
clothingDiscount = 0.0
if clothingItems > 5:
  clothingDiscount = 0.09
elif clothingItems >= 2:
  clothingDiscount = 0.05

for line in cart.LineItems:
  if line.Product.Category == 'Clothing':
    line.Discount = clothingDiscount
  if totalItems >= 7:
    line.Discount = line.Discount + 0.03
```

Not knowing anything in particular about the pseudocode in listing 8.9, most developers can recognize what this script might do. In fact, many savvy business users will follow along, too, given the sheer simplicity of the code. Reading it in English, it goes something like this:

- Set up a couple of variables for counting items.
- Loop over the LineItems contained in something named the cart.
  - Set the Discount level of each LineItem to zero.
  - Accumulate the Quantity of each LineItem into totalItems.
  - For each LineItem that has the 'Clothing' Category for its Product, accumulate the Quantity of each LineItem into clothingItems.
- Set a discount percentage for all clothing items based on the count tallied within the loop. At least two clothingItems in the cart yields a 5 percent discount on them, whereas 5 or more result in a 9 percent discount being applied.
- Loop over the LineItems in the cart again, setting the calculated discount percentages for the items in the 'Clothing' Product Category. To make things interesting, an additional 3 percent discount is applied to every item in the cart if 7 or more items have been included.

In this pseudocode, the only concept that isn't clear lies in the definition of the cart variable and the LineItem collection it contains. Where was the cart defined? Soon enough, we'll show you how to inject a plain old .NET object (PONO) like the cart into a script like this one using DLR hosting.

If you're comfortable with the pseudocode in listing 8.9 by now, it's time to reveal a little secret. It's not pseudocode at all. It's a working Python program that we'll use in the next section to demonstrate how you can integrate a scriptable rules engine in your own applications with a few dozen lines of code. First, though, understanding the key classes that exist for DLR hosting is important. Let's become familiar with run-times engines and scopes: three of the more important type groups to using DLR hosting effectively.

> **NOTE** Microsoft's Dino Viehland, one of the key contributors to the DLR and the IronPython language implementation, describes the DLR as having two *layers*. The inner layer contains the .NET Framework classes like Dynamic-Object and the various binders examined in the previous section. Those

classes are part of the .NET core, so everyone who installs the .NET Framework has them. The outer layer of the DLR, specifically the hosting API, exists in assemblies that don't ship with the .NET framework. Download the latest stable release from http://ironpython.codeplex.com to complete the exercises in the remainder of this section.

### 8.2.1 Runtimes, engines, and scopes

When you begin working with DLR hosting, the sheer volume of domain-specific classes can make the concepts difficult to grasp. You'll see classes in the `Microsoft .Scripting` namespace like `SourceUnit`, `ScopeVariable`, and `ScriptCode`. From the `Microsoft.Scripting.Hosting` namespace, you'll come across classes like `Compiled-Code`, `ScriptHost`, and `ScriptSource`. All these classes exist in a single assembly named `Microsoft.Scripting.dll` that you need to reference in any application that hosts DLR-compliant scripting languages. You can download that assembly and its source code from http://dlr.codeplex.com.

With so many hosting classes having the word `script` in their names, knowing where to start can be confusing. For simple script hosting scenarios, there are three core types in the DLR that you should understand well: the `ScriptRuntime`, the `ScriptScope`, and the `ScriptEngine`.

#### THE SCRIPTRUNTIME CLASS

As you can see in figure 8.1, the `ScriptRuntime` is something of a master object in the DLR's hosting model.

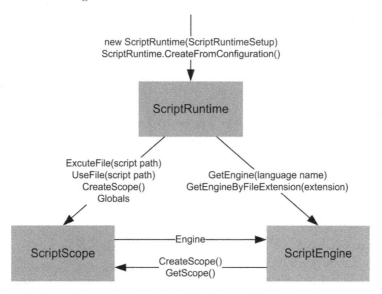

**Figure 8.1   The major classes in the DLR Hosting API are the `ScriptRuntime`, `ScriptScope`, and `ScriptEngine`. To use the hosting API, always start by creating a `ScriptRuntime`, specifying the scripting languages that you intend to make available.**

It represents the global script state for a `ScriptEngine` and its associated scope and executable code objects. Any application hosting a DLR-compliant scripting language will begin by using a constructor for the runtime class or by calling its static factory method `CreateFromConfiguration` to load language setup data from the application's configuration file. The following listing shows a sample configuration file that could be used to set up the assembly for the IronPython language using the `Create-FromConfiguration` factory method.

**Listing 8.10   Application configuration file for enabling IronPython**

```xml
<?xml version="1.0"?>
<configuration>
  <configSections>
    <section name="microsoft.scripting"
      type="Microsoft.Scripting.Hosting.Configuration.Section,
        Microsoft.Scripting"/>
  </configSections>
  <microsoft.scripting>
    <languages>
      <language names="IronPython;Python;py"
        extensions=".py" displayName="IronPython"
        type="IronPython.Runtime.PythonContext, IronPython"/>
    </languages>
  </microsoft.scripting>
</configuration>
```

If you choose to use the configuration file-based factory method to create a `Script-Runtime`, you must include at least one `<language>` element within the `<languages>` collection.

To ensure that the loading and processing of the configuration file shown in listing 8.10 doesn't fault and throw exceptions at runtime, the assemblies `IronPython.dll` and `Microsoft.Scripting.dll` must be available in the application's private assembly path at runtime. But it's common for Visual Studio not to copy these assemblies to the output directory because there may be no mentions of types from those assemblies in the C# or Visual Basic source code. You can avoid this by setting the `Copy Local` property of those references to `True`, as shown in figure 8.2.

Once `Microsoft.Scripting.dll` and language-specific assemblies have been properly referenced, and an application configuration file like the one shown in listing 8.10 is available, the following line of code will create a DLR hosting runtime without exception:

**Figure 8.2   Referenced scripting language assemblies may not be copied to the output directory by Visual Studio during compilation. Set the Copy Local property on the assembly reference to True in the Solution Explorer pane as shown here to make sure they are copied.**

```
ScriptRuntime runtime =
  ScriptRuntime.CreateFromConfiguration();
```

You may include multiple setup sections for hosting more than one scripting language in an application. For example, you could allow your program to be simultaneously scripted with both Python and Ruby. That's not common, but it's certainly possible. If you don't want to use a configuration file to express the scripting language setup, you can also do it in source code, as follows:

```
var language = new LanguageSetup(
  "IronPython.Runtime.PythonContext, IronPython",
  "IronPython",
  new[] { "IronPython", "Python", "py" },
  new[] { ".py" });
var runtimeSetup = new ScriptRuntimeSetup();
runtimeSetup.LanguageSetups.Add(language);
var runtime = new ScriptRuntime(runtimeSetup);
```

In this snippet of code, a LanguageSetup class is constructed passing values similar to those specified in the <language> element of the configuration file shown in listing 8.10. Next, a ScriptRuntimeSetup class is created, and the newly created LanguageSetup is inserted into its LanguageSetups collection. Finally, the ScriptRuntimeSetup instance is passed to the constructor of the ScriptRuntime class.

There's a factory method called ReadConfiguration in the ScriptRuntimeSetup type that you may also find useful for configuring runtime objects. With this static method, a custom configuration file can be loaded to construct a ScriptRuntime with a single line of code:

```
var customRuntime = new ScriptRuntime(
  ScriptRuntimeSetup.ReadConfiguration(
    "custom.config"));
```

You can use an overloaded version of that same factory method to load the configuration from a System.IO.Stream–derived object instead:

```
byte[] buffer;
// fill buffer with configuration here
ScriptRuntime streamRuntime;
using (var stream = new MemoryStream(buffer))
{
  streamRuntime = new ScriptRuntime(
    ScriptRuntimeSetup.ReadConfiguration(stream));
}
```

In this example, a MemoryStream has been loaded with configuration data from some unknown source—perhaps from a remote configuration service. The resulting Stream is read by the ReadConfiguration factory method to create the ScriptRuntimeSetup instance necessary for constructing a new runtime. Any Stream–derived type will do, including a SqlFileStream or a NetworkStream, making this a handy factory method for fetching configuration data for DLR hosting runtimes from a variety of sources.

The `ScriptRuntime` class contains a variety of useful collections and helper methods, covered in the next few pages. But we can't cover all of them. For a more complete reference, download dlr-spec-hosting.pdf from the documentation area of http://dlr.codeplex.com.

### THE SCRIPTENGINE CLASS

After obtaining a reference to a `ScriptRuntime` configured for the IronPython language, you could execute a file containing Python source with one line of code:

```
runtimeObject.ExecuteFile("HelloWorld.py");
```

This may be convenient, but it offers little control over the environment you need to prepare for the script's execution. Loading source code from disk-based storage is also less than ideal in a lot of situations. In sophisticated script-hosting applications with many script assets, source code is often acquired from a database or from a web service instead.

> **NOTE**  As of this writing, the stable, shipping versions of IronPython and Iron-Ruby are v2.7.2.1 and v1.1.3, respectively. All the samples in this section of the book will work with those versions. When you reference the IronPython.dll assembly, you can do it from the Global Assembly Cache (GAC) or directly from the installation folder, typically in C:\Program Files (x86)\IronPython 2.7 or some similar path. IronRuby's main assembly is only installed in the GAC. But you can reference it from a version-specific subfolder under C:\Windows\Microsoft.NET\assembly\GAC_MSIL\IronRuby if you must. Better yet, download the source code for IronPython and IronRuby, then build your own assemblies for these languages.

For finer control, it's usually better to fetch a reference to an engine object that can execute source code in a variety of useful ways. Because a single `ScriptRuntime` can host more than one scripting language simultaneously, you must ask for a specific `Script-Engine` by name or by file type. The next shows the loading of both the IronPython language and the IronRuby language into a single `ScriptRuntime` and then the use of two different methods to obtain the `ScriptEngine` for each language.

**Listing 8.11  `MultiLanguageLoad`: executing in two languages from `ScriptEngines`**

```
public static void MultiLanguageLoad()
{
  var runtimeSetup = new ScriptRuntimeSetup();

  var pythonSetup = new LanguageSetup(
    typeName: "IronPython.Runtime.PythonContext, IronPython",
    displayName: "IronPython",
    names: new[] { "IronPython", "Python", "py" },
    fileExtensions: new[] { ".py" });
  runtimeSetup.LanguageSetups.Add(pythonSetup);

  var rubySetup = new LanguageSetup(
    typeName: "IronRuby.Runtime.RubyContext, IronRuby",
```

```
    displayName: "IronRuby",
    names: new[] { "IronRuby", "Ruby", "rb" },
    fileExtensions: new[] { ".rb" });
runtimeSetup.LanguageSetups.Add(rubySetup);

ScriptRuntime runtimeObject =
  new ScriptRuntime(runtimeSetup);

ScriptEngine pythonEngine =
  runtimeObject.GetEngine("Python");
pythonEngine.Execute("print 'Hello from Python!'");

ScriptEngine rubyEngine =
  runtimeObject.GetEngineByFileExtension(".rb");
rubyEngine.Execute("puts 'Hello from Ruby!'");
}
```

The `MultiLanguageLoad` example in listing 8.11 starts by creating `LanguageSetup` objects for IronPython and IronRuby and then loads them into a new `Script-Runtime`. Because we're not using types from Iron-Python and IronRuby in the compiled code, be sure to set the `Copy Local` property to `True` for the Iron-Python.dll and IronRuby.dll assemblies in your Visual Studio project, as shown in figure 8.2. The remaining lines of code in the `MultiLanguageLoad` example demonstrate how you can obtain language engine references using the `GetEngine` and `GetEngineByFileExtension` methods on the runtime object. Using those engine references, executing simple bits of Python and Ruby code is easy, as shown in figure 8.3.

**Figure 8.3 The output from the `MultiLanguageLoad` example in listing 8.11 shows that Python and Ruby can be executed from a single `ScriptRuntime` using two language-specific `ScriptEngine` objects.**

As you observed in the `MultiLanguageLoad` example, the `ScriptEngine` `Execute` method takes a string parameter containing the text of the script to execute. What you can't see in that example is that the `Execute` method also returns the result of the script as a `System.Object` value. Moreover, in a DLR-compliant host language like C#, the object returned is also treated as a dynamic object:

```
string name = pythonEngine.Execute(
  "raw_input('What is your name? ')");
```

This snippet would query users for their name using Python's `raw_input` function and return the supplied string as a dynamic object. Because the return type from `Execute` is marked as `dynamic`, the C# compiler emits the necessary call site code at the point of assignment to coerce the return value into a `System.String`. That coercion of dynamic objects is handy but comes at a cost, typically in performance. What if you wanted to strongly type the result to avoid the overhead of dynamic typing in the C# code? As it turns out, an overloaded version of the `Execute` method exists to do that. Consider the following line of C# code:

```
int age = engine.Execute<int>(
  "input('How old are you? ')");
```

In this example, a generic method named `Execute` is used to strongly type the result. Inside the Python script that's executed, also note that instead of using the `raw_input` function, the `input` function is used instead. The `input` function in Python is a convenience that combines `raw_input`, which returns a string, with `eval`, which evaluates the expression provided to it as a new Python code expression. Because you expect the user to type in a number as the response to the prompt, Python's `input` (`eval`) function treats it as numeric literal and *compiles* it into the correct type.

This runtime evaluation of code expressions becomes clear when you look at figure 8.4, which demonstrates the output of the `ReturnScalar-FromScript` example. Notice that the age supplied for the second question is an expression that adds two integers. Python's input function evaluates that expression to yield a single integer value, which is returned to the caller strongly typed. The complete code for that example can be found in listing 8.12.

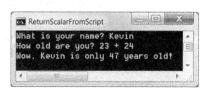

**Figure 8.4  The `Execute` methods in the `ScriptEngine` class can be used to run scripts and return values to the host application.**

**Listing 8.12  `ReturnScalarFromScript`: experimenting with `ScriptEngine`'s `Execute`**

```
public static void ReturnScalarFromScript()
{
  var runtimeSetup = new ScriptRuntimeSetup();
  var languageSetup = new LanguageSetup(
    "IronPython.Runtime.PythonContext, IronPython",
    "IronPython", new[] { "Python" }, new[] { ".py" });
  runtimeSetup.LanguageSetups.Add(languageSetup);
  var runtime = new ScriptRuntime(runtimeSetup);
  ScriptEngine engine = runtime.GetEngine("Python");

  string name = engine.Execute(
    "raw_input('What is your name? ')");
  int age = engine.Execute<int>(
    "input('How old are you? ')");

  Console.WriteLine(
    "Wow, {0} is only {1} years old!", name, age);
}
```

#### THE SCRIPTSOURCE AND COMPILEDCODE CLASSES

Two more DLR hosting types that are useful when working with the `ScriptEngine` class are `ScriptSource` and `CompiledCode`. So far, we've only shown the passing of strings containing script code. But a real-world application may have dozens of scripts to load simultaneously from files, databases, or network streams. It's useful to store these code assets in an object model that has properties and methods for managing the code programmatically. Moreover, the `ScriptSource` is a gateway class for compiling scripts for reuse throughout an application. To obtain a reference to a `Script-Source`, use the following `ScriptEngine` methods:

- `CreateScriptSource`
- `CreateScriptSourceFromFile`
- `CreateScriptSourceFromString`

The following listing shows an example of obtaining a `ScriptSource` from a Python `ScriptEngine` and using it to load a script file from a string before compiling and executing it.

**Listing 8.13 `PassingVariablesToCompiledCode`**

```
public static void PassingVariablesToCompiledCode(
  string question, object correctResponse)
{
  var runtimeSetup = new ScriptRuntimeSetup();
  var languageSetup = new LanguageSetup(
    "IronPython.Runtime.PythonContext, IronPython",
    "IronPython", new[] { "Python" }, new[] { ".py" });
  runtimeSetup.LanguageSetups.Add(languageSetup);
  var runtime = new ScriptRuntime(runtimeSetup);
  ScriptEngine engine = runtime.GetEngine("Python");

  ScriptSource source =
    engine.CreateScriptSourceFromString(@"
import Question
import CorrectResponse
input(Question) == CorrectResponse
");

  CompiledCode AskQuestion = source.Compile();

  runtime.Globals.SetVariable("Question", question);
  runtime.Globals.SetVariable(
    "CorrectResponse", correctResponse);

  Console.WriteLine("You chose... {0}",
    AskQuestion.Execute<bool>()
      ? "wisely."
      : "poorly");
}
```

In listing 8.13, after setting up the `ScriptRuntime` for IronPython and obtaining a `ScriptEngine` reference, a short Python script of three lines is loaded using the engine's `CreateScriptSourceFromString` method. The `ScriptSource` is then compiled using an instance method aptly named `Compile`. This yields a `CompiledCode` object that can be executed over and over again.

However, notice in the listing that before executing the `CompiledCode` object, the `Globals` property on the `ScriptRuntime` is used to *inject* two variables into the execution scope that the script can access. The next section gets into script scopes in more detail. For now, think of the `Globals` scope as a place where the hosting C# application can store variables for the script to access when it runs. The two variables that are injected using the `SetVariable` method take their values from function parameters and are named `"Question"` and `"CorrectResponse."` The tiny, three-line Python script loaded into the ScriptSource in listing 8.13 references those same names:

```
import Question
import CorrectResponse
input(Question) == CorrectResponse
```

The two import statements are required because the IronPython engine doesn't automatically load variables from the Globals scope into the execution context. These two import statements pull the variables injected using the SetVariable method used in listing 8.13 into the local scope so that the remaining script can access them. In the next section, when you instantiate a ScriptScope instance of your own, the import statements aren't necessary because the variables you inject will already be available in the local scope.

For the remaining single line of script code used in listing 8.13, remember that Python's input function prints the supplied string to the console, reads the raw input typed in response, and runs it through the eval function to compile and execute it as a new expression. Lastly, that evaluated expression is compared to the correct (or expected) response to yield a Boolean result. The last C# code line in listing 8.13 performs the execution step and reads that Boolean response value from the script execution:

```
Console.WriteLine("You chose... {0}",
  AskQuestion.Execute<bool>()
    ? "wisely."
    : "poorly");
```

The Execute<T> method on the CompiledCode object named AskQuestion is used to execute the script. In this instance, the generic function is made concrete as Execute<bool> to fetch the result of the comparison done on the last line of the Python script. When the user answers the posed question correctly, they're deemed wise. You could give a short chemistry quiz by calling the PassingVariablesToCompiledCode function in succession like this:

```
PassingVariablesToCompiledCode(
  "Platinum has 6 naturally-occuring " +
  "iostopes. True or False? ", true);

PassingVariablesToCompiledCode(
  "By ascending rank, where does the mass " +
  "of calcium in the Earth's\r\ncrust fall " +
  "as compared to the other elements? ", 5);
```

The result of calling the function like this can be seen in figure 8.5. Note that the responses given by the user are a bit cheeky, taking advantage of the fact that Python's input function will be used to evaluate the text before comparing it to the correct response. For the first quiz question, the response "1 == 1" evaluates to the Boolean value of True, which is expected. For the second question, the response "2 + 3" evaluates to the integer value of 5, which is the correct value for answering that question.

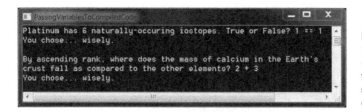

**Figure 8.5  Calling the PassingVariablesTo-CompiledCode function from listing 8.13 in direct succession to create a short chemistry quiz.**

Now that you've seen how to pass variables into a compiled script and get a result, it's time to refine the code using a local `ScriptScope` and other optimizations. You may have noticed that the code in listing 8.13 is inefficient, creating new runtime and engine instances each time the function is called. That's not necessary. Also, the `ScriptSource` and `CompiledCode` objects are recreated every time the function is called, defeating the real value of compiling the script code in the first place. You'll fix all of those problems in the next section as you examine the DLR's `ScriptScope` class.

### THE SCRIPTSCOPE CLASS

You've already seen how you can use the `Globals` property on the `ScriptRuntime` class to pass variables to an executed script. What we didn't reveal in the discussion of listing 8.13 was the data type of the `Globals` property: a `ScriptScope` instance from the `Microsoft.Scripting.Hosting` namespace. Each `ScriptRuntime` contains a single object of type `ScriptScope` for managing so-called global variables. But you can create your own `ScriptScope` objects for managing variables that belong together according to your application's overall architecture. To show how this works, the following listing instantiates a `ScriptScope` to manage the `Question` and `Correct-Response` values shown in the previous listing.

**Listing 8.14  PoseQuizQuestion: using a custom ScriptScope**

```
private static ScriptEngine _pythonEngine = null;
private static ScriptEngine PythonEngine
{
  get
  {
    if (_pythonEngine == null)
    {
      var runtimeSetup = new ScriptRuntimeSetup();
      var languageSetup = new LanguageSetup(
        "IronPython.Runtime.PythonContext, IronPython",
        "IronPython", new[] { "Python" }, new[] { ".py" });
      runtimeSetup.LanguageSetups.Add(languageSetup);
      var runtime = new ScriptRuntime(runtimeSetup);
      _pythonEngine = runtime.GetEngine("Python");
    }
    return _pythonEngine;
  }
}

private static CompiledCode _askQuestion = null;
private static CompiledCode AskQuestion
```

```
{
  get
  {
    if (_askQuestion == null)
    {
      ScriptSource source =
        PythonEngine.CreateScriptSourceFromString(
        "input(Question) == CorrectResponse");

      _askQuestion = source.Compile();
    }
    return _askQuestion;
  }
}
private static ScriptScope _questionScope = null;
private static ScriptScope QuestionScope
{
  get
  {
    if (_questionScope == null)
    {
      _questionScope =
        PythonEngine.CreateScope();
    }
    return _questionScope;
  }
}
public static void PoseQuizQuestion(
  string question, object correctResponse)
{
  QuestionScope.SetVariable("Question", question);
  QuestionScope.SetVariable("CorrectResponse",
    correctResponse);

  Console.WriteLine("You chose... {0}",
    AskQuestion.Execute<bool>(QuestionScope)
      ? "wisely."
      : "poorly");
}
```

To clean up the code from listing 8.13, making it more efficient, the PoseQuiz-
Question function shown in listing 8.14 takes advantage of three properties implemented as singletons:

1  PythonEngine—A singleton property of type ScriptEngine that ensures that
   only one IronPython engine is instantiated by the application
2  AskQuestion—A property of type CompiledCode that encapsulates the concept of
   a script required for asking questions and evaluating a response from the user
3  QuestionScope—A property of type ScriptScope that holds the Question to be
   asked and the CorrectResponse to be evaluated against the response

With these singleton properties available, posing successive questions to the user in a
more efficient way is straightforward. The PoseQuizQuestion function invokes the

SetVariable method on the ScriptScope returned by the QuestionScope property to inject the two required variables into the local scope, not the global scope as shown earlier. If the scope hasn't yet been created, the singleton property accessor performs the instantiation as required. The call to the Execute<T> method that follows should look familiar:

```
Console.WriteLine("You chose... {0}",
  AskQuestion.Execute<bool>(QuestionScope)
    ? "wisely."
    : "poorly");
```

Did you spot the difference as compared to the last line of C# code in listing 8.13? Rather than pass no parameters to Execute<T>, the analog call in listing 8.14 instead passes the value obtained from the QuestionScope singleton. This allows the Question and CorrectResponse variables referenced in the Python script to be treated as local instead of global variables. Accordingly, the small script buried within the AskQuestion property in listing 8.14 doesn't include import statements as the Python script in listing 8.13 did.

Because you pass your own ScriptScope when executing the script, the import statements are no longer required. With these changes in place, subsequent calls to the PoseQuizQuestion function will reuse the cached ScriptEngine, the cached CompiledCode, and the cached ScriptScope objects to present each question to the user. This is much more efficient, as you can imagine.

In addition to the SetVariable method shown in this example, the ScriptScope class contains other useful methods for managing scope variables:

- bool ContainsVariable(string name)—Test to see if a named variable exists
- T GetVariable<T>(string name)—Fetch the specified variable's value as a specific type, throwing an exception when not found
- dynamic GetVariable(string name)—Fetch the specified variable's value as a dynamic object, throwing an exception when not found
- IEnumerable<string> GetVariableNames()—Iterate over the names of all of the variables in the scope
- bool RemoveVariable(string name)—Eliminate the specified variable within the scope
- bool TryGetVariable<T>(string name, out T value)—Attempt to fetch the specified variable's value as a specific type, returning true when found or false otherwise
- bool TryGetVariable(string name, out dynamic value)—Attempt to fetch the specified variable's value as a dynamic object, returning true when found or false otherwise

Some of these ScriptScope methods are demonstrated in an upcoming example, which shows how to create a simple, yet fully functional rules engine to an application using the DLR.

### 8.2.2 Adding a rules engine to your application

Scripting the behavior of an application in a completely open-ended way can be useful. Using DLR hosting, exposing the entirety of a program's object model to end-user control in that way is possible. But it's typically safer and more valuable to provide users some restricted, domain-specific structures instead. For example, consider an e-commerce program that needs complex, perpetually changing rules to be applied for the discounting of items in a shopping cart. The Python code shown in listing 8.9 could be such a rule for a system like that. In essence, the rule in listing 8.9 says the following:

- If there are two or more clothing type items in the cart, apply a 5 percent discount to the clothing items.
- However, if more than five clothing items are in the cart, apply a 9 percent discount to them.
- If there are more than seven items in the shopping cart in total, apply an extra 3 percent discount to *all* the items in the cart, regardless of their category.

Now think about how you might write such a rule in a way that your business users can understand. You probably couldn't make any XML-based expression of this rule discernible to the folks in your merchandising department. Although it's certainly possible to concoct a new dialect that's friendlier to business users than what's shown in listing 8.9, the Python language comes pretty close without much effort. This is even more true if the business users adhere to using the absolute basics of the Python language for writing their rules: if-else statements and for loops, for example. In the next section, we'll show you how to create a generic rules engine that allows rules like the one shown in listing 8.9 to execute in your own applications.

#### AN E-COMMERCE EXAMPLE

Consider an object model that contains types called Cart, LineItem, and Product. The user of the program has a single shopping Cart to which they add items for purchase as they browse your store. Inside the Cart are zero or more LineItem objects, representing the items in the cart. Each LineItem has a Quantity and a Product as well as a Discount percentage to be applied during checkout.

Figure 8.6 shows our sample ECommerceExample program executing the rule from listing 8.9. Notice that the five Clothing type items have received a 5 percent discount with an additional 3 percent discount applied to all of the items in the cart. This is in keeping with the merchandising rule expressed in listing 8.9.

Based on that merchandising rule, the customer would save $13.93 at checkout. To make this possible, a class called UnsafeRuleEngine (partially shown in listing 8.15) and an associated interface called IRule (shown in listing 8.16) are used to do the work. The code in this simple example isn't necessarily *unsafe*, but there's a better, potentially safer way we'll you show later that makes the naming of this sample appropriate.

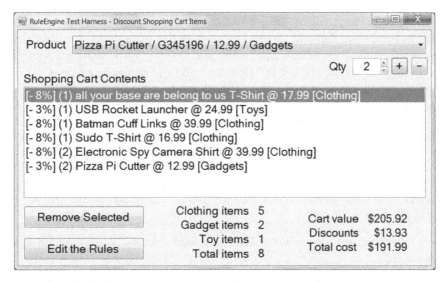

**Figure 8.6** The running of the `EcommerceExample` sample. Using the rule shown in listing 8.9, eight items added to a shopping cart have been discounted.

---

**Listing 8.15  The basis of the `UnsafeRuleEngine` class**

```
public class UnsafeRuleEngine
{
  private readonly ScriptRuntimeSetup _runtimeSetup;
  private readonly ScriptRuntime _sharedRuntime;
  private readonly Dictionary<int, RuleContext>
    _rulesContexts;
  private static int _nextHandle = 0;

  private struct RuleContext
  {
    internal IRule Rule;
    internal CompiledCode Code;
    internal ScriptScope SharedScope;
  }

  public UnsafeRuleEngine()
  {
    _runtimeSetup = new ScriptRuntimeSetup();
    _runtimeSetup.LanguageSetups.Add(
      new LanguageSetup(
        "IronPython.Runtime.PythonContext, IronPython",
        "IronPython",
        new[] { "IronPython", "Python", "py" },
        new[] { ".py" }));
    _sharedRuntime =
      new ScriptRuntime(_runtimeSetup);
    _rulesContexts =
      new Dictionary<int, RuleContext>();
  }
}
```

The `UnsafeRuleEngine` class shown in the previous listing defines a private structure called `RuleContext` that will be used to manage the rules that run within the engine, the compiled versions of the rule code, and references to shared `ScriptScope` for exchanging variables between the DLR host and the scripting engines. The `Unsafe-RuleEngine` maintains a dictionary of these contexts to serve as a cache of precompiled script code.

> **TIP**  It's certainly possible to run more than one type of scripting language within a single rule engine, as shown in the `MultiLanguageLoad` example earlier. For sheer simplicity, the example in listing 8.15 only shows the addition of the Python language to the `UnsafeRuleEngine`. To include another language, you only need to add the appropriate `LanguageSetup` during rule engine construction.

The `IRule` interface shown in the following listing serves as the basis for any kind of business rule.

**Listing 8.16  The `IRule` interface describes the script for a business rule**

```
public interface IRule
{
    string Name { get; set; }
    string Address { get; set; }
    string Body { get; set; }
    string ContentType { get; set; }
    string[] ExpectedReturnValueNames { get; set; }
}
```

Every rule executed by the `UnsafeRuleEngine` must conform to this standard:

- `Name`—The name of the rule (used strictly for convenience)
- `Address`—The filename, database key, or user name that sourced the rule
- `Body`—The source code of the rule
- `ContentType`—The type of code expressed in the `Body` ( Python, Ruby, and so on)
- `ExpectedReturnValueNames`—An array of variable names for which the rule engine should fetch the associated values after executing the rule

The `UnsafeRuleEngine` stores references to newly added rules using the two methods shown in the following listing. These insert and update methods use a private helper method named `UpsertRule` shown in the listing.

**Listing 8.17  The `InsertRule` and `UpdateRule` methods of the `UnsafeRuleEngine`**

```
public int InsertRule(IRule rule)
{
    int handle = -1;
    UpsertRule(rule, ref handle);
    return handle;
}
```

```
public void UpdateRule(int handle, IRule rule)
{
  UpsertRule(rule, ref handle);
}

private void UpsertRule(IRule rule,
  ref int handle)
{
  CompiledCode compilation = null;
  ScriptScope sharedScope = null;
  ScriptEngine engine = _sharedRuntime
    .GetEngineByFileExtension(
      rule.ContentType);
  sharedScope = engine.CreateScope();
  ScriptSource source = engine
    .CreateScriptSourceFromString(
      rule.Body);
  compilation = source.Compile();

  if (_rulesContexts.ContainsKey(handle))
    _rulesContexts.Remove(handle);
  else
    handle = System.Threading
      .Interlocked.Increment(
        ref _nextHandle);

  _rulesContexts[handle] =
    new RuleContext()
    {
      Rule = rule,
      Code = compilation,
      SharedScope = sharedScope,
    };
}
```

When a rule is inserted, an integer handle is returned to the caller. This handle can be used to update the rule later. The UpsertRule method is where all the real work happens. After locating the relevant scripting language by the rule's ContentType property, the engine compiles the code and stores it in a new RuleContext, along with a shared ScriptScope for use during future executions of the rule. Lastly, you need to be able to execute rules within the UnsafeRuleEngine cache.

The following listing shows the Execute method of the UnsafeRuleEngine class, which allows the host application to run a rule by its integer handle, obtained from an earlier insert or update operation.

**Listing 8.18  The Execute method of the UnsafeRuleEngine class**

```
public IDictionary<string, dynamic> Execute(
  int handle, IDictionary<string, object> parameters)
{
  RuleContext context =
    _rulesContexts[handle];
  ScriptScope scope = context.SharedScope;
```

```
    foreach (var kvp in parameters)
      scope.SetVariable(kvp.Key, kvp.Value);

    context.Code.Execute(scope);

    var results = new Dictionary<string, dynamic>();
    if (context.Rule.ExpectedReturnValueNames != null
      && context.Rule.ExpectedReturnValueNames.Length > 0)
    {
      dynamic result;
      foreach (var valueName in
        context.Rule.ExpectedReturnValueNames)
      {
        if (valueName == null
          || valueName.Trim().Length == 0)
        {
          continue;
        }
        if (scope.TryGetVariable(
          valueName.Trim(), out result))
        {
          results.Add(valueName, result);
        }
      }
    }

    return results;
}
```

The `Execute` method also accepts a dictionary of named parameters to insert into the `ScriptScope` before running the rule.

Notice that the `Execute` method returns a dictionary of named dynamic objects based on the names expressed in the property named `ExpectedReturnValueNames` in the rule's context.

> **CODE SOURCE**  The full source code to the `ECommerceExample` discussed here is lengthy, so we've decided to print only the most relevant portions of it. To get the full source code, visit http://metadotnetbook.codeplex.com and open the chapter 8 samples.

After loading the merchandising rule shown in listing 8.11 into an `IRule`-derived variable named `discountRule`, the following small bit of C# code will run the rule inside any .NET object that implements a collection of properly structured `LineItems`:

```
var engine = new UnsafeRuleEngine();
var ruleHandle = engine.InsertRule(
  discountRule);
engine.Execute(
  handle: ruleHandle,
  parameters: new Dictionary<string, object>
    {{"cart", this}});
```

Notice that the `parameters` passed to the rule contain a single name-value pair named `cart`. The value of that parameter is `this`, meaning that the object executing the code must be the so-called shopping cart that contains LineItems with Quantity, Discount, and Product properties. Each of those Product objects must also implement a Category property. As long as those conditions are satisfied, the rule will work as expected. Looking back at listing 8.11, you'll see that the Python script references such a cart variable in that way. The Python script will update the Discount property of each LineItem based on the merchandising preferences of its author.

**A SAFER E-COMMERCE EXAMPLE**

Now that you've seen how simple it is to execute a Python-based business rule against an arbitrary .NET object, we unfortunately owe it to you to make things a bit more complex. The problem with your UnsafeRuleEngine is that it gives too much authority to executing scripts. The discount rule as shown in listing 8.11 is okay because it only updates the Discount property of the line items in the cart. But what if it weren't so well behaved? What if the script modified the Price property of each Product in a way that caused the company to lose money on each transaction? Outside of the issues related to the script's own authority, what if a near-simultaneous execution of the same script inserted a different cart object into the shared ScriptScope at the wrong moment?

The DLR hosting model offers three levels of *isolation* to address these concerns. At the highest level, each execution event can be assigned a different ScriptScope. This will allow a single ScriptEngine to isolate the variables used during execution from all other executions that may be occurring at the same time. Scope isolation won't solve the *errant script problem* described previously, but it can address some other concerns. Lower in the DLR hosting stack, the programmer could choose to create a new ScriptRuntime each time script code is executed. That would be highly inefficient, so you might instead cache a ScriptRuntime per rule instead. That would tackle the same set of problems that scope isolation addresses and potentially some others by giving each rule its own private runtime. But runtime isolation still allows scripts to modify any objects they gain access to in ways that may not be appropriate.

The DLR hosting model provides a third type of isolation, which can solve the *errant script problem*. As depicted in figure 8.7, the programmer may create an application domain that separates the execution environment of scripts from that of the host application.

Various .NET objects to be injected into the script scope must be serialized across the AppDomain boundary or marshaled as reference types as desired. The following listing shows the complete RuleEngine class to replace the UnsafeRuleEngine described earlier.

**Listing 8.19  A (potentially) safer RuleEngine class**

```
using System;
using System.Dynamic;
using System.Collections.Generic;
using Microsoft.Scripting.Hosting;
```

```csharp
namespace DevJourney.Scripting
{
  public enum IsolationMode { Shared, Private }
  public class RuleEngine
  {
    private readonly ScriptRuntimeSetup _runtimeSetup;
    private readonly ScriptRuntime _sharedRuntime;
    private readonly Dictionary<int, RuleContext>
      _rulesContexts;
    private readonly AppDomain _remoteAppDomain;
    private static int _nextHandle = 0;

    private struct RuleContext
    {
      internal IRule Rule;
      internal CompiledCode Code;
      internal ScriptScope SharedScope;
      internal bool IsIsolatedRuntime;
    }

    public RuleEngine(IsolationMode appDomainMode)
    {
      _runtimeSetup = new ScriptRuntimeSetup();
      _runtimeSetup.LanguageSetups.Add(
        new LanguageSetup(
          "IronPython.Runtime.PythonContext, IronPython",
          "IronPython",
          new[] { "IronPython", "Python", "py" },
          new[] { ".py" }));
      if (appDomainMode == IsolationMode.Private)
        _remoteAppDomain = AppDomain.CreateDomain(
          DateTime.UtcNow.ToString("s"));
      _sharedRuntime =
        (_remoteAppDomain != null)
          ? ScriptRuntime.CreateRemote(
            _remoteAppDomain, _runtimeSetup)
          : new ScriptRuntime(_runtimeSetup);
      _rulesContexts =
        new Dictionary<int, RuleContext>();
    }

    public IRule SelectRule(int handle)
    {
      lock (_rulesContexts)
      {
        if (!_rulesContexts.ContainsKey(handle))
        throw new ArgumentOutOfRangeException(
          "handle", String.Format("The rule " +
          "context with handle {0} cannot be " +
          "selected from the cache because it " +
          "does not exist.", handle));
        return _rulesContexts[handle].Rule;
      }
    }

    public int InsertRule(IRule rule,
      IsolationMode runtimeMode)
```

```
{
  lock (_rulesContexts)
  {
    int handle = -1;
    UpsertRule(rule, ref handle,
      runtimeMode);
    return handle;
  }
}

public void UpdateRule(int handle, IRule rule,
  IsolationMode runtimeMode)
{
  lock (_rulesContexts)
  {
    if (!_rulesContexts.ContainsKey(handle))
      throw new ArgumentOutOfRangeException(
        "handle", String.Format("The rule " +
        "context with handle {0} cannot be " +
        "updated in the cache because it " +
        "does not exist.", handle));
    UpsertRule(rule, ref handle,
      runtimeMode);
  }
}

public void DeleteRule(int handle)
{
  lock (_rulesContexts)
  {
    if (!_rulesContexts.ContainsKey(handle))
      throw new ArgumentOutOfRangeException(
        "handle", String.Format("The rule " +
        "context with handle {0} cannot be " +
        "deleted from the cache because it " +
        "does not exist.", handle));
    if (_rulesContexts[handle].IsIsolatedRuntime)
    {
      _rulesContexts[handle].Code.Engine
        .Runtime.Shutdown();
    }
    _rulesContexts.Remove(handle);
  }
}

public IDictionary<string, dynamic> Execute(
  int handle,
  IDictionary<string, object> parameters,
  IsolationMode scopeMode)
{
  RuleContext context;
  lock (_rulesContexts)
  {
    if (!_rulesContexts.ContainsKey(handle))
      throw new ArgumentOutOfRangeException(
        "handle", String.Format("Rule handle " +
```

```
          "{0} was not found in the rule cache.",
          handle));
      context = _rulesContexts[handle];
  }

  ScriptScope scope =
    (scopeMode == IsolationMode.Private)
      ? context.Code.Engine.CreateScope()
      : context.SharedScope;
  foreach (var kvp in parameters)
    scope.SetVariable(kvp.Key, kvp.Value);
  context.Code.Execute(scope);
  var results = new Dictionary<string, dynamic>();
  if (context.Rule.ExpectedReturnValueNames != null
    && context.Rule
        .ExpectedReturnValueNames.Length > 0)
  {
    dynamic result;
    foreach (var valueName in
      context.Rule.ExpectedReturnValueNames)
    {
      if (valueName == null
        || valueName.Trim().Length == 0)
      {
        continue;
      }
      if (scope.TryGetVariable(
        valueName.Trim(), out result))
      {
        results.Add(valueName, result);
      }
    }
  }
  return results;
}

private void UpsertRule(IRule rule,
  ref int handle, IsolationMode runtimeMode)
{
  if (rule == null)
    throw new ArgumentNullException("rule");
  lock (_rulesContexts)
  {
    CompiledCode compilation = null;
    ScriptScope sharedScope = null;
    ScriptRuntime runtime =
      (runtimeMode == IsolationMode.Private)
        ? (_remoteAppDomain != null)
          ? ScriptRuntime.CreateRemote(
              _remoteAppDomain,
              _runtimeSetup)
          : new ScriptRuntime(_runtimeSetup)
        : _sharedRuntime;
    ScriptEngine engine = runtime
      .GetEngineByFileExtension(
        rule.ContentType);
```

```
    sharedScope = engine.CreateScope();
    ScriptSource source = engine
      .CreateScriptSourceFromString(
        rule.Body);
    compilation = source.Compile();

    if (_rulesContexts.ContainsKey(handle))
      DeleteRule(handle);
    else
      handle = System.Threading
        .Interlocked.Increment(
          ref _nextHandle);

    _rulesContexts[handle] =
      new RuleContext()
      {
        Rule = rule,
        Code = compilation,
        SharedScope = sharedScope,
        IsIsolatedRuntime =
          (runtimeMode == IsolationMode.Private)
      };
    }
  }
 }
}
```

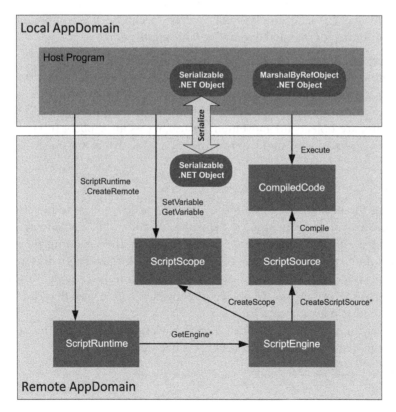

**Figure 8.7
Executing script
code in a separate
`AppDomain`**

Highlighting the differences between the `UnsafeRuleEngine` and the new `RuleEngine` class, the first thing to notice is the existence of an enumerated type called `Isolation-Mode`. Values of this type can be used in the `RuleEngine` class to enable all three isolation modes supported by the DLR hosting model. The first and most important of these is `AppDomain` isolation, which you can enable by passing `IsolationMode.Private` to the `RuleEngine` constructor. Doing so forces the `RuleEngine` to create a new `App-Domain` on behalf of the host application in which all the rules inserted into the `RuleEngine` will be run.

The next type of DLR hosting isolation that can be enabled using the `RuleEngine` class is `ScriptRuntime` isolation. To do so, pass `IsolationMode.Private` as the `runtimeMode` parameter when calling the `InsertRule` or `UpdateRule` methods. This will cause that particular rule to be run in its own `ScriptRuntime` each time it's executed. Understand, though, that runtime isolation is separate and distinct from `AppDomain` isolation. You could force the creation of a separate `AppDomain` and then use a shared `ScriptRuntime` for all the rules that run within it, for example. You may also run multiple rules within the local `AppDomain` but separate their execution by using different runtimes. You're free to choose the isolation models to suit your needs.

The new `RuleEngine` class also supports `ScriptScope` isolation. To enable that, pass `IsolationMode.Private` as the `scopeMode` parameter when calling the `Execute` method. Scope isolation is orthogonal to both `AppDomain` and `ScriptRuntime` isolation. With the new `RuleEngine` class, you're free to choose the combination of all three isolation strategies that make sense for your application.

### MARSHALING AND SERIALIZATION OF .NET TYPES VIA SCRIPTSCOPE

The `RuleEngine` class allows for the execution of rules in a separate `AppDomain`, which is much safer than allowing them to run inside your host program's `AppDomain`. But enabling rules to run remotely is half the battle. As depicted in figure 8.7, there are two ways to prepare objects for movement or use across an `AppDomain` boundary. In the `ECommerceExample`, you might derive the `Cart` class from `MarshalByRefObject` like this:

```
public class Cart : MarshalByRefObject
```

After invoking the `SetVariable` method of the `ScriptScope` class to inject the `Cart` object into the execution scope, the DLR Hosting API code will be able to marshal the object reference into the remote `AppDomain`. The script code running there will be able to access the `Cart` object as if had been instantiated locally. This works well, but it still allows the script to modify properties of the cart's line items which it shouldn't have access to. Also, if your domain objects already have a base class that can't be marshaled, this solution may not work for you.

Another way to move the .NET `Cart` objects back and forth across the `AppDomain` boundaries is to mark them as `[Serializable]`, like this:

```
[Serializable] public class Cart
```

This also allows the DLR Hosting API to copy the `Cart` into the remote `AppDomain` for access by the script. The word *copy* here is the key to understanding the major difference between the `MarshalByRefObject` method and the `[Serializable]` method for setting and fetching variables in the `ScriptScope`. When a `[Serializable]` `Cart` object is inserted into the `ScriptScope`, a copy of it is made available in the remote `AppDomain`. If the script modifies the `Cart` in any way, it will have modified only its copy, not the original.

There's even more work to be done when using such pass-by-value semantics for your .NET types. Some members of those types may not serialize properly, so you'll have to mark them as `[NonSerialized]` to keep them from making the trip across the `AppDomain` boundary. Furthermore, you'll have to fetch the modified `Cart` from the `ScriptScope` when the rule execution is complete. Lastly, because the modified `Cart` is a copy, you'll need to compare it to the one you sent over before execution to see what changes were made. In the following listing you see two new `Cart` methods that handle this work: `CompareModifiedLineItem` and `UpdateFromModifiedCart`.

**Listing 8.20   Methods for comparing and updating a modified shopping cart**

```
private bool CompareModifiedLineItem(
  LineItem original, LineItem modified, int ndx)
{
  if (modified == null)
    throw new ApplicationException(
      String.Format("After recalculating " +
        "the cart value, line item {0} was " +
        "null. The discount script must not " +
        "remove line items.", ndx));
  if (modified.Product == null)
    throw new ApplicationException(
      String.Format("After recalculating " +
        "the cart value, the product on " +
        "line {0} was null. The discount " +
        "script must not modify the " +
        "products.", ndx));
  if (!original.Product.Equals(modified.Product))
    throw new ApplicationException(
      String.Format("After recalculating " +
        "the cart value, the product on " +
        "line {0} was different from the " +
        "original. The discount script " +
        "must not modify the products.", ndx));
  if (original.Quantity != modified.Quantity)
    throw new ApplicationException(
      String.Format("After recalculating " +
        "the cart value, the quantity on " +
        "line {0} was different from the " +
        "original. The discount script " +
        "must not modify quantities.", ndx));
  return (original.Discount != modified.Discount);
}
```

```
private void UpdateFromModifiedCart(
  Cart modifiedCart)
{
  if (modifiedCart == null)
    throw new ApplicationException(
      "The modified cart was not returned " +
      "from the discount script as expected.");
  if (LineItems.Length !=
      modifiedCart.LineItems.Length)
    throw new ApplicationException(
      String.Format("After recalculating the " +
        "cart value, {0} line items were " +
        "expected but {1} items were found. " +
        "The discount script must not add " +
        "or remove line items.", LineItems.Length,
        modifiedCart.LineItems.Length));
  for (int ndx = 0; ndx < LineItems.Length; ndx++)
  {
    LineItem original = LineItems[ndx];
    LineItem modified =
      modifiedCart.LineItems[ndx];
    if (CompareModifiedLineItem(
      original, modified, ndx))
    {
      original.Discount = modified.Discount;
    }
  }
}
```

The `UpdateFromModifiedCart` method should be called immediately after execution of the discount rule. This will check that the script did not attempt to modify properties other than each `LineItem Discount`. Such a safety check is optional, but it's highly recommended for catching rogue scripts during preproduction and debugging. After the safety checks are complete, only the modified `Discount` properties are allowed to be updated in the original `Cart` object's `LineItems`. Perhaps you can see why App-Domain isolation using [Serializable] objects is the safest way to integrate a rules engine into your .NET application. The full source code of the `ECommerceExample` available at http://metadotnetbook.codeplex.com contains complete working Rule-Engine and `Cart` classes that demonstrate `AppDomain`, `ScriptRuntime`, and `ScriptScope` isolation as well as the selectable use of pass-by-reference or pass-by-value semantics.

## 8.3    *Summary*

In closing this chapter, we note that Microsoft's DLR represents something of a conundrum in the history of the .NET Framework. The DLR appeared with some fanfare at the MIX conference in 2007, and by the time of Microsoft's Professional Developer Conference (PDC) in 2008, the industry was abuzz about the impossible coming true. Microsoft was finally going to embrace dynamic languages as first-class citizens in the .NET Framework. Or so it seemed. In some rather high-profile demonstrations at PDC 2008, we saw how a statically typed language like C# could evolve by adopting some dynamic language features, too. We also saw evocative demonstrations of C# and Visual Basic working seamlessly with JavaScript, Python, and Ruby by way of the DLR. For those who appreciate the power of dynamic languages, a sense of eagerness and hope was growing in those days.

But as the saying goes, if something seems too good to be true, it probably is. By the time Visual Studio 2010 shipped with a dynamic version of C# in April 2010, the IronPython and IronRuby teams had been dramatically reduced in size. The budding, DLR-based JavaScript engine seen only briefly in 2008 had vanished entirely by 2010. A few voluntary departures from those teams lent credence to the rumors that the "Iron Languages" were dead on arrival. By October 2010, when Microsoft moved the DLR source code into the public domain under the Apache License V2.0 and the "father of IronPython" left the company, the death knell for dynamic languages on the .NET Framework seemed to be ringing loud and clear for most people.

However, not everyone saw those developments with complete pessimism. In late 2009, key members of the DLR and IronPython teams had been moved to a secret project in the Windows OS group. Members of various language teams had joined them, working on related and equally secret projects. Based strictly on the talent and experiences of the people involved, something good seemed to be brewing at Microsoft. At the BUILD 2011 conference, Microsoft finally let the cat out of the bag, as the saying goes, when it announced Windows 8, a new OS-specific JavaScript engine (WinJS), and the new Windows Runtime (WinRT). Yet few people recognized the sublime connection between the underpinnings of DLR and the new development framework for Windows 8.

At some point in mid-2009, someone important inside Microsoft probably realized what the DLR was truly all about. It wasn't about Python. It wasn't about Ruby. The DLR wasn't even about adding dynamic features to languages like C# and Visual Basic. The DLR's *raison d'être*, they likely surmised, was to provide a *language of languages* for the .NET Framework. The plumbing that the DLR team defined to enable IronPython and IronRuby would allow any set of compliant languages to communicate and to interoperate. The DLR had enabled something wonderful to happen between languages that even the rich metadata model of the CLR could not enable on its own.

The beauty of such an idea is apparent: many programming languages interoperating without expensive ceremony, exchanging data and invoking functions freely between them. That sounds wonderful, right? So why did Microsoft *abandon* the DLR, and how does Windows 8 help to accomplish the same objectives in better fashion? Unfortunately, the DLR language-interoperability features are implemented in the wrong way and at the wrong level of the capability stack to make them truly useful for non-dynamic languages.

In large measure, the interface-level conventions of the DLR described in this chapter have been superseded in Windows 8 by metadata-level conventions in WinRT. In fact, the same metadata model of .NET, known as ECMA 335 Partition II, has been implemented at the OS level in Windows 8 with a few new extensions. Having the rich metadata to which we've become accustomed in .NET at the lowest levels of the OS allows for excellent, native interoperability between languages like JavaScript (WinJS), C++, C#, and Visual Basic.

Rather than seeing the "death of the DLR" as catastrophic, we see hope instead. With .NET's metadata model in place at the lowest level of the OS, future WinRT-specific implementations of Python, Ruby, and other programming languages could be developed for Windows 8. Those as-yet-unseen WinRT implementations of Python and Ruby won't require a hosting model at all. They will interoperate with other WinRT languages as first-class citizens, putting to rest the rumors about Microsoft's commitment to language choice once and for all.

We hope you'll join us in being optimistic about the future of dynamic languages and metaprogramming in general within the Microsoft ecosystem.

# Languages and tools

**This chapter covers**

- An introduction to languages that contain native metaprogramming constructs
- An overview of tools that provide dynamic programming facilities for C#

Throughout this book, you've seen C# used (and potentially abused!) to facilitate metaprogramming. In some cases, external components (like NRefactory and Cecil) were used because they provided functionality necessary to support metaprogramming. Although C# is a powerful programming language that you can use to create concise, flexible programs, at times in this book C# may have felt twisted and bent to service metaprogramming needs.

This isn't too surprising, because you could argue that C# wasn't designed with metaprogramming as a deep, core aspect. But programming languages have been created that allow you to modify the language as it executes. These languages, created after the initial 1.0 release of .NET, have metaprogramming facilities built in. Furthermore, tools have been created for .NET languages to allow you to handle concepts such as code injection and aspect-oriented programming (AOP). This chapter introduces you to languages that make metaprogramming straightforward and easy to use, and to tools that lower the barrier of dynamic programming in C#.

Let's start by looking at a couple of different metaprogramming-based languages that target the CLR.

## 9.1    *A survey of languages*

In this section, you'll see how metaprogramming works in two languages—Boo and Nemerle—but the first stop is back in C#. You'll revisit the idea of *code as data* that you saw in chapter 6 and see how it works in C#. With this little expression refresher in mind, you'll have a solid base to understand how these other languages lift metaprogramming from an expression API into a first-class language feature.

### 9.1.1    *C# and expression limitations*

In chapter 6, you saw how the Expression API let you manipulate coding structures at runtime. For example, consider the following statement:

```
Expression<Func<int, int, int>> add = (x, y) => x + y;
var result = add.Compile()(2, 3);
```

You know that the add variable refers to an expression tree. This tree consists of a BinaryExpression for the add operation and two ParameterExpression nodes that represent the x and y parameters to the expression. The expression tree isn't executable in its current form; you have to compile it to create a method that you can invoke.

Most of the content in chapter 6 revolves around expressions from an API standpoint. You didn't create expressions using the preceding inline coding approach; you formulated expressions by using static methods on the Expression class. Although this works, wouldn't it be nice if C# handled expressions within the language itself? For example, let's look at a fictitious bit of C# code that contains a symbol that doesn't exist within C#, but imagine for a second if the backtick character worked like this:

```
var add = `(x, y) => x + y;
```

Note that this isn't the single-quote character used to define char values in C#. This is that "bent" character called the backtick. Either way, it doesn't matter because it isn't valid C#. The point is this: right now, you can't declare an expression and assign it to a variable type via inference in C#. You have to explicitly type the variable so C# knows you want an expression, not a lambda. But that's a fair amount of ceremony to get your expression. Having one character would make it far easier to generate expressions in C#.

Here's another limitation of expressions. Consider this piece of C# that isn't valid and won't compile:

```
Expression<Func<TextWriter, int>> a = (writer) =>
{
  var x = new Random().Next();
  writer.WriteLine(x);
  var q = 11 + x;
  writer.WriteLine(q);
  return q;
};
```

Why won't it compile? C# doesn't support multiline expressions. You can create complex expressions via the Expression API, but you can't do it as a declared expression in C# code. It has to be one line of code.

The beauty of expressions is that they give you the ability to create dynamic code without the mess and fuss of learning IL. But you don't get that beauty natively in C#, and frankly, once you start playing with expressions, you start to wish that C# would somehow get that elegance right into the language in the next version.

To be honest, the creators and maintainers of C# get lots of requests from developers to add all sorts of features into the language, so it's understandable that it can't do everything one may hope for. But other .NET languages have built expression-building capabilities directly into their feature set. These languages make it almost trivial to come up with functions that can be manipulated at runtime, and in some cases allow you to redefine the language itself. Let's start your language journey with Boo.

### 9.1.2 *Boo and metaprogramming*

The first language you'll look at is called Boo. If you've ever worked with (or at least seen) Python, you'll feel right at home with Boo. Boo has quite a few metaprogramming facilities that you can take advantage of in a natural way within the language itself. Let's start by seeing a simple Boo code snippet so you can get a feel for the structure of the language.

#### A SIMPLE CLASS IN BOO

Although Boo isn't a strict derivative of Python, there are a fair amount of similarities. Here's a simple class definition in Boo:

```
import System

class Data:
  def constructor():
    pass

  def constructor(value as Guid):
    _value = value

  [Getter(Value)]
  _value as Guid

[STAThread]
def Main(args as (string)):
  print(Data().Value)
  print(Data(Guid.NewGuid()).Value)
```

As in Python, whitespace is key to define and scope code in Boo. That's why the methods are indented from the class definition, and the method's implementation is indented from the method definition. It doesn't take long to read Boo code and understand what it's doing. You know you have a class called `Data` with two constructors. You also have a `Main()` method where you print information to the console window. Creating an object in Boo doesn't require the `new` keyword like you have in C#—you type the name of the class with parenthesis and you're done.

There's one odd bit of code in Boo that may take some getting used to: the GetterAttribute. In Boo, if all you want is a getter for a property, you can use the GetterAttribute. If you want a write-only field, you can use a SetterAttribute—the PropertyAttribute defines a read-write property. Note that the name of the attribute is specified as an argument to the attribute, and the code right after it defines the backing field for the property.

It isn't strictly true that you must use attributes for property definitions. The following Boo code defines a Value property that acts the same way as the Value property in the Data class:

```
Value as Guid:
  get:
    return _value

_value as Guid
```

The GetterAttribute class is a special kind of attribute that's treated much differently in Boo than other attributes. It's a kind of AbstractAstAttribute that modifies the code as it's compiled. This kind of power can lead to all sorts of cool code manipulation, but before you dive into these special attributes in detail, let's take a look at how you can define chunks of Boo code directly in AST format.

### UNDERSTANDING CODE LITERALS IN BOO

One of the cool things Boo lets you do is define functions as trees, as you can in C# with the Expression API. But although Boo has its own API that's similar to the LINQ Expression API, you're not confined to going through API calls to create a tree. Let's start with a simple addition method in Boo:

```
def Add(x as int, y as int):
  return x + y
```

If you represented this as a tree structure via Boo's AST API, it would look something like the code in the following listing.

---

**Listing 9.1    Representing a Boo method with the AST API**

```
import Boo.Lang.Compiler.Ast

xParameter = ParameterDeclaration(
  Name: 'x',
  Type: SimpleTypeReference(Name: 'int'))
yParameter = ParameterDeclaration(
  Name: 'y',
  Type: SimpleTypeReference(Name: 'int'))
parameters = ParameterDeclarationCollection()
parameters.Add(xParameter)
parameters.Add(yParameter)

apiAdd = Method(
  Name: 'LiteralAdd',
  Parameters: parameters,
  Body: Block(ReturnStatement(BinaryExpression(
```

```
    Left: Expression.Lift(xParameter),
    Right: Expression.Lift(yParameter),
    Operator: BinaryOperatorType.Addition))))
```

This should feel like creating a LINQ expression. You create parameters with the `ParameterDeclaration` class, specifying their names and types. Then you add them to a `Method`, which also specifies the name of the method. The `Block` class contains the implementation of the method, which is a `BinaryExpression` that adds the two parameter values together.

Now here's the fun part:

```
literalAdd = [|
  def QuotedAdd(x as int, y as int):
    return x + y
|]
```

That's the same thing as the code in listing 9.1! Boo defines the quasi-quotation markers, `[|` and `|]`, to let you specify code literals in your code without having to go through the gyrations of an API. You express your intention as naturally as you would any other piece of Boo code, except that in this case, this isn't executable code; it's code in tree format.

Now that you have an expression tree, you want to be able to execute it. In the next section, you'll see how you can compile Boo code.

### COMPILING BOO CODE AT RUNTIME

To compile Boo fragments, you use the `compile()` method from the `Boo.Lang.Compiler .MetaProgramming` assembly. Here's how it looks:

```
import Boo.Lang.Compiler.MetaProgramming

literalAdd = [|
  class QA:
    static def QuotedAdd(x as int, y as int):
      return x + y
|]
compiledLiteralAdd as duck = compile(literalAdd)
print(compiledLiteralAdd.QuotedAdd(5, 6))
```

This code is slightly modified from the `literalAdd` fragment from the last section. It's been redefined as a `static` on a class called `QA`. Now, when you `compile()` the fragment, you assign it to a variable using the `duck` keyword. Boo supports duck typing such that method calls are resolved at runtime. Therefore, as long as there's a `QuotedAdd` method on the class, the method call will resolve correctly.

What's nice about Boo is that it also has the parser exposed as an API. This means you can compile code fragments that are contained within strings if you want. Consider the following code:

```
import Boo.Lang.Compiler.MetaProgramming
import Boo.Lang.Parser

stringifiedAdd = """
class SA:
```

```
    static def stringifiedAdd(x as int, y as int):
      return x + y
"""
```

```
compiledStringifiedAdd as duck = compile(BooParser.ParseString(
  'SA', stringifiedAdd)).GetType('SA')
print(compiledStringifiedAdd.stringifiedAdd(11, 22))
```

The triple double quotes allow you to span a string across multiple lines—you get the same effect in C# if you put the @ symbol in front of a string declaration. Within the `stringifiedAdd` string, you define a class with a method. That code is compiled with the `ParseString()` method on `BooParser`. That method returns a `CompileUnit` object, which you can pass into the `compile()` method you saw in the last section. In this case, you're getting a standard `System.Reflection.Assembly` object from the `compile()` call, so a simple call to `GetType()` is all it takes to duck-type the return value so your call to `stringifiedAdd()` works.

At this point, hopefully it's clear that Boo provides a lot of dynamic programming capabilities. But your brief Boo tour isn't over yet. Now that you know how code fragments and code generation work in Boo, let's revisit the concept of AST attributes.

### INJECTING BOO CODE AT COMPILATION WITH AST ATTRIBUTES

In the subsection "A simple class in Boo," you saw the `GetterAttribute`. This is a class that has `AbstractAstAttribute` as its base class. Technically, this isn't a .NET attribute that you're used to, like the `STAThreadAttribute` used on the `Main()` method from the code sample. It doesn't get compiled into the assembly as metadata. Rather, these AST attributes are detected by the Boo compiler and inject code into the resulting assembly. Therefore, you can control the shape and behavior of code by putting reusable bits of code generation in AST attributes. Let's create a simple method-tracing attribute to see how easy it is to add code to your applications. The following listing shows what that attribute looks like.

---

**Listing 9.2   Creating a trace attribute in Boo**

```
import Boo.Lang.Compiler
import Boo.Lang.Compiler.Ast
import System

class TraceAttribute(AbstractAstAttribute):
  def Apply(type as Node):
    target = type as ClassDefinition

    if target is null:
      raise ArgumentException(
        "TraceAttribute can only be applied to classes.",
        "type")

    for member in target.Members:
      method = member as Method
      continue if method is null
      method.Body = [|
        Console.Out.WriteLine(string.Format(
```

```
      "Method {0} started.", $(method.FullName)))
    $(method.Body)
    Console.Out.WriteLine(string.Format(
      "Method {0} finished.", $(method.FullName)))
  |]
```

The intent of this attribute is to add tracing to every method in a class. Therefore, the first thing you need to do is make sure the attribute has been associated with a class. The `Apply()` method is called by the Boo compiler, and `type` is the AST node that the attribute is associated with. That's why `type` is cast as a `ClassDefinition` object—if that fails, `Apply()` will throw an `ArgumentException`. If `TraceAttribute` is associated with a class, you need to iterate over every method in the class. Here's where Boo's metaprogramming facilities shine. When you find a method, you transform its implementation by altering the `Body` property. You inject two calls to the `Console`, before and after the original body definition (you definitely can't lose that original code!). You use the splice operator (the dollar sign, $) to inject expressions into the expression tree, such as the method's name and body.

To use this attribute, you have to compile it into a separate assembly first. Boo can't have the attribute definition in a Boo file that wants to use the attribute. Once you have the compiled attribute, using it is a line of code away:

```
import System

[Trace]
class TracedClass:
  def TraceMe():
    Console.Out.WriteLine("I should have been traced.")

TracedClass().TraceMe()
```

Figure 9.1 shows what happens when you run this code.

Even with a simple example, you can immediately see how powerful a language becomes when metaprogramming is in the forefront. With code fragments, splicing, and AST attributes, you have the freedom in Boo to separate and combine code as you see fit.

We'll wrap up our discussion of metaprogramming in Boo with a quick look at macros.

**Figure 9.1  Method tracing in Boo. By moving the tracing logic to an attribute that's injected into a method at compile time, your code is reusable and easier to read.**

**MACROS IN BOO**

Macros are powerful constructs that act like functions. They work on statements during the compilation process. Take a look at this simple macro:

```
import Boo.Lang.Compiler
import Boo.Lang.Compiler.Ast
import System

macro power:
  yield [| Console.Out.WriteLine(
    Math.Pow($(power.Arguments[0]), $(power.Arguments[1]))) |]
```

You define macros via the macro keyword. Notice that you don't explicitly declare the arguments to the macro, though you can do that if you want. In this example, you're generating code that will write the results of a Math.Pow() call. Macros are like AST attributes in that you have to compile them into a separate assembly first and then you reference them in another code file:

```
[STAThread]
def Main(args as (string)):
  power 3.2, 4.2
```

If you use a decompiler like ILSpy, you can see what ends up in the Main() method (in C# format):

```
[STAThread]
public static void Main(string[] args)
{
   Console.Out.WriteLine(Math.Pow(3.2, 4.2));
}
```

Boo adds the macro expansion to the compiler pipeline, so the entire line of code is now part of the resulting implementation.

This example is quite simple—in fact, you may wonder why you wouldn't make a call to Math.Pow() directly. The reason you want to use macros is to provide a way to add keywords to Boo to provide simplicity to code structures. Here's what the using macro in Boo does:

```
using file=File.OpenText(name):
  print(file.ReadLine())
```

Code-generation constructs such as the using statement in C# are done internally—you have no way to provide code during the compilation process. With macros, you're free to add implementations to your Boo programs as you see fit. In this case, the using macro generates all the code to make sure the file object is disposed of correctly within a finally block.

Now that you've seen what can be done in Boo, let's shift gears and take a look at Nemerle, a C#-like language that has similar metaprogramming constructs.

### 9.1.3  *Nemerle and metaprogrammg*

There's another CLR-based language that you can use to satisfy your metaprogramming needs, in particular if you feel comfortable in a language that uses C-like constructs, like curly braces and semicolons. Nemerle uses macros as its vehicle to drive metaprogramming in its language. Let's see how macros work in Nemerle.

#### MACROS IN NEMERLE

Nemerle has macros similar to Boo. In fact, macros are the key to metaprogramming in Nemerle. You'll see in the next section how you can use macros to modify types, but let's start by looking at a deceptively simple Nemerle macro:

```
using System;

macro @^^(x, y)
  syntax(x, "^^", y) {
    <[ Math.Pow($x, $y) ]>
}
```

The `<|` and `|>` operators are similar to the ` (backtick) in Boo. Therefore, you can deduce that this macro will perform the power operation on x and y. Also, macros need to be compiled into their own assemblies before they can be referenced in Nemerle code, like in Boo. The interesting difference in Nemerle is that you can provide a syntax keyword that Nemerle understands when it's used in code. In this macro, the syntax is `"^^"` with the two arguments on either side of the syntax node. This is what it looks like when you use the macro:

```
System.Console.WriteLine (3.0 ^^ 5.0);
```

That's slick. It looks like you added a new operator to Nemerle, and, in fact, you have. As long as a developer uses your macro assembly, they can use `"^^"` whenever they want to perform a power function.

Not every code transformation works at a statement level. Adding method-tracing–like functionality such as the Boo Trace AST attribute you saw in the section "Injecting Boo code at compilation with AST" requires access to the type itself. Fortunately, Nemerle provides this support with custom attributes. Let's see how you can create a Nemerle attribute to add tracing to all methods in a class.

#### USING MACROS FOR TYPE MODIFICATION

Macros in Nermele can be used to perform all sorts of code modifications. The following listing shows a macro that adds tracing to every method in a type.

> **Listing 9.3   A tracing macro in Nemerle**

```
using Nemerle;
using Nemerle.Compiler;
using Nemerle.Compiler.Parsetree.ClassMember;
using System;

[MacroUsage(MacroPhase.WithTypedMembers, MacroTargets.Class,
  Inherited = true, AllowMultiple = false)]
```

```
macro Trace (type : TypeBuilder)
{
  foreach (method : IMethod in type.GetMethods(
    BindingFlags.Public | BindingFlags.Instance | BindingFlags.Static))
  {
    match(method)
    {
      | builtMethod is MethodBuilder =>
        builtMethod.Body =
          <[
            Console.Out.WriteLine(string.Format(
              "Method {0} entered.", $(method.Name : string)));
            $(builtMethod.Body);
            Console.Out.WriteLine(string.Format(
              "Method {0} finished.", $(method.Name : string)));
          ]>;
      | _ => { }
    }
  }
}
```

Although Nemerle looks like C#, it has some distinct differences, so let's cover this code in detail. The first thing you do is mark this macro with a `MacroUsageAttribute`. You need to specify what phase of the compilation process you're interested in having this macro execute with the `MacroPhase` enumeration. You could specify a value like `BeforeInheritance`, but in this case, you want to wait until all the methods have been declared, which is why `WithTypedMembers` is used. You also need to specify the target; in this macro, the target is a class. You also need to provide some arguments so you can get access to the right members in your macro code, which is what the `Type-Builder`-based type argument is for.

Once your macro is invoked, you need to visit all the methods in the type. The `GetMethods()` call returns a list of `IMethod`-based objects, but you need to work with methods that are of type `MethodBuilder`. That's what the `match()` statement is for. It's a pattern-based approach to invoke code based on certain conditions. In this case, your code modification will run only if the current method is of the `MethodBuilder` type. Otherwise, the macro does nothing to that method.

Once you have a `MethodBuilder` object, adding tracing to the method is pretty simple. You create the code with the appropriate `WriteLine()` calls, keeping the original body of the method intact. Like the Boo tracing macro, you're not diving into the body of the method to ensure the "finished" message happens whenever the method returns control to the calling method, but you could visit the method body and put the messages in the right spots.

Using this macro is an attribute declaration away:

```
using System;

module Program
{
  [Trace]
  public class TracedTest
```

```
  {
    public TraceMe() : void
    {
      Console.Out.WriteLine("I should have been traced.");
    }
  }

  Main() : void
  {
    TracedTest().TraceMe();
  }
}
```

**TIP** Both Boo and Nemerle produce .NET assemblies that contain their compiler pipeline, AST definitions, and so on. It's definitely possible to define the macros for both languages in C# or VB by referencing the appropriate Boo or Nemerle assemblies, though you still need to understand how these target languages work so that you're producing the right statements. You can also use their compiler engines to provide a scripting or DSL framework for you in C# or VB. To learn about how you can use Boo to create DSLs, see *DSLs in Boo: Domain-Specific Languages in .NET* by Ayende Rahien (Manning, 2010). Check out the book's website at www.manning.com/rahien/.

You've now seen how other languages use metaprogramming directly in their feature sets. But although these languages may seem appealing and interesting, using these languages at your current place of employment may not be possible. Development shops aren't always willing to have their developers switch languages whenever they see fit, so you may have to find other ways to extend C# or VB. Fortunately, there are tools and frameworks that can add some of the features that Boo and Nemerle have. In the next section, you'll see what these tools are and how they work in C#.

## 9.2 A survey of tools

Throughout this chapter, you've seen a number of languages that have metaprogramming embedded deeply within their structure. But it's probably a good bet that, although you may have heard of Boo or Nemerle before, you haven't used them. At the end of the day, most .NET developers code in C# or VB. It's fun to learn about what other languages have to offer, but it's doubtful that you'll switch to another .NET language.

That's where tools come in. They extend C# with the ability to weave aspects into your code so you can separate out reusable pieces of code with relative ease. Moreover, you don't need to know the details of IL to do it either. In this section, you'll see what Spring.NET and PostSharp can do to employ metaprogramming in C#, starting with Spring.NET.

### 9.2.1 What is Spring.NET?

The first tool you're going to look at is called Spring.NET (www.springframework.net). Spring.NET is an interesting collection of frameworks and tools, such as Spring.Data and Spring.Messaging, but this chapter focuses on the Spring.Aop component. This assembly

provides you with the capability of weaving code into a
class at runtime. It does this by creating a dynamic
proxy of an interface at runtime. Figure 9.2 illustrates
what Spring is doing to add aspects to your code.

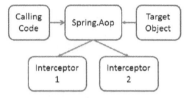

Spring adds interceptors around method invocations so you can easily layer facets like logging and
security on top of your code. The main limitation is
that it only works with virtual methods because the
generated proxy classes can't override nonvirtual
members. Let's take a look at building a simple interceptor that will notify you whenever a property is used.

**Figure 9.2   Spring produces
wrappers around the object you want
to use. These wrappers add facilities to
the methods that are transparent
to the caller and the callee.**

**NOTE**   Spring.Aop is available in NuGet, at www.nuget.org/packages/
Spring.Aop.

### 9.2.2   *Intercepting property usage with Spring.NET*

To give you a taste for the facilities Spring.Aop has to offer, you'll create an interceptor that you can use to find out whenever a property is used on an object. It doesn't
take much to know when properties are used in code via Spring—you need to create a
class that implements IMethodInterceptor. The following code listing shows how you
can get this to work.

**Listing 9.4   Using IMethodInterception for property usage**

```
public sealed class PropertyInterceptor
  : IMethodInterceptor
{
  private static bool IsPropertyMethod(MethodBase method)
  {
    return (from property in method.DeclaringType.GetProperties(
          BindingFlags.Public | BindingFlags.Instance)
        where (property.GetGetMethod() == method ||
        property.GetSetMethod() == method)
        select property).Any();
  }

  public object Invoke(IMethodInvocation invocation)
  {
    if (PropertyInterceptor.IsPropertyMethod(invocation.Method))
    {
      Console.Out.WriteLine(
        "Property {0} was invoked.",
        invocation.Method.Name);
    }

    return invocation.Proceed();
  }
}
```

The only method in IMethodInterception that you need to implement is Invoke().
You use the Method property on the invocation argument to determine whether the
method is one that's used as a getter or setter on a property. That's what the IsProperty-
Method() does. If it is, you print the property name to the console window. The
Proceed() method tells Spring that it should continue with any other interceptors
that may want to do something with this invocation. If this interceptor is the last one
in the chain, the underlying implementation is invoked.

You can test this using the following simple class definitions:

```
public interface IClassWithData
{
  Guid GetData();
  Guid Data { get; }
}
public class ClassWithData
  : IClassWithData
{
  public ClassWithData()
    : base() { }

  public ClassWithData(Guid data)
    : base()
  {
    this.Data = data;
  }

  public Guid Data { get; private set; }
}
```

The following code uses the interceptor with a ProxyFactory class:

```
var factoryData = new ProxyFactory(new ClassWithData(Guid.NewGuid()));
factoryData.AddAdvice(new PropertyInterceptor());
var dataWithInterceptor = (IClassWithData)factoryData.GetProxy();
Console.Out.WriteLine(dataWithInterceptor.Data);
```

The ProxyFactory class allows you to add interceptors to the factory via AddAdvice().
Then you call GetProxy(), and that returns a dynamic object that implements the
interface you cast the return value to. Once the Data property is used, the interceptor
code is invoked, and the property value is printed to the console. You should see
something like Figure 9.3.

Although Spring.Aop provides a decent framework for dynamic code, it carries
with it the traditional limitations that most frameworks do: you can only hook virtual
members or nonsealed classes. In the next section, you'll use a tool that provides a
higher level of flexibility for developers to add reusable pieces of code.

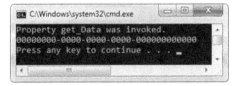

**Figure 9.3  Receiving notifications of property usage.
When the Data property is retrieved, the interceptor's
Invoke() method is called, providing you with the
ability to provide extra functionality to the application
(which, in this case, is logging that action to the
console window).**

### 9.2.3   *What is PostSharp?*

PostSharp is a product that uses metadata to hook into your code and do a number of things, including:

- Adding traditional aspect code, like logging and tracing for a method
- Implementing methods and interfaces for a class

PostSharp provides an API that makes applying code at specific points in an application straightforward, without having to understand the low-level details of .NET. It also integrates into Visual Studio to provide you with IDE helpers so you know when a code member may be affected by PostSharp. One main difference between PostSharp and Spring is that PostSharp isn't limited to virtual members because PostSharp can inline its hooks in both virtual and nonvirtual methods. Later in this chapter you'll crack open an assembly that's been modified by PostSharp to get a feel for what it's doing to your code, but for now, let's write a simple aspect that informs you when an instance of a class is created.

> **NOTE** If you want to play with PostSharp, visit www.sharpcrafters.com. It offers free and paid versions of its product, though you'll quickly find that the free version is fairly limited. In this book you'll see us use PostSharp that requires the paid version in only a couple of cases. We feel it's beneficial to see code that uses features in the paid version because you can do some cool things with that particular version. In no way do we expect you to buy PostSharp to run the code based on the paid-for features—we don't get any royalties from the makers of PostSharp.

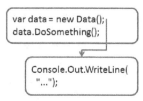

### 9.2.4   *Intercepting object creation with PostSharp*

The first thing you'll do with PostSharp is write code to tell you whenever a constructor is called and to specify the argument values. You'll write this information to the console window to keep things simple. Figure 9.4 provides a flow for what this aspect does.

The following listing shows the code that you need to write to do this. As you can tell, PostSharp makes this easy to accomplish.

**Figure 9.4   Adding object creation notifications to your code. Whenever a constructor is called, PostSharp injects code so that information about the creation is sent to the console window.**

> **Listing 9.5   Creating a constructor weaver with PostSharp**

```
[Serializable]
public sealed class CreationAttribute
  : OnMethodBoundaryAspect
{
  public override void OnEntry(MethodExecutionArgs args)
  {
    if (args.Method.IsConstructor)
    {
```

```
    Console.Out.WriteLine(
      "Object {0} was instantiated with the following arguments:",
      args.Method.DeclaringType.Name);

    foreach (var argument in args.Arguments)
    {
      Console.Out.WriteLine("Type: {0} || Value: {1}",
        argument.GetType().Name, argument);
    }
  }
 }
}
```

As stated in the previous section, PostSharp uses attributes to define the points where code will be modified in some way. In this case, you use the OnMethodBoundaryAspect attribute. Note that PostSharp doesn't follow the normal .NET naming convention with attributes. Normally you'd expect the attribute to be named OnMethodBoundary-AspectAttribute, but that's not the case with PostSharp.

The PostSharp attributes provide a number of overrides you can use to know when a specific event has occurred in code. By overriding OnEntry(), you're notified when a method has been invoked. You only care about constructor invocations, so you use the IsConstructor property on Method, which is a System.Reflection.MethodBase reference. If it's a constructor, you post the name of the method to the console window along with all the argument values. Note that the Arguments property is a collection of objects; it's not a collection of objects typed to something like an Argument class that provides information like the name and position of the argument. You get the values of the arguments.

Using this attribute is pretty simple:

```
[Creation]
public sealed class ClassWithCreation
{
  public ClassWithCreation()
    : base() { }

  public ClassWithCreation(Guid data)
    : base()
  {
    this.Data = data;
  }

  public Guid Data { get; private set; }
}
```

Now all it takes is writing some code like this to see it in action:

```
var noData = new ClassWithCreation();
Console.Out.WriteLine(noData.Data);
var data = new ClassWithCreation(Guid.NewGuid());
Console.Out.WriteLine(data.Data);
```

Figure 9.5 shows what the results are when you run that code. In the first case, the no-argument constructor is called, but in the second case, you see the constructor's argument values in the console window.

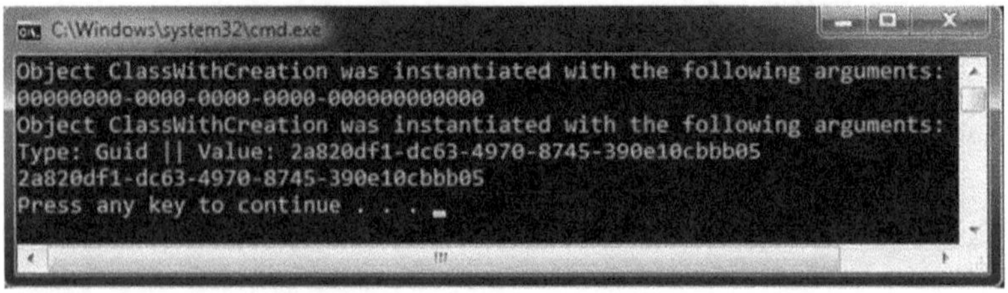

**Figure 9.5   Using PostSharp to intercept object creation. You can be notified by PostSharp whenever an object of a marked class is created.**

The `CreationAttribute` is a stripped-down version of the canonical example typically seen whenever AOP is discussed: tracing. In this case, you only care about constructor entry, but `OnMethodBoundaryAspect` provides `OnExit` to inform you when the method is completed. There's also an `OnException` method override that you can use if an exception is thrown from the method. It's easy to imagine how you can use these methods to create an attribute that encapsulates the aspect of logging such that you can quickly apply it to any type in your application.

In fact, making your aspect work for any class in your code is easy. Try this: remove the `CreationAttribute` from any class in your code and add this one line of code somewhere within your project:

```
[assembly: Creation]
```

Now every class in that project will have an object initialization notification! The reason is due to the way attributes work in .NET. You can specify where an attribute can be used via the `AttributeUsageAttribute`. It so happens that PostSharp's aspects don't limit you to a specific type with attributes like `OnMethodBoundaryAspect`. You can tell PostSharp to make its usage assembly-wide, and presto: constructor notification for every type. That's pretty slick.

But PostSharp's feature set isn't limited to intercepting method calls. In the next section, you'll see how you can add functionality to a class where it didn't exist before by defining complete method implementations.

### 9.2.5   *Implementing Equals() and GetHashCode()*

You've seen how you can intercept method calls with PostSharp. It's not hard to envision how you can use that feature to capture specific method requests to provide custom implementations of methods at runtime. Say you wanted to have a standard way to implement the `Equals()` method for all classes by comparing the values of all public properties. You could create a custom aspect that watched for the invocation of the `Equals()` method, invoking your reflection-based code at that particular moment. But this isn't ideal because you'd have to intercept every method invocation to find the `Equals()` one you want. There's a much cleaner way to do that in PostSharp via instance-level aspects and member introduction. The following listing defines an `EqualsAttribute` that provides a custom implementation of `Equals()` for any class (along with GetHashCode(), because you should always override both when you override one or the other).

Listing 9.6  **Providing implementation of** Equals() **and** GetHashCode()

```
[Serializable]
public sealed class EqualsAttribute
  : InstanceLevelAspect
{
  [IntroduceMember(IsVirtual = true,
    OverrideAction = MemberOverrideAction.OverrideOrIgnore,
    Visibility = Visibility.Public)]
  public override bool Equals(object obj)
  {
    var areEqual = false;

    if (obj != null && this.Instance.GetType()
      .IsAssignableFrom(obj.GetType()))
    {
      var result =
        (from prop in this.Instance.GetType().GetProperties(
          BindingFlags.Instance | BindingFlags.Public)
        where prop.CanRead
        select prop.GetValue(this.Instance, null)
          .Equals(prop.GetValue(obj, null)))
        .Distinct().ToList();

      areEqual = result.Count != 1 ? false : result[0];
    }

    return areEqual;
  }

  [IntroduceMember(IsVirtual = true,
    OverrideAction = MemberOverrideAction.OverrideOrIgnore,
    Visibility = Visibility.Public)]
  public override int GetHashCode()
  {
    return
      (from prop in this.Instance.GetType().GetProperties(
        BindingFlags.Instance | BindingFlags.Public)
      where prop.CanRead
      select prop.GetValue(this.Instance, null).GetHashCode())
      .Aggregate(0, (counter, item) => counter ^= item);
  }
}
```

**NOTE**   The preceding example requires the paid version of PostSharp.

The first step is to inherit from InstanceLevelAspect for your custom attribute. This means that the attribute works at the instance level and not at the method level like our previous CreationAttribute did. The next step is to provide an implementation for Equals(). To do that, you override Equals() in the attribute itself and then mark that method with the IntroduceMemberAttribute. That may seem confusing at first, but what you're doing is literally *introducing* the marked member to the instance of the class that has this attribute on it. Therefore, any classes with the EqualsAttribute will have any calls to Equals() redirected to this Equals() method.

The implementation of Equals() is fairly straightforward. You ensure that the given object is the same type as the instance and then you iterate through all the public property values via Reflection. The result of the LINQ statement is either one distinct Boolean value or two. If you get two back, you know the objects aren't equal—otherwise, you return the one Boolean value you got from the query. Note that you must be careful *not* to use this if you want to reference an object member, because this is the attribute's this. If you do use this directly in Equals(), you're using the attribute instance, which isn't what you want.

It's natural to use this, but you have to remember that you're writing code that's targeting another object instance. Therefore, you use the Instance property to get a reference to the object currently in scope. Figure 9.6 illustrates how the current object is exposed via the Instance property.

The GetHashCode() method is handled like the Equals() method is—it's *introduced* into the marked object. All the hash code values are XOR'ed together with the Aggregate() function.

Now that you have the two methods that handle equality overridden, adding them to a class is easy:

```
[Equals]
public sealed class ClassWithEquals
{
  public int IntData { get; set; }
  public string StringData { get; set; }
}
```

With this attribute in place, you can run the following code:

```
var equals1 = new ClassWithEquals { IntData = 10, StringData = "10" };
var equals2 = new ClassWithEquals { IntData = 20, StringData = "20" };
var equals3 = new ClassWithEquals { IntData = 10, StringData = "10" };

Console.Out.WriteLine(equals1.Equals(equals2));
Console.Out.WriteLine(equals1.Equals(equals3));
```

You'll see that the first and third objects are equal and have the same hash code values. Keep in mind that this is an instance-level attribute, so you can't apply this assembly-wide like you could with the CreationAttribute class.

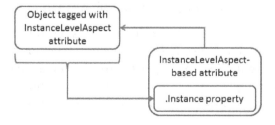

**Figure 9.6  Getting a reference to the "real" object. In the attribute, you use the Instance property to reference the object that the aspect is on. PostSharp handles setting that reference for you.**

You've now seen how PostSharp can make metaprogramming clean and simple. But you may be wondering how PostSharp does what it's doing. The next section takes a brief look under the covers to find out.

### 9.2.6 *A quick dive into the internals of PostSharp*

As you can probably guess, it takes more than referencing PostSharp.dll to enable all the fancy gyrations you saw in the last two sections. PostSharp ties into the compilation process to create all the necessary hooks and custom implementation specified by your custom attributes. Let's see what PostSharp does to your code by looking at the `ClassWithCreation` class created in section 9.2.4. The following listing shows the code that exists in the constructor for `ClassWithCreation` that takes a `Guid` after Post-Sharp does its magic.

**Listing 9.7   Code modified by PostSharp**

```
public ClassWithCreation(Guid data)
{
  this.<>z__InitializeAspects();
  MethodExecutionArgs methodExecutionArgs =
    new MethodExecutionArgs(null, new Arguments<Guid>
    {
      Arg0 = data
    });
  MethodExecutionArgs arg_2A_0 = methodExecutionArgs;
  MethodBase m = ClassWithCreation.<>z__Aspects.m7;
  arg_2A_0.Method = m;
  ClassWithCreation.<>z__Aspects.a4.OnEntry(methodExecutionArgs);
  this.Data = data;
}
```

The preceding code was produced by the tool ILSpy (http://ilspy.net). PostSharp puts a fair amount of code into the method to support its features—remember that the original method only had one line of code: the property setter. PostSharp also uses some strange variable names to minimize the chance that they will collide with any names you've used, but once you get past them figuring out what's going on is straightforward. PostSharp first gathers up the argument values with a `MethodExecutionArgs` reference. Then it captures a `MethodBase` reference that refers to the currently executing method. Finally, it passes them on to the `OnEntry()` method you overrode in the `CreationAttribute` attribute.

PostSharp is free to change how it performs its code modification, so you shouldn't necessarily rely on anything you see here being the same from version to version. Yet given all that you know about metaprogramming in .NET, you probably weren't surprised to see how PostSharp does what it does. Although PostSharp doesn't give you the ability to modify the IL of a method, for most AOP techniques you don't need such fine-grained control. Having an API and toolset that sit at a reflection-like level is easier for a C# developer to comprehend, which makes it quicker for them to start performing all sorts of useful gyrations in their code.

## 9.3    *Summary*

In this chapter, you investigated languages that lifted metaprogramming into the forefront via expressions and tools that provided interception and code weaving to make your code succinct and reusable.

In the final chapter, you're going to get a glimpse into the future of .NET. Although dynamic capabilities exist in .NET, there's never been a unified way to manage your code from parsing to execution. That's what Project Roslyn is all about, that's what chapter 10 is all about too.

# Managing
# the .NET Compiler

# 10

**This chapter covers**

- The evolution of the compilers
- Using the Roslyn API to generate code

By now, we hope you've seen that metaprogramming in .NET isn't only possible, it's something you should always consider using whenever you create new applications. Metaprogramming requires more care and thought than "normal" .NET development, but the payoff comes with succinct, reusable, dynamic pieces of code. One recurring theme of this book is the use of frameworks to support these techniques—frameworks that provide you with a lot of power, but don't come with an installation of .NET. With Project Roslyn—a framework from Microsoft that allows you to compile your C# or VB code with a managed API—that's going to change in a big way.

This chapter gives you a quick tour of the history of compilers within the Microsoft world, how they've been done in the past, and what Roslyn does to change that traditional architecture. You'll also get an overview of key features within the Roslyn API that will help you understand how you'll be able to use Roslyn to support the metaprogramming techniques discussed in this book. Finally, you'll see how Roslyn can make program analysis easier.

First, let's see what Roslyn is doing to change the compiler world in .NET.

## 10.1   *Opening up the compiler*

Metaprogramming in .NET usually requires you to understand low-level APIs like System.Reflection.Emit or find frameworks like Cecil or NRefactory. There isn't a consistent, unified approach for you to support metaprogramming techniques like dynamic code execution and code parsing. This fragmentation occurs because the compiler's inner workings aren't visible to you. In this section, you'll see how compilers have traditionally worked in .NET, why this makes metaprogramming hard to do, and how Roslyn addresses this issue by opening up the compiler.

### 10.1.1   *The current state of affairs: a black box*

Ever since the first version of .NET, the compiler has existed as a simple executable. You invoke it to morph your code, contained in text files, into an assembly. Figure 10.1 illustrates this simplistic process that goes on when you compile C# code.

At first glance, a compiler may seem somewhat trivial, but the inner workings are incredibly complex. The rules that a compiler writer must follow to change your C# code into metadata and IL can be daunting to say the least. Imagine the last lines of C# code you wrote on a recent big project and think of all the things the compiler has to keep track of correctly: generic definitions, lambda expressions, and variable definitions, to name a few (and semicolons). Writing compilers can be one of the hardest things to do correctly, and it'll show if it has bugs. There's probably no other executable you run more in your day-to-day activities as a C# developer than csc.exe, and if it doesn't work as expected, you'll know right away.

> **NOTE**   For a description of the passes the C# compiler does, see the article at http://mng.bz/8dWX.

Even though a lot of work goes on in the background, you don't have a lot of options for controlling what the compiler does. In fact, you have fewer than 50 options, some of which have nothing to do with the compilation process itself; they tell the compiler to create extraneous files (such as /doc). When it comes to metaprogramming, this creates challenges you have to overcome.

> **NOTE**   The complete list of command line options for the C# compiler is available at http://mng.bz/xML9.

### 10.1.2   *Limitations for metaprogramming*

The architecture of a compiler is complex, but over the years not having access to this process has started to show limitations in various areas of development, and not only with metaprogramming. Think about a code analysis engine. Right now, the engine

Figure 10.1   Compiling code files with csc.exe. It's a fairly easy process: you specify what files the compiler works with, and it gives you an assembly.

has to wait for the compiler to finish its job before it can analyze the assembly to tell you whether you may have subtle issues with your implementation. For example:

```
[OperationContract(IsOneWay = true)]
public string MyOperation() { }
```

The C# compiler will happily compile this with no issues because it doesn't know about the WCF rule that one-way operations (methods marked with the `Operation-ContractAttribute`) can't return a value. Sure, you can write a unit test to exercise your code and catch this issue before it gets farther than your machine, but wouldn't it be better if you knew about this when compilation was happening, and not when the analysis engine kicked in? Or even better—how about knowing about these kinds of errors while you were typing your code?

A lot of services and features that you use as a .NET developer have to work around the fact that they can't tie in to the compilation process. Code formatting services, code analysis engines—they need ways to determine what's wrong with your code without having explicit, rich knowledge of your code. Without a standardized way of getting this information from code, developers have resorted to creating their own libraries and tools to fill the gaps. This had led to duplication in effort in many areas related to parsing code and creating assemblies (for example, Cecil and CCI).

This is also a key issue when it comes to metaprogramming. There's no way for a .NET developer to access the compiler passes and workflows to influence and manipulate what the compiler does. Think about that for a moment, as it pertains to all the techniques and ideas you've read about in this book. For example, when you looked at adding code via assembly rewriting techniques in chapter 6, you needed to use a library called NRefactory to parse C# code. If .NET provided that parse-related information for you, you wouldn't need to create it yourself (or use what someone else has created). If you had the ability to add a `ToString()` implementation or weave in code that checked arguments for a null value when the code was compiling, you wouldn't need to add in another step after compilation occurs. You could do it when compilation was happening!

Fortunately, Microsoft has been working on a new, managed compiler with a plethora of APIs behind it waiting for you to play with. This is called Project Roslyn.

### 10.1.3 What Roslyn provides: a white box

Project Roslyn finally opens up the compiler box to let you see all the steps and paths the compiler takes when it takes your code and creates an assembly. Figure 10.2 illustrates what is now available to you with Project Roslyn.

You now have access to parsing information, symbolic details, and so on. Although the next version of csc.exe may not have this kind of extensibility, its internals are no longer *internals*—they're externalized with the Roslyn APIs. We cover the details of how Roslyn works in upcoming sections. But it's not only about seeing what the compiler is doing. With this kind of extensive insight into your code, you can reason about

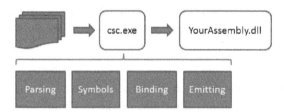

**Figure 10.2  Seeing the internals of the compiler. Having access to this level of detail opens up a whole new set of dynamic possibilities to the .NET developer.**

it to give immediate feedback to a developer to fix potential issues, or provide code generation facilities, or generate code at runtime—the possibilities are enormous. Roslyn brings a lot to the table for those interested in metaprogramming techniques, but it also provides a unified view for code analysis adventures.

You'll see examples in this chapter on how you can use Roslyn to execute and examine code to support metaprogramming. Before we dive into the Roslyn APIs, let's spend time covering what's not in Roslyn. This will help level-set any expectations you may have about what you're hoping it can do.

### 10.1.4  *What's in (and not in) the CTP*

Roslyn is a major step forward for developers who want that intimate view of code, but it does have limitations. Let's cover some of them before you see what Roslyn can do.

First, Roslyn only works with C# and VB. If you like F#, you're out of luck when it comes to analyzing your code with the Roslyn APIs. The same goes for any other language that targets the .NET world. That's not to say that Roslyn won't change in a future version to let others create providers and extensions to Roslyn for other languages, but Microsoft has to ship the first version.

Second, Roslyn isn't about extending the C# and VB languages. As you play with the Roslyn APIs, you may start having ideas like this:

```
public disposed class DisposableItem
{
  public void DoSomething()
  {
    // Important code goes here...
  }

  public string Data { get; set; }
}
```

Notice the addition of the new keyword, `disposed`, in that code snippet. Having the compiler generate all the code you need to implement `IDisposable`, including the rules around `ObjectDisposedException`, all based on the existence of a custom token— that would be nice! Or what about doing something like this?

```
var x = 23.2;
var y = 4.2;
var z = x ^^ y;
```

Instead of having to type `Math.Pow`, you could use something like a double-caret (`^^`), and let your custom parsing implementation translate that token into a `Math.Pow` call.

You think, hey, I have access to the compiler engine—why don't I add my own keywords and operations and pick them up when the code is parsed?

That would be problematic, mainly because you've extended the language in a way that would require anyone else that wants to compile your code to have your specific extensions in place to handle that syntax. Plus, even if you were able to make it extremely simple to provide these extensions to any developer who compiles your code, what about the hordes of developers who are creating their own extensions to the language? Or, even worse, what if someone uses a double-caret to mean something entirely different from something you meant?

That's not to say you can't use metadata to extend C# like this:

```
[Disposable]
public sealed class DisposableItem
  : IDisposable
{
  public void Dispose()
  {
    // Dispose code goes here...
  }

  public void DoSomething()
  {
    // Important code goes here...
  }

  public string Data { get; set; }
}
```

Then you can use the existence of that metadata to generate code with Roslyn. There's nothing wrong with that. But Roslyn isn't about letting you extend C# or VB.

**NOTE** For a full description of Roslyn's limitations, check out http://mng.bz/PXRO.

With the limitations out of the way, let's see what Roslyn *can* do. We'll start creating pieces of executable code by compiling code as text and work our way deeper into more of its parts. The first example will mirror an example you've seen before in this book, but it won't involve understanding IL or expressions trees. All you'll need is your knowledge of C#, which, as you'll see, allows you to focus on the skills you already have.

## 10.2 *Understanding the basics of Roslyn*

Let's start your journey of looking at how Roslyn works by creating executable code fragments at runtime. You'll do it in two ways: you'll use a scripting engine first, and then you'll see how it's done by compiling and executing the code.

### 10.2.1 *Running code snippets with the script engine*

One of the prevalent examples used in this book was to create dynamic code to implement ToString(). The output is a double-pipe delimited set of property name and

**Installing Roslyn**

To play with Roslyn, visit the Roslyn site (http://msdn.microsoft.com/en-us/roslyn) and download the bits from there. The material in this chapter was based on the June 2012 CTP. Because this is a CTP, you may not want to run this on your main installation of VS 2010 or 2012; a safer bet is to create a virtual PC and work with Roslyn there. It's slower, but you won't have to deal with any uninstallation issues that a CTP may have.

value pairs, which is what you see in figure 10.4. Let's do the same thing with Roslyn. We won't concern ourselves with caching or other performance improvements or tweaks for now. This is a CTP, and trying to gain any insight into performance numbers you gather is suspect at best.

Let's start by defining the extension method that will be used:

```
public static class ToStringViaRoslynExtensions
{
  public sealed class Host<T>
  {
    public Host(T target)
    {
      this.Target = target;
    }

    public T Target { get; private set; }
  }

  public static string Generate<T>(this T @this)
  {
```

You'll see the definition for `Generate()` momentarily, but notice there's also a class called `Host` that has a read-only property of the same type as `@this`. That's needed for your scripting environment so it can reference the object you've been given in `@this`.

Let's see the code that's generated to create a meaningful object description from `ToString()`:

```
var code = "new StringBuilder()" +
  string.Join(".Append(\" || \")",
    from property in @this.GetType().GetProperties(
      BindingFlags.Instance | BindingFlags.Public)
    where property.CanRead
    select string.Format(
    ".Append(\"{0}: \").Append(Target.{0})",
      property.Name)) + ".ToString()";
```

This reflection code is similar to what you've seen in the other examples that handle `ToString()` on the fly. The difference is that you're creating C# code as the output and not something like IL in a dynamic method. What ends up in the `code` variable looks something like this:

```
new StringBuilder().Append("Age: ").Append(Target.Age).Append(" || ")
  .Append("Name: ").Append(Target.Name).ToString()
```

The last piece is bringing Roslyn's scripting engine into play to execute the code:

```
    var hostReference =
      new AssemblyFileReference(typeof(
        ToStringViaRoslynExtensions).Assembly.Location);
    var engine = new ScriptEngine(
      references: new[] { hostReference },
      importedNamespaces: new[] { "System", "System.Text" });
    var host = new Host<T>(@this);
    var session = Session.Create(host);
    return engine.Execute<string>(code, session);
  }
}
```

**1** Get assembly reference to host

**2** Create scripting engine

**3** Create session

**4** Execute code

First you need to get an `AssemblyFileReference` to the assembly that contains the `Host` type so the scripting engine will know what `Target` means in the code you give it **1**. Next, create a `ScriptEngine` object, passing it the assembly references it needs to know about, as well as any namespaces. You're using `StringBuilder`, so that's why `System.Text` is passed into the engine **2**. A `Session` object is also required because you need to pass in a host object that the code can use—namely, an instance of `Host`— and `Session` is what ties the dynamic code to your code that's currently executing **3**. The last step is to execute the code, done by calling `Execute()` **4**. Figure 10.3 lays out the flow and interaction between these parts so you can see at a higher level how they work together to run your dynamic code.

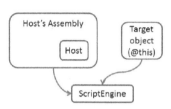

**Figure 10.3 Interaction with the `ScriptEngine`. Your code passes a reference to the assembly that contains the `Host` class, along with the target object, to the `ScriptEngine`. The script that's executed will use both parts to run correctly.**

To test it, create a simple class with a couple of properties and `ToString()` overridden to call the extension method:

```
public sealed class Person
{
  public Person(string name, uint age)
  {
    this.Name = name;
    this.Age = age;
  }

  public override string ToString()
  {
    return this.Generate();
  }

  public uint Age { get; private set; }
  public string Name { get; private set; }
}
```

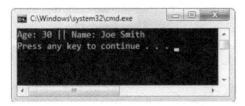

**Figure 10.4   Calling** `ToString()` **implemented via Roslyn. By compiling C# at runtime, you can implement anything you want at the abstraction level where you always write.**

When you run `ToString()` in a console application like this

```
static void Main(string[] args)
{
  Console.Out.WriteLine(
    new Person("Joe Smith", 30).ToString());
}
```

you should see the output in Figure 10.4.

The end result may look simple, but think about what you did. You created code on the fly, but it wasn't IL, or an expression tree. It was C# code! The Roslyn engine happily compiled that little piece of code and executed it on the fly. No knowledge of opcodes or expressions is necessary—you can write code that literally writes more code and executes it.

One could argue that this can be mimicked with what's currently available in the C# compiler. Create the code snippet in a file, run the compiler, load the resulting assembly, and execute a method via reflection. With Roslyn, though, it's all in-memory, and you don't have to mess with things like assembly loading and file creation if you don't want to. To be fair, Roslyn can compile code files and generate assemblies—it has to if it's going to replace csc.exe. But the point is, Roslyn brings code analysis and manipulation to a much higher level than was ever available before.

Now that you have your feet wet with Roslyn, let's take a deeper dive into its API and see how to create a simplistic dynamic mock at runtime.

### 10.2.2  *Creating dynamic assemblies with Roslyn*

In the preceding section, you saw how to use the scripting engine to run C#. Now you'll see how you can compile a mock C# into an assembly. Before you look deeper into the Roslyn API again, let's define what a mock is.

### 10.2.3  *What is a mock?*

Generally speaking, a *mock* is an object that can stand in place of another object. The mock is typically used in unit-testing scenarios, where a developer uses a mock instead of an object that does a number of long-running or complex calculations. Rather than include these dependencies in the unit test, the developer will inject a mock into the test such that the test can focus on the code at hand. You can also use a mock object to verify that the code under test used it in an expected manner.

Let's use a simple example to illustrate how mocks are used. Let's say you had a class called `Person` that used a service to look up address information for that person. Figure 10.5 shows the dependency `Person` has on the service.

**Figure 10.5   Using a dependency directly. Using an object that has complex setup needs or takes a long time to execute can make unit testing difficult and time-consuming.**

Now, whenever a developer needs to test a `Person` object, she needs to also ensure that the service is up and running and will return the expected data. This is time-consuming and brittle. A better approach would be to break the direct dependency on `Address-Service`, as figure 10.6 shows.

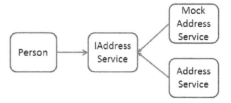

**Figure 10.6   Using an interface in code. Now the `Person` object doesn't care how `IAddressService` is implemented, and you can use mocks for `Person`-based unit tests.**

In this case, `Person` now has a dependency on the `IAddressService` interface. The code doesn't care how the class that implements `IAddressService` works; it cares about the contract that the interface specifies. During a test, a `MockAddressService` object is used, and in production, `AddressService` is used.

> **TIP**  If want to learn more about unit testing, please check out *The Art of Unit Testing* by Roy Osherove (Manning, 2009) (http://manning.com/osherove/) and *Dependency Injection in .NET* by Mark Seemann (Manning, 2011) (http://manning.com/seemann/).

You can hand-roll the mocks if you want; you can write the code that implements an interface and notifies you when a method has been called. You can also use metaprogramming techniques to synthesize a class at runtime that does this for you. Let's see how you can use Roslyn to create a mock at runtime.

### 10.2.4  Generating the mock code

In this section, you'll see how you can create a mock using C#-generated code at runtime. You'll compile the code and create an instance of the mock, passing that back to the caller. The caller will use a class with methods that match the signature of the methods in the interface you want to handle in the test. This arrangement will allow you to provide a mocked implementation of the interface method, which is useful in testing scenarios.

> **Mock frameworks in .NET**
>
> The mock structure you're going to create is fairly simplistic compared to some of the frameworks that currently exist in the .NET world.
>
> Some of the ones we recommend are NSubstitute (http://nsubstitute.github.com), Moq (http://code.google.com/p/moq/), and RhinoMocks (http://hibernatingrhinos.com/open-source/rhino-mocks).
>
> Hopefully, once Roslyn is officially released, these frameworks will spend time updating their engines to use the Roslyn API to generate their mocks.

The first thing you want to do is create a string that represents the structure of the class you want to dynamically create at runtime:

```
public sealed class MockCodeGenerator
{
  private const string Template = @"
    [System.Serializable]
    internal sealed class {0}
      : {1}
    {{
      private {2} callback;

      public {0}({2} callback)
      {{
        this.callback = callback;
      }}

      {3}
    }}";
```

Each mock needs a new type name ({0}), the interface it's implementing ({1}), a reference to the callback object ({2}), and a list of interface methods with an implementation based on the methods that exist in the callback object ({3}). Let's fill these holes in the code:

```
public MockCodeGenerator(string mockName,
  Type interfaceType, Type callbackType)
  : base()
{
  this.MockName = mockName;
  this.InterfaceType = interfaceType;
  this.InterfaceTypeName = InterfaceType.FullName;
  this.CallbackType = callbackType;
  this.Generate();
}

private void Generate()
{
  this.Code = string.Format(MockCodeGenerator.Template,
    this.MockName, this.InterfaceTypeName,
    this.CallbackType.FullName,
    this.GetMethods());
}
```

Other than generating the methods, everything else is fairly boilerplate. Note that we use the FullName property for both the interface and callback types. This makes it a little easier to generate the code because you don't need to include using statements. The following listing illustrates how you generate the methods that implement the interface.

**Listing 10.1  Generating methods for an interface**

```
private string GetMethods()
{
  var methods = new StringBuilder();
```

```
   var callbackMethods = this.CallbackType.GetMethods(
     BindingFlags.Public | BindingFlags.Instance);

   foreach (var interfaceMethod in
     this.InterfaceType.GetMethods())
   {
     methods.Append("public " +
       MockCodeGenerator.GetMethod(interfaceMethod) + "{");

     var callbackMethod = this.FindMethod(
       callbackMethods, interfaceMethod);

     if (callbackMethod != null)
     {
       if (callbackMethod.ReturnType != typeof(void))
       {
         methods.Append("return ");
       }

       methods.Append("this.callback." +
         MockCodeGenerator.GetMethod(
           callbackMethod, false) + ";");
     }
     else
     {
       if (interfaceMethod.ReturnType != typeof(void))
       {
         methods.Append("return " + (
           interfaceMethod.ReturnType.IsClass ?
           "null;" : string.Format("default({0});",
             interfaceMethod.ReturnType.FullName)));
       }
     }

     methods.Append("}");
   }

   return methods.ToString();
}
```

❶ Create implementation for each method

❷ Call method on callback object if match exists

❸ Return default value for interface method if return type isn't void

You need to generate a method for each method on the interface ❶. The key aspect to notice is the way the implementation is done. You look to see if the callback object has a method that matches the signature of the interface method. If so, call the method on the callback object ❷. Otherwise, you return the default value of the interface method's return type if it's not void ❸.

You call FindMethod() to find a match on the callback object, as shown in the following listing.

**Listing 10.2 Finding a method match on the callback object**

```
private MethodInfo FindMethod(
  MethodInfo[] callbackMethods, MethodInfo interfaceMethod)
{
  MethodInfo result = null;

  foreach (var callbackMethod in callbackMethods)
  {
```

```
    if (callbackMethod.ReturnType ==
      interfaceMethod.ReturnType)
    {
      var callbackParameters =
        callbackMethod.GetParameters();
      var interfaceParameters =
        interfaceMethod.GetParameters();

      if (callbackParameters.Length ==
        interfaceParameters.Length)
      {
        var foundDifference = false;

        for (var i = 0;
          i < interfaceParameters.Length; i++)
        {
          if (callbackParameters[0].ParameterType !=
            interfaceParameters[0].ParameterType)
          {
            foundDifference = true;
            break;
          }
        }

        if (!foundDifference)
        {
          result = callbackMethod;
          break;
        }
      }
    }
  }
}

return result;
}
```

**❶ Make sure return types are the same**

**❷ Ensure all parameter types match**

**❸ Return current method if all types match**

You iterate through each method on the callback object. First, you check the return types to see if they match ❶. If they do, then you look at each parameter's type to see if they match ❷. If there are no differences in the parameter types, you've found a match, and that's what you return ❸.

The GetMethod() method returns a stringified version of a MethodInfo that can be used in C# code generation, as shown in the following listing.

**Listing 10.3  Generating C# for a method definition**

```
private static string GetMethod(
  MethodInfo method, bool includeTypes = true)
{
  var result = new StringBuilder();

  if (includeTypes)
  {
    result.Append(method.ReturnType == typeof(void) ? "void " :
      method.ReturnType.FullName + " ");
  }
```

```
      result.Append(method.Name + "(");
      result.Append(string.Join(", ",
        from parameter in method.GetParameters()
        select (includeTypes ?
          parameter.ParameterType.FullName + " " + parameter.Name :
          parameter.Name)));
      result.Append(")");
      return result.ToString();
    }

  private Type CallbackType { get; set; }
  public string Code { get; private set; }
  private Type InterfaceType { get; set; }
  private string MockName { get; set; }
  private string InterfaceTypeName { get; set; }
}
```

Again, note that you're using full type names for the return type (if it's not void) and the parameter types.

Let's go through a quick example to see what the generated code looks like. Consider the following interface:

```
public interface ITest
{
  void CallMe(string data);
  int CallMe();
}
```

And let's say you defined a callback object like this:

```
public sealed class TestCallback
{
  public int Callback()
  {
    return new Random().Next();
  }
}
```

Note that the Callback() method matches the signature of CallMe() in ITest, but TestCallback doesn't implement ITest. A generated mock for ITest that uses Test-Callback would look something like this:

```
[System.Serializable]
internal sealed class TestCallbackMock
  : DynamicMocks.Roslyn.Tests.ITest
{
  private DynamicMocks.Roslyn.Tests.TestCallback callback;

  public TestCallbackMock(
    DynamicMocks.Roslyn.Tests.TestCallback callback)
    {
      this.callback = callback;
    }

    public void CallMe(System.String data){}

    public System.Int32 CallMe()
    {
```

```
            return this.callback.Callback();
        }
    }
```

The mock defines two methods to implement the ITest method, but the CallMe()
method that takes a string doesn't do anything. The CallMe() methods calls Callback
on the TestCallback object as the signature matches.

  Now you have the ability to generate a mock in C#. In the next section, you'll see
how you can compile this with Roslyn.

### 10.2.5  *Compiling the mock code*

You have the ability to create a C#-based mock. The following listing shows how you
can compile that code with Roslyn.

---
**Listing 10.4  Compiling code at runtime with Roslyn**
---

```
public static class Mock
{
  private static readonly Lazy<ModuleBuilder> builder =
    new Lazy<ModuleBuilder>(() => Mock.CreateBuilder());

  public static T Create<T>(object callback)
    where T : class
  {
    var interfaceType = typeof(T);

    if (!interfaceType.IsInterface)                              ❶ Ensure generic
    {                                                              type is an
      throw new NotSupportedException();                           interface
    }

    var callbackType = callback.GetType();
    var mockName = callbackType.Name +                          ❷ Create
      Guid.NewGuid().ToString("N");                               mock
                                                                  code
    var template = new MockCodeGenerator(mockName,
      interfaceType, callbackType).Code;
    var compilation = Compilation.Create("Mock",
      options: new CompilationOptions(
        OutputKind.DynamicallyLinkedLibrary),
      syntaxTrees: new[]
      {
        SyntaxTree.ParseCompilationUnit(template)
      },
      references: new MetadataReference[]                       ❸ Compile
      {                                                           mock
        new AssemblyFileReference(                                code
          typeof(Guid).Assembly.Location),
        new AssemblyFileReference(
          interfaceType.Assembly.Location),
        new AssemblyFileReference(
          callbackType.Assembly.Location)
      });
```

```
    var result = compilation.Emit(Mock.builder.Value);

    if (!result.Success)
    {
      throw new NotSupportedException(
        string.Join(Environment.NewLine,
          from diagnostic in result.Diagnostics
          select diagnostic.Info.GetMessage())));
    }

    return Activator.CreateInstance(
      Mock.builder.Value.GetType(mockName), callback) as T;
  }

  private static ModuleBuilder CreateBuilder()
  {
    var name = new AssemblyName
    {
      Name = Guid.NewGuid().ToString("N")
    };

    var builder = AppDomain.CurrentDomain.DefineDynamicAssembly(
      name, AssemblyBuilderAccess.Run);
    return builder.DefineDynamicModule(name.Name);
  }
}
```

**4** Emit mock code into dynamic assembly, check for success

**5** Return new instance of mock

**6** Create new dynamic assembly

The first thing to do is check that T is an interface **1**. Once you've verified that, you use the MockCodeGenerator class to create the mock code **2**. You pass that generated code to the Create() method of the Compilation class via a syntax tree. This syntax tree is created by SyntaxTree.ParseCompilationUnit() (we cover trees in the next section). You also pass AssemblyFileReference objects so the compiler knows where the types are that are referenced in the mock code **3**. Once Create() is done, you can emit the results into a dynamic module. If Emit() wasn't successful, you can examine the Diagnostic property to find out what isn't correct in your code **4**. Finally, a new instance of the mock is created with a reference to the callback object **5**. Note that the dynamic assembly is lazily created **6**.

With all this in place, you can now create a mock using the ITest and TestCallback classes like this:

```
var callback = new TestCallback();
var mock = Mock.Create<ITest>(callback);
var result = mock.CallMe();
```

When this code executes, result will contain a random integer value.

With Roslyn, you can easily create dynamic code that does complex activities. Rather than resort to System.Reflection.Emit and IL, you can write your C# and compile that instead. The barrier to entry to perform powerful metaprogramming-based implementations is much lower with Rolsyn than with other approaches you've seen in this book.

The last thing you need to look at are the trees that Roslyn produces. This will become important when you start writing code that interacts with code written in Visual Studio.

### 10.2.6 Understanding trees

In the last example, you used `SyntaxTree.ParseCompilationUnit()` to create a tree structure that represents the code you pass into the method. As you can imagine, these trees are rich and complex—in fact, when you install Roslyn, you get a couple of visualizers to help you easily see the tree. Figure 10.7 is the debug visualizer that's a representation of the mock code as a tree.

**TIP** To learn more about using the Roslyn visualizers, visit http://mng .bz/59EU.

The syntax tree is a complete representation of the code you parsed, including whitespace (known as *trivia*). This is necessary because if you want to retain code formatting as you change it, you need to know what kind of whitespace exists in the document (and how much of it).

Trees in Roslyn are immutable. You can't change the contents of a tree. Immutable structures have many advantages—for example, they can make concurrent programming much easier to reason about—but, because they're immutable, you can't change them. Thankfully, Roslyn ships with a couple of visitor classes: you can use `Syntax-Walker` and `SyntaxWriter` to search the contents of a tree and create a new tree based on a given tree. You'll use trees and visitors a lot more in the next section, when you interact with code written in Visual Studio.

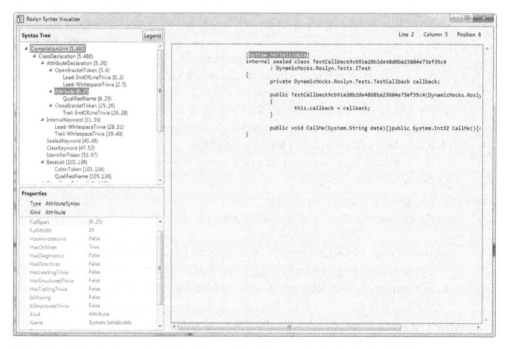

**Figure 10.7 The Roslyn syntax debugging visualizer. If you look at certain objects in the `SyntaxTree` view, you can look at the tree (and its corresponding code) in the visualizer.**

**NOTE** This is the same technique that you used to change an expression tree in chapter 6.

## 10.3 Interacting with code in Visual Studio

You've now seen how to generate code on the fly with Roslyn. This can have a tremendous, positive impact on you as a developer who wants to incorporate metaprogramming techniques in your code because you can generate code in C#, compile it, and execute it. You're using knowledge you already have, rather than having to understand the details of IL. But you can do a lot more with Roslyn than compile code. You can use it to analyze code while code is being written and provide alternatives and fixes. You can also generate code for a developer to make it easier to implement patterns and idioms. Let's take a look at what it would take to fix a WCF issue, and then you'll see how you can generate code in the editor.

### 10.3.1 Creating a IsOneWay warning

In section 10.1.2 you saw a code snippet where the code violated a WCF rule but the C# compiler considered the code valid. Let's use Roslyn to create a couple of classes that will integrate into the Visual Studio editor to provide a developer with a custom error and a couple workarounds.

### 10.3.2 Defining the Code Issue

The first thing you need to do is create a Code Issue project. That's pretty simple, as figure 10.8 shows.

Once you have your project set up, you need to create a Code Issue. This is a class that implements the `ICodeIssue` interface with a couple of MEF attributes, as shown in the following listing.

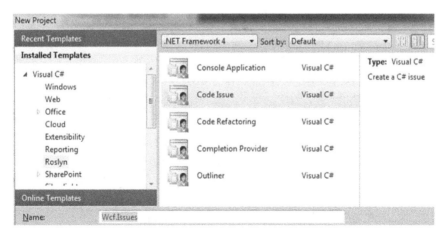

**Figure 10.8 Creating a Code Issue project. Project Roslyn provides a number of project templates to make it easy to create specific kinds of Roslyn-based solutions.**

**Listing 10.5    Creating a Code Issue project**

```
namespace Wcf.Issues
{
  [ExportSyntaxNodeCodeIssueProvider(
    "Wcf.Issues.OneWayOperationIssueProvider",
    LanguageNames.CSharp,
    typeof(MethodDeclarationSyntax))]
  public sealed class OneWayOperationCodeIssueProvider
    : ICodeIssueProvider
  {
```

❶ Create MEF export to define item issue will use

❷ Define supporting language

You state that your class is a code issue provider with ExportSyntaxNodeCode-IssueProvider. The type of the node stated (MethodDeclarationSyntax) means you're looking for method declarations that have been made or changed in the editor ❶. Note that this code is for C#. You could easily create a provider for VB, but you'd have to use the VB version of Roslyn to do it ❷.

The ICodeIssueProvider defines three GetIssues() methods. You're concerned only with the one that takes a CommonSyntaxNode as its second parameter; the other methods you can implement by throwing NotImplementedException. To implement this method, you need to check for a few things with the method you've been given:

- It must have the OperationContractAttribute defined.
- IsOneWay must be set to true.
- The return type of the method must be something other than System.Void.

The following listing suggests how you'd handle the first two requirements.

**Listing 10.6    Searching for WCF metadata on a method**

```
var methodNode = (MethodDeclarationSyntax)node;
if (methodNode.Attributes != null)
{
  var model = document.GetSemanticModel();
  var operationContractType =
    typeof(OperationContractAttribute);
  var operationSyntax = (
    from attribute in methodNode.Attributes
    from syntax in attribute.Attributes
    let attributeType = model.GetTypeInfo(syntax).Type
    where
      attributeType != null &&
      attributeType.Name ==
        operationContractType.Name &&
      attributeType.ContainingAssembly.Name ==
        operationContractType.Assembly.GetName().Name
    from argument in syntax.ArgumentList.Arguments
    where (
      argument.NameEquals.Identifier.GetText() ==
        "IsOneWay" &&
      argument.Expression.Kind ==
        SyntaxKind.TrueLiteralExpression)
    select new { syntax, argument }).FirstOrDefault();
```

If the method has any attributes, you get type info from the semantic model for that attribute and compare its name and containing assembly name to `OperationContract-Attribute`'s values. Look through the argument list of the attribute, and if one of the identifiers is `IsOneWay`, and its expression type is a `SyntaxKind.TrueLiteralExpression`, you know you should definitely check the return type of the method.

The third requirement is to check the return type of the method, as shown in the following listing.

**Listing 10.7   Checking the return type of a method**

```
        if (operationSyntax != null)
        {
          var returnType = model.GetSemanticInfo(
            methodNode.ReturnType).Type;

          if (returnType != null &&
            returnType.SpecialType != SpecialType.System_Void)
          {
            return new[]
            {
              new CodeIssue(CodeIssue.Severity.Error,
                methodNode.ReturnType.Span,
                "One-way WCF operations must return System.Void.",
                new ICodeAction[]
                {
                  new OneWayOperationReturnVoidCodeAction(
                    editFactory, document,
                    methodNode.ReturnType),
                  new OneWayOperationMakeIsOneWayFalseCodeAction(
                    editFactory, document,
                    operationSyntax.argument)
                })
            };
          }
        }
      }

    return null;
  }
```

Once you have semantic information about the method's return type, you can check `SpecialType` to see if it equals `SpecialType.System_Void`. If so, you need to tell the developer that the code has an error, and that's what you do when you return a `Code-Issue` object. In this case, it's definitely an error, which is why `Severity.Error` is used. You want the user to focus on the return type portion of the method declaration, which is why you pass the `Span` property value of the `ReturnType` property. This will put the red squiggle error line under the return type in the code editor—you'll see a screen shot of that in a moment.

The other thing you'll notice is that you're passing in two objects via an `ICode-Action` array to the `CodeIssue` object. This provides developers with ways to address the issue they're seeing. In the next section, you'll see what these actions are doing.

### 10.3.3  *Defining the OneWayOperation code actions*

It's one thing to tell developers what they're doing is wrong. But if you can provide them with ways to fix the issue, that's a big win. There are at least two ways you can fix this WCF issue:

- Change the value of IsOneWay to false.
- Change the return type to be System.Void.

Let's look at how you can fix the problem with the first approach. The first thing you need to do is create a class that implements ICodeAction. You don't need to put any MEF attributes on your implementation this time. You need to create a constructor that will capture a couple of objects from the code issue and help in creating a fix for the issue:

```
public sealed class OneWayOperationMakeIsOneWayFalseCodeAction
  : ICodeAction
{
  private IDocument document;
  private AttributeArgumentSyntax attributeArgumentSyntax;

  public OneWayOperationMakeIsOneWayFalseCodeAction(
    IDocument document,
    AttributeArgumentSyntax attributeArgumentSyntax)
  {
    this.document = document;
    this.attributeArgumentSyntax = attributeArgumentSyntax;
  }
```

There are three members in ICodeAction that you have to implement. The two properties, Description and Icon, are easy to handle:

```
public string Description
{
  get { return "Make IsOneWay = false"; }
}

public ImageSource Icon
{
  get { return null; }
}
```

The main member, GetEdit(), is the method where you'll create your resolution, as shown in the following listing.

**Listing 10.8   Making IsOneWay false**

```
public CodeActionEdit GetEdit(
  CancellationToken cancellationToken)
{
  var trueToken =
    this.attributeArgumentSyntax.Expression.GetFirstToken();

  var falseToken = Syntax.Token(trueToken.LeadingTrivia,
    SyntaxKind.FalseKeyword, trueToken.TrailingTrivia);
```

```
      var tree = (SyntaxTree)this.document.GetSyntaxTree();
      var newRoot = tree.GetRoot().ReplaceToken(trueToken, falseToken);
      return new CodeActionEdit(document.UpdateSyntaxRoot(newRoot));
  }}
```

It's pretty straightforward. You need to get a reference to the first token in the
Expression portion of the attribute, because that's what you'll replace in code (the
false token). Next, create a new token via Syntax.Token() that uses Syntax-
Kind.FalseKeyword to define the token. You want to preserve any leading or trailing
trivia (for example, whitespace) so that your new token will easily fit in where the old
token was. Then you get a reference to the syntax tree via GetSyntaxTree() on your
document object. That's used to replace the old token (true) with the new one
(false) via ReplaceToken(). The last step is to return a CodeActionEdit object,
which defines what the new code would look like—you'll see an example of this in
action in the next section.

Note the power of immutable tree design that's prevalent in Roslyn. You create a
new tree based on the one that represents what's in the code editor, but Replace-
Token() doesn't change the original tree. If the user decides to not use your code
action, nothing in their current code file changes.

The other action changes the return type of the method to System.Void. The
following listing shows what the GetEdit() implementation looks like with this
code action.

**Listing 10.9  Implementing `GetEdit()` to change the return type to `System.Void`**

```
public CodeActionEdit GetEdit(
  CancellationToken cancellationToken)
{
  var returnToken = this.typeSyntax.GetFirstToken();

  var voidToken = Syntax.Token(returnToken.LeadingTrivia,
    SyntaxKind.VoidKeyword, returnToken.TrailingTrivia);

  var tree = (SyntaxTree)this.document.GetSyntaxTree();
  var newRoot = tree.GetRoot().ReplaceToken(
    returnToken, voidToken);
  return new CodeActionEdit(document.UpdateSyntaxRoot(newRoot));
}
```

Listing 10.9 is virtually the same as listing 10.8. The main difference is you're making a
new token that uses the VoidKeyword value on SyntaxKind to change the return type
to void.

With all the code in place, let's see what the experience is like in Visual Studio.

### 10.3.4  Viewing the results

Launch your Code Issue project under the debugger. This launches a new instance of
Visual Studio with Roslyn integration enabled. It also includes your Code Issue in the
process so you can debug your code in action. Next, create a project that references

### Ramifications of changing the return type

When you want to fix a problem, the fix can often introduce other issues. This is the case when you change the return type to `System.Void`. The new problem is that the method may have multiple return statements, so now you've introduced a number of errors that the developer has to fix.

There are a couple of things you can do. You can change the return type and let the developer handle any return statements in code. Or you can change the code action to parse the method body and remove all return statements as well. This may be too invasive of an action because a return statement may contain side effects (like calling a function that changes state). Writing code issues and actions requires a fair amount of analysis to ensure you're providing a true positive with the issue and an effective fix with the action.

`System.ServiceModel` so you can use `OperationContractAttribute`. Finally, add the following text to your class:

```
[OperationContractAttribute(IsOneWay = false)]
public string MyOperation() { return null; }
```

You'll notice that no errors show up in the Error List window. Now, change `IsOneWay` to true, and you should see a new error in the Error List window, as shown in figure 10.9.

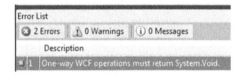

Remember when you passed in the `Span` value of the `ReturnType` property? That was so Visual Studio would add a squiggle in code, which also provides a place for the developer to fix the error. Figure 10.10 shows what the actions look like in Visual Studio.

**Figure 10.9   Integrating custom errors in Visual Studio. You don't have to wait until a postcompile step to statically analyze your code with Roslyn; you can do it as a developer is writing code.**

Note the little code window to the right of the code action description. You get a preview of what the code would look like if the developer decides to invoke the action.

This kind of power and Visual Studio integration is enabled by the Roslyn parsing engines. You're probably already thinking of other ways to enhance your development experience by fixing issues as you code. But you can also use Roslyn to suggest refactorings so your code is easier to read and maintain. Let's see how you can create a code refactoring such that code will automatically follow a particular coding standard.

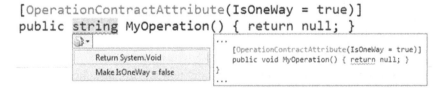

**Figure 10.10   Selecting code actions for code issues in Visual Studio. The preview window is a nice touch to see what the change will look like.**

### 10.3.5  *Autoarrange code*

On most software development projects, it's common to have a coding standards document that defines the conventions and idioms that all developers should follow. Having a consistent approach in a project is a good idea, not only with the implementation techniques used, but also in the formatting styles for the code. But let's be honest—keeping track of whether or not the opening curly brace goes after the method definition or on the next line is tedious. Sure, you want everyone to use the same style, but you want rules like this to be handled by something else, like the computer. Easy coding styles are easy to forget to do right. With Roslyn, it doesn't take much to put together some sophisticated rules.

Let's use an example where a coding standard is in place where the members of a class are grouped together like this:

- Events
- Fields
- Constructors
- Methods
- Properties
- Enums
- Nested classes or structs

Let's go through what it's supposed to do first, and then you'll see how it's done in C#.

### 10.3.6  *Specifying the algorithm to reformat the code*

Consider the following code snippet:

```
public class MyClass
{
  public string Data { get; private set; }

  public void AMethod() { }

  public struct NestedStruct { }

  private int aField;
}
```

This doesn't fit the format specified in the previous section. How can you transform it so it does?

First, read the contents of the class and find all the members. You don't need to move anything around yet—you're only capturing references to those members in an object like a list. You'll also need to handle nested classes and structures with their own capturing object, because their members need to be processed within the scope of that class.

Once you know how many members you have, you put them in the order that you want to see them in the class or structure definition. Then, you reread the definition of the type and whenever you run into a member that could be rearranged, you replace it with the next member in your list.

For example, with `MyClass`, you'll find four members: a property (`Data`), a method (`AMethod`), a nested type (`NestedStruct`), and a field (`aField`). When you reread the class contents, you'll put the members in the desired order: `aField`, `AMethod`, `Data`, and `NestedStruct`. Then, you look for members that could be replaced. The first one you find is `Data`. You replace that with `aField`. The next member is `AMethod`, which you replace with itself: `AMethod`. You finish out the last two members, which leaves you with a reordered definition of `MyClass`:

```
public class MyClass
{
  private int aField;

  public void AMethod() { }

  public string Data { get; private set; }

  public struct NestedClass { }
}
```

As you'll see in the following sections, Roslyn makes implementing this pretty painless.

### 10.3.7  *Defining the core parts of the refactoring project*

The first thing you do is create a Code Refactoring project from the Roslyn Visual Studio template. Once you have your project defined, you need to create a class that implements an interface from the Roslyn API and use a MEF export attribute, similar to what you did with the Code Issue provider. The following code snippet shows what that looks like:

```
[ExportCodeRefactoringProvider(
  "Core.Refactorings.AutoAlphabetizeCodeRefactoringProvider",
  LanguageNames.CSharp)]
public sealed class AutoArrangeCodeRefactoringProvider
  : ICodeRefactoringProvider
{
```

The `ICodeRefactoringProvider` interface defines one method that you need to implement: `GetRefactoring()`. The following code snippet shows how you define it to find type definitions.

#### Listing 10.10  Finding class and struct definitions

```
public CodeRefactoring GetRefactoring(IDocument document,
  TextSpan textSpan, CancellationToken cancellationToken)
{
  var token = document.GetSyntaxTree(cancellationToken)
    .Root.FindToken(textSpan.Start);
  var parent = token.Parent;

  if (parent != null && (
    parent.Kind == (int)SyntaxKind.ClassDeclaration ||
    parent.Kind == (int)SyntaxKind.StructDeclaration))
  {
    return new CodeRefactoring(
```

```
        new []
        {
          new AutoArrangeCodeAction(
            this.editFactory, document,
            parent as TypeDeclarationSyntax)
        });
    }

    return null;
  }
}
```

Remember, you need to reformat classes or structures to fit a defined style, so you need to ensure that the text the user has highlighted in Visual Studio is part of a type declaration. That's what you're doing when you examine the Parent node of the token that maps to the provided TextSpan (the highlighted text in the IDE). Once you've determined that the parent's Kind is either a ClassDeclaration or a Struct-Declaration, you pass the parent node as a TypeDeclarationSyntax object to an AutoArrangeCodeAction object (along with the editFactory and document objects). This code action object does the heavy lifting in terms of rearranging your class into the right format.

### 10.3.8  *Creating a code action*

You saw how to create a ICodeAction-based class in section 10.3.3, so let's focus on the implementation of GetEdit():

```
public CodeActionEdit GetEdit(
  CancellationToken cancellationToken)
{
  var captureWalker = new AutoArrangeCaptureWalker();
  captureWalker.VisitTypeDeclaration(this.token);
  var result = new AutoArrangeReplaceRewriter(
    captureWalker).VisitTypeDeclaration(this.token);

  var tree = (SyntaxNode)this.document.GetSyntaxRoot(
    cancellationToken);
  var newTree = tree.ReplaceNodes(new [] { this.token },
    (a, b) => result);
  return new CodeActionEdit(document.UpdateSyntaxRoot(newTree));
}
```

You can probably guess what the AutoArrangeCaptureWalker and AutoArrange-ReplaceWriter classes do, based on their names. The first one finds all the members you want to relocate, and the second one performs the relocations. Let's see how the walker works by looking at the VisitTypeDeclaration():

```
public void VisitTypeDeclaration(TypeDeclarationSyntax node)
{
  this.Target = node;

  var classNode = node as ClassDeclarationSyntax;

  if (classNode != null)
  {
```

```
    base.VisitClassDeclaration(classNode);
  }
  else
  {
    base.VisitStructDeclaration(
      node as StructDeclarationSyntax);
  }
}
```

What you want to do is visit all the members within the target type node. Therefore, you tell the base implementation to visit either the class or structure, depending on what the node type is. The SyntaxWalker then visits all the child nodes within the type definition, which means you need to override a handful of VisitXYZDeclaration() methods to capture the members. Here's what VisitEnumDeclaration() looks like (the other member overrides are virtually the same):

```
protected override void VisitEnumDeclaration(
  EnumDeclarationSyntax node)
{
  this.Enums.Add(node);
}
```

A number of lists are initialized on construction to store nodes that you care about. You put the node in that list when that node is visited.

The only exception to this pattern is nested types. Here's how you handle those nodes:

```
protected override void VisitClassDeclaration(
  ClassDeclarationSyntax node)
{
  var capture = new AutoArrangeCaptureWalker();
  capture.VisitTypeDeclaration(node);
  this.Types.Add(capture);
}
```

You create a new AutoArrangeCaptureWalker object for that nested type and let that walker find all of the nested type's members. Then you store that walker in a list you'll use when you reorder the root type definition. Note that the VisitStructDeclaration() method is done in the exact same way as VisitClassDeclaration().

Once you've walked the target type, you need to transform the target type to contain the reordered members. The first thing to do is resort each list, as shown in the following listing.

**Listing 10.11 Resorting all the type members**

```
public AutoArrangeReplaceRewriter(
  AutoArrangeCaptureWalker rewriter)
{
  rewriter.Constructors.Sort(
    (a, b) => a.Identifier.ValueText.CompareTo(
      b.Identifier.ValueText));
  rewriter.Enums.Sort(
    (a, b) => a.Identifier.ValueText.CompareTo(
```

```
          b.Identifier.ValueText));
  rewriter.Events.Sort(
    (a, b) => a.Identifier.ValueText.CompareTo(
      b.Identifier.ValueText));
  rewriter.Fields.Sort(
    (a, b) => a.Declaration.Variables[0]
      .Identifier.ValueText.CompareTo(
        b.Declaration.Variables[0]
          .Identifier.ValueText));
  rewriter.Methods.Sort(
    (a, b) => a.Identifier.ValueText.CompareTo(
      b.Identifier.ValueText));
  rewriter.Properties.Sort(
    (a, b) => a.Identifier.ValueText.CompareTo(
      b.Identifier.ValueText));
  rewriter.Types.Sort(
    (a, b) => a.Target.Identifier.ValueText.CompareTo(
      b.Target.Identifier.ValueText));

  this.nodes = new List<SyntaxNode>();
  this.nodes.AddRange(rewriter.Events);
  this.nodes.AddRange(rewriter.Fields);
  this.nodes.AddRange(rewriter.Constructors);
  this.nodes.AddRange(rewriter.Methods);
  this.nodes.AddRange(rewriter.Properties);
  this.nodes.AddRange(rewriter.Enums);
  this.nodes.AddRange(
    from typeRewriter in rewriter.Types
    select new AutoArrangeReplaceRewriter(typeRewriter)
      .VisitTypeDeclaration(typeRewriter.Target)
        as TypeDeclarationSyntax);
}
```

Each member is resorted in its list, and a new list is created that contains the resorted members in the correct order. The nested types are handled by creating an Auto-ArrangeReplaceRewriter for that type and putting the results of VisitType-Declaration() into the nodes list.

As was the case with AutoArrangeCaptureRewriter, a custom VisitType-Declaration() method is created to visit (and subsequently replace) all the members with the members in proper order:

```
public TypeDeclarationSyntax VisitTypeDeclaration(
  TypeDeclarationSyntax node)
{
  var classNode = node as ClassDeclarationSyntax;

  if (classNode != null)
  {
    return base.VisitClassDeclaration(classNode)
      as ClassDeclarationSyntax;
  }
  else
  {
    return base.VisitStructDeclaration(
```

```
        node as StructDeclarationSyntax)
        as StructDeclarationSyntax;
  }
}
```

Similarly, the desired `VisitXYZDeclaration()` methods are overridden to handle the replacement strategy. You can see how that's done with `VisitEnumDeclaration()` as an example:

```
protected override SyntaxNode VisitEnumDeclaration(
  EnumDeclarationSyntax node)
{
  return this.Replace(node);
}
```

The `Replace()` method is what handles the reordering:

```
private SyntaxNode Replace(SyntaxNode node)
{
  SyntaxNode result = null;

  if (this.count < this.nodes.Count)
  {
    result = this.nodes[this.count];
    this.count++;
  }
  else
  {
    throw new NotSupportedException();
  }

  return result;
}
```

At this point, it's simple. You need to keep track of how many members you've already visited (which is done with the count field) and replace the current one with the right one in the nodes list.

That's pretty much it. Now let's see what it looks like when you use it in Visual Studio.

### 10.3.9  *Viewing the results*

Once your project launches a Roslyn-based Visual Studio instance, you can create a new project with a class that has its members in any kind of order. Then, select the sealed text for a given class definition—you should see a small, blue-ish rectangle to the left of the highlighted text. If you hit Ctrl+. (the period key), you'll get a preview window of the results, as figure 10.11 demonstrates.

If you accept the changes, the members will move around in the IDE, and you'll have a result that looks something like figure 10.12.

With Roslyn, you can do pretty much whatever you want to do with your code in the editor. It's a matter of figuring out how to work the API to produce the results you desire.

```
public sealed class SortedClassWithNestedClass
{                                          {
    pub        Auto-arrange                   private int someProperty;
    public void Metho                         internal string yetAnotherField;
    public enum DataV                         //internal event EventHandler LoudEvent;
    public Guid MyPro                         public SortedClassWithNestedClass(Guid va
    public SortedClas                         public SortedClassWithNestedClass() { }
                                              public void Method() { }
```

**Figure 10.11  Previewing the auto-arrange refactoring. As you can see, the position of the members has already changed—it's a matter for the user to accept the change.**

```
public sealed class SortedClassWithNestedClass
{

    private int someProperty;
    internal string yetAnotherField;

    //internal event EventHandler LoudEvent;
    public SortedClassWithNestedClass(Guid value) { }
    public SortedClassWithNestedClass() { }
    public void Method() { }
    public string AProperty { get; set; }
    public Guid MyProperty { get; private set; }
```

**Figure 10.12  Autoarranging code. Once the refactoring is done, the members are in the right order.**

### What about the CodeDOM?

As you saw in chapter 4, there's already an API in .NET called CodeDOM that may seem similar to Roslyn at first glance. But CodeDOM is more limiting in what it can do than Roslyn. For a thorough description of the differences between these APIs, visit http://mng.bz/Tx53.

## 10.4   Summary

This chapter gave you a preview of the Roslyn API. You saw how Roslyn provides you with a rich view of your code with parsers that provide tokens and trees. You were able to use this functionality to generate and execute C# code at runtime. You also wrote code that interacted with the Visual Studio IDE to not only provide near real-time feedback to developers to warn them of potential errors, but also to provide solutions as well. Although Roslyn is only in a CTP state, it's encouraging to see what Microsoft is doing with their compilers. Developers like you who love metaprogramming have lots to play with!

# appendix A
## Metaprogramming
## in Windows 8

Two years ago, when we first envisioned writing this book, we didn't consider the next version of Windows to be a big deal. Frankly, we thought you would be reading *Metaprogramming in .NET* well before the next versions of Windows (and Visual Studio) were released, and we had no idea just how much Windows would change. Fate intervened. We finished this book's content just as Windows 8 and Visual Studio 2012 were released to manufacture. Although we didn't want to refocus the entire book on these two new versions for multiple reasons, we felt we should briefly mention some differences you'll run into if you decide to develop applications for Windows 8 using Visual Studio 2012.

It's important to be aware of the changes as you enter the brave new world of Windows 8.

## A.1 The limits of emitting code

A whole new API called the Windows Runtime is the foundation upon which all Windows 8 applications are built and you will definitely encounter changes when you start to work on a Windows 8 application. If you're using C# or JavaScript or C++, it doesn't matter in Windows 8: every language binds to these functions in one way or another. The main difference in Windows 8 is how the runtime API is projected to a language. A simple example is with function names. In JavaScript, function names are typically formatted in camel case; in .NET, Pascal case is the convention. These conventions are adhered to in the language projections, so the API feels natural to the developer.

There are also limitations in terms of what you can and cannot do in a Windows 8 application. One has to do with isolated storage. You can't just open a file from the C drive as you could in a typical .NET application. You must use the Windows .Storage namespace, which restricts file use to an isolated area for your application. For the metaprogramming enthusiast, there's another limitation, and it has to do with Reflection.Emit.

As you saw in chapter 5, to create dynamic types at runtime, you must use the types within the System.Reflection.Emit namespace. In a Windows 8 application, these types are not projected to you. If you type *System.Reflection.Emit* in Visual Studio 2012, you'll see that only a small handful of enumerations are available; you don't have access to `AssemblyBuilder`, `TypeBuilder`, and so on. Proxy libraries, mocking frameworks, dynamic serialization generators ... there's no way to generate dynamic types in Windows 8. This API is not available for a number of reasons, but at the end of the day, there's no fighting it.

Well, that's not exactly true. You can't load code generated at runtime, but you can load code generated with all the code you package together and ship to the Windows Store. So it's possible that you could generate all the types you'd need in an application, then load them as needed as your Windows 8 application runs. However, this seems to defeat the purpose of "dynamic code generated at runtime." Maybe when your code runs you don't need to generate types based on what the user does. Maybe you only need to generate a couple of types. But with the architecture of the Windows 8 sandbox, you have no choice. If your application needed 145 dynamic types, you'd have to create all 145 through some kind of pre- or postcompile procedure, and include those types and the assembly that contains them in your package. This is only true of Windows 8 applications.

> **TIP** There are a couple of attempts to overcome the absence of Reflection.Emit in Windows 8. One is MoqRT (https://github.com/mbrit/moqrt#readme) which analyzes your code to figure out what mocks you'll need in your tests and creates those mocks in a static assembly that you reference in code. Another is a precompiler for a serialization engine called protobuf (http://mng.bz/eD7u), which generates an assembly you can use in Windows 8 applications. It's also conceivable to use the Roslyn APIs to generate code based on source code analysis from Windows 8 applications and automatically add assembly references to those autogenerated assemblies as well.

If you want to create a .NET 4.5-based application that will run in Windows 8 through the Windows 7 Desktop, you can. In this case, all the System.Reflection.Emit goodness is available to you.

## A.2 *Expressions are supported*

Before you bemoan the Windows 8 programming model too much, especially as it relates to metaprogramming, keep in mind that all is not lost. As you know from chapter 6, there's another way to create new functions as your code is running, and that's through LINQ expressions. This is still available in a Windows 8 application. In fact, running code like the following (lifted from section 6.1.1) produces the expected output of 5:

```
Expression<Func<int, int, int>> add = (x, y) => x + y;
var result = add.Compile()(2, 3);
```

If your applications depend on expressions to support some kind of metaprogramming concept, you can still use that in Windows 8.

## A.3    *Changes with Reflection*

There are a couple of changes that happen with Windows 8 and .NET 4.5 with respect to the Reflection API. The first one is how the `Type` class is projected into Windows 8. There's a new class called `TypeInfo`, and you'll use it a lot in Windows 8 if you do any Reflection-based programming, because it's the only way to access and invoke members at runtime. You don't see methods like `IsAssignableFrom` on a `Type` object like this:

```
typeof(object).IsAssignableFrom(typeof(Math))
```

You have to do it this way:

```
typeof(object).GetTypeInfo().IsAssignableFrom(typeof(Math).GetTypeInfo())
```

The `GetTypeInfo()` takes you from a `Type` to a `TypeInfo`, and the `AsType()` extension method brings you back from a `TypeInfo` to a `Type`.

As you've probably already guessed with a Windows 8 application and its security model, you can only access public members; you can't access private members. Again, these changes are strictly for Windows 8 applications. If you're targeting .NET 4.5 outside of Windows 8, you can still use the full `Type` class.

The following table lists guidelines for using the techniques demonstrated in chapters 2–10. These should aid you in making decisions as to when to use a particular framework or approach, depending on your architecture and design parameters at hand. Chapter 1 is not included because it is essentially an introductory chapter.

| Chapter | Technique(s) | Guidelines |
|---------|--------------|------------|
| 2 Exploring code and metadata with Reflection | Using the System.Reflection API | Using arbitrary code members (for example, methods, properties, etc.) based on base class definitions or standard naming conventions, composing dynamic code paths at runtime, or executing code based on the existence of metadata |
| 3 The Text Template Transformation Toolkit | Using the T4 engine | Generating new text (usually code) via templates to simplify creating similar code |
| 4 Generating code with the CodeDOM | Using the System.CodeDom API | Generating new code from an expression-based API for different languages |
| 5 Generating code with Reflection.Emit | Using the System.Reflection.Emit API | Creating and executing new code at runtime at the IL level, either as whole types or distinct methods, or compiling dynamic, discovered code path execution based on Reflection for performance gains |
| 6 Generating code with Expressions | Using the System.Linq.Expressions API | Creating new methods at runtime using a higher-level API, or creating new methods based on Expressions at runtime |

| Chapter | Technique(s) | Guidelines |
|---|---|---|
| 7  Generating code with IL rewriting | Using the Cecil API | Static analysis of assemblies, full control of assembly content, or post-compilation weaving of new code into any assembly |
| 8  The Dynamic Language Runtime | Using the DLR | Provides support for dynamic/scripting languages in .NET, or to handle dynamic code execution in .NET without directly using Reflection |
| 9  Languages and tools | Using alternate languages (e.g., Boo) and third-party libraries (e.g., PostSharp) | Experimentation of coding concepts (such as quotations) that are not supported in C# or VB, or using existing frameworks to handle metaprogramming concepts |
| 10  Managing the .NET compiler | Using Project Roslyn | Access to compiler services for code modification techniques, real-time analysis of C# or VB code for code analysis and refactorings, or Visual Studio integration of custom code issues and refactorings |

# *index*